ADVANCEMENTS IN MENTAL SKILLS TRAINING

Advancements in Mental Skills Training presents contemporary evidence-based intervention approaches from leading sport psychology researchers and practitioners.

The book comprehensively examines the use of mental skills training for athletic performance and well-being from a cross-cultural perspective. It begins by introducing theoretical advancements related to mental toughness, cultural factors, performance optimization, and mindfulness. It goes on to examine the technological advancements related to mental skills training, outlining how mobile technologies can be used to measure and train perceptual-cognitive skills, and the effectiveness of virtual reality in mental training. The book concludes by discussing emerging topics, such as how sports psychology can incorporate spirituality, minority groups in sport and the impact of prejudice, and referee career development.

This insightful text introduces the potential for sport psychology to be integrated into our daily functioning and provides strategies for athletes to optimize their performance and bolster their mental health. It will be an essential read for all sport psychology researchers as well as professionals working in the field.

Maurizio Bertollo is Rector's delegate for international affairs and Associate Professor of Motor Behavior at the University G. d'Annunzio of Chieti and Pescara, Italy. He is Vice-President of the European Federation of Sport Psychology and has been consultant for some Italian Sport Federations and some National Olympic Committees.

Edson Filho is currently a Lecturer in Sport and Exercise Psychology at the University of Central Lancashire. He has authored over 70 peer-reviewed manuscripts and book chapters in the field of Sport, Exercise, and Performance Psychology, and has worked as a consultant for college and amateur athletes.

Peter C. Terry is Dean of the Graduate Research School and Professor of Psychology at the University of Southern Queensland, Australia. He is past-President of the Asian-South Pacific Association of Sport Psychology and a veteran of nine Olympic Games as an applied sport psychologist.

International Perspectives on Key Issues in Sport and Exercise Psychology

Series Editors: Robert J. Schinke, Thomas Schack and Athanasios Papaioannou

International Perspectives on Key Issues in Sport and Exercise Psychology is a series of edited books published in partnership with the International Society of Sport Psychology. Each title reflects cutting edge research in the psychological study of high level sport, written by key researchers and leading figures in the field of sports psychology.

Books in this series:

Athletes' Careers across Cultures
Edited by Natalia B. Stambulova and Tatiana V. Ryba

Routledge Companion to Sport and Exercise Psychology
Global Perspectives and Fundamental Concepts
Edited by Athanasios Papaioannou and Dieter Hackfort

The Psychology of Sub-Culture in Sport and Physical Activity
Critical Perspectives
Edited by Robert J. Schinke and Kerry R. McGannon

Psychology in Professional Sports and the Performing Arts
Challenges and Strategies
Edited by Robert J. Schinke and Dieter Hackfort

Encyclopedia of Sport and Exercise Psychology
Volume 1: Theoretical and Methodological Concepts
Edited by Dieter Hackfort and Robert J. Schinke

Encyclopedia of Sport and Exercise Psychology
Volume 2: Applied and Practical Measures
Edited by Dieter Hackfort and Robert J. Schinke

Advancements in Mental Skills Training
Edited by Maurizio Bertollo, Edson Filho, and Peter C. Terry

ADVANCEMENTS IN MENTAL SKILLS TRAINING

Edited by
Maurizio Bertollo, Edson Filho, and Peter C. Terry

Routledge
Taylor & Francis Group
LONDON AND NEW YORK

First published 2021
by Routledge
2 Park Square, Milton Park, Abingdon, Oxon OX14 4RN

and by Routledge
52 Vanderbilt Avenue, New York, NY 10017

Routledge is an imprint of the Taylor & Francis Group, an informa business

British Library Cataloguing-in-Publication Data
A catalogue record for this book is available from the British Library

Library of Congress Cataloging-in-Publication Data
A catalog record has been requested for this book

ISBN: 978-0-367-11155-7 (hbk)
ISBN: 978-0-367-11158-8 (pbk)
ISBN: 978-0-429-02511-2 (ebk)

Typeset in Bembo
by codeMantra

CONTENTS

FIGURES

TABLES

CONTRIBUTORS' NOTES (SHORT BIOS)

EDITORS

Maurizio Bertollo is Rector's delegate for international affairs and Associate Professor of Motor behavior at the University G. d'Annunzio of Chieti and Pescara, Italy. He is Vice-President of the European Federation of Sport Psychology and has been consultant for some Italian Sport Federations and some National Olympic Committees.

Edson Filho is currently a Lecturer of Sport and Exercise Psychology at the University of Central Lancashire. He has authored over 70 peer-reviewed manuscripts and book chapters in the field of Sport, Exercise, and Performance Psychology, and has worked as a consultant for college and amateur athletes.

Peter C. Terry is Dean of the Graduate Research School and Professor of Psychology at the University of Southern Queensland, Australia. He is past-President of the Asian-South Pacific Association of Sport Psychology and a veteran of nine Olympic Games as an applied sport psychologist.

AUTHORS

Itay Basevitch is a Lecturer at Anglia Ruskin University, Cambridge, UK. He is a Certified Mental Performance Consultant (CMPC) through the Association for Applied Sport Psychology. Itay's main research interests are in the areas of decision-making and perceptual-cognitive skills in team sports. Itay received his PhD from Florida State University and has worked in the UK, USA and Israel as a professor, researcher, and applied practitioner.

Nataniel Boiangin is an Assistant Professor at Barry University Miami Shores, FL, USA and Director at MindTap, LLC. Nataniel's main research interests focus on enhancing sport-related decision-making and the application of technology in psychological skills training protocols. As a consultant, he has worked with athletes at various levels (NCAA, Club, Olympic, etc.), coaches, and musicians.

Howie J. Carson is a Lecturer in Motor Learning and Control at the University of Edinburgh, UK. Howie's research addresses motor skill acquisition and refinement, talent development in sport and dance, and coach decision-making. From an applied perspective, Howie is an Accredited Sport and Exercise Scientist (BASES) and a professional golf coach (The PGA of GB & NI).

Ming-Yang (Dylan) Cheng is an Associate Professor in the School of Psychology at Shanghai University of Sport, China. He received a Ph.D. in Psychology and Sport Science from Bielefeld University, Germany. His research focuses on using neurofeedback training to enhance sports performance and its underlying neurocognitive mechanism.

Suzete Chiviacowsky is a Research Professor in the School of Physical Education at the Federal University of Pelotas, Brazil. She is the author of over 100 articles and book chapters with the main focus being on motivational factors that affect motor performance and learning

Dave Collins is a Professorial Fellow at the University of Edinburgh, UK and Director at Grey Matters Performance Ltd. As an academic, Dave has over 350 peer review publications and 70 books/chapters. As a practitioner, he has worked with over 70 World or Olympic medalists plus professional teams and performers.

Stewart Cotterill is a Professor of Sport and Performance Psychology at AECC University College, UK and owner of Think Performance consultancy services. Stewart has worked with national and international athletes and teams across a broad range of sports including football, rugby and cricket. He also has experience working in other performance domains including the military, surgery, musical performance, acting, emergency services, and business.

Richard G. Cowden is a social-personality psychologist and a Research Fellow in the Department of Psychology at the University of the Free State, South Africa. His research agenda focuses on a wide variety of areas (e.g., mental toughness, resilience, forgiveness) that intersect more broadly with well-being. He has written over 10 scholarly articles on mental toughness in sport.

Emily Crowe completed her BSc, MSc and PhD in Psychology in the United Kingdom at the Universities of Bristol, Exeter and Bristol, respectively. During this time, she developed an interest in the sensory basis of motor control and the application of science to sport which led to her current position as a Postdoctoral

Researcher in Human Movement Sciences at the Vrije Universiteit Amsterdam in The Netherlands.

Lee Crust is an Associate Fellow of the British Psychological Society, a Chartered Sport and Exercise Psychologist, an Accredited Practitioner Psychologist, and a Chartered Scientist. He has published more than 30 peer-reviewed papers concerning mental toughness and has taught in higher education for over 20 years.

Brad Donohue is a Professor in the Department of Psychology at the University of Nevada, Las Vegas, USA and Director of The Optimum Performance Program. His research focus involves the development and evaluation of mental health interventions and assessment tools for athletes and other populations evidencing unique cultures and specialized skill sets.

Jean Fournier is an Associate Professor at Paris Nanterre University, and the President of the French Society of Sport Psychology. His research has focused on mental training, imagery, and mindfulness. Jean has consulted in mental training with Olympic athletes and coaches at the French Institute of Sports, Paris, and at the National Institute of Sport in Montréal.

Cornelia Frank is a Postdoctoral Researcher at Bielefeld University, Germany. Her primary research interest is on motor learning via overt, imagined and virtual (inter)action. At the interdisciplinary Center of Cognitive Interaction Technology, Cornelia has worked on virtual reality for learning and coaching in sports.

Marina Galante Harris graduated with her doctorate in clinical psychology from the University of Nevada, Las Vegas, USA. She interned at Duke University Medical Center and is a Postdoctoral Clinical Fellow at the University of North Carolina Chapel Hill Center of Excellence for Eating Disorders. Her specialty areas include athlete mental health, eating disorders, mindfulness, and dialectical behavior therapy.

Yulia Gavrilova, graduated from the University of Nevada Las Vegas, USA with a degree in clinical psychology. She completed her residency at the Brown University Clinical Psychology Training Consortium. Currently, she is a Postdoctoral Fellow at the Medical University of South Carolina (MUSC). Her research focuses on development, evaluation, and dissemination of culturally tailored interventions for populations that underutilize mental health services.

Yang Ge is a Lecturer in the Psychology School of Beijing Sport University, China. She received her doctoral degree from Laurentian University, Canada, and has experience working with both Chinese and Canadian athletes. Her research interests focus on cultural aspects of athletes' careers and sport performance.

Megan E. Gilchrist recently completed her PhD at the University of Queensland, Australia. Her research focused on team culture and leadership within underperforming professional football teams. Megan's ongoing research interests include understanding and enhancing high performance environments with a specific focus on leadership.

Michelle D. Guerrero is a Postdoctoral Fellow at the Children's Hospital of Eastern Ontario Research Institute, Canada. She was the recipient of the 2017–18 Governor General's Gold Medal at the University of Windsor in recognition of her academic excellence at the graduate level. In 2018, she was awarded the Reviewer of the Year for *Adapted Physical Activity Quarterly*.

Maria Luisa M. Guinto is an Associate Professor, Research Director, and Sport Psychologist in the Department of Sports Sciences at the University of the Philippines College of Human Kinetics. Her research interests include champion mindset, community resilience, sport for development and peace, spirituality, and mindfulness.

Stephanie Hanrahan, a Registered Psychologist, is the Convenor of the Sport and Exercise Psychology Master's program at The University of Queensland in Australia. She has worked in more than 10 countries, primarily with her physical activity-based life skills program, LifeMatters.

David Harris completed his BSc in Psychology at the University of Nottingham, UK and MSc and PhD at the University of Exeter, UK. David's research focuses on attentional processes and skill learning, and he has a particular interest in the use of virtual reality for both training and studying visually guided skills. David is currently working as a Royal Academy of Engineering Research Fellow at the University of Exeter.

Tsung-Min (Ernest) Hung is a Research Chair Professor at the Department of Physical Education, National Taiwan Normal University, Taipei, Taiwan. He was inducted as a Fellow for the National Academy of Kinesiology (USA) in 2018. His research focuses on the EEG signature of superior sport performance and the neurocognitive effects of physical activity.

Patricia C. Jackman is a Lecturer in Sport and Exercise Psychology at the University of Lincoln, UK, where she also received her PhD. Her research coheres around the area of optimal psychological states in sport, exercise, and physical activity. Patricia's research on this topic focuses on flow states, performance under pressure, goal-setting, and attentional focus.

Clifford J. Mallett is a Professor of Sport Psychology and Coaching at the University of Queensland (UQ), Australia where he completed his undergraduate and doctoral studies in psychology. He is an Olympic and World Championships medal-winning coach in athletics. In 2002, he created then convened the Master of Sports Coaching at UQ. In addition to his teaching and research activities, Cliff has consulted widely to national and international sporting organisations as well as professional franchises in Australia.

Jeffrey Martin is a Professor at Wayne State University. He has published over 200 research articles and chapters as well as the *Handbook of Disability Sport and Exercise Psychology*. He was the founding editor of *Sport, Exercise, and Performance Psychology*, and the current editor of the *Adapted Physical Activity Quarterly*.

Bryan McCann is a Lecturer in Psychology at Glasgow Caledonian University, UK, a Chartered Sport & Exercise Psychologist and a Practitioner Psychologist. He is an experienced academic, with research interests in motivation, mental health and wellbeing, and youth sport.

Paul McCarthy is the Director of the taught Doctorate pProgramme in Sport and Exercise Psychology at Glasgow Caledonian University, UK. He is a Chartered Psychologist and works in private practice at St Andrews Links Golf Academy. He publishes research on attention, emotion and motivation in sport and exercise settings.

Giulia Prete is a Research Fellow at the "G. d'Annunzio" University of Chieti-Pescara, Italy. As a psychologist working in the neurosciences, her main focus is on the study of human cerebral asymmetries concerning perceptual and emotion processing, in healthy participants and in neurological patients.

Eva Prokesova is an academic in the Department of Adapted Physical Education and Sport Medicine at the Charles University, Faculty of Physical Education and Sport, Czech Republic. Her primary interest as a practitioner is in the area of adapted indoor skydiving for people after spinal cord injury.

Claudio Robazza is a Professor at the "G. d'Annunzio" University of Chieti-Pescara, Italy. As a sport psychologist, he has been working with high-level athletes of different sports. His primary research interest is in the area of performance-related emotions, performance optimization, and motor learning.

Camilo Sáenz-Moncaleano is in private practice in Malmö, Sweden. She is a certified Specialist in Applied Sport Psychology by the European Federation of Sport Psychology (SASP-FEPSAC), and a Performance Coach with more than 10 years' experience working in a variety of domains such as athletics (including World Champions and Olympic athletes), professional gamers, music, dance, and corporate leaders.

Roy David Samuel is a Lecturer in Sport Psychology at the Interdisciplinary Center Herzliya, Israel. His research focuses on career change-events in various populations and the psychology of soccer refereeing. He is a Chartered Psychologist, mainly consulting with professional and Olympic athletes and teams, national teams, and soccer referees.

Stephanie J Tibbert, is based in the UK following her doctoral years in Melbourne, Australia. Her work on the social construction and potential negative consequences of mental toughness has helped move this area of research into new territories. Dr. Tibbert's research interests include continued investigation of mental toughness and examining strategies to enhance sports cultures to improve athletes' experiences in elite sport.

Luca Tommasi is a Professor of Psychobiology at the "G. d'Annunzio" University of Chieti-Pescara, Italy. His main research interests range from the cognitive neurosciences of hemispheric lateralization to the evolutionary roots of perception and emotion, investigated by means of behavioural, neuroimaging and neurostimulation techniques.

John Toner is a Lecturer in Sports Coaching and Performance at the University of Hull, UK. He has published a number of articles on the role conscious processes play in facilitating 'continuous improvement' among skilled performers. His recent work on this topic has been published in *Body & Society* and the *Psychology of Sport and Exercise*.

Samuel J. Vine completed his BSc and PhD in the United Kingdom at the University of Exeter. His research focuses on how visual attention and other physiological processes mediate motor skill and decision-making performance. At the heart of this is the use of eye tracking technology to explore focus of attention during skilled aiming performance. Sam is currently an Associate Professor in Psychology, within the Sport and Health Sciences department at the University of Exeter.

Mark Wilson is a Professor of Performance psychology at the University of Exeter, UK and a Registered Sport and Exercise Psychologist with the Health and Care Professions Council. He is a leading expert in visuomotor skill acquisition and has an applied and theoretical interest in understanding the influence of pressure on performance and developing training that might mitigate against negative effects.

Liwei Zhang is a Professor of Psychology at the Beijing Sports University, China, and a former President of the Asian-South Pacific Association of Sport Psychology and the China Sport Psychology Association. An ex-international table tennis player, his research interests are related to self-concept, self-control and burnout. His consultation work includes delivering mental training programs to Chinese Olympic teams in table tennis, rhythmic gymnastics, tennis, trampoline, windsurfing, and freestyle skiing aerials.

FOREWORD

The International Society of Sport Psychology (ISSP) continues to work closely with Taylor & Francis in securing world-class editors for their series *International Perspectives on Key Issues in Sport and Exercise Psychology*. The broader series continues to evolve, based on the series editors' and the ISSP's strategic vision that any book included must have the widest possible reach by recruiting scholars from a breadth of continents and with diverse identities (i.e., gender, nationality, language, race, ethnicity). Enveloped in whether a book project is to be included within the series are a few key considerations. The deliberation begins by focusing on the thematic topic being proposed. Does the topic have meaning, or "wings," as an attractive offering for a wide, learned prospective readership? Next, and of equal importance, do the proposed editors for the book project have sufficient notoriety and credibility to pull off the project? Should the answer to these initial questions be "yes," then discussion with the book project editors turns to topic matter. Do the proposed topics align with the overarching focus of the book? Once the topics are deemed suitable, a further deliberative question is whether the structure of the book makes sense. Should the book meet all of the markers above, it then satisfies our increasingly stringent requirements.

The information above prefaces the book project titled *Advancements in Mental Skills Training*, co-edited by Maurizio Bertollo, Edson Filho, and Peter C. Terry. The ISSP is privileged to have these co-editors as book project leads. Dr. Bertollo is recognized worldwide for his innovative research. Not long ago, my colleague and friend Dr. Gershon Tenenbaum, Past President of the ISSP, invited me to join a symposium where Dr. Bertollo was a co-presenter. What became abundantly clear to me was his capacity to bridge science and practice like few others. As he spoke about his innovative research with elite shooters, I felt honored to be involved in the symposium, given the quality of his content and delivery. Edson Filho brings a second perspective to the book. He is a relatively young and highly successful scholar. Dr. Filho's writings have included a breadth of emerging topics that have spanned team and individual sports, from a multiplicity of methodologies. These writings, much like Dr. Bertollo's, can be found in Q1 journals, both within and beyond sport and exercise psychology. Dr. Filho brings a wonderful balance of youth and breadth of knowledge to the project. Peter C. Terry is a world-renowned scholar and practitioner. His research portfolio is expansive, and many know his innovative scholarship in the topic area of moods and emotions. What they might not know about Dr. Terry is the expansive list of Olympic medal-winning performers who were supported by him in training and onsite at too many Olympic Games to list in this foreword. Dr. Terry has also worked with many successful professional athletes, originally in the United Kingdom and now in Australia, where he currently resides and works. The editorial team for this book is unquestionably world class.

Delving into the book's content, the reader will find three sections, ordered in a manner that speaks to sound scientific and practical logic. Section 1 is comprised of world-class authors from around the world, tasked with "Theoretical Advancements." The topics include optimal performance, mental toughness, motivation, mindfulness, clinical issues, cultural factors, and team dynamics. Clearly, the subjects listed are sufficiently broad and overarching to cover discussion areas that will enthuse researchers and practitioners alike. The second section is focused on "Technological Advancements." Technology is an important, emerging, and essential part of today's sport psychology. As someone who works with several Olympic teams and professional sports, I find that technology is becoming more of how athletes are being prepared for performance, worldwide, though especially in developed countries. An understanding of these technologies is a necessity for every sport psychology professional who wishes to be at the forefront of the field. The topics in the broader section include social media, mobile technologies, neuro-cognitive tracking, biofeedback and neurofeedback, brain stimulation and neural entrainment, and virtual reality. The listed topics are the most prevalent known today, and they are indeed being heavily used by the next guard of Olympians preparing for the 2020 Tokyo Olympics, and beyond. The third and final section is aptly titled "Emerging Topics and Understudied Populations." This closing section to the book not only speaks to what is currently at the vanguard of the discipline but, moreover, unpacks with clarity the future of sport psychology. The topics included are spirituality, minorities, athletes with disabilities, youth, coaches, and referees. There is a lovely balance of foci in Section 3 that speak to diversity, something the ISSP also advocates.

So, where does the description above leave this book? I find a progressive book with contemporary topics that will challenge and stimulate all levels of reader to think outside the box and beyond what is traditionally known about our field. Should this book be an indication of the broader future of the domain, there is much to be enthused about. I strongly encourage you to engage with this world-class offering. The challenge in sport psychology is to stay abreast of its quickly expanding content. *Advancements in Mental Skills Training* delivers a learned, practical, and cutting-edge series of contributions that will push this field forward in a fast, technological age, where professionals need to remain current to advance their own understanding and, then, deliver the best possible interventions to their clients.

Robert Schinke
President of the International Society
of Sport Psychology

1

ADVANCEMENTS IN MENTAL SKILLS TRAINING

An introduction

Peter C. Terry, Maurizio Bertollo, and Edson Filho

This book has been produced as part of Routledge publisher's *Key Issues in Sport and Exercise Psychology* series, endorsed by the International Society of Sport Psychology. The book presents a range of contemporary evidence-based intervention approaches used by leading sport psychology researchers and practitioners from around the world. In this introductory chapter, we set out to provide past, present, and future perspectives on applied sport psychology, in particular, the use of mental skills training for athlete performance and well-being. In doing so, we offer both historical and current contextual overviews, followed by a forecast of future approaches to mental skills training provision in sport.

Most elite athletes recognize that their performance is influenced by psychological variables. Even the great Roger Federer, renowned as the epitome of on-court control, enlisted help in the early days of his tennis career: "At 17, my family decided that I had to go to a psychologist because I was so angry on the court. From that moment on, my growth has been constant" (Federer, quoted in Otway, 2017). It is increasingly acknowledged that sport psychology is not necessarily about developing sporting titans. In its broadest sense, sport psychology is about using psychological principles, knowledge, strategies, and techniques to address a wide range of performance and well-being issues in sport and in life.

Applied practitioners adopt many different approaches when working with athletes, coaches, and others in the sporting community. Some focus on optimizing athletic performance via the application of psychological techniques, an approach often referred to as psychological skills training, mental skills training, or simply as mental training. Others emphasize the psychological well-being of athletes and the avoidance of potential harmful consequences of involvement in sport, in the form of anxiety, depression, or burnout. Clinically trained professionals are often oriented toward mental health in athletes and the prevention of psychological disorders or the treatment of pathogenic behaviors, such as disordered eating or compulsive exercising, whereas other practitioners take a holistic approach toward their clients, implementing interventions to promote happiness, quality of life, and enhanced self-esteem, anticipating that such personal development may also provide benefits to athletic performance. More recently, multidisciplinary perspectives have led others to adopt a psychophysiological approach using brain/body technologies during practice for performance optimization (e.g., Bertollo, Doppelmayr, & Robazza, 2020; di Fronso, Robazza, Bortoli, & Bertollo, 2017).

Historical overview of sport psychology

The historical roots of sport psychology can be traced back to the 19th century and beyond. "Control the controllables" is a ubiquitous catchcry of modern sport psychologists, but it is not a new principle. The challenge of distinguishing controllable internal influences on physical performance from uncontrollable external forces was understood even in ancient times, as the words of Roman Emperor Marcus Aurelius (AD 121–180) testify, "You have power over your mind - not outside events. Realize this, and you will find strength."

Moreover, some of the topics covered in this book were evident in traditional Chinese culture, particularly those related to "skill formation, physical competition, competitive tactics, and mental training" (Smith & Si, 2005, p. 397). Indeed, a number of the techniques applied by contemporary practitioners to assist physical and emotional control, including meditation, centering, and mindfulness, all have their origins in ancient Eastern philosophies. Similarly, the existential approach to sport psychology espoused by some modern writers (e.g., Nesti, 2004) has its origins in the Socratic tradition of Ancient Greece.

Uncertainty shrouds the exact birthplace of sport psychology, although its recorded origins lie in Europe. A publication appeared in Germany as early as 1830 on the psychology of calisthenics, written by Carl Friedrich Koch, and sport psychology experiments were conducted in the world's first psychology laboratory, established by Wilhelm Wundt at the University of Leipzig in 1879. Some sources erroneously credit Norman Triplett of Indiana University as having published the first journal article in sport psychology in 1898, based on his research into social facilitation in cycle racing, but publications addressing the effect of hypnosis on muscular endurance (Rieger, 1884), the effect of mental fatigue on physical performance (Mosso, 1891), and the reaction times of fencers (Scripture, 1894) and athletes (Fitz, 1895) were produced prior to Triplett's article (see Table 1.1).

In 1908, Robert Yerkes and John Dodson published their classic paper on the relationship between stimulus strength and rapidity of habit formation. Their experiments involved teaching mice to successfully navigate mazes of increasing difficulty, using electric shocks as a disincentive for making errors. They concluded that "an easily acquired habit, ...which does not demand difficult sense discriminations or complex associations, may readily be formed under strong stimulation, whereas a difficult habit may be acquired readily only under relatively weak stimulation" (Yerkes & Dodson, 1908, p. 482). Somewhat bewilderingly, this was extrapolated by the sport psychology community as demonstrating an inverted-U relationship between physiological arousal and athletic performance that is moderated by skill complexity, and the Yerkes-Dodson hypothesis has been mentioned in most sport psychology textbooks ever since.

Pierre de Coubertin, the aristocratic French educator best known for organizing the first modern Olympic Games in 1896, was very influential in the early development of sport psychology (Kornspan, 2007), not least because his article *La Psychologie du Sport*, published at the dawn of the 20th century, may have been the first time that the term "sport psychology" was used (Coubertin, 1900). Carl Diem, a former athlete and fervent admirer of Coubertin, established the first laboratory dedicated to investigating psychological aspects of sport in Germany in 1920.

Avksenty Puni and Piotr Roudik set up similar laboratories in Russia during 1925, at the Institute of Physical Culture in Leningrad (now Saint Petersburg) and the State Central Institute of Physical Culture in Moscow (see Ryba, Stambulova, & Wrisberg, 2007) around the same time that the celebrated University of Illinois psychologist Coleman Griffith established the first sport psychology laboratory in America. Griffith published two seminal books on sport psychology, the *Psychology of Coaching* in 1926 – acknowledged as the first ever sport psychology textbook – and *Psychology and Athletes* in 1928. Developments occurred in Asia during the same decade, with a paper on the psychological value of sport published in 1926 by Chinese sport pioneer Ma Yuehan, known in English as John Ma. The paper, titled "Transfer Value of Sports" in translation, addressed the character-building and personality development qualities of sport participation.

Key developments in sport psychology and mental skills training

Sport psychology gained considerable momentum during the latter half of the 20th century and has been organized on a global scale since 1965, when the International Society of Sport Psychology (ISSP; www.issponline.org) was formed during the 1st International Congress of Sports Psychology in Rome with Ferruccio Antonelli, an Italian psychiatrist, as its first President. Several continental organizations have followed, as shown in Table 1.2, including the North American Society for the Psychology of Sport and Physical Activity (NASPSPA; www.naspspa.org) in 1966 and the European Federation of Sport Psychology (FEPSAC: www.fepsac.com) in 1969.

From the 1980s, Olympic teams regularly included sport psychologists among their on-site support staff. The Soviet Union was a pioneer in this respect at the 1980 Olympic Games in Moscow, with Australia following suit by appointing its first team psychologist to the 1984 Olympics in Los Angeles. The United States Olympic Committee established a sport psychology advisory board in 1980 and

TABLE 1.1 Selected Historical Developments in the Early Years of Sport Psychology

Date	*Author*	*Development*
1830	Koch	Paper published in Germany on psychology of calisthenics
1884	Rieger	Case study published on hypnosis and muscular endurance
1891	Mosso	Paper published on mental fatigue and physical performance
1894	Scripture	Paper published on reaction time of fencers
1895	Fitz	Paper published on reaction time of athletes
1898	Triplett	Paper published on social facilitation in cycling
1900	De Coubertin	*La Psychologie du Sport* published
1908	Yerkes and Dodson	Paper published on relationship between stimulus strength and rapidity of habit formation
1920	Diem	Sport psychology laboratory established in Berlin, Germany
1925	Puni	Sport psychology laboratory established in Leningrad (now St. Petersburg), Russia
1925	Roudik	Sport psychology laboratory established in Moscow, Russia
1925	Griffith	Sport psychology laboratory established at the University of Illinois, USA
1926	Ma	Paper published in Chinese on psychological benefits of sport
1926	Griffith	*Psychology of Coaching* textbook published
1928	Griffith	*Psychology of Athletics* textbook published

Adapted from Terry (2011).

appointed its first full-time sport psychologist in 1985. By 1996, more than 20 sport psychologists were working with the US athletes in preparation for the Atlanta Olympics (Terry, 2011).

Public understanding of the role of a sport psychologist remains incomplete at best. Practitioners are often characterized in the media as someone brought in to "motivate" teams or to deal with "problem" athletes (perceptions originally encouraged by Ogilvie and Tutko's seminal book, titled *Problem Athletes and How to Handle Them*, published in 1966). More recently, the profession has made sufficient inroads into the culture of elite sport to be seen as a valuable, perhaps essential, part of a support team and has received enough public accolades from grateful athletes and coaches for the profession as a whole to have demonstrated its worth.

Nowadays, several of the same research questions and applied challenges from the infancy of the sport psychology field continue to occupy the attention of today's professionals, although many new avenues of investigation and technological advances have emerged. However, most research and resource material in sport psychology are published in English and reflect a North American, European, and Australasian orientation. In this book, we have recruited prominent

TABLE 1.2 Development of International Organizations in Sport Psychology

Organization	*Formed*	*Congress Frequency*	*Number of Congresses*
Asian South Pacific Association of Sport Psychology (ASPASP)	1989	Quadrennial	8 to 2018
Association of Applied Sport Psychology (AASP)	1986	Annual	33 to 2019
European Federation of Sport Psychology (FEPSAC)	1969	Quadrennial	15 to 2019
International Association of Applied Psychology (IAAP) Division 12	1994	Quadrennial	7 to 2018
International Society of Sport Psychology (ISSP)	1965	Quadrennial	14 to 2017
North American Society for the Psychology of Sport and Physical Activity (NASPSPA)	1966	Annual	53 to 2019
South American Society of Sport Psychology (SOSUPE)	1986	Variable	13 to 2013

Adapted from Terry (2011).

sport psychology and skill acquisition specialists from 16 countries across five continents to contribute overviews of the latest research findings and to provide recommendations for how to apply this knowledge for the benefit of athlete performance and well-being. The result is a state-of-the-art summary of the latest advancements in sport psychology from across the globe.

Advancements in mental skills training

The book is divided into three sections. The first section covers theoretical advancements related to optimal performance, mental toughness, motivation, mindfulness, clinical issues, team dynamics, and cultural factors. The second section addresses technological advancements related to mental skills training in the areas of social media, mobile technologies, neuro-cognitive tracking, biofeedback and neurofeedback, brain stimulation and neural entrainment, and virtual reality. The final section focuses on emerging topics and understudied populations in mental skills training, covering spirituality, minorities, athletes with disabilities, youth sport, coaches, and referees.

Theoretical advancements in mental skills training

The first section opens with an innovative chapter, titled "Optimizing Performance in Sport: An Action-Based Perspective," which originated from a collaboration between researchers from the University of Chieti in Italy (Claudio Robazza and Maurizio Bertollo) and British scholars (Dave Collins, John Toner, and lead author Howie Carson, from the University of Edinburgh, Scotland). This chapter focuses on motoric factors during the execution of sports skills, providing evidence to support the desirability of attentional control interventions to optimize performance under pressure situations.

Another multinational team, led by Richard Cowden from the University of the Free State in South Africa, penned the next chapter, titled "Mental Toughness Development and Training in Sport." Although mental toughness now features prominently in elite sport narratives, it largely escaped the attention of researchers until the past two decades. Mental toughness is now seen as a key driver of several performance and well-being indicators; hence interventions designed to build mental toughness are highly valued in the sport community although, as Cowden and colleagues attest, evidence of their efficacy remains equivocal.

The third chapter in this section was composed by Suzete Chiviacowsky from the Universidade Federal de Pelotas in Brazil and is titled "The Motivational Role of Feedback in Motor Learning: Evidence, Interpretations, and Implications." Chiviacowsky provides a comprehensive overview of experimental findings, addresses the underlying mechanisms for the motivational role of feedback, and discusses the importance of feedback after successful performance to optimize motor skill learning.

In the fourth chapter, "Mindfulness and Mental Preparation," Jean Fournier from the Université Paris Nanterre in France first describes the nature of mindfulness and its burgeoning use in sport, then reviews emerging evidence supporting the efficacy of mindfulness training for improving sport performance and the pursuit of athlete well-being. Finally, Fournier details a mindfulness intervention program, delivered for the benefit of an elite fencer.

Clinical psychologist Brad Donohue and colleagues from the University of Nevada Las Vegas, USA, present the next chapter, titled "An Optimization Approach to Mental Health in Athletes," in which they outline The Optimum Performance Program in Sports (TOPPS), designed to address the stigma associated with the pursuit of mental health care by athletes. TOPPS includes a cognitive-behavioral rationale to inform mental health assessment and screening procedures, and promote sport performance optimization in athletes.

The penultimate chapter of this section sees co-editor Edson Filho from the University of Central Lancaster, UK, address the topic of "Team Dynamics Theory." Filho tackles this wide-ranging area by first presenting an ontogenetic thesis to inform the development of high-performing teams, followed by the presentation of a nomological network linking cohesion, team mental models, coordination, collective efficacy, and team outcomes. A series of recommendations to aid applied practice in the group dynamics area is also provided.

The first section concludes with a chapter titled "Cultural Codes Provide Novel Strategies for Mental Training," written by Chinese researchers and applied practitioners Yang Ge and Liwei Zhang from Beijing Sport University, in which they explicate the fundamental influence of culture on applied sport psychology practice. In a profession often dominated by Western worldviews, it is refreshing to read the perspective of Ge and Zhang. They emphasize how their work with athletes is infused with the cultural principles of sacrifice, inner peace, and the concept of *Jingjie*, referring to a spiritual ideal of achieving perfect characteristics by becoming conscientious, selfless, responsible, and beloved in dealing with hardships.

Technological advancements in mental skills training

The second section kicks off with a chapter titled "Social Media and Sport Psychology Practice" by Stewart Cotterill from the AECC University College, Bournemouth, UK. Cotterill chronicles the challenges and opportunities presented to sport psychology practitioners by social media, explains how new technology can be used to assist behavior change and enhance performance, and discusses some of the professional, ethical, and moral issues associated with an ever-changing technological world.

Following on is a chapter titled "Mobile Technologies and Perceptual-Cognitive Training," produced by an international collaboration, led by Itay Basevitch from Manhattanville College, New York, focusing on achieving expertise in team sports via the ability to read the game and make optimal decisions. Specifically, Basevitch and colleagues address how mobile technologies can be used innovatively to measure and train perceptual-cognitive skills, such as anticipation, option generation, optimization and response-selection, and pattern recognition and recall.

Colleagues from the Vrije Universiteit Amsterdam, Holland, and the University of Exeter, UK, with Emily Crowe as lead author, contributed the subsequent chapter, titled "Eye Tracking and Cardiovascular Measurement to Assess and Improve Sporting Performance." Eye tracking methodologies developed originally for research purposes are now being applied creatively to explore concentration and attention in competitive environments, providing coaches with unprecedented insights into athlete performance. Specific examples of how eye tracking can benefit athletes and coaches are described in relation to laser shooting, one of the five elements in the sport of modern pentathlon.

Ming-Yan Cheng, from the Shanghai Sport University, China, and Tsung-Min (Ernest) Hung, from the National Taiwan Normal University, continue the contributions from Asia with a chapter titled "Biofeedback and Neurofeedback for Mental Skills Training in Sports." The authors first review contemporary evidence of the effectiveness of biofeedback training, especially multimodal and heartrate variability techniques, followed by an insightful review of neurofeedback training using electroencephalography (EEG). Cheng and Hung then evaluate the strength of the evidence base, identify its limitations, and offer directions for future research.

In an authoritative account of a rapidly developing field, a trio of Italian researchers from the University of Chieti-Pescara, with Giulia Prete as lead author, elucidates the subject of "Brain Stimulation Techniques and Sports Performance."

The authors first review a range of neurostimulation methods and the associated evidence base for their effectiveness in clinical and sport settings, before considering the ethical issues related to their application as a performance-enhancing strategy.

The final chapter of this section is "Virtual Reality and Mental Training" by Cornelia Frank from Bielefeld University, Germany. The author first provides an introduction to the vast potential of virtual reality and its technical components, before explaining the factors that help create embodied, immersive, and interactive experiences. In the latter part of the chapter, recent applications of virtual reality to mental skills training are described and evaluated.

Emerging topics and understudied populations

The first chapter in this section, by Maria-Luisa Guinto from the University of the Philippines, addresses the oft-neglected subject of "Spirituality in Sport Psychology Consulting." Combining 20 years of applied work with Filipino athletes with her qualitative research into the lived experience of several elite athletes, Guinto vividly illuminates how spirituality pervades the lives and sporting careers of many athletes, and how sport psychologists can weave spiritual elements into the support they provide.

Stephanie Hanrahan from the University of Queensland, Australia, compiled the next chapter, "Minorities," as an understudied population. Hanrahan first describes the characteristics that distinguish minority groups before addressing the nature and enduring impact of white privilege, and how systematic oppression and continued stigmatization of minorities stagnate their progress in many sports. As a passionate advocate for cultural competence among sport psychologists, she goes on to discuss the benefits of diversity, introduce cultural competence models, and emphasize the need for culturally targeted interventions.

Continuing the theme of understudied populations, a multinational writing team from Canada, USA, and Czech Republic, with Michelle Guerrero from the Children's Hospital of Eastern Ontario Research Institute as lead author, scribed a chapter titled "Psychological Interventions with Paralympic Athletes." The authors first summarize the literature on mental skills for athletes with disabilities, before providing detailed recommendations for sport psychologists planning to embark on work in this field. Guerrero and colleagues address the sensitive issues of disability classification, injury, and pain among Paralympians before presenting mindfulness and gratitude as potential interventions.

Paul McCarthy and Bryan McCann from Glasgow Caledonian University in Scotland contribute an engaging chapter, titled "Innovations in Mental Skills Training for Young Athletes," in which they explain how the benefits of mental skills training extend well beyond the performance domain into the territory of psychological well-being and transferable life skills. The authors take pains to emphasize the importance of building the therapeutic alliance between athlete and sport psychologist in order to optimize the benefits of mental skills training, and the necessity for practitioner approaches to be individualized to the needs of the athlete.

The penultimate chapter, titled "Contemporary Approaches to Sport Leadership," is written by Megan Gilchrist and Clifford Mallett from the University of Queensland, Australia. Focusing primarily on the "wicked problems" faced by coaches and players as leaders, the authors discuss leadership from a social identity vantage point. The chapter is liberally sprinkled with lessons learned from successful leadership interventions, and promotes the concepts of leaderful teams and engendering followership.

Roy Samuel from Kibbutzim College in Tel Aviv, Israel, wraps up the book with his chapter, titled "Referees: Developmental, Performance, and Training Considerations." With a focus on refereeing in soccer and basketball, Samuel provides a lively discussion of the motivational and developmental aspects of refereeing careers, before devoting attention to examples of psychological skills training for referees. Multiple performance considerations of referees are then addressed, including decision-making, game management, human-technology interface, and match evaluations; and finally, several future avenues for research, training, and applied practice are presented.

Future directions in sport psychology and mental skills training

Weir (2018) writing in *Monitor on Psychology*, the American Psychological Association's monthly professional journal, identifies a growing demand for sport psychology services, due to an increasing recognition that applied practitioners are well placed to help athletes navigate life issues and address mental health challenges in addition to enhancing performance, coupled with escalating requests for services from high-performance domains outside of sport, including business, medical, and military environments.

Broadening the influence of sport psychology in society as a whole, by strengthening the nexus between mental skills training and daily life, represents an excellent opportunity for the profession. Sport psychologists routinely help athletes to handle pressure, to become more resilient, to enhance self-esteem, and to fulfil potential. Applying these processes to life challenges outside of sport by expanding the concept of performance to include daily functioning at work, interpersonal relationships, or leisure pursuits, sport psychologists have the capacity to influence the psychological well-being of a much wider spectrum of society.

An inevitable future development for the sport psychology field will be to optimize strategies for utilizing the internet in the provision of effective web-based mental skills training and other psychological interventions, including online mood profiling (e.g., www.moodprofiling.com) for sport, education, business, military, or health contexts (see Lane & Terry, 2016; van Wijk, Martin, & Hans-Arendse, 2013). Furthermore, as sport psychology and mental skills training evolve into the future, it is clear that the further integration of technological advancements into the profession will occur (Schack, Bertollo, Koester, Maycock, & Essig, 2014). For example, brain technologies, such as EEG neurofeedback, are becoming progressively more portable, user-friendly, and affordable, opening up potential uses in the field that were previously impossible, such as assessing brain activity associated with optimum performance in self-paced sports and developing multi-brain (or hyper-brain) analyses and interventions (see Bertollo et al., 2020; Filho & Tenenbaum, 2019).

Similarly, the ever-expanding capacity of smart devices offers a range of future applications, including remote delivery by practitioners of individualized interventions for athletes combining music, video clips, and personalized instructions. Virtual reality technology similarly offers potential for more sophisticated use of simulation training, allowing athletes to "practice" in venues they have not yet visited, in environmental conditions they have not yet experienced, and against competitors they have not yet faced.

The field of mental skills training has come a very long way since its origins more than a century ago, but as the chapters of this book attest, it is striving to set new goals, develop new techniques, and identify new directions as it moves through the 21st century.

References

Bertollo, M., Doppelmayr, M., & Robazza, C. (2020). Using brain technologies in practice. In G. Tenenbaum & R. Eklund (Eds.), *Handbook of sport psychology* (pp. 666–693) Hoboken, NJ: Wiley-Blackwell.

Coubertin, P. de (1900). La psychologie du sport. *Revue Des Deux Mondes, 70,* 161–179. Retrieved from https://fr.wikisource.org/wiki/La_Psychologie_du_sport

di Fronso, S., Robazza, C., Bortoli, L., & Bertollo, M. (2017). Performance optimization in sport: A psychophysiological approach. *Motriz: Revista De Educacao Fisica, 23,* e1017138. doi:10.1590/S1980-6574201700040001

Filho, E., & Tenenbaum, G. (2019). We think, therefore we are: A social neuroscience perspective on team dynamics, hyperbrains, and collective minds. In R. A. Carlstedt, & M. Balconi (Eds.), *Handbook of sport neuroscience and psychophysiology* (pp. 320–332). New York, NY: Routledge.

Fitz, G. W. (1895). A location reaction apparatus. *Psychological Review, 2,* 37–42.

Griffith, C. R. (1926). *The psychology of coaching.* New York, NY: Scribner.

Griffith, C. R. (1928). *The psychology of athletics.* New York, NY: Scribner.

Koch, C. F. (1830). *Die gymnastik aus dem gesichtspuncte der diätetik und psychologie* [Callisthenics from the viewpoint of dietetics and psychology]. Magdeburg, Germany: Creutz.

Kornspan, A. S. (2007). The early years of sport psychology: The work and influence of Pierre de Coubertin. *Journal of Sport Behavior, 30,* 77–94. Retrieved from https://www.researchgate.net/profile/Alan_Kornspan/publication/266327149

Lane, A. M., & Terry, P. C. (2016). Online mood profiling and self-regulation of affective responses. In R. Schinke, K. McGannon, & B. Smith (Eds.), *The Routledge international handbook of sport psychology* (pp. 324–334). Milton Park, UK: Routledge.

Ma, J. (1926). *Transfer value of sports.* Springfield, MA: Springfield College.

Mosso, A. (1891, trans. 1904). *La fatica.* Milan, Italy: Treves.

Nesti, M. (2004). *Existential psychology and sport: Theory and application*. London, UK: Routledge. doi:10.4324/9780203483435

Ogilvie, B. C., & Tutko, T. A. (1966). *Problem athletes and how to handle them*. London, UK: Pelham.

Otway, J. (2017, November 21). Roger Federer: My family had to stop me being so angry after I was chased off court. *Express*. Retrieved from https://www.express.co.uk/sport/tennis/882440/Roger-Federer-family-court-news

Rieger, K. (1884). *Der hypnotismus: psychiatrische beiträge zur kenntniss der sogenannten hypnotischen zustände* [Hypnotism: Psychiatric contributions to the knowledge of the so-called hypnotic states]. Würzburg, Germany: University of Würzburg.

Ryba, T. V., Stambulova, N., & Wrisberg, C. (2007). The Russian origins of sport psychology: A translation of an early work of A. C. Puni. *Journal of Applied Sport Psychology, 17*, 157–169. doi:10.1080/10413200590932461

Schack, T., Bertollo, M., Koester, D., Maycock, J., & Essig, K. (2014). Technological advancements in sport psychology. In A. G. Papaioannou & D. Hackfort (Eds.), *Routledge companion to sport and exercise psychology* (pp. 953–966). London, UK: Routledge.

Scripture, E. W. (1894). Tests of mental ability as exhibited in fencing. *Studies from the Yale Psychology Laboratory, 2*, 122–124. Retrieved from http://echo.mpiwg-berlin.mpg.de/ECHOdocuView?url=/permanent/vlp/lit23175/index.meta&viewMode=index

Smith, D. E., & Si, G. (2005). Educational programs for sport psychologists in Asia. In D. Hackfort, J. L. Duda, & R. Lidor (Eds.), *Handbook of research in applied sport and exercise psychology: International perspectives* (pp. 397–409). Champaign, IL: Human Kinetics.

Terry, P. C. (2011). Applied sport psychology: Beware the sun, Icarus. In P. R. Martin, F. M. Cheung, M. C. Knowles, M. Kyrios, L. Littlefield, J. B. Overmier, & J. M. Prieto (Eds.), *The IAAP handbook of applied psychology* (pp. 386–410). Oxford, UK: Blackwell.

Triplett, N. (1898). The dynamogenic factors in pacemaking and competition. *American Journal of Psychology, 9*, 507–533. Retrieved from https://psychclassics.yorku.ca/Triplett/

van Wijk, C. H., Martin, J. H., & Hans-Arendse, C. (2013). Clinical utility of the Brunel Mood Scale in screening for post-traumatic stress risk in a military population. *Military Medicine, 178*, 372-376. doi:10.7205/MILMED-D-12-00422

Weir, K. (2018). A growing demand for sport psychologists. *Monitor on Psychology, 49*(10), 50. Retrieved from https://www.apa.org/monitor/2018/11/cover-sports-psychologists

Yerkes, R. M., & Dodson, J. D. (1908). The relation of strength of stimulus to rapidity of habit-formation. *Journal of Comparative Neurology and Psychology, 18*, 459–482. Retrieved from https://onlinelibrary.wiley.com/doi/10.1002/cne.920180503

SECTION 1

Theoretical advancements

2

OPTIMIZING PERFORMANCE IN SPORT

An action-based perspective

Howie J. Carson, Claudio Robazza, Dave Collins, John Toner, and Maurizio Bertollo

Athletes are often required to execute motor skills under conditions of competitive pressure. Consequently, achieving and maintaining high levels of performance under dynamic, stressful, and demanding situations is an essential characteristic of successful performance (Collins & Kamin, 2012; Swann, Keegan, Crust, & Piggott, 2016). Indeed, the provision of services to achieve such outcomes has been a long-standing and primary purpose of performance sport psychology (Moran & Toner, 2017).

Presently, there are two key paradigms informing the knowledge used to help performers in pressure situations, respectively concerning *anxiety* and *attention*. In the former, strategies usually aim to control the dysfunctional impact of anxiety on performance through, for instance, teaching cognitive reappraisal techniques to promote a positive attitude (Balk, Adriaanse, de Ridder, & Evers, 2013). Reflecting this approach, a substantial literature has developed, focused on the nature, timing, and impact of anxiety on performance in its many forms (e.g., Causer, Holmes, Smith, & Williams, 2011). The literature seems to emphasize anxiety as the primary concern in preventing athletes from achieving high-level performance.

Regarding attention, efforts are directed toward either (a) the execution experience, by addressing athletes' thought processes during skill acquisition; or (b) the actual performance, for example, through directing attention either internally (i.e., on bodily movements) or externally (i.e., on the intended movement effect; Masters & Maxwell, 2008; Wulf, 2013). Recommendations largely espouse benefits from not thinking about the movement during execution, whether it be in a controlling or reinvesting manner (Baumeister, 1984; Beilock, Carr, MacMahon, & Starkes, 2002). Relevant theoretical perspectives include the *constrained action hypothesis*, *reinvestment theory*, and the *explicit monitoring hypothesis*. The state of not consciously processing bodily movements has been described as a "sine qua non" for all athletes in any situation (Wulf, 2016, p. 1293), due purportedly to imposed disruptions on self-organization processes caused by an internal focus on the movement.

Something is missing in this perspective, however. We point to the neglect of motoric factors despite a growing case for their impact across performance contexts (e.g., Filho et al., 2015; Wolpert, Diedrichsen, & Flanagan, 2011). Perhaps this is unsurprising considering that sport (and even general) psychology and motor control domains are infrequently presented or understood in tandem (Moran & Toner, 2017; Rosenbaum, 2005). Crucially, however, motoric consideration affords several key alternatives and advantages to existing applied practice, reflecting a move towards more complex conceptualizations of athletes' needs and, therefore, decision-making efficacy (Collins, Burke, Martindale, & Cruickshank, 2015; Martindale & Collins, 2012).

Accordingly, in this chapter we; first, focus on fundamental influences of motoric factors during execution; second, provide evidence to support the desirability and applicability of conscious motor processing under pressure conditions; and, finally, suggest some empirically informed guidelines for what could be considered good practice and explain future research required.

Contribution of motoric factors toward proficient execution

Motoric factors relate to structures involved during the execution process, and, although there is justification for peripheral considerations (e.g., the hard-wired ability of the motor system to adjust movements under stress or fatigue; see Kiely, 2017), we focus here on centralized control structures. Specifically, we focus on representations that underlie cognitive processes.

Consistent with a grounded cognition perspective (i.e., the view that modal simulations, bodily states, and situated action underlie cognition; Barsalou, 2008), Schack and colleagues' (Bläsing, Tenenbaum, & Schack, 2009; Schack & Mechsner, 2006) explanation of actions as being formed through the interaction of multi-level structures (i.e., mental control, mental representation, sensorimotor representation, and sensorimotor control) is a useful exemplar model for understanding motor preparation and execution. Of interest here are the internal representations within the multi-level structure. Mental representations provide a scaffold (or guide) for cognitive processing and transform planned intentions into a structured working model of the technique required. Central to this process are basic action concepts (BACs), which are considered as major representation units for action control stored within long-term memory (LTM). Specifically, BACs are conceptualized as "the mental counterparts of functionally relevant elementary components or transitional states (body postures) of movements" (Seegelke & Schack, 2016, p. 2) that are chunked (or associated; see Fitts & Posner, 1967, associative stage of learning) based on commonality in realizing a movement goal.

Examples of BACs during the golf swing might include: (1) club face position, (2) grip control, (3) address position, (4) ball position, (5) locking, (6) push club away, (7) pressure inside right foot, (8) bend right knee, (9) arms make wide circle, (10) wrist cock, (11) back points to target, (12) clear the left side, (13) head behind the ball, (14) acceleration through impact, (15) let go, and (16) balanced finish (Seegelke & Schack, 2016). Furthermore, the functional organization of these BACs into movement phases might progress for this golf example as follows: preparation (1–5), backswing (6–11), forward swing (12–14), and attenuation (15–16). Put simply, BACs represent procedural knowledge that is directly related to the skill.

Reflecting non-observable changes to execution processes that underpin performance gains, data show a restructuring of cognitive architecture with skill improvements (e.g., Bläsing et al., 2009). For example, experts have a more detailed account of skills stored within LTM, movements are more strongly associated, BACs are clustered into temporally and functionally based phase structures, and there is a closer match between the representation and physical skill execution (Seegelke & Schack, 2016).

Similar to Paivio's (1986) "nonverbal" system within the dual-coding theory, sensorimotor representations also exist within the multi-level structure; that is, modality-specific information resulting from the movements' structure. Information coding can span multiple senses as skills become more detailed within memory (Lang, 1979; Williams, Cooley, & Cumming, 2013), as well as pertaining to perceptual patterns within near-peripersonal and far-extrapersonal space. With this knowledge, it is then possible to compare criteria with afferent feedback and regulate control processes (the role of sensorimotor control and mental control levels within the multi-level structure). In summary, sensorimotor representations play an important role in knowing how a certain movement should "feel, look, or be like" when integrated with BACs (the mental representation).

Importantly for competitive athletes, Carson and Collins (2016) explored the role of experience and confidence in successfully activating these representations to increase the level and permanence of automated control within LTM; referred to as skill establishment. Contrary to traditional information-processing theory (Fitts & Posner, 1967) and the dichotomy put forward within the more recent attention paradigm (Masters & Maxwell, 2008; Wulf, 2013), automaticity is conceptualized to be nonuniform across the different movement phases and for each BAC making up the movement's entirety. For example, novice participants involved in combined mental and physical practice of golf putting for three consecutive days showed nonuniform movement clustering in a retention test (Frank, Land, & Schack, 2016). Some movements (e.g., impact with the ball, club face square to target line at impact, and rotate shoulders through the ball) were clustered together, while other movements (e.g., rotate shoulders away from the ball and smooth transition) were not.

Accordingly, successful and automatic activation of one movement (e.g., golf swing takeaway) does not guarantee that all others will desirably follow. Indeed, Scholz and Schöner (1999) introduced the uncontrolled manifold approach from a nonlinear dynamics perspective to explain that the central nervous system differentially controls movement components based on their importance for achieving the task goal. Activating these components correctly would, therefore, appear even more essential for success under pressurized conditions. However, for executions to be effortless (i.e., seemingly undemanding of attentional resources), fluent, and reliable (e.g., during "flow"), both automaticity of and confidence in the activation process need to be high (Swann, Crust, Keegan, Piggott, & Hemmings, 2015). Conversely, when skill establishment is low, this can result in lower consistency and a higher risk of getting movements "muddled-up," or confused. Note that this risk is not synonymous with lower-skill athletes. Experienced and high-level athletes who frequently attempt to refine their highly automated skills can suffer equally due to the low-level establishment for that specific movement version (Carson & Collins, 2014).

Based on the ideas presented, it seems that effective and easily accessible motor representations provide an excellent scaffold to guide mental and sensorimotor control processes. A clear understanding of the skills to be performed, an understanding of their contribution, and knowing how to activate them would therefore derive from this body of work.

Desirability and applicability of an action-focus approach under pressure

At the top-flight of any sport, the consequences and meaningfulness of performance are often great, especially when the stakes are at their highest. As such, routine and relatively easy executions performed under training conditions often become more difficult, effortful, and resource demanding as situational awareness and pressure increase (e.g., Eysenck, Derakshan, Santos, & Calvo, 2007). Christensen, Sutton, and McIlwain (2016) have even argued that such situations represent a more typical level of challenge for high-level athletes than previous theory has considered (Fitts & Posner, 1967). Furthermore, and on this basis, Carson and Collins (2011, 2016) emphasized the need to establish motor skills under realistic conditions if they are to be most effectively transferred into competition following their acquisition and subsequent refinement. This idea of training with the purpose to achieve high levels of transfer presumably underpins the notion of representative learning design (i.e., ensuring functionality and action fidelity; Pinder, Davids, Renshaw, & Araújo, 2011), at least from an application perspective.

From a process perspective, as pressure increases, execution failure can often occur due to distraction by task-irrelevant thoughts (e.g., thoughts of winning) or cues (e.g., a sudden focus on one element of the movement to the detriment of the whole), prompting athletes to exert (or attempt to exert) step-by-step conscious processing over the skill (Beilock, Jellison, Rydell, McConnell, & Carr, 2006). Thus, poor execution by high-level athletes is underpinned by counterproductive and inefficient use of resources, similar to lesser-skilled athletes, which disrupts the balance of control across the entire skill (e.g., MacPherson, Collins, & Morriss, 2008). Accordingly, the presenting problem is one of needing to effectively execute a (usually complex) movement in what is essentially a different, less familiar, and/or less comfortable bodily state (e.g., Toner, Jones, & Moran, 2016).

As mentioned earlier, current recommendations would attempt to reduce symptoms of pressure through reappraisal of the symptoms (anxiety paradigm, e.g., challenge vs. threat states) and/or avoid them entirely by focusing elsewhere (attention paradigm, e.g., external focus of attention or implicit motor learning). However, applied research suggests that success can be characterized by athletes "making it happen" as opposed to always "letting it happen" (Swann et al., 2016). In other words, pressure symptoms are also part of high-level and successful performances. Accordingly, we propose that existing paradigms fail to explain and cater for interventions to help maintain, or even enhance, such pressurized performance, especially when athletes do start thinking about technique in a dysfunctional fashion.

The multi-action plan (MAP) model (Bortoli, Bertollo, Hanin, & Robazza, 2012; Robazza, Bertollo, Filho, Hanin, & Bortoli, 2016) exemplifies how motoric factors can positively inform mental training as part of psychological provision to athletes. Contrary to theory-driven models of attentional control, an underpinning of the MAP is that high performance effectiveness does not rely solely on the coupling of high processing efficiency with low cognitive resource use (Eysenck et al., 2007). Rather, high performance effectiveness is based on proficiency in switching from efficient/effortless to more effortful elaborations, and vice versa, by consciously activating the desired representations (Bertollo et al., 2016). Therefore, despite a performance state not always being effortless or occurring in a flow-like state (Csikszentmihalyi, 1990), it can still result in optimal outcomes (e.g., score, distance, height, time) providing the representations are entirely and accurately activated. The MAP also acknowledges both the idiosyncratic nature of representations and their nonuniform levels of automaticity. Crucial considerations, which contrast with fundamental research (Christensen et al., 2016), relate to the nature of manipulations applied through mental control, including what, when, how, and how much is attended to (Bobrownicki, MacPherson, Coleman, Collins, & Sproule, 2015; Carson & Collins, 2016).

Depicted as a 2 × 2 interaction between optimal/suboptimal (performance outcome) and automatic/controlled (level of conscious movement control) states, the MAP explains four different execution types. The MAP model also considers a 2 × 2 interplay between performance (optimal/suboptimal) and hedonic tone of emotions (pleasure/displeasure) as conceptualized in the individual zones of optimal functioning (IZOF) model (Hanin, 2007). This performance-hedonic tone relationship leads to functional pleasant, functional unpleasant, dysfunctional unpleasant, and dysfunctional pleasant emotional states. However, we only address the nuanced contribution offered from a cognitive–motoric interaction (see Bortoli et al., 2012; Robazza et al., 2016, for full coverage of the MAP), since emotional components of pressure situations are well covered elsewhere within the literature. Optimal/automatic (Type-1) is essentially a state in which peak performance is reached in an effortless manner; actions are consistent, smooth, and effortless with minimal/supervisory conscious control during execution. Optimal/controlled (Type-2) executions are also successful, although they require effortful conscious focus toward core action components.

We suggest that core action components are complementary with and could be derived from BACs, consisting of one or two distinctive, task-relevant actions (e.g., the downswing in golf) and action parameters (e.g., absolute timing, force production). Importantly, selection of an appropriate core action component should specify one that is not completely automatized and, therefore, in need of control for an accurate execution, especially under pressurized conditions. Stabilizing these components ensures retrieval of important conditions for success, and, through subconscious association (i.e., high skill establishment), the entire skill is activated with the avoidance of excessive movement rumination, namely, unnecessary, repetitive thoughts about the action that interfere with higher levels of mental activity and task execution (Bobrownicki et al., 2015; Masters & Maxwell, 2008). Such an idea is also compatible with a "positive self-focus" (i.e., motorically oriented attention that accurately resonates with the to-be-performed skill; Carson & Collins, 2016, p. 10) or "action gist" (i.e., a cognitive specification of an action type and a particular way of performing the action appropriate to the circumstances; Christensen et al., 2016, p. 43) and, we suggest, represents a key step in managing performance as pressure symptoms arise.

In contrast, a Type-3 performance is also consciously controlled but suboptimal. Specifically, focus is directed toward irrelevant and/or too many BACs (i.e., not core and/or in a step-by-step manner); therefore, attention is dysfunctional in activating the motor representation as desired (i.e., a "negative self-focus," Carson & Collins, 2016), consequently disrupting any benefit of high skill establishment. Finally, Type-4 (suboptimal/automatic) executions reflect a lack of focus, involvement, interest, energy, or effort toward the task (Bortoli et al., 2012), a condition leading to "untuned" skill establishment. Notably, we also suggest that wallowing in self-pity and an inability to change things also typify this state. Thus, at its extreme, Type-4 experiences might lead an athlete to exclaim, or simply think, "I give up," "what's the point," "I don't care," "I've tried everything and nothing works," or "why me?" Amotivated to continue, escaping the situation (i.e., through a rapid defeat or simply diverting the attention of others away from oneself) often seems the most desirable course of action. Clearly, consideration of these execution states calls into question the veracity of claims that thinking about the movement is always bad (Type-2 vs. Type-3) and that not thinking about the movement is always good (Type-1 vs. Type-4; Collins et al., 2015).

Growing empirical evidence supports the presence of these different performance states in elite athletes and the psychophysiological factors that underpin them (e.g., Bertollo et al., 2015, 2016; Filho et al., 2015; di Fronso et al., 2016). For example, Bertollo et al. (2016) found the greatest similarity in cortical synchronization between Type-1 and Type-4 states and cortical desynchronization between Type-2 and Type-3 states. Type-2 performances were underpinned by a focus on idiosyncratic core action components (e.g., aiming or triggering) and a distinctively different neural signature to Type-1 performances. Similarly, and extending the motoric concept to lesser-experienced recreational athletes, Bertollo et al. (2015) found that focusing on core action components (i.e., individual optimal pacing; Type-2) or being in a flow-like state (an individually tailored metronome rhythm; Type-1) during an endurance cycling task elicited a functional influence over performance, as measured by a time-to-exhaustion test, whereas a focus on muscular fatigue symptoms (Type-3) resulted in worse performances. These data demonstrate that successful and functional performance can be generated by multiple states, some of them consciously regulated.

The Control Continuum (Figure 2.1) draws on both the motoric perspective (Carson & Collins, 2016; Schack & Mechsner, 2006) and the MAP model (Robazza et al., 2016). To clarify, "control" here relates to the influence over the performance situation and not the skill itself. Influenced by the MAP, the extremities of the continuum represent Optimal (Type-1/Type-2; upper half) and Dysfunctional (Type-3/Type-4; lower half) states as may be experienced during pressurized conditions. An athlete's positioning between these two extremities can be bi-directional depending, partly, on what, how, and how much thought is consciously applied, as explained earlier. However, there are several essential skill development and sport psychology principles for athletes to understand when interpreting the Control Continuum. These are addressed in the following section.

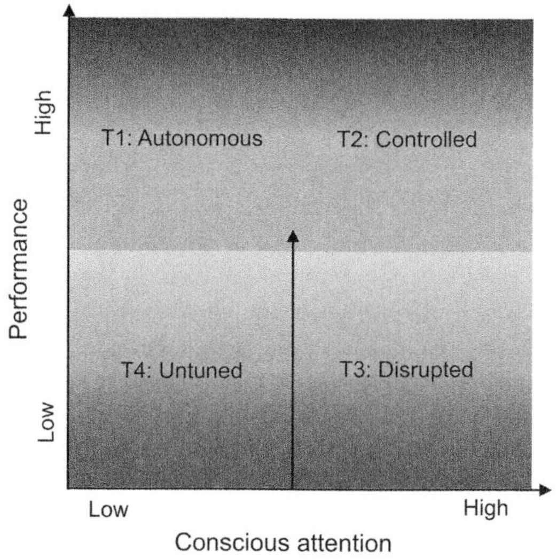

FIGURE 2.1 The control continuum. T1 (Type-1), T2 (Type-2), T3 (Type-3), and T4 (Type-4) are performance states, and the central arrow depicts the desired executional change when experiencing dysfunctional control. T3 and T2 show higher levels of conscious attention toward movement components, where different performance levels are due to contrasting control styles. The same is true for T4 and T1 states.

Practical considerations

As discussed earlier, Schack and colleagues' work (e.g., Bläsing et al., 2009) has revealed several underpinning changes to the motor representations as skills are acquired. The notion of motor representations is related to the concept of long-term working memory, a mechanism based on skilled use of storage in long-term memory in addition to the temporary storage of information referred to as short-term working memory (Ericsson & Kintsch, 1995). Long-term working memory enables expert knowledge to be retrieved quickly and effectively. Motor representations are responsible for transforming planned intentions into a structured working model of the technique required.

Important implications derive from these notions. First, it follows that representations should be taught and developed with performers in a highly individualized and personally relevant way for optimal understanding of the movement required (Carson & Collins, 2011). As such, in working to promote performance, psychologists must address what the athlete "thinks is happening" during their successful competitive executions against an accurate depiction of the effective action, and sensibly incorporate coach perceptions to develop a shared understanding as to what is actually causing the outcome. To do this, performance psychologists may use what Carson, Collins, and Jones (2014) refer to as a "best self-model" (p. 65), presenting the athlete with their most accurate of desired techniques, for example using video feedback. In this way, information provided to structure the representation is most relevant to the movement execution process (i.e., it is the athlete's own movement) and the athlete is motivated by receiving positive motor feedback. The development of understanding is an essential step in this process, empowering the athlete to take charge of their own outcomes.

Second, it would be important to ensure sufficient flexibility within the representations so that athletes are capable and confident in adapting their movement template to novel performance situations or changing the style of control under pressure (Toner & Moran, 2015). This would necessitate exposure to a variety of training situations and challenges (Collins, Button, & Richards, 2011), including training under pressure. Indeed, evidence supports training under these conditions as benefiting later pressurized performance (e.g., Collins, Doherty, & Talbot, 1993). Notably, selecting and monitoring the appropriate level of challenge is a key factor in determining that sufficient quality and quantity of executions are made (Carson & Collins, 2016), whilst avoiding demotivation or overtraining ineffective technique.

Furthermore, the desired level of skill establishment may also depend on the nature, complexity, and longevity of movement required (Toner & Moran, 2015) and, therefore, vary in the amount of time needed for its development. When attempting to broaden an athlete's repertoire of skills, it is crucial to make sure that the athlete understands and can delineate the different performance outcomes with important execution variations. Primarily this is because levels of automatic association will not be consistent for all BACs; some BACs will share more in common to achieve a specific outcome than others. So, an athlete must know, "If I want this outcome, these BACs are important and this is how I do it." Structuring and establishing these activation processes to a high degree under pressurized conditions can assist in "buffering" against dysfunctional states, thereby increasing the likelihood of realizing an Optimal state (see Figure 2.1).

Supporting the interactive relationship between the multi-levels, representational changes have been shown to be facilitated by mental control in the forms of imagery practice and action observation (Kim, Frank, & Schack, 2017). Accordingly, both would seem sensibly deployed to assist athletes with their execution process. Recent research that builds on the earlier work of Lang (1979) has demonstrated benefits from layered (progressive) stimuli-response training when compared to motor or visual imagery only (Cumming et al., 2017), including when executing under pressure (Carson et al., 2014). Typically, athletes will focus their imagery on behavioral (e.g., the image of a golf shot) and physiological (e.g., the intensity of muscle activation, or feelings, during the shot) components of a meaningful scenario (or stimuli) and gradually include more details between sessions (e.g., environmental sounds, preparatory sensations during a pre-performance routine). If the scripts/images used were depicting the athlete's actual performance through a self-model, this should serve to increase the necessary meaningfulness originally described by Lang (1979).

Layering is also suggested to extend beyond the stimulus details to the response propositions (e.g., not only the feeling of the movement but also introducing the impact of club with ball). As such, we suggest integrating mental simulation of movement with auditory, kinesthetic, and visual propositions included. Indeed, generating multiple codes within the sensorimotor representations can be beneficial in providing a more vivid representation and, therefore, a greater number of associated retrieval cues for the athlete. Crucially, however, these codes should include both stimulus (e.g., performing against a specific opponent or at a particular venue, the sound of the crowd) and response propositions (e.g., symptoms of somatic anxiety, movement intensity, rhythm) of the pressurized context for optimal training preparation (Beaumont, Maynard, & Butt, 2015).

Other than identifying individually important BACs, attention should be directed to the temporal aspects of the entire skill, or holistic rhythm (MacPherson, Collins, & Obhi, 2009). Previous studies have identified that focusing on rhythm is not unusual for athletes as they attempt to cope with symptoms of competitive pressure (Nicholls, Holt, Polman, & James, 2005) and has been shown to provide a stabilizing effect on movement kinematics (MacPherson et al., 2008). Holistic thoughts may not only be acoustic in modality; professional golfers have reported focusing kinesthetically on the proximal and larger body segments as opposed to very specific and distal elements of the skill along the kinematic chain (Carson, Collins, & MacNamara, 2013). However, we suggest that further layering of visual and acoustic propositions may serve to enhance this process. Either way, technically focused work should be explicit in nature, increasing the familiarity with practice under pressurized conditions, and supported by quality feedback to demonstrate causal relationships between process and outcome.

Conclusions and future directions

Future research should employ longitudinal interventions to examine the effect of the recommendations provided above, aimed at improving performances under pressure. We suggest that such undertaking be conducted on an intraindividual basis (e.g., Carson & Collins, 2015) to acknowledge the idiosyncratic nature of motor representations. Interventions should combine existing precepts of the MAP, detailed guidelines for constructing imagery scripts (e.g., PETTLEP; Holmes & Collins, 2001), the development of metacognitive skills (e.g., reflection within an activity to evaluate and adjust cognitions, and judgments of learning) to recognize and regulate psycho-emotional states (MacIntyre, Igou, Campbell, Moran, & Matthews, 2014), and practice variables to target increased confidence and embedding of the skill to LTM. The role of athlete understanding is another key factor worthy of more attention. For applied purposes, it is important to consider the relationship between psychology and motor control domains, thereby integrating more "mental-focused" perspectives with action-based approaches to performance improvement and optimization.

References

Balk, Y. A., Adriaanse, M. A., de Ridder, D. T. D., & Evers, C. (2013). Coping under pressure: Employing emotion regulation strategies to enhance performance under pressure. *Journal of Sport and Exercise Psychology, 35*, 408–418. doi:10.1123/jsep.35.4.408

Barsalou, L. W. (2008). Grounded cognition. *Annual Review of Psychology, 59*, 617–645. doi:10.1146/annurev.psych.59.103006.093639

Baumeister, R. F. (1984). Choking under pressure: Self consciousness and paradoxical effects of incentives on skilful performance. *Journal of Personality and Social Psychology, 46*, 610–620. doi:10.1037/0022-3514.46.3.610

Beaumont, C., Maynard, I. W., & Butt, J. (2015). Effective ways to develop and maintain robust sport-confidence: Strategies advocated by sport psychology consultants. *Journal of Applied Sport Psychology, 27*, 301–318. doi:10.1080/10413200.2014.996302

Beilock, S. L., Carr, T. H., MacMahon, C., & Starkes, J. L. (2002). When paying attention becomes counterproductive: Impact of divided versus skill-focused attention on novice and experienced performance of sensorimotor skills. *Journal of Experimental Psychology: Applied, 8*, 6–16. doi:10.1037/1076-898x.8.1.6

Beilock, S. L., Jellison, W. A., Rydell, R. J., McConnell, A. R., & Carr, T. H. (2006). On the causal mechanisms of stereotype threat: Can skills that don't rely heavily on working memory still be threatened? *Personality and Social Psychology Bulletin, 32*, 1059–1071. doi:10.1177/0146167206288489

Bertollo, M., di Fronso, S., Filho, E., Conforto, S., Schmid, M., Bortoli, L., … & Robazza, C. (2016). Proficient brain for optimal performance: The MAP model perspective. *PeerJ, 4*, e2082. doi:10.7717/peerj.2082

Bertollo, M., di Fronso, S., Filho, E., Lamberti, V., Ripari, P., Reis, V. M., … & Robazza, C. (2015). To focus or not to focus: Is attention on the core components of action beneficial for cycling performance? *The Sport Psychologist, 29*, 110–119. doi:10.1123/tsp.2014-0046

Bläsing, B., Tenenbaum, G., & Schack, T. (2009). The cognitive structure of movements in classical dance. *Psychology of Sport and Exercise, 10*, 350–360. doi:10.1016/j.psychsport.2008.10.001

Bobrownicki, R., MacPherson, A. C., Coleman, S. G. S., Collins, D., & Sproule, J. (2015). Re-examining the effects of verbal instructional type on early stage motor learning. *Human Movement Science, 44*, 168–181. doi:10.1016/j.humov.2015.08.023

Bortoli, L., Bertollo, M., Hanin, Y., & Robazza, C. (2012). Striving for excellence: A multi-action plan intervention model for shooters. *Psychology of Sport and Exercise, 13*, 693–701. doi:10.1016/j.psychsport.2012.04.006

Carson, H. J., & Collins, D. (2011). Refining and regaining skills in fixation/diversification stage performers: The Five-A Model. *International Review of Sport and Exercise Psychology, 4*, 146–167. doi:10.1080/1750984x.2011.613682

Carson, H. J., & Collins, D. (2014). Effective skill refinement: Focusing on process to ensure outcome. *Central European Journal of Sport Sciences and Medicine, 7*, 5–21.

Carson, H. J., & Collins, D. (2015). Tracking technical refinement in elite performers: The good, the better, and the ugly. *International Journal of Golf Science, 4*, 67–87. doi:10.1123/ijgs.2015-0003

Carson, H. J., & Collins, D. (2016). The fourth dimension: A motoric perspective on the anxiety–performance relationship. *International Review of Sport and Exercise Psychology, 9*, 1–21. doi:10.1080/1750984X.2015.1072231

Carson, H. J., Collins, D., & Jones, B. (2014). A case study of technical change and rehabilitation: Intervention design and interdisciplinary team interaction. *International Journal of Sport Psychology, 45*, 57–78. doi:10.7352/IJSP2014.45.057

Carson, H. J., Collins, D., & MacNamara, Á. (2013). Systems for technical refinement in experienced performers: The case from expert-level golf. *International Journal of Golf Science, 2*, 65–85. doi:10.1123/ijgs.2.1.65

Causer, J., Holmes, P. S., Smith, N. C., & Williams, A. M. (2011). Anxiety, movement kinematics, and visual attention in elite-level performers. *Emotion, 11*, 595–602. doi:10.1037/a0023225

Christensen, W., Sutton, J., & McIlwain, D. (2016). Cognition in skilled action: Meshed control and the varieties of skill experience. *Mind and Language, 31*, 37–66. doi:10.1111/mila.12094

Collins, D., Burke, V., Martindale, A., & Cruickshank, A. (2015). The illusion of competency versus the desirability of expertise: Seeking a common standard for support professions in sport. *Sports Medicine, 45*, 1–7. doi:10.1007/s40279-014-0251-1

Collins, D., Button, A., & Richards, H. (Eds.). (2011). *Performance psychology: A practitioner's guide.* Oxford, UK: Elsevier.

Collins, D. J., Doherty, M. D., & Talbot, S. (1993). Performance enhancement in moto cross: A case study of the sport science team in action. *The Sport Psychologist, 7*, 290–297.

Collins, D., & Kamin, S. (2012). The performance coach. In S. M. Murphy (Ed.), *The Oxford handbook of sport and performance psychology* (pp. 692–706). New York, NY: Oxford University Press.

Csikszentmihalyi, M. (1990). *Flow: The psychology of optimal experience.* New York, NY: Harper & Row.

Cumming, J., Cooley, S. J., Anuar, N., Kosteli, M.-C., Quinton, M. L., Weibull, F., & Williams, S. E. (2017). Developing imagery ability effectively: A guide to layered stimulus response training. *Journal of Sport Psychology in Action, 8*, 23–33. doi:10.1080/21520704.2016.1205698 di Fronso, S., Robazza, C., Filho, E., Bortoli, L., Comani, S., & Bertollo, M. (2016). Neural markers of performance states in an olympic athlete: An EEG case study in air-pistol shooting. *Journal of Sports Science and Medicine, 15*, 214–222.

Ericsson, K. A., & Kintsch, W. (1995). Long-term working memory. *Psychological Review, 102*, 211–245. doi:10.1037/0033-295X.102.2.211

Eysenck, M. W., Derakshan, N., Santos, R., & Calvo, M. G. (2007). Anxiety and cognitive performance: Attentional control theory. *Emotion, 7*, 336–353. doi:10.1037/1528-3542.7.2.336

Filho, E., Di Fronso, S., Mazzoni, C., Robazza, C., Bortoli, L., & Bertollo, M. (2015). My heart is racing! Psychophysiological dynamics of skilled racecar drivers. *Journal of Sports Sciences, 33*, 945–959. doi:10.1080/02640414.2014.977940

Fitts, P. M., & Posner, M. I. (1967). *Human performance*. Belmont, CA: Brooks/Cole.

Frank, C., Land, W. M., & Schack, T. (2016). Perceptual-cognitive changes during motor learning: The influence of mental and physical practice on mental representation, gaze behavior, and performance of a complex action. *Frontiers in Psychology, 6*, 1981. doi:10.3389/fpsyg.2015.01981

Hanin, Y. L. (2007). Emotions in sport: Current issues and perspectives. In G. Tenenbaum & R. C. Eklund (Eds.), *Handbook of sport psychology* (3rd ed., pp. 31–58). Hoboken, NJ: John Wiley & Sons.

Holmes, P. S., & Collins, D. J. (2001). The PETTLEP approach to motor imagery: A functional equivalence model for sport psychologists. *Journal of Applied Sport Psychology, 13*, 60–83. doi:10.1080/10413200109339004

Kiely, J. (2017). The robust running ape: Unraveling the deep underpinnings of coordinated human running proficiency. *Frontiers in Psychology, 8*, 892. doi:10.3389/fpsyg.2017.00892

Kim, T., Frank, C., & Schack, T. (2017). A systematic investigation of the effect of action observation training and motor imagery training on the development of mental representation structure and skill performance. *Frontiers in Human Neuroscience, 11*, 499. doi:10.3389/fnhum.2017.00499

Lang, P. J. (1979). A bio-informational theory of emotional imagery. *Psychophysiology, 16*, 495–512. doi:10.1111/j.1469-8986.1979.tb01511.x

MacIntyre, T. E., Igou, E. R., Campbell, M. J., Moran, A. P., & Matthews, J. (2014). Metacognition and action: A new pathway to understanding social and cognitive aspects of expertise in sport. *Frontiers in Psychology, 5*, 1155. doi:10.3389/fpsyg.2014.01155

MacPherson, A. C., Collins, D., & Morriss, C. (2008). Is what you think what you get? Optimizing mental focus for technical performance. *The Sport Psychologist, 22*, 288–303. doi:10.1123/tsp.22.3.288

MacPherson, A. C., Collins, D., & Obhi, S. S. (2009). The importance of temporal structure and rhythm for the optimum performance of motor skills: A new focus for practitioners of sport psychology. *Journal of Applied Sport Psychology, 21*, 48–61. doi:10.1080/10413200802595930

Martindale, A., & Collins, D. (2012). A professional judgment and decision making case study: Reflection-in-action research. *The Sport Psychologist, 26*, 500–518. doi:10.1123/tsp.26.4.500

Masters, R., & Maxwell, J. (2008). The theory of reinvestment. *International Review of Sport and Exercise Psychology, 1*, 160–183. doi:10.1080/17509840802287218

Moran, A., & Toner, J. (2017). *A critical introduction to sport psychology* (3rd ed.). London, UK: Routledge.

Nicholls, A. R., Holt, N. L., Polman, R. C. J., & James, D. W. G. (2005). Stress and coping among international adolescent golfers. *Journal of Applied Sport Psychology, 17*, 333–340. doi:10.1080/10413200500313644

Paivio, A. (1986). *Mental representations: A dual-coding approach*. New York, NY: Oxford University Press.

Pinder, R. A., Davids, K., Renshaw, I., & Araújo, D. (2011). Representative learning design and functionality of research and practice in sport. *Journal of Sport and Exercise Psychology, 33*, 146–155. doi:10.1123/jsep.33.1.146

Robazza, C., Bertollo, M., Filho, E., Hanin, Y., & Bortoli, L. (2016). Perceived control and hedonic tone dynamics during performance in elite shooters. *Research Quarterly for Exercise and Sport, 87*, 284–294. doi:10.1080/02701367.2016.1185081

Rosenbaum, D. A. (2005). The Cinderella of psychology: The neglect of motor control in the science of mental life and behavior. *American Psychologist, 60*, 308–317. doi:10.1037/0003-066X.60.4.308

Schack, T., & Mechsner, F. (2006). Representation of motor skills in human long-term memory. *Neuroscience Letters, 391*, 77–81. doi:10.1016/j.neulet.2005.10.009

Scholz, J. P., & Schöner, G. (1999). The uncontrolled manifold concept: Identifying control variables for a functional task. *Experimental Brain Research, 126*, 289–306. doi:10.1007/s002210050738

Seegelke, C., & Schack, T. (2016). Cognitive representation of human action: Theory, applications, and perspectives. *Frontiers in Public Health, 4*, 24. doi:10.3389/fpubh.2016.00024

Swann, C., Crust, L., Keegan, R., Piggott, D., & Hemmings, B. (2015). An inductive exploration into the flow experiences of European tour golfers. *Qualitative Research in Sport, Exercise and Health, 7*, 210–234. doi:10.1080/2159676X.2014.926969

Swann, C., Keegan, R., Crust, L., & Piggott, D. (2016). Psychological states underlying excellent performance in professional golfers: "Letting it happen" vs. "making it happen." *Psychology of Sport and Exercise, 23*, 101–113. doi:10.1016/j.psychsport.2015.10.008

Toner, J., Jones, L., & Moran, A. (2016). Bodily crises in skilled performance: Considering the need for artistic habits. *Performance Enhancement & Health, 4*, 50–57. doi:10.1016/j.peh.2015.10.001

Toner, J., & Moran, A. (2015). Enhancing performance proficiency at the expert level: Considering the role of 'somaesthetic awareness'. *Psychology of Sport and Exercise, 16*, 110–117. doi:10.1016/j.psychsport.2014.07.006

Williams, S. E., Cooley, S. J., & Cumming, J. (2013). Layered stimulus response training improves motor imagery ability and movement execution. *Journal of Sport and Exercise Psychology, 35*, 60–71. doi:10.1123/jsep.35.1.60

Wolpert, D. M., Diedrichsen, J., & Flanagan, J. R. (2011). Principles of sensorimotor learning. *Nature Reviews Neuroscience, 12*, 739–751. doi:10.1038/nrn3112

Wulf, G. (2013). Attentional focus and motor learning: A review of 15 years. *International Review of Sport and Exercise Psychology, 6*, 77–104. doi:10.1080/1750984x.2012.723728

Wulf, G. (2016). An external focus of attention is a conditio sine qua non for athletes: A response to Carson, Collins, and Toner (2015). *Journal of Sports Sciences, 34*, 1293–1295. doi:10.1080/02640414.2015.1136746

3

MENTAL TOUGHNESS DEVELOPMENT AND TRAINING IN SPORT

Richard G. Cowden, Lee Crust, Stephanie J. Tibbert, and Patricia C. Jackman

In the past two decades, the concept of mental toughness (MT) has been studied extensively by scholars and practitioners interested in the psychology of performance excellence. As the literature on MT has grown, resolution of early ambiguities surrounding the concept has led to improvements in conceptual clarity and increased consensus among researchers about its definition (Cowden, Crust, Joynt, Hook, & Worthington, 2018). Most scholars agree that MT represents a psychological resource that enables individuals to initiate and sustain efforts toward attaining optimal levels of performance despite exposure to adversity (e.g., Coulter, Mallett, & Gucciardi, 2010; Gucciardi, Hanton, Gordon, Mallett, & Temby, 2015; Hardy, Bell, & Beattie, 2014). As such, MT is a key psychological attribute associated with various indicators of success in sport (for a review, see Cowden, 2017a).

Mental toughness: a brief overview

A number of conceptual models of MT have been proposed in the literature, which differ primarily in theoretical grounding and dimensionality (see Table 3.1, for a comparative summary of select MT models). Despite distinctions, several features have frequently been identified as central to the concept of MT. To illustrate key similarities in existing conceptualizations of MT, Mahoney, Ntoumanis, Mallett, and Gucciardi (2014) applied broad thematic categories of surviving (e.g., psychological buoyancy, coping adaptively), striving (e.g., persevering through obstacles, self-belief), and thriving (e.g., growth-oriented mindset, accepting personal responsibility) to synthesize and organize core attributes of MT delineated in the literature.

TABLE 3.1 Summary of Select Models Used to Conceptualize Mental Toughness

Author	*Model Description*	*Working Definition*	*Dimensionality*	*Contextual Utility*	*Superordinate and Subordinate Dimensions*
Clough, Earle, & Sewell (2002)	A tri-dimensional theory of hardiness (i.e., control, commitment, and challenge) was appropriated into a model of MT, with *confidence* added as a key dimension distinguishing MT from hardiness.	"Mentally tough individuals tend to be sociable and outgoing; as they are able to remain calm and relaxed, they are competitive in many situations and have lower anxiety levels than others. With a high sense of self-belief and an unshakeable faith that they control their own destiny, these individuals can remain relatively unaffected by competition of adversity" (p. 38).	Multidimensional	General (athletes and non-athletes)	Control (emotion; life) Commitment Challenge Confidence (interpersonal; abilities)
Jones, Hanton, & Connaughton (2002, 2007)	A multi-phased qualitative approach informed by personal construct theory was used to organize attributes identified into a sport-general framework of MT.	"...having the natural or developed edge that enables you to: (a) generally, cope better than your opponents with the many demands (competition, training, lifestyle) that sport places on a performer; (b) specifically, be more consistent and better than your opponents in remaining determined, focused, confident, and in control under pressure" (Jones et al., 2002, p. 209).	Multidimensional	Sport-general	Attitude/mindset (belief; focus) Training (using long-term goals as the source of motivation; controlling the environment; pushing yourself to the limit) Competition (belief; staying focused; regulating performance; handling pressure; awareness and control of thoughts and feelings; controlling the environment) Post-competition (handling failure; handling success)

(*Continued*)

Author	*Model Description*	*Working Definition*	*Dimensionality*	*Contextual Utility*	*Superordinate and Subordinate Dimensions*
Gucciardi, Gordon, & Dimmock (2008)	Guided by personal construct theory, an explanatory model of MT within Australian rules football was constructed from the three inductively-derived thematic areas that emerged from qualitative inquiry.	"Mental toughness in Australian football is a collection of values, attitudes, behaviours, and emotions that enable you to persevere and overcome any obstacle, adversity, or pressure experienced, but also to maintain concentration and motivation when things are going well to consistently achieve your goals" (p. 278).	Multidimensional	Sport-specific	Characteristics (self-belief; work ethic; personal values; self-motivated; tough attitude; concentration/focus; resilience; handling pressure; emotional intelligence; sport intelligence; physical toughness) Behaviors General (recover well from injury; preparation; consistent performances) Competition (repeatable good performances; play well no matter the position; superior decision-makers; do the "one percenters") Situations General (injury and rehabilitation; preparation; challenges) Competition (external pressures (environment, playing environment); internal pressures (fatigue/endurance, confidence))

Author	*Model Description*	*Working Definition*	*Dimensionality*	*Contextual Utility*	*Superordinate and Subordinate Dimensions*
Hardy et al. (2014)	Neuropsychological research and personality theory (i.e., reinforcement sensitivity theory) were applied in developing a perspective of MT predicated on the occurrence of mentally tough behavior.	"…the ability to achieve personal goals in the face of pressure from a wide range of different stressors" (p. 70).	Unidimensional	Sport-general	–
Gucciardi et al. (2015)	Central indicators of MT identified (e.g., generalized self-efficacy) by integrating existing evidence on MT, with linkages drawn between each indicator and relevant theoretical perspectives (e.g., self-efficacy theory) to support those identified.	"...a personal capacity to produce consistently high levels of subjective (e.g., personal goals or strivings) or objective performance (e.g., sales, race time, GPA) despite everyday challenges and stressors as well as significant adversities" (p. 28).	Unidimensional	General (athletes and non-athletes)	–

Another area of contention among scholars concerns the temporal stability of MT. Behavioral genetic research involving twins (e.g., Horsburgh, Schermer, Veselka, & Vernon, 2009) identified that individual differences in MT are primarily attributable to genetic and non-shared environmental factors, suggesting that MT is comparable to other trait-like constructs. Other studies have reported state-like fluctuations in MT across situations (e.g., Weinberg, Butt, Mellano, & Harmison, 2017). In one study that acquired weekly measurements of MT from a sample of undergraduate students over a 10-week period, Gucciardi et al. (2015) found that within-person variability in MT was 12% higher compared to variability between persons. Collectively, existing research resonates with a person × environment interactionist approach to MT (Harmison, 2011) in which expressions in MT are relatively stable (i.e., trait-like) across similar types of situations, yet may vary (i.e., state-like) across situations that differ.

Beyond achievement: mental toughness and well-being

The implications of MT for competitive performance are highly attractive to personnel involved in sport (e.g., athletes, coaches). However, there are also broader benefits of MT for mental and physical health. First, MT functions as a protective mechanism against ill health. To illustrate, a number of studies (e.g., Cowden et al., 2018; Gerber et al., 2018) have yielded relations between MT and lower levels of self-reported stress, and more adaptive responses to general stress (e.g., fewer symptoms of burnout and depression) or specific kinds of stress (e.g., underperformance). Second, MT has been described as a marker of a person's tendency to self-actualize (Mahoney et al., 2014) and promotes personal flourishing. Such theorizing has been supported by research that has drawn links between MT and indicators of optimal human functioning (e.g., eudaimonic well-being), desirable character strengths (e.g., honesty, zestfulness), and seeking or advantageously using circumstances for self-growth (Gucciardi et al., 2015; Mahoney et al., 2014; Stamp et al., 2015).

Although the bulk of scholarly activity has focused on the intrapersonal significance of MT, there is also growing support for the advantages of MT to interpersonal functioning. Specifically, recent studies have connected MT with socially adaptive virtues that promote relational well-being, including gratitude (Coulter, Mallett, & Singer, 2018) and interpersonal forgivingness (Cowden, Clough, & Oppong Asante, 2017). In studies that have examined MT in relation to aspects of interpersonal functioning (e.g., relationships with peers) more directly (e.g., Stamp et al., 2015; St Clair-Thompson et al., 2015), findings suggest that MT may perform an integral role in developing and maintaining quality relationships with others.

Developing mental toughness in sport: evidence from targeted interventions

If the practical utility of MT is to be advanced, evidence-based interventions targeting MT are needed to enable performers to effectively navigate, and perhaps thrive on, the demands of training, competition, and life outside of sport. Given the potential for training in MT to be misused by pseudo-experts, it is critical that such interventions are grounded in scientific evidence, have sound theoretical foundations, and are evaluated empirically. Numerous qualitative studies (for a review, see Anthony, Gucciardi, & Gordon, 2016) have used retrospective approaches to report on the experiences of athletes, coaches, and sport psychologists in developing MT. Most findings identified a long-term developmental process that could be facilitated (or restricted) through features of the sporting environment (e.g., challenging training conditions, high coach expectations) but also through more short-term targeted learning of psychological skills. Knowledge acquired through exploratory, qualitative studies has begun to be tested experimentally. Although much work remains in designing and implementing interventions aimed at developing MT, we review some of the more theoretically driven evidence that currently exists.

Environmental and coaching-based approaches

Qualitative research has highlighted important features of the environment that operate as mentally toughening mechanisms (Anthony et al., 2016). There appears to be potential for coaches to manipulate the environment to provide both challenging and supportive learning experiences that could influence MT. Research indicates that MT can be cultivated by challenging participants, moving beyond established comfort zones, and creating discomfort (e.g., Cook, Crust, Littlewood, Nesti, & Allen-Collinson, 2014). These conditions create opportunities for athletes to learn from setbacks, engage in problem-solving, and become more self-reliant. Nevertheless, such approaches need to be implemented with appropriate guidance from a support network (hence, the term "autonomy-supportive"), especially as athletes are developing new skills and abilities. In applying an autonomy-supportive approach, athletes are systematically exposed to situations where they are challenged appropriately in a form of guided discovery. This is similar to a child learning to ride a bike: the use of stabilizers enables them to avoid falling off, but they begin to experience the sensation of cycling on their own, and they learn from being unbalanced and make requisite adjustments.

Findings of numerous qualitative studies suggest that autonomy-supportive coaching behaviors (as opposed to controlling behaviors) have the potential to promote MT (see Anthony et al., 2016). Theoretically, an autonomy-supportive approach to developing MT is in line with self-determination theory (Ryan & Deci, 2000) and the satisfaction of fundamental psychological needs associated with optimal human functioning. Mahoney, Ntoumanis, Gucciardi, Mallett, and Stebbings (2016) utilized a sample of 18 rowing coaches who were randomly assigned to either an immediate or a delayed treatment condition, which involved attending autonomy-supportive workshops over eight weeks. As part of the intervention process, coaches were asked to apply the autonomy-supportive approach to working with their athletes. Although the coaches identified several benefits of the intervention (e.g., increased insight) and expressed an appreciation for the autonomy-supportive approach, the intervention was unsuccessful at enhancing the MT of the rowers. Qualitative feedback from coaches indicated that the taught behaviors might not have been applied due to contextual pressures and challenges in applying workshop content to the performance context. For example, coaches reported reverting to habitual ways of coaching that included controlling-type behaviors in order to be time efficient, thus highlighting the potential challenges of applying this type of intervention to increase MT.

Taking a somewhat different approach, Anthony, Gordon, Gucciardi, and Dawson (2018) targeted increasing the frequency of mentally tough behaviors in team sports using behavioral coaching workshops over a five-month period. This process included the use of an autonomy-supportive framework to identify and encourage coaches to promote sport-specific behaviors linked to MT (e.g., responding effectively to setbacks or criticism). Coaches then applied this new approach to working with their athletes. They also rated the mentally tough behavior of their athletes at several points before, during, and after the intervention. Coaches reported an initial increase in mentally tough behavior after baseline, followed by a plateau and minor decreases.

Although existing evidence highlights the potential for autonomy-supportive coaching to enhance MT, further testing is necessary to evaluate the effectiveness of this approach. As most studies have based evaluations on self- and informant-ratings (approaches that are inherently susceptible to bias without the use of independent and impartial assessors), multi-pronged measurement approaches for assessing efficacy are necessary. Few studies have explored the prospect of leveraging broader social support networks to develop MT. For example, findings identify the role of parents in providing athletes with an appropriate level of involvement and support (e.g., encouragement, guidance) to cultivate MT (e.g., Connaughton, Wadey, Hanton, & Jones, 2008). By focusing on a selection of key personnel involved in athletes' lives, autonomy-supportive climates may be nurtured across different environments to increase opportunities for developing MT.

In contrast to autonomy-supportive approaches, Bell, Hardy, and Beattie (2013) adopted a behavioral intervention predicated on punishment. The authors reported the results of a two-year longitudinal study that aimed to enhance MT in elite young cricketers. Bell and colleagues argued that elite sport is a demanding setting in which developing players need to be aware that negative consequences follow undesirable behavior or performance. To mitigate some of the potential drawbacks of using punishment, the intervention also employed a transformational approach delivered by a range of staff (e.g., coaches, psychologists, medical staff), which allowed performers opportunities to practice under pressure. Athletes were also taught supplemental coping skills to assist them with navigating various challenges. Importantly, the intervention group of 20 elite young players was compared to a matched control group that took part in more traditional cricket practices. At the end of the study, coach-rated MT was found to be significantly higher in the intervention group. Performance statistics also supported the benefits of the intervention. Despite these promising findings, use of a multi-modal intervention meant that it remained unclear whether the results were due to the use of punishment, the transformational approach to delivery, teaching the participants coping skills, or a combined effect.

Psychological skills training

Psychological skills training (PST) has a long history of being applied to enhance performance in sports. Although the validity of supporting evidence for PST has been criticized due to study design and methodological issues (Gardner & Moore, 2006), PST continues to be used in applied settings where sport psychologists work with athletes to address performance-related issues. Evidence from cross-sectional studies involving samples of athletes (e.g., Crust & Azadi, 2010) has revealed positive relations between MT and use of psychological skills.

Other studies have used experimental approaches to assess whether PST programs led to improvements in MT. One of the first studies to examine the effects of PST on MT sampled 36 national-level junior swimmers aged between 10 and 18 years old (Sheard & Golby, 2006). Improvements in self-reported MT and performance times were found following a seven-week training program (45 minutes per week) that included goal-setting, visualization, relaxation, concentration training, and thought-stopping. However, findings were limited by the use of a one-group, pretest-posttest design and concerns that subsequent testing has raised over the validity of the instrument used to measure MT (see Gucciardi, 2012).

Some scholars have argued that interventions should be developed specifically to target the key elements of MT. To test this proposition, Gucciardi, Gordon, and Dimmock (2009a) compared the effects of a targeted mental toughness training (MTT) program with a more traditional PST program. A sample of 75 adolescent Australian football players were divided between two experimental groups (six weeks of single two-hour sessions) and a control group that was not exposed to either intervention. Subjective ratings of MT were found to be higher post-intervention in both training groups compared to the control group. However, no differences in MT were found between the PST and targeted MTT groups, likely owing to overlap in the type of psychological skills (e.g., self-regulation) that were targeted in both experimental groups (Gucciardi et al., 2009a). A qualitative follow-up study (Gucciardi, Gordon, & Dimmock, 2009b) reported some of the key benefits of the MTT (as perceived by athletes, parents, and coaches), which included valuing the importance of quality preparation, being more receptive to criticism, team cohesion, increased work ethic, and tougher attitudes. Although the evidence did not support the hypothesis that MTT would be more effective in enhancing MT than traditional PST, findings suggested that MT can be developed through relatively short-term interventions focused on psychological skills development.

Using a slightly different approach, Slack, Maynard, Butt, and Olusoga (2015) targeted MT development in early-career English Football League referees. To facilitate the development of more robust and better performing referees, Slack and colleagues implemented a workshop-based education and training program for three referees over an eight-month period. A staggered, multiple baseline approach was taken to establish initial baseline measures before introducing an intervention phase. A series of individual and group workshops aimed to develop awareness of the psychological issues involved in officiating, as well as developing traditional skills such as positive thinking, thought stopping, relaxation, and general coping. Referees' self-reported MT and external ratings of referee performance were higher following the intervention when compared with baseline scores. Interestingly, MT was reported to fluctuate from time to time, which supports previous assertions that MT needs to be maintained (see Connaughton et al., 2008). Thus, future studies incorporating appropriate follow-up are needed to determine the extent to which gains in MT are maintained following intervention.

A key challenge in assessing the effectiveness of multi-modal intervention approaches is determining the role of individual components in the development of MT. One study that purported to evaluate the effects of a specific skill (attributional retraining) on the MT development of seven male rugby players has been conducted (Parkes & Mallett, 2011). Although qualitative and quantitative assessments identified more optimistic thinking, greater resilience in the face of adversity, and enhanced confidence, the omission of any recognized measure of MT makes the evidence difficult to evaluate. As such, additional studies are required to assess the effects of enhancing specific kinds of psychological skills on MT.

Alongside the traditional change-based focus of PST approaches, there is a need to examine the effectiveness of alternative models to developing MT. A growing body of research (for a review, see Noetel, Ciarrochi, Van Zanden, & Lonsdale, 2019) advocates mindfulness- and acceptance-based approaches for improving mental health and athletic performance. Based on evidence relating MT to dimensions of self-awareness, attentional control, and mindfulness more generally (e.g., Cowden, 2017b; Jones & Parker, 2018), mindfulness and experiential acceptance approaches appear to be potential avenues through which MT can be developed and maintained.

Strengths-based approaches

As an alternative to traditional PST interventions that focus on overcoming weaknesses or performance deficits, strengths-based approaches that aim to identify and capitalize on strengths have been applied within sport. Strengths-based approaches begin with the identification of strengths (realized or unrealized) that the individual or team is passionate about and progress toward making greater use of such strengths. Previously, Gordon (2012) outlined the theoretical rationale behind the use of strengths-based approaches to develop MT in sport. More recently, Gordon, Anthony, and Gucciardi (2017) evidenced the effectiveness of such an approach using an elite cricketer and comparing baseline and intervention measures of MT with control participants. Gordon and Gucciardi (2011) also identified how strengths-based approaches could be used in team settings. Importantly, such approaches require individualized coaching (limiting large-scale application), and the range of different approaches to strengths-based training make it challenging to evaluate. Although the limited evidence available generally supports the effectiveness of strengths-based coaching for developing MT, further empirical testing is necessary before more substantive conclusions about efficacy are made.

Drawbacks to mental toughness: implications for interventions

Although researchers and practitioners are primarily interested in the adaptive features and outcomes linked to MT, existing research has identified a number of potentially maladaptive MT attributes. Therefore, training and intervention initiatives focused on developing MT should be accompanied by an awareness of possible negative outcomes (Levy, Polman, Clough, Marchant, & Earle, 2006). One attribute of MT that has been linked to potentially undesirable outcomes is physical toughness, which includes behaviors related to pushing through pain, injury, and illness in pursuit of a goal (see Coulter et al., 2010). Similar behaviors are espoused by traditional masculine ideals prevalent in sport, many of which (e.g., performing while in pain, ignoring injury, denying fatigue) are associated with physiological and psychological distress in athletic populations (Young & White, 2000).

Physical toughness has been incorporated into prior MT interventions (see Gucciardi et al., 2009a), but teaching athletes these methods may increase susceptibility to overtraining, burnout, and injury (Richardson, Andersen, & Morris, 2008). For example, Brown, Wilson, and Sharp (2006) investigated MT and burnout qualitatively in a sample of seven elite athletes. They found that the MT norm of pushing through fatigue and pain can be beneficial to performance, but there was a point at which ignoring or denying fatigue becomes unhealthy and could develop into unexplained underperformance syndrome (Budgett et al., 2000). Thus, MT training programs ought to emphasize the importance of recovery when in pain rather than reward or teach athletes to push through injury, illness, or pain (Richardson et al., 2008). To avoid the traditional masculine imperatives that may lead to physical and psychological distress, practitioners are encouraged to teach athletes and coaches how to recognize the difference between physical pain associated with improving fitness and physical pain associated with damage, overtraining, and burnout (Jaeschke, Sachs, & Dieffenbach, 2016).

Another MT characteristic that resonates with traditional sporting masculinity is suppressing and controlling emotions. Although controlling unhelpful emotions can be beneficial for performance, there is a risk of embracing an extreme version of this response that endorses unrealistic expectations where mentally tough athletes hide unwanted feelings at all times. In one study, Coulter, Mallett, and Singer (2016) identified an Australian Football League (AFL) player who asserted that being mentally tough meant not showing emotion: "I tend to keep my problems to myself. That's what the coaches want to see in players…" (p. 104). Uphill and Hemmings (2017) suggested that an unintended consequence of suppressing emotions under the banner of MT is that athletes who are struggling with their emotions are silenced. Swann, Crust, and Allen-Collinson (2016) reported the consequences of emotional suppression in a group of elite mountaineers. Those who suppressed emotions following a tragic event, behavior that was considered mentally tough, were more likely to experience long-term difficulties adjusting to post-tragedy life. Ramaeker and Petrie (2019) found that individuals who conformed most to the masculine ideal of suppressing emotion appeared susceptible to experiencing mental and physical distress and were also the individuals least likely to seek out assistance. Because emotional suppression does not appear compatible with psychological well-being over the long-term, training for MT needs to incorporate facets that teach athletes to regulate rather than silence emotion.

An important consideration for designing effective interventions is the contextual nature of MT (Eubank, Nesti, & Littlewood, 2017). Researchers (e.g., Coulter et al., 2016; Tibbert, Andersen, & Morris, 2015) have found that, in AFL, demonstrating excessive physical and mental perseverance to overcome any obstacle to reach goals is a common behavior and a prerequisite for acceptance within the sport culture. Conversely, in Crust, Swann, and Allen-Collinson's (2019) investigation of elite mountaineers, they found that MT in this environment meant *not* persevering to overcome any obstacle. Rather, MT involved being able to abandon goals when there was a risk to personal safety. This contradiction between perseverance as never quitting and knowing when to quit showcases the different ideals that exist about MT, leading to questions concerning the appropriateness of constructing generic MT training programs.

Contextual influences may also explain why numerous unique attributes of MT have been identified by research teams in different sport environments. The vast number of idiosyncratic characteristics and behaviors has direct consequences for developing effective MT training programs. For example, in one environment MT may mean overtraining and playing in pain (Tibbert et al., 2015), while in another it may mean having presence and self-awareness (Wilson, Bennet, Mosewich, Faulkner, & Crocker, 2019). Eubank et al. (2017) suggested that the unique aspects related to understanding MT within a sport culture carried greater importance than a generic understanding of MT. To comprehend fully what MT means in one sport setting, practitioners and researchers need to immerse themselves in each individual sporting environment armed with an understanding that knowledge of MT acquired in one setting may not fully transfer to another.

Given the complex nature of MT, practitioners may find themselves walking a fine line between athlete well-being and sport performance. Although the applied practitioner may be able to provide a safe, nonjudgmental environment where athletes can learn about emotion, vulnerability, injury, and pain, this environment has to align with the cultural context. To be effective, interventions should be designed to fit within the sport culture but primarily have individual well-being in mind. Interventions may need to be directed toward educating key stakeholders, including governing bodies and coaching personnel, about the benefits and potential drawbacks of MT for athlete performance and well-being. Identifying and modifying unrealistic ideals about MT within specific sport cultures will likely promote healthy decision-making among athletes, both during training and competition.

Conclusions

In summary, MT has the potential to enhance sport performance and promote athletes' well-being. Although evidence has offered some support for the efficacy of selected MT interventions, current approaches require further empirical evaluation. Importantly, opportunities exist to examine the utility of currently unexplored avenues for developing MT among athletes. As sport personnel (e.g., coaches, practitioners) explore available approaches and implement MT training initiatives, careful consideration should be given to sport-specific contextual factors that are likely to affect the type, degree, and manner in which MT should be targeted and the short- and long-term implications of interventions that aim to nurture MT.

References

Anthony, D. R., Gordon, S., Gucciardi, D. F., & Dawson, B. (2018). Adapting a behavioural coaching framework for mental toughness development. *Journal of Sport Psychology in Action*, *9*, 32–50. doi:10.1080/21520704.2017.1323058

Anthony, D. R., Gucciardi, D. F., & Gordon, S. (2016). A meta-study of qualitative research on mental toughness development. *International Review of Sport and Exercise Psychology*, *9*, 160–190. doi:10.1080/1750984X.2016.1146787

Bell, J. J., Hardy, L., & Beattie, S. J. (2013). Enhancing mental toughness and performance under pressure in elite young cricketers: A 2-year longitudinal intervention. *Sport, Exercise, and Performance Psychology*, *2*, 281–297. doi:10.1037/a0033129

Brown, J. F. M., Wilson, M. A., & Sharp, N. C. C. (2006). "Down but not out": An exploration of the psychological factors that impact unexplained underperformance syndrome (UPS). *International Journal of Sports Science and Coaching, 1*, 163–176. doi:10.1260/174795406777641212

Budgett, R., Newsholme, E., Lehmann, M., Sharp, C., Jones, D., Peto, T., … White, P. (2000). Redefining the overtraining syndrome as the unexplained underperformance syndrome. *British Journal of Sports Medicine, 34*, 67–68. doi:10.1136/bjsm.34.1.67

Clough, P. J., Earle, K., & Sewell, D. (2002). Mental toughness: The concept and its measurement. In I. Cockerill (Ed.), *Solutions in sport psychology* (pp. 32–43). London, UK: Thomson Publishing.

Connaughton, D., Wadey, R., Hanton, S., & Jones, G. (2008). The development and maintenance of mental toughness: Perceptions of elite performers. *Journal of Sports Sciences, 26*, 83–95. doi:10.1080/02640410701310958

Cook, C., Crust, L., Littlewood, M., Nesti, M., & Allen-Collinson, J. (2014). What it takes: Perceptions of mental toughness and its development in an English Premier League soccer academy. *Qualitative Research in Sport, Exercise and Health, 6*, 329–347. doi:10.1080/2159676X.2013.857708

Coulter, T. J., Mallett, C. J., & Gucciardi, D. F. (2010). Understanding mental toughness in Australian soccer: Perceptions of players, parents, and coaches. *Journal of Sports Sciences, 28*, 699–716. doi:10.1080/02640411003734085

Coulter, T. J., Mallett, C. J., & Singer, J. A. (2016). A subculture of mental toughness in an Australian football league club. *Psychology of Sport and Exercise, 22*, 98–113. doi:10.1016/j.psychsport.2015.06.007

Coulter, T. J., Mallett, C. J., & Singer, J. A. (2018). A three-domain personality analysis of a mentally tough athlete. *European Journal of Personality, 32*, 6–29. doi:10.1002/per.2129

Cowden, R. G. (2017a). Mental toughness and success in sport: A review and prospect. *The Open Sports Sciences Journal, 10*, 1–14. doi:10.2174/1875399X01710010001

Cowden, R. G. (2017b). On the mental toughness of self-aware athletes: Evidence from competitive tennis athletes. *South African Journal of Science, 113*, 1–6. doi:10.17159/sajs.2017/20160112

Cowden, R. G., Clough, P. J., & Oppong Asante, K. (2017). Mental toughness in South African youth: Relationships with forgivingness and attitudes towards risk. *Psychological Reports, 120*, 271–289. doi:10.1177/0033294116687516

Cowden, R. G., Crust, L., Joynt, S., Hook, J. N., & Worthington, E. L., Jr. (2018). How do mentally tougher athletes overcome self-directed anger, shame, and criticism? A self-forgiveness mediation analysis. *International Journal of Sport Psychology, 49*, 327–348.

Crust, L., & Azadi, K. (2010). Mental toughness and athletes' use of psychological strategies. *European Journal of Sport Science, 10*, 43–51. doi:10.1080/17461390903049972

Crust, L., Swann, C., & Allen-Collinson, J. (2019). Mentally tough behaviour in extreme environments: Perceptions of elite high-altitude mountaineers. *Qualitative Research in Sport, Exercise, and Health, 11*, 334–347. doi:10.1080/2159676X.2018.1494622

Eubank, M. R., Nesti, M. S., & Littlewood, M. A. (2017). A culturally informed approach to mental toughness development in high performance sport. *International Journal of Sport Psychology, 48*, 206–222. doi:10.7352/IJSP 2017.48

Gardner, F. L., & Moore, Z. E. (2006). *Clinical sport psychology*. Champaign, IL: Human Kinetics.

Gerber, M., Best, S., Meerstetter, F., Walter, M., Ludyga, S., Brand, S., … Gustafsson, H. (2018). Effects of stress and mental toughness on burnout and depressive symptoms:

A prospective study with young elite athletes. *Journal of Science and Medicine in Sport, 21*, 1200–1205. doi:10.1016/j.jsams.2018.05.018

Gordon, S. (2012). Strengths-based approaches to developing mental toughness: Team and individual. *International Coaching Psychology Review, 7*, 210–222.

Gordon, S., Anthony, D. R., & Gucciardi, D. F. (2017). A case study of strengths-based coaching of mental toughness in cricket. *International Journal of Sport Psychology, 48*, 223–245.

Gordon, S., & Gucciardi, D. F. (2011). A strengths-based approach to coaching mental toughness. *Journal of Sport Psychology in Action, 2*, 143–155. doi:10.1080/21520704.2011.598222

Gucciardi, D. F. (2012). Measuring mental toughness in sport: A psychometric examination of the Psychological Performance Inventory–A and its predecessor. *Journal of Personality Assessment, 94*, 393–403. doi:10.1080/00223891.2012.660292

Gucciardi, D. F., Gordon, S., & Dimmock, J. A. (2008). Towards an understanding of mental toughness in Australian football. *Journal of Applied Sport Psychology, 20*, 261–281. doi:10.1080/10413200801998556

Gucciardi, D. F., Gordon, S., & Dimmock, J. A. (2009a). Evaluation of a mental toughness training program for youth-aged Australian footballers: I. A quantitative analysis. *Journal of Applied Sport Psychology, 21*, 307–323. doi:10.1080/10413200903026066

Gucciardi, D. F., Gordon, S., & Dimmock, J. A. (2009b). Evaluation of a mental toughness training program for youth-aged Australian footballers: II. A qualitative analysis. *Journal of Applied Sport Psychology, 21*, 324–339. doi:10.1080/10413200903026074

Gucciardi, D. F., Hanton, S., Gordon, S., Mallett, C. J., & Temby, P. (2015). The concept of mental toughness: Tests of dimensionality, nomological network and traitness. *Journal of Personality, 83*, 26–44. doi:10.1111/jopy.12079

Hardy, L., Bell, J. J., & Beattie, S. J. (2014). A neuropsychological model of mentally tough behavior. *Journal of Personality, 81*, 344–364. doi:10.1111/jopy.12034

Harmison, R. J. (2011). A social-cognitive framework for understanding and developing mental toughness in sport. In D. F. Gucciardi & S. Gordon (Eds.), *Mental toughness in sport: Developments in theory and research* (pp. 47–68). New York, NY: Routledge.

Horsburgh, V. A., Schermer, J. A., Veselka, L., & Vernon, P. A. (2009). A behavioural genetic study of mental toughness and personality. *Personality and Individual Differences, 46*, 100–105. doi:10.1016/j.paid.2008.09.009

Jaeschke, A. C., Sachs, M. L., & Dieffenbach, K. D. (2016). Ultramarathon runners' perceptions of mental toughness: A qualitative inquiry. *The Sport Psychologist, 30*, 242–255. doi:10.1123/tsp.2014-0153

Jones, G., Hanton, S., & Connaughton, D. (2002). What is this thing called mental toughness? An investigation of elite sport performers. *Journal of Applied Sport Psychology, 14*, 205–218. doi:10.1080/10413200290103509

Jones, G., Hanton, S., & Connaughton, D. (2007). A framework of mental toughness in the world's best performers. *The Sport Psychologist, 21*, 243–264. doi:10.1123/tsp.21.2.243

Jones, M. I., & Parker, J. K. (2018). Mindfulness mediates the relationship between mental toughness and pain catastrophizing in cyclists. *European Journal of Sport Science, 18*, 872–881. doi:10.1080/17461391.2018.1478450

Levy, A. R., Polman, R. C. J., Clough, P. J., Marchant, D. C., & Earle, K. (2006). Mental toughness as a determinant of beliefs, pain, and adherence in sport injury rehabilitation. *Journal of Sport Rehabilitation, 15*, 245–254. doi:10.1123/jsr.15.3.245

Mahoney, J. W., Ntoumanis, N., Gucciardi, D. F., Mallett, C. J., & Stebbings, J. (2016). Implementing an autonomy-supportive intervention to develop mental toughness in adolescent rowers. *Journal of Applied Sport Psychology, 28*, 199–215. doi:10.1080/10413200.2015.1101030

Mahoney, J. W., Ntoumanis, N., Mallett, C. J., & Gucciardi, D. F. (2014). The motivational antecedents of the development of mental toughness: A self-determination theory perspective. *International Review of Sport and Exercise Psychology, 7*, 184–197. doi:10.1080/1750984X.2014.925951

Noetel, N., Ciarrochi, J., Van Zanden, B., & Lonsdale, C. (2019). Mindfulness and acceptance approaches to sporting performance enhancement: A systematic review. *International Review of Sport and Exercise Psychology, 12*, 139–175. doi:10.1080/1750984X.2017.1387803

Parkes, J. F., & Mallett, C. J. (2011). Developing mental toughness: Attributional style retraining in rugby. *The Sport Psychologist, 25*, 269–287. doi:10.1123/tsp.25.3.269

Ramaeker, J., & Petrie, T. A. (2019). "Man up!": Examining intersections of sport participation, masculinity, psychological distress, and help-seeking attitudes and intentions. *Psychology of Men & Masculinities, 20*, 515–527. doi:10.1037/men0000198

Richardson, S. O., Andersen, M. B., & Morris, T. (2008). *Overtraining athletes: Personal journeys in sport*. Champaign, IL: Human Kinetics.

Ryan, R. M., & Deci, E. L. (2000). Self-determination theory and the facilitation of intrinsic motivation, social development, and well-being. *American Psychologist, 55*, 68–78. doi:10.1037/0003-066X.55.1.68

Sheard, M., & Golby, J. (2006). Effect of psychological skills training program on swimming performance and positive psychological development. *International Journal of Sport and Exercise Psychology, 4*, 149–169. doi:10.1080/1612197X.2006.9671790

Slack, L. A., Maynard, I. W., Butt, J., & Olusoga, P. (2015). An evaluation of a mental toughness education and training program for early-career English Football League referees. *The Sport Psychologist, 29*, 237–257. doi:10.1123/tsp.2014-0015

Stamp, E., Crust, L., Swann, C., Perry, J., Clough, P., & Marchant, D. (2015). Relationships between mental toughness and psychological wellbeing in undergraduate students. *Personality and Individual Differences, 75*, 170–174. doi:10.1016/j.paid.2014.11.038

St Clair-Thompson, H., Bugler, M., Robinson, J., Clough, P. J., McGeown, S. P., & Perry, J. (2015). Mental toughness in education: Exploring relationships with attainment, attendance, behaviour and peer relationships. *Educational Psychology, 35*, 886–907. doi:10.1080/01443410.2014.895294

Swann, C., Crust, L., & Allen-Collinson, J. (2016). Surviving the 2015 Mount Everest disaster: A phenomenological exploration into lived experiences and the role of mental toughness. *Psychology of Sport and Exercise, 27*, 157–167. doi:10.1016/j.psychsport.2016.08.012

Tibbert, S. J., Andersen, M. B., & Morris, T. (2015). What a difference a "mentally toughening" year makes: The acculturation of a rookie. *Psychology of Sport and Exercise, 7*, 68–78. doi:10.1016/j.psychsport.2014.10.007

Uphill, M. A., & Hemmings, B. (2017). Vulnerability: Ripples from reflections on mental toughness. *The Sport Psychologist, 31*, 299–307. doi:10.1123/tsp.2016-0034

Weinberg, R., Butt, J., Mellano, K., & Harmison, R. J. (2017). The stability of mental toughness across situations: Taking a social-cognitive approach. *International Journal of Sport Psychology, 48*, 280–302. doi:10.7352/IJSP.2017.48.280

Wilson, D., Bennett, E. V., Mosewich, A. D., Faulkner, G. E., & Crocker, P. R. E. (2019). "The zipper effect": Exploring the interrelationship of mental toughness and self-compassion among Canadian elite women athletes. *Psychology of Sport and Exercise*, *40*, 61–70. doi:10.1016/j.psychsport.2018.09.006

Young, K., & White, P. (2000). Researching sport injury: Reconstructing dangerous masculinities. In J. McKay, M. A. Messner, & D. Sabo (Eds.), *Masculinities, gender relations, and sport* (pp. 108–126). Los Angeles, CA: Sage.

4

THE MOTIVATIONAL ROLE OF FEEDBACK IN MOTOR LEARNING

Evidence, interpretations, and implications

Suzete Chiviacowsky

Learning new motor skills is a critical aspect of life, and there is little disagreement that feedback and motivation play important roles in this process. Feedback is information about one's performance, usually provided by an external source (e.g., teacher, coach, therapist, computer), by which learners can confirm, adjust, or reorganize not only performance but also knowledge, strategies, conceptions, and views about one's self, abilities, and skills. Feedback is an essential tool to optimize learning and is delivered in many different practical settings. Motor learning contexts can vary from children acquiring new skills in physical education to patients adapting or relearning movements in clinical rehabilitation. Other motor learning contexts involve expert athletes, dancers or musicians improving their skills, professionals learning and refining working skills (e.g., a surgical technique), skill learning in human-computer interactions, among many others, in which skilled performance is expected to develop, adapt, and improve.

After decades of research investigating the informational impact of feedback on the acquisition of motor skills, evolving from a dominance of information processing perspectives (see Swinnen, 1996 for a review), it is now well accepted that feedback is not neutral information to be processed by the learner. Rather, feedback plays a critical motivational role in the learning of motor skills. Congruent with numerous findings showing the impact of feedback on motivation and learning in several different practice environments (e.g., Koka & Hein, 2003), the motivational role of feedback has evolved, after two decades of investigation, into a strong and robust topic of research in motor learning.

Motivation is the disposition of individuals to play, explore, engage, interact, understand, master, and persist in activities, with such behaviors being supported, notably in its intrinsic form, by the interest and enjoyment that accompanies such activities (Ryan & Deci, 2000). Motivated learners demonstrate increased energy, direction, persistence of behavior, and enhanced curiosity that results in more exploratory behavior. In terms of neural activity, motivated learners show patterns of activity in neural networks that support salience detection, attentional control, and self-referential cognition, and higher activation in major dopaminergic pathways or reward brain systems that support memory and learning (e.g., Di Domenico & Ryan, 2017; Wise, 2004).

Numerous experiments from behavioral research suggest that motivational levels can be increased and sustained, but also decreased, by distinct factors, including the type, meaning, and content of feedback. Higher motor performance and learning can result from practice conditions in which the use of feedback increases motivation, helping individuals to build confident and self-determined mindsets. In this chapter, an overview of experimental findings from four different lines of investigation evidencing the motivational impact of feedback on motor learning is presented. Potential underlying mechanisms explaining the observed effects are discussed. Implications of the reviewed findings are also highlighted to identify new research perspectives and guidelines to maximize motor skill learning.

Feedback after successful trials

Over the past two decades, scholars in the motor learning domain have tried to identify and understand when and why learners prefer to receive feedback (e.g., whether it is mainly to confirm good performance or to correct mistakes), and when feedback would be more effective for motor learning (e.g., when informing about trials with relatively small errors or with large errors). In fact, if learners are adequately instructed about what needs to be learned and are typically able to discriminate between "good" and "poor" performance, feedback informing about larger errors would be redundant and probably frustrating, and would potentially decrease motivation and learning. In contrast, feedback provided after more successful trials or that informs learners about the best aspects of performance would perhaps help them to confirm that the movement (or part of it) is correct or on the "right track," guiding them to fine-tune it and potentially increasing motivation and learning.

The first motor learning experiment to look at this question revealed that learners are often effective in estimating their errors and discriminating between good and poor trials, and show a clear preference to receive feedback to confirm successful performance (Chiviacowsky & Wulf, 2002). These findings were followed up by an experiment that examined more directly whether learning is enhanced if participants received feedback mainly after smaller rather than larger errors (Chiviacowsky & Wulf, 2007). Participants received feedback on the best half or on the worse half of trials in each practice block, and the former group demonstrated more effective task learning. Together, the findings of both experiments revealed the important motivational role of feedback in motor learning. Notably, these findings were in contrast with the prevailing theoretical view (guidance hypothesis; Salmoni, Schmidt, & Walter, 1984), according to which feedback provided after larger relative to smaller errors would be more important for the acquisition of motor skills.

Several studies have since endorsed the findings described above in different tasks and populations, showing learners' general preference for receiving feedback mainly to confirm good instead of poor performance (e.g., Fairbrother, Laughlin, & Nguyen, 2012) and that deliberately providing feedback after trials with relatively small versus larger errors facilitates learning (e.g., Abbas & North, 2018). Feedback indicating increased success through use of criteria of "good" performance (e.g., Chiviacowsky, Wulf & Lewthwaite, 2012) or the provision of positive short feedback statements (e.g., Stoate, Wulf, & Lewthwaite, 2012) also benefits motor performance and learning. These and many other studies have advanced the knowledge on the motivational effects of feedback after more successful trials in distinct settings, types of tasks, kinds of measures, moments of practice, and populations.

Feedback after good trials benefit learning because it influences learners' perceptions of competence. Competence refers to the need to feel confident, capable of skillfully mastering challenges, rather than feeling ineffective and incompetent in one's environment, and is considered a basic psychological human need (Ryan & Deci, 2000). The feeling of improving and demonstrating success or competence is considered fundamentally satisfying and motivating (Bandura, 1982). Higher perceived competence can inspire learners to set higher performance goals and increase effort tolerance and attention paid during practice (Locke & Latham, 2006; Themanson & Rosen, 2015). Perceived success is expected to increase self-efficacy, thereby breeding subsequent success (e.g., Iso-Ahola & Dotson, 2014). Feedback after more successful trials can also enhance learners' expectancies for performance, strengthening goal-action coupling, a mechanism suggested to enhance motor learning (Wulf & Lewthwaite, 2016).

Motor performance and learning research has, in fact, demonstrated that feedback after good trials results in increased intrinsic motivation (Abbas & North, 2018), positive affect (Stoate et al., 2012), self-confidence (Badami, VaezMousavi, Wulf, & Namazizadeh, 2012), and self-efficacy (Saemi, Porter, Ghotbi-Varzaneh, Zarghami, & Maleki, 2012). Self-efficacy has been found to be a predictor of motor learning (Chiviacowsky et al., 2012). Thus, different opportunities to confirm successful performance through feedback affects motivation, impacting motor learning in a direction whereby learning is enhanced or undermined when participants' perceptions of competence are respectively increased or reduced.

Choices over feedback

Over the past 20 years, motor learning research has also focused on the effects of providing learners with some form of autonomy support over the learning setting, starting with choices over feedback (Janelle, Barba, Frehlich, Tennant, & Cauraugh, 1997). In such studies, participants are typically allowed to choose when to receive feedback during practice (also called self-controlled feedback) and are compared with a control group that is not allowed the chance to choose. The control group usually receives a "yoked" feedback schedule; that is, matching the feedback schedule requested by the choice group.

The positive effects on motor learning of providing choices over feedback have been verified consistently in diverse types of tasks and different populations, such as young adults (Janelle et al., 1997); children (Chiviacowsky, Wulf, Medeiros, Kaefer, & Tani, 2008); individuals more or less extroverted (Kaefer, Chiviacowsky, Meira Júnior, & Tani, 2014); those with high or low physical activity levels (Fairbrother et al., 2012); individuals with disabilities (Hemayattalab, Arabameri, Pourazar, Ardakani, & Kashefi, 2013); and older adults given the choice to control, or not control, when to receive feedback (Chiviacowsky & Lessa, 2017).

Distinct motivational pathways explain why allowing learners choice over feedback may benefit motor learning. One mechanism concerns the satisfaction of the learners' need for autonomy, experienced when people act according to their own beliefs and values. Autonomy is considered a key element of optimal human psychological well-being, linked with increased intrinsic motivation through the satisfaction of a basic psychobiosocial need (Catania, 1975; Ryan & Deci, 2000). The experience of choice, or the anticipation of the opportunity to choose, has been observed to activate reward mechanisms, increasing activity in corticostriatal regions involved in affective and motivational processes (Leotti & Delgado, 2011). Autonomy can also enhance performance by increasing attention and neuroaffective reactions to performance errors (Legault & Inzlicht, 2013), and has been observed to enhance performance expectancies and positive affect (Lemos, Wulf, Lewthwaite, & Chiviacowsky, 2017). An augmentation in learners' perceived competence and subsequent self-efficacy, even independent of actual performance, can also result from choice or perceived control (Chiviacowsky, 2014).

A second important motivational pathway explaining choices over feedback effects relates to an overlay with learners' competence need. Considering that feedback usually carries competence information to be processed for task learning, allowing choices over feedback enables learners to confirm successful performance when desired, thus increasing motivation and facilitating learning by directly satisfying the learners' competence need. Indeed, motor learning research has established the preferences of learners for receiving feedback, mainly in order to confirm good performance when allowed choice (e.g., Chiviacowsky & Wulf, 2002; Fairbrother et al., 2012). In other studies, participants allowed choice were not only observed to ask for feedback mainly after more successful trials but also showed higher attention (EEG activity) while processing the requested feedback and increased intrinsic motivation relative to no-choice groups (e.g., Grand et al., 2015).

Few studies have tried specifically to disaggregate autonomy from competence motivational effects resulting from practice with choices over feedback. The findings indicate the existence of two distinct pathways, with both playing critical roles in motor learning. In the Chiviacowsky (2014) study, competence was controlled in such a way that both groups were able to confirm successful performance at the same rate, while autonomy was manipulated by comparing choice and no-choice (yoked) groups. Even confirming good performance at the same rate, the choice group reported higher self-efficacy levels and increased learning of the task relative to the yoked group. These findings confirmed that autonomy over feedback results in inherent rewards and a greater sense of agency with the exercise of control, protecting learners' perceptions of competence, thus boosting confidence and increasing motivation and motor learning.

In the Chiviacowsky et al. (2012) experiment, autonomy was controlled in such a way that three choice groups could request feedback at the same rate while competence was manipulated by informing participants different subjective criterion of "good" performance (difficult, easy, or no criteria). While all groups, as expected, asked for feedback mainly after good trials, the group that practiced with the difficult criterion rarely confirmed successful performance. This group demonstrated decreased self-efficacy and task learning relative to the other groups. These findings showed that satisfaction of the competence need is critical to the benefits of practice with choices over feedback and that competence frustration can cause deleterious learning effects, even in the presence of autonomy support. Not surprisingly, participants practicing with choices over feedback but not allowed to confirm good performance, either by being prevented from processing the requested feedback or by not receiving feedback based on performance (e.g., Chiviacowsky & Wulf, 2005), were observed to not take full advantage of practice with choices over feedback.

Although distinct motivational pathways for the effects of choices over feedback have been detected, they probably work in parallel to benefit learning when practice is organized for, and results in, the satisfaction of learners' psychological needs. Thus, providing learners with choices over feedback can satisfy their psychological needs, leading to increased motivation and facilitating motor learning. However, practice with autonomy over feedback that somehow frustrates other learners' needs may decrease motivation, thus harming learning.

Positive comparative feedback

For a number of reasons, including the desire for self-improvement or self-knowledge, people generally evaluate themselves against others or their own past selves. Conceptually, social comparison involves self-evaluation via comparison of outcomes of an individual with those of others (Festinger, 1954), while temporal comparison involves the set of opinions and abilities that constitutes an individual self-description at different points in time (Albert, 1977). In several domains, social and temporal comparisons are considered fundamental sources of information for evaluating one's competences, satisfying the learner's self-evaluation goals (e.g., Brown & Middendorf, 1996).

Given the drive in the human organism to compare and evaluate his/her own competence, opinions, and abilities (Festinger, 1954), alongside the motivational value of feedback in providing such information, motor learning research has looked at the potential benefits of providing learners with positive self-evaluative information through social and temporal-comparative feedback. The impact of comparative feedback on motor learning was first examined in the form of social comparison. Lewthwaite and Wulf (2010) provided two groups of participants with (false) comparative feedback suggesting that their performance was in the top or bottom 10th percentile relative to the average performance of a group of peers, while a third group did not receive comparative feedback. The results showed more automatic control of movement and higher balance learning among the former relative to the other groups. Subsequent studies in young adults reported similar effects on the learning of different tasks (e.g., Wulf, Chiviacowsky, & Lewthwaite, 2010). These positive learning effects were also replicated in other populations, including older adults (Wulf, Chiviacowsky, & Lewthwaite, 2012) and children (Ávila, Chiviacowsky, Wulf, & Lewthwaite, 2012; Gonçalves, Cardozo, Valentini, & Chiviacowsky, 2018). Positive social-comparative feedback was also found to increase muscular stability and efficacy at different task difficulty levels in participants learning the stabilometer balance task (Navaee, Farsi, & Abdoli, 2016).

Previous research suggesting that social-comparative feedback affects motor learning has focused attention on temporal-comparative feedback, a more useful form of information for intervention in practical settings, especially considering the logical nature of performance improvements observed in learning settings. Social and temporal comparisons were observed in other domains to independently influence individuals' evaluations of their own skills (Zell & Alicke, 2009). Temporal comparisons were also seen to be preferred among different age groups relative to social comparisons, with their importance increasing throughout life while the importance of social comparison remained constant (Brown & Middendorf, 1996). Given these observations, Chiviacowsky and Drews (2016) evaluated whether temporal-comparative feedback would also affect motor learning. The results of an experiment using a coincident anticipation-timing task showed enhanced learning among participants who received feedback informing them that their performance had gradually improved across blocks of practice, relative to participants who were informed that their performance had slightly degraded over time. A follow-up experiment using a sport task (i.e., golf putting) showed that positive temporal-comparative feedback also benefits motor learning relative to a control group not receiving comparative feedback (Chiviacowsky, Harter, Gonçalves, & Cardozo, 2019). Similar results were observed in an experiment in older adults learning a timing walk task (Lessa, Tani, & Chiviacowsky, 2018). In this way, similar to findings on social comparison, positive temporal-comparative feedback (i.e., informing participants that their performance is improving over time) can enhance the learning of motor skills in different tasks and populations.

Positive comparative feedback affects motor learning because social and temporal comparisons are pervasive and, therefore, can inform individuals about their standing relative to others or past selves, serving as a means for the development of a positive self-concept (e.g., Cheng & Lam, 2007). Research has demonstrated that young adults reported greater tolerance for sustained effort, enhanced motor learning, and higher perceived competence when informed that their performance was above average or temporally improving across blocks of practice (e.g., Chiviacowsky & Drews, 2016; Chiviacowsky et al, 2019; Lewthwaite & Wulf, 2010). Children similarly reported significantly higher levels of perceived competence, importance of doing well, and persistence related to a task relative to control groups (Ávila et al., 2012; Gonçalves et al., 2018). Older adults who received feedback implying that their performance was better than that of their peers, or informed of temporal self-improvements across blocks of practice, reported being less nervous while balancing or learning a walk timing task and less concerned about their ability (Lessa et al., 2018; Wulf et al., 2012). Hence, positive temporal and social comparative feedback act through motivational pathways while satisfying learner's self-evaluation goals, protecting learners' perceptions of competence, increasing task interest and persistence, and alleviating nervousness or self-related efficacy concerns that degrade performance and learning.

Feedback inducing a learnable view of skills

Research in different domains has attempted to explain why some learners tend to be more focused on task learning, reacting to difficult situations by increasing their effort and seeing mistakes as a natural part of the learning process, while others tend to avoid challenging situations that might demonstrate low ability, striving to demonstrate their abilities by outperforming others and showing less effort and persistence when confronted with errors. The results of this research have shown that specific attitudes usually result from individuals' contrasting views on the learnability of skills or how personal competence is constructed – that is, people's conceptions of ability (Ross, 1989). These distinct conceptions of ability can consider competence as learnable/malleable abilities, with improvements being strongly dependent on effort and learning, or as inherited/fixed capacities that cannot be improved beyond a set limit (Dweck & Leggett, 1988). Critical to note is that such dispositional or induced conceptions of ability can be affected simply by different positive feedback statements provided by teachers, instructors, or coaches, developing these two distinct, adaptive or maladaptive, behaviors.

While research in the psychology domain on conceptions of ability has a long history, few experiments have evaluated whether inducing learnable versus inherent conceptions of ability can affect motor performance and learning, and only a couple of these have looked at feedback effects. In one feedback study, children practicing a soccer-kicking task (Chiviacowsky & Drews, 2014, experiment 1) received positive generic (person-related) feedback statements to induce an inherent conception of ability (e.g., "You are a great soccer player!") or non-generic (process-related) feedback statements inducing a learnable view of the skill (e.g., "Your last kicks were very good!"). After a few blocks of trials receiving these distinct positive feedbacks, participants of both groups received the same negative feedback statement ("Those last kicks were not very good!"), and the authors evaluated the subsequent kicks as a function of the different induced conceptions. Participants receiving feedback that induced the learnable view of skill during practice outperformed participants induced to the inherent view. In another experiment (Chiviacowsky & Drews, 2014, experiment 2), the earlier results were confirmed and extended by observing the learning of throwing beanbags to a target, evaluating the more permanent effects of the manipulated views of skills after 24 hours.

Although still limited and deserving of further research, the findings on feedback to induce a learnable versus an inherent view of skills in motor learning show that even young children are sensitive to these kinds of feedback with respect to their behavior and that not all positive feedback is beneficial for motor performance and learning. Subtle wording differences in positive feedback statements can produce different motivational and learning consequences. These findings are in agreement with those of the Cimpian, Arce, Markman, and Dweck (2007) study, where children who received generic positive feedback while drawing showed more helpless behavior regarding persistence and lower competence self-evaluation when criticized than children who received positive non-generic feedback. The findings are also in line with results from motor learning experiments in which different ability conceptions were induced using instructions (e.g., Wulf, Lewthwaite, & Hooyman, 2013).

The learnable view of skill induced by instructions has been observed to result in lower nervousness levels and concerns about ability reported by adult participants while learning a balance task (Wulf et al., 2013) and higher self-efficacy, task interest, and positive affect levels while performing a pursuit-rotor tracking task (Jourden, Bandura, & Banfield, 1991) than the induced inherited/fixed view of ability. The provision of positive feedback suggesting a learnable view of skill likely affects motor learning via similar pathways, potentially protecting learners against setbacks when exposed to errors or mistakes, a situation frequently encountered in motor skill learning contexts (e.g., Chiviacowsky & Drews, 2014). These learners tend to persist and increase efforts when confronted with errors during practice, while others in the same scenario do not persist and instead respond with helpless behavior. In a recent study looking at the neural mechanisms underlying conceptions of ability-related differences in learning, participants with a fixed view of skills showed stronger "punishment" responses (performance and striatal responses) to negative feedback than participants with a learnable view of skills (Bejjani, DePasque, & Tricomi, 2019). Results of a meta-analysis have indicated that conceptions of abilities are associated with measures of intrinsic motivation in the motor domain (Vella, Braithewaite, Gardner, & Spray, 2016). Thus, different conceptions of ability induced by feedback may distinctly affect learners' motivation, facilitating motor learning when promoting a learnable view of skills.

Conclusions, future directions, and practical implications

In this chapter, four lines of behavioral research showing the motivational impact of feedback on motor learning developed over the past 20 years were reviewed. Consistent with theoretical expectations (Ryan & Deci, 2000), the reviewed findings indicate that positive motivational effects of feedback are mediated by the satisfaction of learners' basic psychological needs, with studies performed to date predominantly confirming the competence and autonomy needs. Higher feelings of autonomy and enhanced perceived competence or expectations of future successful performance have been suggested to trigger dopaminergic responses that enhance memory consolidation and neural pathway development, as well as to strengthen the coupling of goals to actions at several different levels, thus optimizing motor learning (Wulf & Lewthwaite, 2016).

Future research on the motivational impact of feedback in motor learning can not only generalize the findings to different settings (e.g., dance, music, sports, martial arts, physical therapy, medical skills) and populations, but also follow many directions and levels of analysis. For example, research has been developed that mainly observes the impact on learners' competence and autonomy psychological needs. Still lacking experimentation is the potential importance of relatedness-supportive feedback in motor skill acquisition. Social relatedness has been observed to affect motor learning when manipulated through instructions (e.g., Gonzalez & Chiviacowsky, 2018), with positive learning outcomes detected when learners felt genuinely liked, connected, and respected during practice. Thus, feedback provided in a way that emphasizes acknowledgment, caring, and interest in participants' experiences may potentially result in higher motivation and learning relative to feedback disregarding learners' satisfaction of the relatedness need. It is also worth noting that the reviewed findings involved learning mainly at an individual level, with participants practicing the task alone, while motor skill learning is often taught in groups or teams. Hence, further studies could focus on how individuals collaboratively sharing the acquisition of a motor skill in groups may be affected by motivational feedback. The application of neuroscience methods may also help to identify the neural underpinnings of motivational states resulting from feedback manipulation (e.g., Reeve & Lee, 2019).

These findings have applicability in multiple learning settings. As reviewed, the way in which feedback is handled during practice can substantially affect the learning process. Increased motivation and positive effects on learning can be expected when feedback affords opportunities for learners to experience feelings of success and efficacy, supports learners' need for autonomy and competence by allowing choices over the feedback delivery, helps learners to be aware of self-improvements over time through evaluative comparative feedback, and highlights a learnable view of skills or conception of ability. Contrarily, practice conditions in which feedback emphasizes greater errors or mistakes, in which the learner is never allowed to exercise control over the feedback provision, in which feedback does not highlight improvements over time, and which induce an entity or fixed view of skills most certainly decrease learners' motivation and impair learning. Observing the interplay between motivational feedback research and real-world learning settings may allow more efficient practice methods to be designed, thus answering several specific problems in intervention (e.g., Winstein, Lewthwaite, Blanton, Wolf, & Wishart, 2014). Understanding how the type, content, and meaning of feedback can influence motivation and learning may allow professionals in many contexts to develop more effective learning environments.

References

Abbas, Z. A., & North, J. S. (2018). Good-vs. poor-trial feedback in motor learning: The role of self-efficacy and intrinsic motivation across levels of task difficulty. *Learning and Instruction, 55*, 105–112. doi:10.1016/j.learninstruc.2017.09.009

Albert, S. (1977). Temporal comparison theory. *Psychological Review, 84*, 485–503. doi:10.1037/0033-295X.84.6.485

Ávila, L. T. G., Chiviacowsky, S., Wulf, G., & Lewthwaite, R. (2012). Positive social-comparative feedback enhances motor learning in children. *Psychology of Sport and Exercise, 13*, 849–853. doi:10.1016/j.psychsport.2012.07.001

Badami, R., VaezMousavi, M., Wulf, G., & Namazizadeh, M. (2012). Feedback about more accurate versus less accurate trials: Differential effects on self-confidence and activation. *Research Quarterly for Exercise and Sport*, *83*, 196–203. doi:10.1080/02701367.2012.10599850

Bandura, A. (1982). Self-efficacy mechanism in human agency. *American Psychologist, 37*, 122–147. doi:10.1037/0003-066X.37.2.122

Bejjani, C., DePasque, S., & Tricomi, E. (2019). Intelligence mindset shapes neural learning signals and memory. *Biological Psychology, 156*, e107715. doi:10.1016/j.biopsycho.2019.06.003

Brown, R., & Middendorf, J. (1996). The underestimated role of temporal comparison: A test of the life-span model. *The Journal of Social Psychology, 136*, 325–331. doi:10.1080/00224545.1996.9714011

Catania, A. C. (1975). Freedom and knowledge: An experimental analysis of preference in pigeons. *Journal of Experimental Analysis of Behavior, 24*, 89–106. doi:10.1901/jeab.1975.24-89

Cheng, R. W. Y., & Lam, S. F. (2007). Self-construal and social comparison effects. *British Journal of Educational Psychology, 77*, 197–211. doi:10.1348/000709905X72795

Chiviacowsky, S. (2014). Self-controlled practice: Autonomy protects perceptions of competence and enhances motor learning. *Psychology of Sport and Exercise, 15*, 505–510. doi:10.1016/j.psychsport.2014.05.003

Chiviacowsky, S., & Drews, R. (2014). Effects of generic versus non-generic feedback on motor learning in children. *PLoS ONE, 9*, e88989. doi:10.1371/journal.pone.0088989

Chiviacowsky, S., & Drews, R. (2016). Temporal-comparative feedback affects motor learning. *Journal of Motor Learning and Development, 4*, 208–218. doi:10.1123/jmld.2015-0034

Chiviacowsky, S., Harter, N. M., Gonçalves, G. S., & Cardozo, P. L. (2019). Temporal-comparative feedback facilitates golf putting. *Frontiers in Psychology, 9*, e2691. doi:10.3389/fpsyg.2018.02691

Chiviacowsky, S., & Lessa, H. T. (2017). Choices over feedback enhance motor learning in older adults. *Journal of Motor Learning and Development, 5*, 304–318. doi:10.1123/jmld.2016-0031

Chiviacowsky, S., & Wulf, G. (2002). Self-controlled feedback: Does it enhance learning because performers get feedback when they need it? *Research Quarterly for Exercise and Sport, 73*, 408–415. doi:10.1080/02701367.2002.10609040

Chiviacowsky, S., & Wulf, G. (2005). Self-controlled feedback is effective if it is based on the learner's performance. *Research Quarterly for Exercise and Sport, 76*, 42–48. doi:10.1080/02701367.2005.10599260

Chiviacowsky, S., & Wulf, G. (2007). Feedback after good trials enhances learning. *Research Quarterly for Exercise and Sport, 78*, 40–47. doi:10.1080/02701367.2007.10599402

Chiviacowsky, S., Wulf, G., & Lewthwaite, R. (2012). Self-controlled learning: The importance of protecting perceptions of competence. *Frontiers in Psychology, 3*, e458. doi:10.3389/fpsyg.2012.00458

Chiviacowsky, S., Wulf, G., Medeiros, F. L., Kaefer, A., & Tani, G. (2008). Learning benefits of self-controlled knowledge of results in 10-year-old children. *Research Quarterly for Exercise and Sport, 79*, 405–410. doi:10.1080/02701367.2008.10599505

Cimpian, A., Arce, H. M. C., Markman, E. M., & Dweck, C. S. (2007). Subtle linguistic cues affect children's motivation. *Psychological Science, 18*, 314–316. doi:10.1111/j.1467-9280.2007.01896.x

Di Domenico, S. I., & Ryan, R. M. (2017). The emerging neuroscience of intrinsic motivation: A new frontier in self-determination research. *Frontiers in Human Neuroscience, 11*, e145. doi:10.3389/fnhum.2017.00145

Dweck, C. S., & Leggett, E. L. (1988). A social-cognitive approach to motivation and personality. *Psychological Review, 95*, 256–73. doi:10.1037/0033-295X.95.2.256

Fairbrother, J. T., Laughlin, D. D., & Nguyen, T. V. (2012). Self-controlled feedback facilitates motor learning in both high and low activity individuals. *Frontiers in Psychology, 31*, e323. doi:10.3389/fpsyg.2012.00323

Festinger, L. (1954). A theory of social comparison processes. *Human Relations, 7*, 117–140. doi:10.1177/001872675400700202

Gonçalves, G. S., Cardozo, P. L., Valentini, N. C., & Chiviacowsky, S. (2018). Enhancing performance expectancies through positive comparative feedback facilitates the learning of basketball free throw in children. *Psychology of Sport and Exercise, 36*, 174–177. doi10.1016/j.psychsport.2018.03.001

Gonzalez, D. H., & Chiviacowsky, S. (2018). Relatedness support enhances motor learning. *Psychological Research, 82*, 439–447. doi:10.1007/s00426-016-0833-7

Grand, K. F., Bruzi, A. T., Dyke, F. B., Godwin, M. M., Leiker, A. M., Thompson, A. G., … & Miller, M. W. (2015). Why self-controlled feedback enhances motor learning: Answers from electroencephalography and indices of motivation. *Human Movement Science, 43*, 23–32. doi:10.1016/j.humov.2015.06.013

Hemayattalab, R., Arabameri, E., Pourazar, M., Ardakani, M. D., & Kashefi, M. (2013). Effects of self-controlled feedback on learning of a throwing task in children with spastic hemiplegic cerebral palsy. *Research in Developmental Disabilities, 34*, 2884–2889. doi:10.1016/j.ridd.2013.05.008

Iso-Ahola, S. E., & Dotson, C. O. (2014). Psychological momentum: Why success breeds success. *Review of General Psychology, 18*, 19–33. doi:10.1037/a0036406

Janelle, C. M., Barba, D. A., Frehlich, S. G., Tennant, L. K., & Cauraugh, J. H. (1997). Maximizing performance feedback effectiveness through videotape replay and a self-controlled learning environment. *Research Quarterly for Exercise and Sport, 68*, 269–279. doi.org/10.1080/02701367.1997.10608008

Jourden, F. J., Bandura, A., & Banfield, J. T. (1991). The impact of conceptions of ability on self-regulatory factors and motor skill acquisition. *Journal of Sport and Exercise Psychology, 13*, 213–226.

Kaefer, A., Chiviacowsky, S., Meira Júnior, C. M., & Tani, G. (2014). Self-controlled practice enhances motor learning in introverts and extroverts. *Research Quarterly for Exercise and Sport, 85*, 226–233. doi:10.1080/02701367.2014.893051

Koka, A., & Hein, V. (2003). Perceptions of teacher's feedback and learning environment as predictors of intrinsic motivation in physical education. *Psychology of Sport and Exercise, 4*, 333–346. doi:10.1016/S1469-0292(02)00012-2

Legault, L., & Inzlicht, M. (2013). Self-determination, self-regulation, and the brain: Autonomy improves performance by enhancing neuroaffective responsiveness to self-regulation failure. *Journal of Personality and Social Psychology, 105*, 123–138. doi:10.1037/a0030426

Lemos, A., Wulf, G., Lewthwaite, R., & Chiviacowsky, S. (2017). Autonomy support enhances performance expectancies, positive affect, and motor learning. *Psychology of Sport and Exercise, 31*, 28–34. doi:10.1016/j.psychsport.2017.03.009

Leotti, L. A., & Delgado, M. R. (2011). The inherent reward of choice. *Psychological Science, 22*, 1310–1318. doi:10.1177/0956797611417005

Lessa, H. T., Tani, G., & Chiviacowsky, S. (2018). Benefits of enhanced expectancies through temporal-comparative feedback for motor learning in older adults. *International Journal of Sport Psychology, 49*, 521–530. doi:10.7352/IJSP.2018.49.521

Lewthwaite, R., & Wulf, G. (2010). Social-comparative feedback affects motor skill learning. *Quarterly Journal of Experimental Psychology, 63*, 738–749. doi:10.1080/17470210903111839

Locke, E. A., & Latham, G. P. (2006). New directions in goal-setting theory. *Current Directions in Psychological Science, 15*, 265–268. doi:10.1111/j.1467-8721.2006.00449.x

Navaee, S. A., Farsi, A., & Abdoli, B. (2016). The effect of normative feedback on stability and efficacy of some selected muscles in a balancing task. *International Journal of Applied Exercise Physiology, 5*, 43–52.

Reeve, J., & Lee, W. (2019). A neuroscientific perspective on basic psychological needs. *Journal of Personality, 87*, 102–114. doi:10.1111/jopy.12390

Ross, M. (1989). Relation of implicit theories to the construction of personal histories. *Psychological Review, 96*, 341–357. doi:10.1037/0033-295X.96.2.341

Ryan, R. M., & Deci, E. L. (2000). Self-determination theory and the facilitation of intrinsic motivation, social development, and well-being. *American Psychologist, 55*, 68–78. doi:10.1037//0003-066x.55.1.68

Saemi, E., Porter, J. M., Ghotbi-Varzaneh, A., Zarghami, M., & Maleki, F. (2012). Knowledge of results after relatively good trials enhances self-efficacy and motor learning. *Psychology of Sport and Exercise, 13*, 378–382. doi:10.1016/j.psychsport.2011.12.008

Salmoni, A. W., Schmidt, R. A., & Walter, C. B. (1984). Knowledge of results and motor learning: A review and critical reappraisal. *Psychological Bulletin, 95*, 355–386. doi:10.1037/0033-2909.95.3.355

Stoate, I., Wulf, G., & Lewthwaite, R. (2012). Enhanced expectancies improve movement efficiency in runners. *Journal of Sports Sciences, 30*, 815–823. doi:10.1080/02640414.2012.671533

Swinnen, S. P. (1996). Information feedback for motor skill learning: A review. In H. N. Zelaznik (Ed.), *Advances in motor learning and control* (pp. 37–66). Champaign, IL: Human Kinetics.

Themanson, J. R., & Rosen, P. J. (2015). Examining the relationships between self-efficacy, task-relevant attentional control, and task performance: Evidence from event-related brain potentials. *British Journal of Psychology, 106*, 253–271. doi:10.1111/bjop.12091

Vella, S. A., Braithewaite, R. E., Gardner, L. A., & Spray, C. M. (2016). A systematic review and meta-analysis of implicit theory research in sport, physical activity, and physical education. *International Review of Sport and Exercise Psychology, 9*, 191–214. doi:10.1080/1750984X.2016.1160418

Winstein, C., Lewthwaite, R., Blanton, S. R., Wolf, L. B., & Wishart, L. (2014). Infusing motor learning research into neurorehabilitation practice: A historical perspective with case exemplar from the accelerated skill acquisition program. *Journal of Neurologic Physical Therapy, 38*, 190–200. doi:10.1097/NPT.0000000000000046

Wise, R. A. (2004). Dopamine, learning and motivation. *Nature Reviews Neuroscience, 5*, 483–494. doi:10.1038/nrn1406

Wulf, G., Chiviacowsky, S., & Lewthwaite, R. (2010). Normative feedback effects on the learning of a timing task. *Research Quarterly for Exercise and Sport, 81*, 425–431. doi:10.1080/02701367.2010.10599703

Wulf, G., Chiviacowsky, S., & Lewthwaite, R. (2012). Altering mindset can enhance motor learning in older adults. *Psychology and Aging, 27*, 14–21. doi:10.1037/a0025718.

Wulf, G., & Lewthwaite, R. (2016). Optimizing performance through intrinsic motivation and attention for learning: The OPTIMAL theory of motor learning. *Psychonomic Bulletin & Review, 23*, 1382–1414. doi:10.3758/s13423-015-0999-9

Wulf, G., Lewthwaite, R., & Hooyman, A. (2013). Can ability conceptualizations alter the impact of social comparison in motor learning? *Journal of Motor Learning and Development, 1*, 20–30. doi:10.1123/jmld.1.1.20

Zell, E., & Alicke, M. D. (2008). Self-evaluative effects of temporal and social comparison. *Journal of Experimental Social Psychology, 45*, 223–227. doi:10.1016/j.jesp.2008.09.007

5

MINDFULNESS AND MENTAL PREPARATION

Jean Fournier

Mindfulness has received a lot of attention in recent years. Evidence suggests that mindfulness is useful for improving performance because it can help maintain focus in problem situations (Gardner & Moore, 2012; Mardon, Richards, & Martindale, 2016) which does not detract from the more general use of mindfulness in the pursuit of well-being. In this chapter, we first review the literature related to the use of mindfulness for improving performance in sport and then present a program of intervention implemented in a case study with an elite fencer.

Psychological skills training

According to Vealey (1988, p. 319), mental training, or psychological skill training (PST), refers to "techniques and strategies designed to teach or enhance mental skills that facilitate performance and a positive approach to sport competition." We consider the idea that psychological skills regulate thoughts, emotions, and behavior. These skills can be reinforced with various, often composite, techniques, such as mental imagery. For example, it has been established that an optimal level of activation is necessary for the production of effective movements in competition. Athletes need to learn to regulate their breathing or their muscular tension to allow the realization of effective movements or the coordination of fluid movements.

Excess thinking – often due to awareness of the stakes or an inappropriate focus on the movement – may disrupt the automatic execution of skills. Based on research results in mainstream psychology, mindfulness-based approaches are founded on a new conception of the relationship maintained with internal experiences (e.g., cognitions, emotions, bodily sensations). Masters and Maxwell (2004) explain "paralysis by analysis" using reinvestment theory, whereby the athletes' thoughts interfere with the production of movements and their performance declines. Paying attention to non-pertinent issues (e.g., the outcome of a competition, or thinking about a technical element of the movement) is responsible for lower than usual performance or lower performance in competition than during a training session. We propose that a mindfulness training program, described in this chapter, can help to focus attention on useful points and improve performance in competitive situations.

Mindfulness

Mindfulness is awareness that arises through paying attention deliberately in the present moment, non-judgmentally (Kabat-Zinn, 2009). Philippot (in Cottraux, 2007, p. 69) advances a more precise definition of mindfulness as "a mental state resulting from a deliberate focus of one's attention on the experience of sensory and mental aspects, cognitive and emotional, without judgment." Mindfulness is a special form of awareness and attention that predisposes the individual to well-being (Brown & Ryan, 2003).

The goal of mindfulness-based interventions is to make the individual aware of his automatic thoughts and accept them, without trying to judge them or modify them. For example, cognitive-behavioral approaches traditionally used in mental preparation recommend that athletes "cope" with their cognitions and emotions that have become harmful or unpleasant by attempting to control, restructure, or suppress them. These coping strategies (see Crocker, Tamminen, & Gaudreau, 2015) aim to modify the content of cognitions and emotions through techniques such as relaxation and cognitive restructuring.

Mindfulness is sometimes defined as a trait and sometimes as a state (Tang, Hölzel, & Posner, 2016). These conceptualizations are not mutually exclusive. Intervention programs include mindfulness as a skill that can be developed with practice. Some researchers, such as Brown and Ryan (2003), believe that mindfulness is based on a single dimension: awareness and attention focused on the present moment. Other authors argue that mindfulness is bi- or multidimensional. Cardaciotto, Herbert, Forman, Moitra, and Farrow (2008), for example, distinguished present-moment awareness from acceptance. These two components, awareness on the one hand and acceptance on the other, constitute together the principal theoretical constructs of mindfulness.

Bishop et al. (2004) proposed a two-component model of mindfulness. The first component of this definition involves the conscious and deliberate direction of attention so that it is maintained on immediate experiences (related to the facets of observing and describing). The second component is named "acceptance" and involves adopting an orientation of curiosity, openness, and acceptance instead of reacting negatively to experience (related to the facets of non-judging and non-reactivity).

Being mindful means being open to all experiences by allowing the appearance of thoughts, emotions, and bodily sensations in the flow of consciousness.

According to these authors, this openness to experience leads to a decrease in the use of cognitive and behavioral strategies to avoid what is experienced in the present moment. In addition, adopting this non-judgmental attitude toward thoughts, emotions, or bodily sensations alters the psychological context in which these elements are experienced, thereby reducing emotional distress and improving well-being. In summary, the consensus developed by Bishop and his colleagues is that mindfulness is a metacognitive skill that allows one to monitor the flow of consciousness and regulate attention, while facilitating a non-judgmental attitude toward the current experience.

Interventions based on mindfulness and acceptance

Our intervention, Mindfulness for Performance (MFP), is inspired by key interventions, such as Acceptance and Commitment Therapy (ACT; Luoma, Hayes, & Walser, 2018), and Mindfulness-Based Cognitive Therapy (MBCT; Zindel, Teasdale, & Williams, 2016). Standardized training programs based on mindfulness are often focused on reducing emotional distress. These addiction reduction programs are typically conducted in groups for approximately eight weeks. Each week, participants are guided by a practitioner trained in different mindfulness practices, including mindfulness breathing and body-mind scans (Dreeben, Mamberg, & Salmon, 2013). This sensitization during sessions is debriefed during subsequent sessions. The sessions often involve practical exercises. Participants do practical and written assignments and measure symptoms, such as "cravings."

Mindfulness in sport psychology

If mindfulness approaches have finally gained acceptance in general psychology, the experience has been quite different within sport psychology. Indeed, Gardner and Moore's (2005) *Clinical Sport Psychology* manual challenged the field of sport psychology not so much by proposing a new approach based on mindfulness but rather by rejecting the old approaches based on techniques that aim to modify thought content or feelings. The authors presented an analysis of 104 articles of adequate methodological quality dealing with sport psychology interventions aimed at improving athletic performance. Results of their analysis (p. 79) showed insufficient demonstration of effectiveness to validate the teaching of mental skills alone or in combination (e.g., imagery, goal setting, self-talk, and regulation of activation). The authors added that their findings were already well known, but practitioners (sport psychologists and mental performance consultants) continued to use these methods. According to Gardner and Moore, these methods of intervention are misrepresented in academic and professional textbooks, which erroneously claim that they are based on empirical evidence incorrectly considered as strongly supportive on scientific grounds. The authors vigorously denounce the gap between low scientific support for the use of mental skills in interventions with athletes and the unanimous enthusiasm for teaching these skills in universities.

The effectiveness of classical interventions in sport psychology has been the subject of numerous publications, literature reviews, and meta-analyses. Two recent publications by Zakrajsek and Blanton (2017) and Brown and Fletcher (2017) clarify the older publications. Overall, the number of studies between 1980 and 2018 grew considerably. Whether Gardner and Moore have exaggerated the scope of their analysis or not, we have observed over the past 15 years that their message has not been embraced by academics and practitioners. The new approach proposed by the aforementioned authors did not lead to changes in research and practice. In addition, conventional methods made up – and still do – a good share of athletes', coaches', and journalists' popular beliefs. For example, traditional sport psychology is still being put forward by popular sport psychology websites (Barraclough, 2019) insisting on restructuring thoughts rather than accepting them. Self-talk itself is still considered a common skill by the Association for Applied Sport Psychology, and modifying the content of self-talk is still advertised: "Changing self-talk is commonly used for (a) prompting a specific behavior, (b) improving self-confidence, (c) attention control, (d) motivation, and (e) arousal control" (AASP, 2019). These beliefs or knowledge are mostly rooted in English-speaking countries, where coaches have been trained in the psychology of sport. This is not the case in countries where the training in sport science departments does not systematically integrate the content of English textbooks.

In addition, the meta-analysis on the effects of interventions in mental preparation by Brown and Fletcher (2017) retained only 35 articles published until March 2015 of more than 1,400 articles considered for inclusion. They concluded that if interventions in mental preparation can improve athletes' performance, it is essential to report more rigorously the interventions to be better able to evaluate their effects on performance. In light of this meta-analysis, we suggest reconsidering the work of Gardner and Moore (2005), who opposed the conservative consensus of the profession.

Our analysis is that after the sport psychology community has advocated for many years the necessity of changing the content of thoughts to regulate thoughts and emotions, it became too challenging to propose a different approach. Athletes being customers, it was necessary to sell them what they asked for. Yet, the arguments for the effectiveness of mindfulness are simple: (a) the cognitive load required to change mental content is higher than that of not changing it; (b) studies on skill acquisition conclude that it is better to focus on external elements of the task than on the execution of the movement itself, which risks disrupting the automatisms that are so difficult to acquire.

The evolution of interventions in sports psychology could have integrated cognitive-behavioral approaches based on mindfulness. Although, since 2005, published studies of mindfulness have not been mentioned in the main academic and professional textbooks, the systematic review by Noetel, Ciarrochi, Van Zanden, and Lonsdale (2017) identified more than 5,000 studies, 129 of which focused on mindfulness in sport psychology. The authors selected 66 studies for their rigor based on the Cochrane tool (Higgins & Altman, 2008) and the GRADE method (Schünemann et al., 2008).

Large effect sizes were found for the improvement of performance and decrease in competitive anxiety. However, the authors concluded that the quality of the research must be improved and that it is difficult to determine whether mindfulness strategies are beneficial for athletes. According to them, additional research is needed to verify and reproduce the observed effects. Noetel et al. (2017) concluded that there is a need for more high-quality research interventions based on mindfulness. Our research group has been trying to achieve this since 2005 via experiments in high performance sport with Olympic athletes and golfers (Bernier, Thienot, Codron & Fournier, 2009, Bernier, Thienot, Pelosse, & Fournier, 2014, Thienot et al., 2014). To support our position, we later present a mindfulness-based intervention (MFP) with an elite fencer.

Structure, measurement, and mechanisms of mindfulness in sport psychology

If the definition of mindfulness seems clear, its structure is less so. Studies are needed not only to refine the identification of the different dimensions but also to specify the underlying processes. These studies should be conducted on large samples in general psychology before being applied to the field of sport and physical activity.

The measurement of mindfulness is still evolving, since it depends on a consensus of its structure. Until there is a model that is universally accepted, our position is based on the model of Bishop et al. (2004), which we have adapted to the needs of sport. We have therefore adopted a model encompassing the two factors, (1) awareness and (2) acceptance, to which we have added refocusing (Bernier et al., 2009). We recommend researchers presenting sport interventions to use the Mindfulness Inventory for Sport (MIS; Thienot et al., 2014), which measures these three dimensions. The measurement of mindfulness could be enriched, on the one hand, by more objective components and, on the other hand, by an increase in the frequency of measurement. In our view, the skill that is most relevant to the practice of sport and physical activity is the ability to detect when attention is not focused on the present moment and then to redirect attention to the task. We propose that the steps of awareness and acceptance are essential to allow the redirection of attention. The idea is to develop automatisms to (1) detect distractions or unpleasant mental events, (2) accept them, and (3) react consciously.

The Mindfulness for Performance (MFP) program

Our studies in sport psychology aim to manage attention in problem situations. One advance based on our research conducted since 2005 is the development of the MFP program. Unlike other mindfulness-based interventions, this program has no clinical focus and is not intended to improve well-being. The aim of the MFP program is to help athletes focus on an effective point of attention in a challenging situation, regardless of the cognitions that create interruptions, or the physical sensations related to stress that occur.

Step 1: Identification of the focus of attention

Knowing that in competition, concentration on movement can disrupt the automatisms that have been so diligently acquired in training (Beilock, Carr, MacMahon, & Starkes, 2002), we favor teaching athletes to focus attention on the result of their actions (Fournier & Farrow, 2014). This consideration is taken into account before undertaking training in mindfulness. Therefore, the first step of the MFP program is the identification of the relevant focus of attention, which will be useful during the implementation phase of the program in the field. This phase of identifying relevant points of attention may continue during the training season for technical or tactical skills.

Step 2: Mindfulness and acceptance training

The second stage first involves learning and practicing mindfulness, mainly with very brief exercises (one-minute body-mind scanning) and 10-minute meditation exercises each day. It is then necessary to become acquainted with the concept of acceptance. Acceptance is presented as experiencing events as they are, without trying to modify them. Examples of what acceptance is not (resignation, judgment) are also given to make sure the concept is understood. Ten-minute daily exercises of acceptance are introduced, so that athletes learn to consider any event (sensation or cognition) as transitory. Metaphors are used, such as observing the train of sensations – without stopping or boarding the train, or the movie of thoughts – without participating in or stopping the movie. So, in this step, athletes are taught how to practice two kinds of exercises: meditation exercises related to awareness of what they feel or think, and acceptance exercises.

Step 3: Integration into training and competition

During this phase, the athlete trains to incorporate mindfulness and acceptance whenever a distraction occurs. Exercises can test the relevance of focus of attention and automate the three steps: (1) becoming aware of distractions; (2) accepting thoughts, sensations, or emotions; and (3) quickly directing attention to a focus that is useful to performance.

During these three stages, an agreement with the coaches makes it possible to set up applied exercises in training and in competition. The MFP program is formatted to be integrated into training over a six-week period. Scripts of each session are recorded so that they can be used by different practitioners or researchers.

Assumptions about the mechanisms involved in the MFP program

We hypothesize that at first, awareness enables athletes to detect thoughts and sensations and treat them like transitory mental events. No action is required to manipulate the content of thoughts. However, if muscular tension is considered unsuitable for competitive sport, the athlete can and should change it. We suggest that the acceptance (of these experiences and thoughts) makes it possible to minimize the disruptive effect of cognitive or physical distractions and to facilitate the processing of information without increasing the cognitive load. We assume that the acceptance phase makes it possible to move to the third step, focusing attention effectively, preferably externally. In summary, our hypothesis is that the succession of the three stages, "mindfulness – acceptance – refocusing," enables the athlete to manage attention in stressful situations; hence, behaviors in competition.

Early results of MFP-based interventions are encouraging in various sports such as judo, taekwondo, figure skating, and archery. However, additional studies are needed to confirm effectiveness on athletic performance and to tailor content to individual athletes. These studies should assess the amount of practice needed because there is no consensus on the optimal dose (Garland & Howard, 2018). Indeed, we have chosen to create ten-minute sessions to facilitate the participation of athletes, who prefer short sessions. Thus, it is possible that daily sessions of different durations would be more effective (Ribeiro, Atchley, & Oken, 2018). Program adherence is a point that also needs studying because concentration on breathing, even with short sessions, is not a practice that athletes spontaneously appreciate, regardless of age or level of competition. In addition, at the beginning of the intervention, it is essential to identify specific targets for behavioral indicators and/or focus of attention that are useful. Indeed, targeting these specific issues concentrates effort in regular and frequent practice sessions.

Finally, it is necessary to specify performance indicators since progress in performance can appear independently from the general results in competition (win/loss). This consideration is valid for both individual and team sports. Performance indicators can evaluate individual progress over time, regardless of the outcome of a competition, and of course individual progress can be masked by the group result. In both cases, it is essential, if the purpose of the intervention is to improve performance, to make all the necessary arrangements to measure performance or its indicators.

Case study: Olga

Olga is a fencer in the national team of a European country. She is 27 years old, has been practicing fencing since she was eight, and is ranked among the top 35 athletes in her sport in the world. Her rank has fluctuated from 200th to 45th over the last seven seasons. The first interview was a need analysis. Olga wanted to figure among the world's top 16, to be selected for the Olympic Games. She had trouble, according to her, "managing the pressure in competition," illustrated by a discrepancy in levels between her training and her performance in international competitions. In the first interview, we noted that she had used different methods of mental preparation (including the use of positive internal dialogue and relaxation). Olga expressed the desire to feel good, less stressed in competition to be able to "fence in peace." We then proposed a new method (the MFP program), out of step with her habits. Our objective was not to make her feel better but rather to help her to achieve better performance, so that her level of fencing in competition would be similar to her level during training. We gave Olga time to understand that the work would be different from what she was used to, that it would be based on daily concentration training, in order to focus on useful elements in competition, without any guarantee of reducing anxiety nor associated unpleasant symptoms. The athlete contacted us four weeks later to give her consent.

We then specified that her commitment involved (1) defining an outcome goal, (2) identifying an observable indicator of progress, and (3) completing ten-minute sessions of mindfulness training per day. Olga reiterated that she wanted, for the season, to reach the top 16 in the world ranking, which would suppress the need to go through preliminary competitions at the World Cup. She indicated that she had to improve against left-handed opponents holding their sword with a straight grip, or French grip. Indeed, Olga is particularly distracted by these opponents and does not live up to her full potential when competing against them. According to her, progress in such matches is essential to improve her world ranking. Therefore, the number of victories against these opponents was chosen as a performance indicator during the competition season. She agreed to practice ten-minute mindfulness (focusing on breathing) sessions each day. We agreed to meet once a month, in an office or in the training room for the duration of the season. In-competition monitoring was done by WhatsApp messages and Skype calls at her request when traveling abroad, before the first fight of a competition and during the competition. Olga gave her consent to report the results of the intervention. She also agreed to complete two questionnaires on mental skills (the Ottawa Mental Skill Assessment Tool; Durand-Bush, Salmela, & Green-Demers, 2001) and the MIS. This initial assessment completed the interview and confirmed the need for improvement in stress management and attention skills.

Application of the MFP program

During the first month, Olga performed a daily session of ten minutes of concentration on breathing. With the help of an audio recording, she focused on the sensations of her breathing, noted if and when she was distracted, and directed her focus of attention on her breathing again. The goal was for her to learn to identify distractions, to accept them without judging them, and then to practice directing attention to an automatic action (breathing). The second month, she integrated a three-minute body-mind scan exercise at the beginning of each fencing training session, prompting her to quickly take note of her sensations, thoughts, and emotions. After three months, and noting that the "scan" was performed at the beginning of each fight, we proposed the exercise of "I know that." This exercise summarizes the three steps of the MFP program by combining awareness of the situation, acceptance, and refocusing in one inhalation and one expiration. It consists of verbalizing useless thoughts while inhaling ("I know that I am thinking about the result of the match ..."), then adding the word "and" before specifying the point of useful attention during the expiration ("... I withdraw and 'flèche'"). The focus of attention ("flèche") was chosen through strategic thinking before the match. The "I know that" exercise was to be used in competition whenever Olga detected that her attention was no longer directed to one of the useful elements of the fight.

Integrating mindfulness into fencing

In addition to her training and lessons, after two months of mindfulness training, Olga aimed to integrate a "scan" phase before each timed and refereed bout, regardless of whether the bout happened during training or in competition. We also organized at least one bout that would be timed and refereed during each daily training sessions. The goal here was to gradually integrate the concentration training into the bouts.

Strategy in competition – focus of attention

Olga chose to focus her attention, during competitive bouts, on a relevant strategic element, tailored to each opponent. It could be an external element, such as a target to hit on the opponent, following a video analysis of the athlete's combat technique. When a target was not specified as a result of the analysis, the point of attention could relate to a strategic solution to apply a combat plan (e.g., maintain distance, change the pace of the bout).

Results in competition

The percentage of wins against left-handed opponents increased during the season, after the intervention. During the previous season, Olga had won 4 times out of 12 against left-handed opponents opting for the straight handle, a success rate of 33%. After the MFP intervention, she won 12 times out of 21, a 57% success rate. The number of bouts increased, because Olga obtained better results in competition, and was therefore eliminated later at competitions. Her world ranking improved, such that by the end of the season, she ranked among the world top 16, which allowed her to enter the final stages of competitions directly and be selected for the world championships. However, an injury prevented her from competing at the end of the season, and she competed while injured at the World Championships.

Mindfulness questionnaire

The MIS results show a rapid improvement (within two months) in the values of the awareness subscale and a later increase (over three and a half months) in the acceptance score. We had to remind her of the difference between acceptance and resignation. Olga finally understood that acceptance means not judging one's thoughts, rather than accepting failure or agreeing with the content of one's thoughts. The refocusing subscale scores did not show any large variations in the quality of attention, whereas the progression was more explicit during interviews. We suggest triangulating sources of information (questionnaires, observations, interviews) to check for variations in mental skills.

Conclusion

Olga fully complied with the MFP intervention program with respect to the daily concentration on breathing sessions. She was also able to integrate body-mind scans during training for bouts with a referee, which allowed her to use scans during competition. It can therefore be considered that the basis of the program was respected. However, the planned number of refereed bouts during training could not be completed because of her injury. The amount of fencing training dropped at the end of the season after she qualified for the World Championship.

The improvement of performance indicator values (from 33% to 57% of bouts won) suggests that attention improved in these targeted stress situations. It seems that the MFP program did indeed contribute to a significant improvement in performance in competition, which enabled Olga to rank among the world's top 16, the performance goal of her season.

However, in addition to the injury that disrupted the end of the season, two variables were considered important for future performance. First, the fitness of a fencer must allow her to perform six bouts in a day in order to win a competition. As it stands, Olga needs to improve her physical condition because it is unclear if she is capable of such a physical performance, since she has not done it recently, even in training. Doubts about her physical condition could be managed with appropriate physical preparation. Second, there were differences in instructions from the coach present at training sessions and from the national coach responsible for coaching in competition. Strategic instructions and combat plans against given adversaries differed between the two coaches. Such differences may interfere with the focus of attention prepared by Olga for each opponent. Improving the focus of attention is thus complicated because Olga must choose between various options, and this choice must sometimes be made during a bout in competition. This situation is not optimal because in addition to different distractions, Olga must choose the set of instructions she wants or is able to apply during a bout. Better communication between the two coaches is desirable and requires diplomacy to obtain their cooperation.

In summary mindfulness can complement traditional mental preparation practices in competitive sport. However, as the principle is not to change thoughts, feelings, or emotions, the MFP intervention should not be coupled with cognitive restructuring. The MFP program is based on the identification of useful points of attention in competition, on training in mindfulness and acceptance, and on the integration of strategies (body-mind scan) in competition. Athletes learn to identify competing distractions (cognitions, emotions, or sensations), to accept them, and to direct attention back to the points of attention useful to performance.

References

AASP (2019, June 10). About applied sport & exercise psychology. Retrieved from https://appliedsportpsych.org/about/about-applied-sport-and-exercise-psychology/

Barraclough, J. (2019, June 10). Self-talk. Retrieved from https://believeperform.com/performance/self-talk/

Beilock, S. L., Carr, T. H., MacMahon, C., & Starkes, J. L. (2002). When paying attention becomes counterproductive: Impact of divided versus skill-focused attention on novice and experienced performance of sensorimotor skills. *Journal of Experimental Psychology Applied, 8*, 6–16. doi:10.1037/1076-898X.8.1.6

Bernier, M., Thienot, E., Codron, R., & Fournier, J. (2009). Mindfulness and acceptance in sport performance. *Journal of Clinical Sports Psychology, 4*, 320–333. doi:10.1123/jcsp.3.4.320

Bernier, M., Thienot, E., Pelosse, E., & Fournier, J. (2014). Effects and underlying processes of a mindfulness-based intervention with young elite figure skaters: Two case studies. *The Sport Psychologist, 28*, 302–315. doi:10.1123/tsp.2013-0006

Bishop, S. R., Lau, M., Shapiro, S., Carlson, L., Anderson, N. D., Carmody, J., ... & Devins, G. (2004). Mindfulness: A proposed operational definition. *Clinical Psychology: Science and Practice, 11*, 230–241. doi:10.1093/clipsy.bph077

Brown, D. J., & Fletcher, D. (2017). Effects of psychological and psychosocial interventions on sport performance: A meta-analysis. *Sports Medicine, 47*, 77–99. doi:10.1007/s40279-016-0552-7

Brown, K. W., & Ryan, R. M. (2003). The benefits of being present: Mindfulness and its role in psychological well-being. *Journal of Personality and Social Psychology, 84*, 822–848. doi:10.1037/0022-3514.84.4.822

Cardaciotto, L., Herbert, J. D., Forman, E. M., Moitra, E., & Farrow, V. (2008). The assessment of present-moment awareness and acceptance: The Philadelphia mindfulness scale. *Assessment, 15*, 204–223. doi:10.1177/1073191107311467

Carmody, J. (2009). Evolving conceptions of mindfulness in clinical settings. *Journal of Cognitive Psychotherapy, 23*, 270–280. doi:10.1891/0889-8391.23.3.270

Cottraux, J. (2007). *Thérapie cognitive et émotions: La troisième vague*. Issy-les-Moulineaux, Francais: Elsevier Masson.

Crocker, P. R. E., Tamminen, K. A., & Gaudreau, P. (2015). Coping in sport. In S. Hanton & S. Mellalieu (Eds.), *Contemporary advances in sport psychology: A review* (pp. 28–67). New York, NY: Routledge.

Dreeben, S. J., Mamberg, M. H., & Salmon, P. (2013). The MBSR body scan in clinical practice. *Mindfulness, 4*, 394–401. doi:10.1007/s12671-013-0212-z

Durand-Bush, N., Salmela, J. H., & Green-Demers, I. (2001). The Ottawa Mental Skills Assessment Tool (OMSAT-3). *Sport Psychologist, 15*, 1–19. doi:10.1123/tsp.15.1.1

Fournier, J., & Farrow, D. (2014). *Seven things we don't know: Coaching challenges in sport psychology and skill acquisition.* Laval, QC: Mindeval.

Gardner, F. L., & Moore, Z. E. (2005). *Clinical sport psychology.* Champaign, IL: Human Kinetics.

Gardner, F. L., & Moore, Z. E. (2012). Mindfulness and acceptance models in sport psychology: A decade of basic and applied scientific advancements. *Canadian Psychology/ Psychologie Canadienne, 53*, 309–318. doi:10.1037/a0030220

Gardner, F. L., & Moore, Z. E. (2017). Mindfulness-based and acceptance-based interventions in sport and performance contexts. *Current Opinion in Psychology, 16*, 180–184. doi:10.1016/j.copsyc.2017.06.001

Garland, E. L., & Howard, M. O. (2018). Mindfulness-based treatment of addiction: Current state of the field and envisioning the next wave of research. *Addiction Science & Clinical Practice, 13*, e14. doi:10.1186/s13722-018-0115-3

Higgins, J. P. T., & Altman, D. G. (2008). Assessing risk of bias in included studies. In J. P. T. Higgins & S. Green (Eds.), *Cochrane handbook for systematic reviews of interventions* (pp. 187–241). Chichester, UK: John Wiley.

Kabat-Zinn, J. (2009). *Au cœur de la tourmente, la pleine conscience - MBSR, la réduction du stress basée sur la mindfulness: programme complet en 8 semaines.* Bruxelles, Belgique: De Boeck.

Luoma, J. B., Hayes, S. C., & Walser, R. D. (2018). *Learning ACT: An acceptance and commitment therapy skills-training manual for therapists.* London, UK: New Harbinger.

Mardon, N., Richards, H., & Martindale, A. (2016). The effect of mindfulness training on attention and performance in national-level swimmers: An exploratory investigation. *The Sport Psychologist, 30*, 131–140. doi:10.1123/tsp.2014-0085

Masters, R. S. W., & Maxwell, J. P. (2004). Implicit motor learning, reinvestment and movement disruption: What you don't know won't hurt you. In A. M. Williams & N. J. Hodges (Eds.), *Skill acquisition in sport: Research, theory and practice* (pp. 207–228). London, UK: Routledge.

Noetel, M., Ciarrochi, J., Van Zanden, B., & Lonsdale, C. (2017). Mindfulness and acceptance approaches to sporting performance enhancement: A systematic review. *International Review of Sport and Exercise Psychology*, 1–37. doi:10.1080/1750984X.2017.1387803

Ribeiro, L., Atchley, R. M., & Oken, B. S. (2018). Adherence to practice of mindfulness in novice meditators: Practices chosen, amount of time practiced, and long-term effects following a mindfulness-based intervention. *Mindfulness, 9*, 401–411. doi:10.1007/s12671-017-0781-3

Schünemann, H. J., Oxman, A. D., Vist, G. E., Higgins, J. P. T., Deeks, J. J., Glasziou, P., & Guyatt, G. H. (2008). Interpreting results and drawing conclusions. In J. P. T. Higgins & S. Green (Eds.), *Cochrane handbook for systematic reviews of interventions* (pp. 359–387). Chichester, UK: John Wiley.

Tang, Y. Y., Hölzel, B. K., & Posner, M. I. (2016). The neuroscience of mindfulness meditation. *Nature Reviews Neuroscience, 17*, 59. doi:10.1038/nrn.2015.7

Thienot, E., Dimmock, J., Jackson, B., Grove, R., Bernier, M., & Fournier, J. (2014). Development and validation of the Mindfulness Inventory for Sport. *Psychology of Sport and Exercise, 15*, 72–80. doi:10.1016/j.psychsport.2013.10.003

Vealey, R. S. (1988). Future directions in psychological skills training. *The Sport Psychologist, 2*, 318–336. doi:10.1123/tsp.2.4.318

Zakrajsek, R., & Blanton, J. (2017). Evaluation of psychological interventions in sport and exercise settings. In E. Acevedo (Ed.), *Oxford research encyclopedia of psychology* (pp. 1–36). New York, NY: Oxford University Press.

Zindel, V. S., Teasdale, J. D., & Williams, M. S. (2013). *Mindfulness-based cognitive therapy for depression*. New York, NY: Guilford.

6

AN OPTIMIZATION APPROACH TO MENTAL HEALTH IN ATHLETES

Brad Donohue, Yulia Gavrilova, and Marina Galante Harris

Athletes and performers share a distinct culture with unique demands, including intense physical exertion, intrusive scheduling and travel, frequent evaluation, and public criticism (Birky, 2007; Filho, Aubertin, & Petiot, 2016; Parham, 1993; Waterhouse, Reilly, & Edwards, 2011), that may impact their performance (Anshel, Williams, & Williams, 2000) and well-being (Brewer & Petrie, 2014). High-level competition inherently necessitates a continuous need to optimize performance through cognitive and behavioral skills. At the elite level, athletic skills increasingly warrant precision, as small errors become more impactful to performance. Similarly, sensitivity to feedback also becomes more important, which may lead to stress and dampen positive perspective. These demands compete with prosocial activities outside of sport and often strain relationships (Parham, 1993).

Seminal studies support these assertions: athletes evidence elevated stress, difficulty managing relationships, mental and physical fatigue, and burnout, making it difficult to fulfill major role obligations (Ferrante, Etzel, & Lantz, 1996; Parham, 1993; Shrier & Hallé, 2011) and sometimes compromising their mental wellness (Donohue et al., 2018a; Petrie, Greenleaf, Reel, & Carter, 2008; Reardon & Factor, 2010). Indeed, athletes tend to experience psychiatric symptoms at similar or higher severity as non-athletes (Gorczynski, Coyle, & Gibson, 2017; Martens, Dams-O'Connor, & Beck, 2006; Rice et al., 2016).

Importantly, athletes tend to underutilize traditional psychological services (López, & Levy, 2013), perhaps due to perceived social stigma associated with the pursuit of mental health services, emphasis of mental health programs on pathology, and lack of evidence-supported mental health assessment and intervention programs adapted to sport culture (Donohue, Pitts, Gavrilova, Ayarza, & Cintron, 2013; Gavrilova & Donohue, 2018; Gulliver, Griffiths, & Christensen, 2012). Indeed, traditional therapies may promulgate a culture of mental health service avoidance among athletes.

In 2012 our research team received a substantial grant award from the National Institute on Drug Abuse in the United States to empirically develop the first sport-specific intervention to explicitly address substance use/mental health disorders in collegiate athletes. The award permitted our team to empirically develop a seamless mental wellness program for collegiate athletes that was named *The Optimum Performance Program in Sports* (TOPPS). TOPPS includes (a) a theoretical rationale to explain mental health and sport performance optimization (Donohue et al., 2015; Gavrilova & Donohue, 2018); (b) standardized outreach efforts focused on developing and maintaining a campus culture that values mental health optimization as a goal-worthy initiative capable of engaging athletes into mental health services (Donohue et al., 2004, 2016a); (c) psychometrically validated mental health assessment and screening procedures (Donohue, Miller, Crammer, Cross, & Covassin, 2007a; Donohue, Silver, Dickens, Covassin, & Lancer 2007b; Donohue et al., 2018a, 2019); and (d) standardized methods of optimizing mental health in athletes, regardless of the presence or severity of symptomatology, which have been supported in clinical trials (Chow et al., 2015; Donohue et al., 2015, 2016b, 2018b; Galante, Donohue, & Gavrilova, in press; Gavrilova, Donohue & Galante, 2017; Pitts et al., 2015). In the next sections, we expand on these components.

Theoretical rationale

The underlying tenets of optimization theory are consistent with those espoused in the cognitive-behavioral triangle thoughts, emotions, and behaviors dynamically influence one another during performance situations that are specific to sports and life outside of sports (see Figure 6.1). Emotions are difficult to control (Beck, 2011; Hu, Zhang, & Wang, 2014). Therefore, skill development is focused on the optimization of behavioral and cognitive skills. Presenting therapeutic goals within the context of optimization is less stigmatizing than the pathological implications that are underscored in traditional psychotherapeutic models, and thus more likely to engage athletes. Outreach does not market the optimization of mental health *per se* and does not ignore or avoid discussion of mental health issues if they are assessed or brought up. Rather, our staff promotes the optimization of skills to assist goal achievement in sports and life in general.

Outreach

It is important to initiate outreach programming to assure the respective community appreciates the benefits of mental wellness optimization. Outreach occurs through performance workshops with teams, performance presentations in classrooms, and campus events. The providers of TOPPS wear t-shirts with program insignia that is consistent with optimization messaging and sport culture.

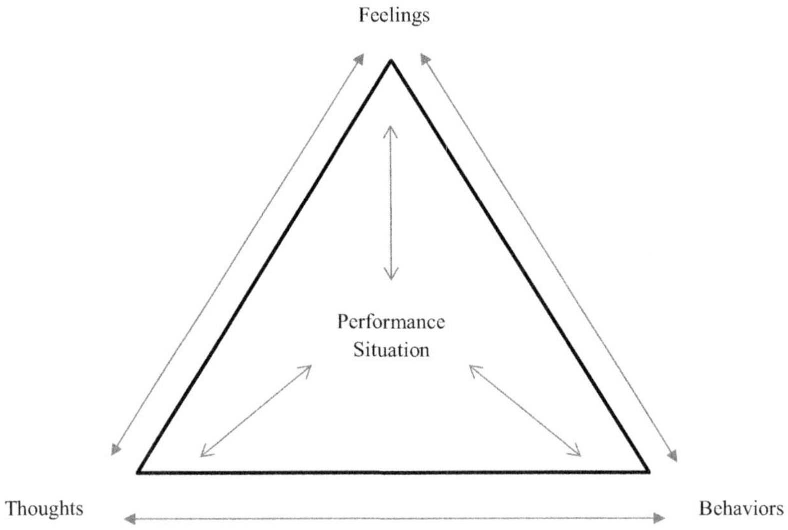

FIGURE 6.1 Cognitive-behavioral triangle adapted to accommodate performance.

Our sport performance workshops for teams are initiated with coaches. We provide the coach a TOPPS t-shirt and a menu of performance options specific to fundamental mental skills that are applicable to sport and life in general (i.e., neutral thinking, positive thinking, motivational communication, cohesion). After workshop content is prioritized, the standardized workshops are customized based on coach's feedback, potential concerns, and team culture. The number of workshop meetings and implementation time are determined by coaches. The workshop series is initiated with a discussion of optimization theory, its benefits and applicability to goal achievement, empirical support, performance plan generated with the coach(es), and opportunity to adapt programming. Each workshop meeting includes a rationale for the skillset to be learned, modeling and behavioral rehearsal specific to the respective skillset, and an opportunity to be scheduled to participate in an engagement meeting to determine if TOPPS might assist goal accomplishment.

The class presentations are negotiated with instructors who teach courses that are likely to involve a relatively high percentage of athletes. The presentations last approximately ten minutes. Content is standardized, focusing on the dissemination of optimization theory; its benefits and applications to goal achievement; and, like in the workshops, an opportunity to participate in the engagement meeting. Presentations in campus or organizational community events are similar, although they occur in an informal context, such as at a booth/table with TOPPS representatives or within the context of competitive games. Competitive games include, for example, throwing bean bags through holes for points while a representative provides "trash talk" or "positive statements." Performance feedback is provided, and athletes are asked to explain why they think they did better or worse in each of the respective conditions. Athletes are told a primary focus of TOPPS is to determine how performance can be optimized (as in the competitive game) and asked if they are interested in learning more about TOPPS. When interest is demonstrated, athletes are immediately invited to the TOPPS facilities to participate in an engagement meeting.

Screening

The National Collegiate Athletic Association (NCAA) recommends that collegiate institutions screen athletes for mental health conditions to facilitate mental health referrals (NCAA Sport Science and the NCAA, 2016). Unfortunately, screening for mental health interventions across student-athletes is currently not standard practice (Sudano, Collins, & Miles, 2017), probably because, with few exceptions, sport-specific mental health screens have yet to be psychometrically validated (Donohue et al., 2019; Hussey, Donohue, Barchard, & Allen, 2019; Rice et al., 2019), screening practices for athletes have been predominantly limited to physical health (Kroshus, 2016), and athletes have been resistant to mental health-focused programming (López, & Levy, 2013).

Athletes are considered a special population with unique mental health intervention and assessment needs (Comeaux, Bachman, Burton, & Aliyeva, 2017; Donohue et al., 2015; Etzel & Watson, 2007). Thus, assessment measures should be culturally specific to encourage engagement and increase accuracy of responses. We have psychometrically developed two mental health assessments that are sport-specific: namely the Sport Interference Checklist (SIC; see Donohue, et al., 2007b) and the Student Athlete Relationship Inventory (SARI; see Donohue et al., 2007a). Both of these scales have been psychometrically validated utilizing factor analysis, and both have demonstrated utility as mental health screens (Donohue et al., 2018a; 2019; Hussey et al., 2019). However, in this chapter we will review the SIC as our preferred screen because it was developed to assess or screen interferences with sport performance in training and competition contexts across a broad range of domains. When relationships with coaches, teammates, and family are concerning, the SARI is a viable option. Both measures are freely available from the first author.

The SIC is a 26-item measure developed for use in collegiate athletes and modified to be applicable to circus artists. The SIC is comprised of three scales (Problems in Sport Training Scale, PSTS; Problems in Sport Competition Scale, PSCS; Desire for Sport Psychology Scale, DSPS). The PSTS and PSCS assess cognitive and behavioral factors that have been determined to interfere with sport performance in training and competition, respectively. In the PSTS and PSCS, athletes report how frequently each item interferes with their performance in training and competition, respectively, utilizing a 7-point Likert scale (1 = Never; 7 = Always). Example items include "negative thoughts about personal performance" and "feeling stressed out." The third scale assesses the extent to which athletes desire sport psychology consultation for each cognitive and behavioral factor (Desire for Sport Psychology Scale, DSPS, where "Yes" is coded "1"; "No" is coded "0"). Scores are summed to obtain total scores, with higher scores indicating greater desire for sport psychology consultation to address performance interferences. Likert scale values are summed to obtain total scores for the PSTS and PSCS, respectively, with higher scores indicating greater cognitive and behavioral interferences in practice and competition domains.

The SIC was initially developed and evaluated in 141 collegiate student-athletes (Donohue et al., 2007b). In this study the SIC demonstrated good internal consistency, convergent validity, and discriminant validity. Responses did not differ significantly by athlete type (NCAA, intramural, club), nor did they differ by gender. A recent study conducted by Donohue and colleagues (2019) evaluated the extent to which the PSTS, and PSCS could predict mental health symptoms and classify athletes as high- and low-risk for mental health concerns based on SIC scores. Two-hundred and eighty-nine student-athletes completed the SIC and the Symptom Checklist-90-Revised (SCL90-R; Derogatis, 1994), which is an empirically validated screen of general mental health symptoms. The SCL90-R yields a Global Severity Index (GSI) score, which is a general indicator of psychiatric functioning. When controlling for gender and sport status (NCAA, intramural, and club), the hierarchical multiple regression revealed that the PSTS, PSCS, and DSPS predicted SCL-90-R GSI scores ($p < .001$). Receiver operating characteristic (ROC) analysis was then used to determine cut-off scores that accurately predicted an athlete's level of risk for mental health concerns (split into low-risk and high-risk groups). The PSTS and PSCS identified high-risk athletes significantly better than chance, with AUCs of .73 and above, using the PSTS cutoff score = 70 and PSCS cutoff core = 65. The DSPS did not significantly classify athletes as high- or low-risk for mental health concerns better than chance. These results indicate that the PSTS and PSCS are capable of predicting mental health concerns and successfully classifying athletes as low-risk or high-risk for mental health concerns. Scores for the SIC also fit directly into the generation of goals when implementing TOPPS (see the "Intervention" section below).

The SIC has also been empirically validated for use as a mental health screening instrument for circus artists. Circus artists have been compared to competitive athletes (Ménard & Hallé, 2014), dancers, and actors (Goudard, 2010; Leroux, 2014) but are considered a special population with unique challenges (Bouissac, 2006; Kristensen, 2004). Both professional- ($n = 88$) and student-artists ($n = 21$) completed the SIC along with a standardized battery of mental, physical, and emotional wellness measures. Among these was the Patient-Reported Outcomes Measurement Information System (PROMIS®), which is a collection of self-report measures developed and validated with support from the National Institutes of Health to assess mental, social, and physical functioning (see www.nihpromis.org). The study conducted by Donohue and colleagues (2018a) utilized the PROMIS Anxiety, Depression, Satisfaction with Social Roles and Activities, Social Isolation, Emotional Support, Informational Support, Fatigue, and Sleep Disturbance. Regression analyses were used to predict SIC scores that were significantly associated with PROMIS measures. Linear regression was used to generate empirical cut-off scores for the PSTS and PSCS corresponding to a *T* score of 60 (or 1 *SD* above the mean) on each PROMIS measure of problems (Anxiety, Depression, Social Isolation, Fatigue, and Sleep Disturbance) or a *T* score of 40 (or 1 *SD* below the mean) on each PROMIS measure of adaptive functioning (Informational Support, Emotional Support, and Satisfaction with Social Roles and Responsibilities). Separate regressions were conducted for professional and student samples.

Regression analyses revealed goal-worthy areas that administrators may consider for follow-up screening and potential treatment. Within the student-artist and professional-artist samples, scores in the 60s and 70s for SIC Training may warrant potential intervention for Fatigue, Anxiety, Depression, Social Isolation, Sleep Disturbance, Informational Support, and Satisfaction with Social Roles and Responsibilities. Scores in the 50s and 60s for SIC Competition (shows/evaluations) suggest follow-up screening for Fatigue, Anxiety, and Depression (see Donohue et al., 2018a for specific scores). Although these findings should be replicated for generalizability and be used as guidelines rather than definitive recommendations, the SIC can be utilized within circus populations to screen for mental health concerns and make appropriate, empirically based referrals.

Engagement

One of the challenging aspects of working with populations that are reluctant to pursue mental health interventions is engagement into services (López, & Levy, 2013). Barriers to recruitment and engagement include perceptions of social stigma, denial of emotional problems, under-reporting of symptoms (Gulliver, Griffiths, & Christensen, 2012; Watson, 2005), lack of time (Parham, 1993), expectations that services will not be helpful (Chandra & Paul, 2003), and concerns about confidentiality and potential negative consequences (Harrison, 1997). To address these concerns and increase athletes' access to mental health care, we recently examined an engagement strategy in a randomized controlled trial (Donohue et al., 2016a). The study involved 79 collegiate athletes who were referred to the study to determine their interest in pursuing one of two goal-oriented programs targeting "performance in sports and life in general" (TOPPS or campus-counseling-as-usual). The study results indicated promise for a engagement interview. The engagement interview is initiated with a solicitation of what the athlete does particularly well in sports and life in general and which aspects of performance in both sports and life outside of sports are desired for optimization. These prompts assist in building rapport and establishing a context for goal development. Next, mental health disorder prevalence rates and negative consequences of substance use for athletes are reviewed to assist in norming these issues. Athletes are asked to indicate why famous professional athletes utilize mental health services, including sport psychologists. They are shown a list of negative consequences that sometimes happen to athletes due to substance use and are informed that most athletes have experienced negative consequences after using alcohol or drugs or experiencing mental health concerns, and the interviewers disclose having experienced at least one of the listed negative consequences (stress is a listed consequence). The interviewer empathizes with expressed concerns and offers opportunities to obtain optimization programming.

The facility in which programming is implemented should be decorated in university or organization paraphernalia, schedules for sport events, and pictures of athletes who have achieved great accomplishments within the organization. Nomenclature is biased to promulgate optimization and empowerment. For instance, treatment plans are labeled performance plans, intervention is performance planning, and so on.

Intervention

As indicated in the Introduction section, TOPPS has shown to be efficacious in seven uncontrolled and controlled clinical trials. The most recent controlled clinical trial (Donohue et al., 2018b) involved 74 collegiate athletes who were formally assessed for mental health/substance use diagnostic severity. Participants were randomly assigned to TOPPS or campus counseling services as usual (SAU) after baseline. Participants were assessed at baseline and four and eight months post-baseline for psychiatric symptoms, mood, mental health factors affecting sport performance in training and competition, days using substances, sex without a condom, happiness in relationships, relationships affecting sport performance, and contributions of relationships to sport performance. Intent-to-treat repeated measures analyses indicated that participants in TOPPS consistently demonstrated better outcomes than participants in SAU up to eight months post-randomization (substance use was lower for participants in TOPPS compared with participants in SAU only during programming, and reductions in the frequency of unprotected sex were similar between participants in TOPPS and SAU). In general, mental health/substance use showed greater improvements in participants who received TOPPS, compared with participants in SAU, as diagnostic severity increased. Results indicated that TOPPS is a viable sport-specific prevention and intervention capable of addressing mental health regardless of presenting symptom severity, gender, or athlete type (NCAA, intramural, or club).

Providers of TOPPS ignore undesired behaviors; empathize with expressed concerns; and passionately and descriptively praise thoughts, behaviors, and character attributes. Humor is utilized, and modeling, behavioral rehearsal, and imagery are used extensively. Prior to formal programming, an orientation meeting is conducted to review limits of confidentiality, format of meetings, conceptualize the optimization approach to fit the athlete's unique situation generate, potential advantages of participation, and goal expectations. Sport background is honored, and methods to assist optimum performance in sport, mental health, and relationships, as well as strategies to avoid substance use, are all reviewed. The potential role of supportive others is underscored, including how they might assist performance goals. These persons include family members, coaches, teammates, and non-teammate friends. These persons encourage meeting attendance, model skills, and assist goal development and monitoring. The extent to which these support persons participate varies, as they can attend some or all meetings in person or through telephone- or video-conferencing.

Programming includes up to 12 weekly performance meetings, each about 60–90 minutes long. There are approximately a dozen intervention components (see Table 6.1). Each of the components includes a rationale that explains the theory and evidence supporting the respective programming, implementation protocol, and provision of handouts or worksheets. Athletes are assigned to practice skills between meetings, and providers encourage participation through supportive text messages and brief telephone calls. Athletes are encouraged to choose the location of programming, including in situ (e.g., athletic facilities, track, court) or office setting.

Athletes select sport and life performance optimization scenarios to be reviewed during performance meetings to ensure programming is pleasurable, relevant, and timely. All meetings are initiated with an exercise to assist optimum mindset in an upcoming sport or life outside of sport scenario (e.g., relaxation prior to test, arousal prior to game). Brainstorming is utilized to facilitate optimum thoughts and emotional intensity for the scenario (i.e., positive personality traits and skills, motivation-, focus-, and relaxation-oriented self-statements). Providers model and instruct role-playing to practice self-statements aloud in a simulated scenario with appropriate timing and intensity. Providers determine agendas with athletes and their supportive others, including intervention components that are planned for the meeting, and estimated time to implement each component. Cultural Enlightenment: The Semi-Structured Interview for Consideration of Ethnic Culture Scale and a similar scale for Sport Culture (Donohue et al., 2006) are administered. These interviews are utilized to prompt questions about athletes' experiences with these cultures, disclose cultural commonalities, potentially empathize with difficult experiences, and determine if program modification is necessary due to culture. This scale includes seven items (four solicit positive experiences regarding ethnic/sport background, three solicit negative experiences). Performance coaches demonstrate interest and compassion through open-ended queries, affirmations, and empathic statements.

Assessment findings, particularly their responses to the SIC, are presented to athletes, and goals are generated and transferred to a monitoring form. Meetings start with athletes reviewing how their goals were achieved since last contact, and contingent rewards and support for goal accomplishment are provided by supportive others. There are several program goals that are reviewed during each performance meeting. These goals are relatively generic (e.g., avoid substance use, doing positive things for others, maintain optimal mental wellness) although reviews of these goals during performance meetings involve solicitation of very specific thoughts and behaviors that were practiced to facilitate goal achievement (e.g., how did you avoid substance use, what did you do to maintain optimal mental wellness on Thursday, what thoughts did you have before you approached that person). Supportive others indicate how goal accomplishment will be encouraged or rewarded. After goals are reviewed in the first meeting, athletes and their supportive others are prompted to determine intervention components to emphasize during future meetings using a menu of options. Interventions are implemented sequentially and cumulatively based on these preferences.

To inspire motivation for goal achievement, athletes are prompted to review positive consequences for their performance of desired behaviors (Gavrilova, Donohue, Galante, & Gavrilova, 2018). Supportive others listen to determine motivational factors. Another intervention component involves athletes and their supportive others exchanging appreciations for one another, and later initiating a series of positive requests to establish reciprocal reinforcement in relationships (e.g., asking a teammate to attend practice on time). When athletes are interested in career development or getting a job out of season or in the future, they are encouraged to discuss career options to assist generation of a "dream job" and review and visualize the experience. Athletes are able to learn job interviewing skills and methods of soliciting job interviews through networking and direct contacts with potential employers. In a stimulus control-based intervention, they learn to create lists of people, places, activities, and emotions that are compatible and incompatible with goal attainment and later review these stimuli to create optimal experiences. Follow-up meetings involve generation of appropriate skills and role-playing to assist optimum actions and thoughts when spending time with these stimuli. A self-control intervention teaches athletes to determine initial thoughts that lead to undesired actions, and sequentially practice cognitive and behavioral skills that are likely to optimize performance in adverse situations. Skills include focus statements, motivational statements, cue-controlled relaxation and diaphragmatic breathing, brainstorming goal-oriented solutions, and imagining goal accomplishment and its positive consequences. All meetings conclude with a review of newly acquired skills and determination of supportive other involvement for the next meeting.

Future directions

TOPPs was developed in clinical trials to be a model sport-specific mental health/substance abuse program, supported by evidence in addressing the full continuum of mental health care, including outreach, screening/assessment, engagement, and intervention implementation. These trials have thus far focused on collegiate athletes. However, the worldwide obesity epidemic and previous empirical support for Family Behavior Therapy (the predecessor of TOPPS) in youth populations (e.g., Azrin, Donohue, Besalel, Kogan, & Acierno, 1994) suggest a controlled evaluation of TOPPS may be particularly warranted in youth athletes who are at-risk for mental health disorders. Indeed, the optimization

TABLE 6.1 TOPPS Performance Interventions

Intervention	*Purpose*
Dynamic goal and rewards	Learn to establish and achieve optimum goals and rewards.
Goal inspiration	Gain motivation for goals.
Environmental control	Learn to manage environment, so more time is spent doing things that optimize performance in sports/life and less time doing things that interfere with optimum performance.
Self-control	Learn to identify things that interfere with optimum performance, increase motivation to avoid interferences, assure calmness while generating and evaluating solutions, and improve imagination of optimal alternatives and rewards for optimum performance.
Performance timeline	Determine when and how to enhance contributions to optimum performance in sport and life situations/events.
Reciprocity awareness	Learn to optimally give and accept appreciation.
Positive request	Learn to optimally request things from others.
Dream job development	Determine an optimum career, including how to prepare for dream job.
Job-getting skills training	Develop skills to achieve optimum employment.
Financial management	Learn how to decrease expenses and increase income.

model is a good fit for school-wide implementation in this age group. Other populations worthy of TOPPS research include those with specified cultures and uniquely shared skillsets, such as professional and amateur athletes, musicians, artists, military, and firefighters.

References

Anshel, M. H., Williams, L. T., & Williams, S. M. (2000). Coping style following acute stress in competitive sport. *Journal of Social Psychology, 140*, 751–773. doi:10.1080/00224540009600515

Azrin, N. H., Donohue, B., Besalel, V., Kogan, E., & Acierno, R. (1994). Youth drug abuse treatment: A controlled outcome study. *Journal of Child and Adolescent Substance Abuse, 3*, 1–16. doi:10.1300/J029v03n03_01

Beck, J. S. (2011). *Cognitive therapy: Basics and beyond* (2nd ed.). New York, NY: Guilford Press.

Birky, I. (2007). Counseling student athletes: Sport psychology as a specialization. In J. A. Lippincott & R. B. Lippincott (Eds.), *Special populations in college counseling* (pp. 21–35). Alexandria, VA: American Counseling Association.

Bouissac, P. (2006, December). Timeless circus in times of change. *Fabulous Risk: Danger in Performance in Circus and Sideshow Conference*, University of Wollongong, Australia (Vol. 1).

Brewer. B. W., & Petrie, T. A. (2014). Psychopathology in sport and exercise. In J. L. Van Raalte & B. W. Brewer (Eds.), *Exploring sport and exercise psychology* (3rd ed., pp. 311–335). Washington, DC: American Psychological Association.

Chandra, A., & Paul, D. P. III. (2003). African American participation in clinical trials: Recruitment difficulties and potential remedies. *Hospital Topics, 81*, 33–38. doi:10.1080/00185860309598020

Chow, G. M., Donohue, B., Pitts, M., Loughran, T., Schubert, K. N., Gavrilova, Y., & Diaz, E. (2015). Results of a single case controlled study of The Optimum Performance Program in Sports in a collegiate athlete. *Clinical Case Studies, 14*, 191–209. doi:10.1177/1534650114548313

Comeaux, E., Bachman, T., Burton, R. M., & Aliyeva, A. (2017). Undergraduate experiences of Division I athlete science, technology, engineering, and mathematics (STEM) graduates. *Journal of Science Education and Technology, 26*, 24–32. doi:10.1007/s10956-016-9648-y

Derogatis, L. R. (1994). *SCL-90-R: Administration, scoring, and procedures manual* (3rd ed.). Minneapolis, MN: Pearson.

Donohue, B., Chow, G. M., Pitts, M., Loughran, T., Schubert, K. N., Gavrilova, Y., & Allen, D. N. (2015). Piloting the Optimum Performance Program in Sports: A family-supported approach to concurrently enhancing mental health and sport performance in athletes. *Clinical Case Studies, 14*, 159–177. doi:10.1177/1534650114548311

Donohue, B., Dickens, Y., Lancer, K., Covassin, T., Hash, A., Miller, A., & Genet, J. (2004). Improving athletes' perspectives of sport psychology consultation: A controlled evaluation of two interview methods. *Behavior Modification, 28*, 181–193. doi:10.1177/0145445503259399

Donohue, B., Galante, M., Hussey, J., Lee, B., Paul, N., Perry, J. E., & Allen, D. N. (2019). Empirical development of a screening method to assist mental health referrals in collegiate athletes. *Journal of Clinical Sport Psychology*. doi.org/10.1123/jcsp.2018-0070

Donohue, B., Gavrilova, Y., Galante, M., Burnstein, B., Aubertin, P., Gavrilova, E., ... & Benning, S. D. (2018a). Empirical development of a screening method for mental, social, and physical wellness in amateur and professional circus artists. *Psychology of Aesthetics, Creativity, and the Arts*. doi: 10.1037/aca0000199

Donohue, B., Gavrilova, Y., Galante, M., Loughran, T., Plant, C., Scott, J., ... & Allen, D. (2018b). Controlled evaluation of an optimization approach to mental health and sport performance. *Journal of Clinical Sport Psychology, 12*, 234–267. doi:101123/jcsp.2017-0054

Donohue, B., Loughran, T., Pitts, M., Gavrilova, Y., Chow, G. M., Soto-Nevarez, A., & Schubert, K. (2016b). Preliminary development of a brief intervention to prevent alcohol misuse and enhance sport performance in collegiate athletes. *Journal of Drug Abuse, 2*, 3–26. doi:10.21767/2471-853X.100035

Donohue, B., Miller, A., Crammer, L., Cross, C., & Covassin, T. (2007a). A standardized method of assessing sport specific problems in the relationships of athletes with their coaches, teammates, family, and peers. *Journal of Sport Behavior, 30*, 375–397.

Donohue, B., Pitts, M., Gavrilova, Y., Ayarza, A., & Cintron, K. I. (2013). A culturally sensitive approach to treating substance abuse in athletes using evidence-supported methods. *Journal of Clinical Sport Psychology, 7*, 98–119. doi:10.1123/jcsp.7.2.98

Donohue, B., Plant, C. P., Dowd, A., Phillips, C., Loughran, T., & Gavrilova, Y. (2016a). Controlled evaluation of a method to assist recruitment of participants into treatment outcome research and engage student athletes into substance abuse intervention. *Journal of Clinical Sport Psychology, 10*, 272–288. doi:10.1123/jcsp.2015-0022

Donohue, B., Silver, N., Dickens, Y., Covassin, T., & Lancer, K. (2007b). Development and initial psychometric evaluation of the sport interference checklist. *Behavior Modification, 31*, 937–957. doi:10.1177/0145445507303827

Donohue, B., Strada, M. J., Rosales, R., Taylor-Caldwell, A., Hise, D., Ahman, S., ... & Laino, R. (2006). The semistructured interview for consideration of ethnic culture in therapy scale: Initial psychometric and outcome support. *Behavior Modification, 30,* 867–891. doi:10.1177/0145445505276096

Etzel, E. F., & Watson, J. C. (2007). Ethical challenges for psychological consultations in intercollegiate athletics. *Journal of Clinical Sport Psychology, 1,* 304–317. doi:10.1123/jcsp.1.3.304

Ferrante, A. P., & Etzel, E., & Lantz, C. (1996). Counseling college student-athletes: The problem, the need. In E. Etzel, A. P. Ferrante, & J. W. Pinkney (Eds.), *Counseling college student-athletes: Issues and interventions* (pp. 3–26). Morgantown, WV: Fitness Information Technology.

Filho, E., Aubertin, P., & Petiot, B. (2016). The making of expert performers at Cirque du Soleil and the National Circus School: A performance enhancement outlook. *Journal of Sport Psychology in Action, 7,* 1–12. doi:10.1080/21520704.2016.1138266

Galante, M., Donohue, B., & Gavrilova, Y. (in press). The optimum performance program in sports: A case of Bulimia Nervosa in a lean sport athlete. In G. Breslin & G. Leavey (Eds.), *Mental health and well-being interventions in sport: A case study analysis* (pp. 9–30). New York, NY: Routledge Taylor & Francis Group.

Gavrilova, Y., & Donohue, B. (2018). Sport-specific mental health interventions in athletes: A call for optimization models sensitive to sport culture. *Journal of Sport Behavior, 41,* 283–304.

Gavrilova, Y., Donohue, B., & Galante, M. (2017). Mental health and sport performance programming in athletes who present without pathology: A case examination supporting optimization. *Clinical Case Studies, 16,* 234–253. doi:10.1177/1534650116689302

Gavrilova, Y., Donohue, B., Galante, M., & Gavrilova, E. (2018). A controlled examination of motivational strategies: Is it better to motivate by reviewing positive consequences for goal accomplishment or negative consequences of not accomplishing goals? *Motivation Science.* doi:10.1037/mot0000118

Gorczynski, P. F., Coyle, M., & Gibson, K. (2017). Depressive symptoms in high-performance athletes and non-athletes: A comparative meta-analysis. *British Journal of Sports Medicine, 51,* 1348–1354. doi:10.1136/bjsports-2016-096455

Goudard, P. (2010). *Le cirque entre l'élan et la chute : Une esthétique du risque [Circus between the rise and the fall: An aesthetic of risk].* Paris, France: Editions Espaces 34.

Gulliver, A., Griffiths, K. M., & Christensen, H. (2012). Barriers and facilitators to mental health help-seeking for young elite athletes: A qualitative study. *BMC Psychiatry, 12,* 157–169. doi:1471-244X/12/157

Harrison, L. (1997). The validity of self-reported drug use in survey research: An overview and critique of research methods. *NIDA Research Monograph, 167,* 17–36.

Hu, T., Zhang, D., & Wang, J. (2014). Relation between emotion regulation and mental health: A meta-analysis review. *Psychological Reports: Measures & Statistics, 114,* 341–362. doi:10.2466/03.20.PR0.114k22w4

Hussey, J., Donohue, B., Barchard, K., & Allen, D. N. (2019). Family contributions to sport performance and their utility in predicting appropriate referrals to mental health optimization programs. *European Journal of Sport Science.* doi:10.1080/17461391.2019.1574906

Kristensen, T. (2004). The physical context of creativity. *Creativity and Innovation Management, 13,* 89–96. doi:10.1111/j.0963-1690.2004.00297.x

Kroshus, E. (2016). Variability in institutional screening practices related to collegiate student-athlete mental health. *Journal of Athletic Training, 51,* 389–397. doi:10.4085/1062-6050-51.5.07

Leroux, L. P. (2014). Contemporary circus research in Quebec: Building and negotiating and emerging interdisciplinary field. *Theatre Research in Canada, 35*, 263–279.

López, R. L., & Levy, J. J. (2013). Student athletes' perceived barriers to and preferences for seeking counseling. *Journal of College Counseling, 16*, 19–31. doi:10.1002/j.2161-1882.2013.00024.x

Martens, M. P., Dams-O'Connor, K., & Beck, N. C. (2006). A systematic review of college student-athlete drinking: Prevalence rates, sport-related factors, and interventions. *Journal of Substance Abuse Treatment, 31*, 305–316. doi:10.1016/j.jsat.2006.05.004

NCAA Sport Science Institute and the NCAA. (2016, January). *Mental health best practices: Inter-Association consensus document: Best practices for understanding and supporting student-athlete mental wellness*. Indianapolis, IN: Author.

Parham, W. D. (1993). The intercollegiate athlete: A 1990s profile. *The Counseling Psychologist, 21*, 411–429.

Petrie, T. A., Greenleaf, C., Reel, J., & Carter, J. (2008). Prevalence of eating disorders and disordered eating behaviors among male collegiate athletes. *Psychology of Men & Masculinity, 9*, 267–277. doi:10.1037/a0013178

Pitts, M., Donohue, B., Schubert, K. N., Chow, G. M., Loughran, T., & Gavrilova, Y. (2015). A systematic case examination of The Optimum Performance Program in Sports in a combat sport athlete. *Clinical Case Studies, 14*, 178–190. doi:10.1037/a0013178

Reardon, C. L., & Factor, R. M. (2010). Sport psychiatry: A systematic review of diagnosis and medical treatment of mental illness in athletes. *Sports Medicine, 40*, 961–980. doi:10.2165/11536580-000000000-00000

Rice, S. M., Parker, A. G., Mawren, D., Clifton, P., Harcourt, P., Lloyd, M., … & Purcell, R. (2019). Preliminary psychometric validation of a brief screening tool for athlete mental health among male elite athletes: The athlete psychological strain questionnaire. *International Journal of Sport and Exercise Psychology*, 1–16 doi:10.1080/1612197X.2019.1611900

Rice, S. M., Purcell, R., De Silva, S., Mawren, D., McGorry, P. D., & Parker, A. G. (2016). The mental health of elite athletes: A narrative systematic review. *Sports Medicine, 46*, 1333–1353. doi:10.1007/s40279-016-0492-2

Shrier, I., & Hallé, M. (2011). Psychological predictors of injuries in circus artists: An exploratory study. *British Journal of Sports Medicine, 45*, 433–436. doi:10.1136/bjsm.2009.067751

Sudano, L. E., Collins, G., & Miles, C. M. (2017). Reducing barriers to mental health care for student-athletes: An integrated care model. *Families, Systems, & Health, 35*, 77–84. doi:10.1037/fsh0000242

Waterhouse, J., Reilly, T., & Edwards, B. (2011). The stress of travel. *Journal of Sports Sciences, 22*, 946–966. doi:10.1080/02640410400000264\

Watson, J. C. (2005). College student-athletes' attitudes towards help-seeking behavior and expectations of counseling services. *Journal of College Student Development, 46*, 442–449. doi:10.1353/csd.2005.0044

7

TEAM DYNAMICS THEORY

Implications for the development of high-performing teams

Edson Filho

High-performing sports teams are said to have "good chemistry," similar to how a complex molecule is formed by several chemical elements, and scholars and practitioners concur that success in team settings hinges on many well-connected team properties (Filho, 2015). To this extent, over the past 30 years, scholars and practitioners from various domains have tried to propose "best-fit models" that explain how myriad team processes are intertwined and influence team outcomes (see Carron, 1982; Filho, 2019). In this chapter, I discuss a recent framework I proposed called team dynamics theory (TDT), which purports that cohesion (CO), team mental models (TMM), collective efficacy (CE), coordination (CD), and team outcomes are connected in a systemic fashion (Filho, 2019, see Figure 7.1). In what follows, I discuss the theoretical roots, propositions, and applied implications of TDT. I conclude by outlining avenues of future research.

Theoretical roots

TDT derives from previous theoretical work in the sport, exercise, and performance psychology field. Since the 1980s, Carron and colleagues have proposed conceptual frameworks describing the reflective indicators of CO and linking it to other team processes (e.g., Carron, 1982; Carron & Spink, 1993; Carron, Widmeyer, & Brawley, 1985). Notably, Carron and Hausenblas's (1998) *conceptual framework for examining sport teams* represents the first well-defined, parsimonious, and testable input-output model linking CO to other team processes and to team performance. Based on this framework, my colleagues and I proposed and tested a nomological network linking CO, TMM, CE, and performance in teams (Filho, Tenenbaum, & Yang, 2015). We observed that CO was exogenous to TMM and CE, which in turn co-varied with and influenced team performance. More recently, research has also suggested that transactive memory

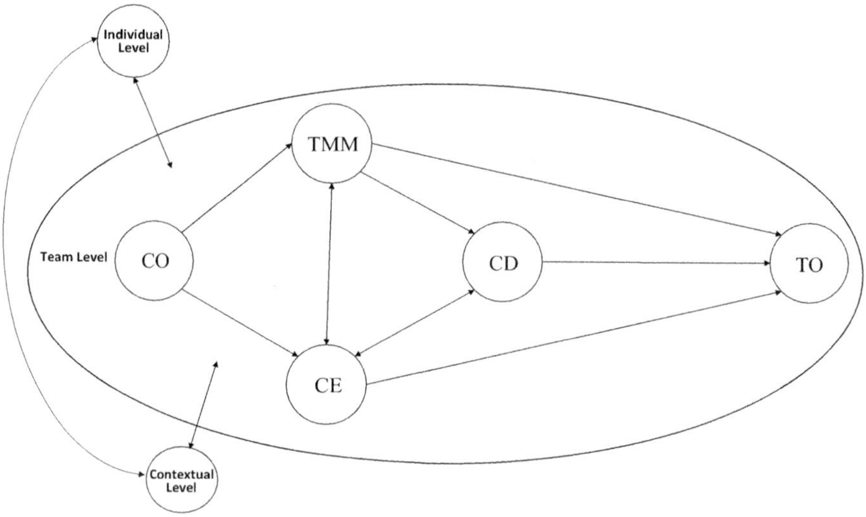

FIGURE 7.1 Team dynamics theory focuses on the team-level of analysis and purports that cohesion (CO) is exogenous to Collective Efficacy (CE) and Team Mental Models (TMM), which in turn co-vary. TMM is a formative indicator of coordination (CD). Collectively, these team processes influence, via direct and indirect means, Team Outcomes (TO).

systems, a similar concept to TMM, is exogenous to CO and co-varies with CE (Leo, González-Ponce, García-Calvo, Sánchez-Oliva, & Filho, 2019).

However, a model of team dynamics without team CD is incomplete (Gorman, 2014). Hence, theoretical work directed at improving team functioning should go beyond CO and social means, and encompass team cognition constructs, such as TMM and CD (Eccles & Tran, 2012; Filho, 2019). In fact, research with circus performers (Filho & Rettig, 2018a), elite police units (Boulton & Cole, 2016), guitar duets (Sänger, Müller, & Lindenberger, 2012), and emergency medical teams (Westli, Johnsen, Eid, Rasten, & Brattebø, 2010) has revealed that TMM and CD are related constructs. To go back one step, TMM is a higher-order construct, with two sub-dimensions – shared mental models and complementary mental models – serving as formative indicators of CD (Filho & Tenenbaum, 2012; Mohammed, Ferzandi, & Hamilton, 2010). Put plainly, to "be at the right place at the right time doing the right thing," teammates need to have both shared and complementary skills (Filho & Tenenbaum, 2020; Mohammed, Hamilton, Sánchez-Manzanares, & Rico, 2017). It follows that in TDT I have added CD to the previous theoretical equations by Carron and colleagues and the empirical works discussed above. In addition, I have outlined the scope and put forth an ontological and nomological proposition to explain the birth and development of high-performing teams, as elaborated upon next.

Ontological and nomological propositions

TDT is a parsimonious systemic framework aimed at explaining part of the complex phenomenon of team birth and development. As such, TDT aims to explain the linkage among key team-level (we/us) processes and team performance. For this reason, leadership, which is central to team performance, is not included in TDT, as some scholars attribute leadership to the individual-level of analysis, while others attribute it to the group-level of analysis (i.e., leader-follower dichotomy). Although the influence of individual (e.g., leadership) and contextual (e.g., social pressure) variables on the linkage among team processes and outcomes can be statistically modelled, TDT focuses on the team-level of analysis. Team processes are emergent "we/us" rather than "I/me" psychobiosocial states because they arise from "the team as a whole" rather than the sum of its individual parts (Gorman, 2014). For instance, a given individual might feel connected to the team, but cohesion in the team as a whole might be low.

By definition, a group of individuals only becomes a team once they have established shared goals (see Carron & Eys, 2012; Pescosolido & Saavedra, 2012). Accordingly, TDT's ontological proposition is that CO is the first team process to emerge because, imagining no previous interaction among individuals ("time = 0"; zero acquaintance condition), a group of people only becomes a team once they have established instrumental task and social goals:

> It is the strength of interdependent shared task and social goals that brings and keeps individuals together as a team. Therefore, CO is the first process to emerge in teams. CO allows for the development of other team processes, which mutually influence one another, and together influence TO.
>
> *(Filho, 2019, p. 8)*

CO will lead to the development of TMM, which in turn leads to the development of CD. Moreover, TMM and CD are theorized to develop alongside CE beliefs, as better mental models and coordination influence team confidence and vice-versa. Together, CO, TMM, CD, and CE influence, via direct or indirect means, TO.

TDT's nomological proposition is that the development of CO allows for the emergence of other processes, which are all bounded to a reciprocal linkage:

> CO will initially foster the development of TMM, which in turn is the basis for CD. CE beliefs will develop simultaneously with TMM and CD; that is, the higher the accuracy and quality of the TMM the higher the teams' CE and CD will be and vice-versa, as in a dynamic systems linkage. Together, these team processes will influence, via direct or direct means, TO.
>
> *(Filho, 2019, p. 9)*

In fact, previous research suggests that CO predicts TMM and CE, which covary, and together predict team performance (Filho et al., 2015; Filho & Rettig,

2018a; Leo, González-Ponce, Sánchez-Miguel, Ivarsson, & García-Calvo, 2015). In turn, TMM form the basis of CD, as extant field and neurological research has shown (Dumas, Nadel, Soussignan, Martinerie, & Garnero, 2010; Filho et al., 2016; Sänger et al., 2012). Together, all of these team processes influence, via direct and indirect means, team performance. These two related propositions are important to inform interventions in team settings, as elaborated upon next.

Applied implications

The goal of individually tailored interventions is to allow performers to find and remain in their "individual zones of optimal functioning" to consistently perform at peak level. Similarly, the goal of applied interventions in team settings is to allow a team to function at an optimal level, which occurs "when team members are able to reach and sustain their performance potential under the most challenging conditions" (Filho & Tenenbaum, 2020, p. 32). To develop a team toward its full performance potential, practitioners should keep in mind that applied interventions should be systemic in nature; that is, they should target several team processes at the same time. As discussed above, the enhancement of one team property leads to the improvement of another team property, akin to TDT's nomological proposition and the overarching notion of *reciprocal determinism* put forth by Bandura (1997). To develop high-performing teams, practitioners must also understand the sub-dimensions or reflective indicators of different team processes. Accordingly, I provide specific recommendations for the development of CO, TMM and CD, and CE.

Developing cohesion

As TDT's ontological proposition suggests, individuals come and stick together (i.e., cohesion) because they share social and task goals (Carron & Eys, 2012; Pescosolido & Saavedra, 2012). Thus, the first step to developing high-performing teams is to help teammates establish high-quality goals. Without high-quality goals, other "psychological contracts," such as leadership (i.e., leading individuals toward a shared goal) and motivation (i.e., intensity and direction of action and effort), cannot be established within a team (see Cashmore, 2006). The next step is to establish team norms, which clarify the rights and responsibilities that apply to all team members. For instance, coaches and practitioners should make clear the standards of conduct expected for training and competition (e.g., practice times, traveling regulations, uniforms). Encouraging open and positive communication among teammates is particularly important to enhance CO and other team processes linked to optimal performance. Developing a team identity or a so-called sense of "we" through different team-building exercises (for a review see Carron & Eys, 2012) is also important to enhance cohesiveness within the team.

Furthermore, coaches and practitioners should ensure that individuals have specific and identifiable roles within the team (Carron & Eys, 2012; Pescosolido & Saavedra, 2012). Role clarity, as opposed to role ambiguity, increases cohesion because every individual team member feels like s/he has something to contribute to the team and because it prevents conflicts about "who does what" in the team (Bosselut, McLaren, Eys, & Heuzé, 2012; Leo et al., 2015). Identifiable roles mean that individuals' contributions to the team should be visible and measurable (e.g., performance statistics) to keep every individual accountable and prevent social loafing within the team. By ensuring that each team member has clear roles within the team, coaches and practitioners should strive for an ideal team size, which depends on the sport type and performance context. Simply put, too many team members leads to social loafing, whereas too few team members do not allow for the development of complementary mental models in the team which, in turn, leads to groupthink (Filho, 2019).

Developing TMM and CD

Once a strong social and task bond among teammates has been established, TMM and CD will develop naturally. By definition, TMM pertain to teammates quantity and quality of different types of knowledge (i.e., know where, when, what, how, and why) about the individual team members, the team tasks, the team as a whole, and the performance context (Filho & Tenenbaum, 2020). As discussed above, TMM form the basis of CD. Put differently, to be at the right place (know-where), at the right time (know-when), doing the right thing (know-what), the right way (know-how) for the right reason (know-why), teammates must possess shared and complementary mental models.

It is important to highlight that TMM are more of a trait construct than a state construct, and thus take time to develop. As such, preventing high turnover of both athletes and coaches is important to enhance the quantity and quality of TMM. To this extent, Shamsie and Mannor (2013) examined performance in professional baseball teams over a 16-year period and concluded that winning percentage is dependent on the number of players that remain on the roster for at least three years. Research also suggests that preventing coach turnover is linked to successful performance in professional soccer (Filho & Rettig, 2018b). Over time, coaches and players learn about their shared and complementary strengths and weaknesses and devise coping strategies to aid team performance. Overall, it is important to find an "optimum balance" to prevent turnover and allow teammates to develop TMM while also recruiting players with shared and complementary skill-sets.

To develop shared and complementary mental models within teams, individuals must also be given problem-solving exercises during practice. It is through problem-solving exercises that teammates will learn how to describe, explain, and predict their fellow teammates' thinking patterns and actions (Filho & Tenenbaum, 2020; Johnson-Laird, 2010). Importantly, these problem-solving exercises should allow individuals to learn more about each other, about the team as a whole, and about the performance context. For instance, during practice, coaches should encourage teammates to think aloud to explain their decisions and actions to their fellow teammates, generate set-plays, and develop non-verbal communication signs (Filho & Tenenbaum, 2012). Cross-training, role-play, and video-analysis also help teammates to develop a shared understanding of each other's tasks and strengths and weaknesses (Eccles & Tran, 2012).

Naturally, the type of problem-solving activity that will help individuals to think as a team depends on the performance context. However, a general guideline applies across the board and consists of teaching performers to use inductive, deductive, and abductive thinking and reasoning strategies. Requiring performers to inductively generate multiple (optimal, moderate, and poor) courses of action and "on-the-fly" responses to the same problem is a way to develop inductive thinking and adaptability in team settings. Providing teammates with top-down ideas (e.g., set-plays, specific game plan, and contingency plans) is paramount to ensure they are on the same page about the key team tasks. Also, similar to the red-team approach in military settings (see Romyn & Kebbell, 2018), teams should develop top-down contingency plan responses to more likely worst-case scenarios (e.g., star player suspended from the final) or less likely worst-case scenarios (e.g., star player, team captain, goalkeeper, and head coach suspended from the final match). Last but not least, abductive thinking consists of teaching teammates to use information beyond themselves (e.g., video-analysis, physiological tracking devices) to generate new insights and knowledge for the team. Altogether, more and better TMM will lead to optimal CO, while also enhancing teammates' CE.

Developing collective efficacy

CE pertains to teammates' confidence in the team's capability to reach its goals and potential, and is dependent on teammates' conjoint levels of ability, preparation, effort, and persistence (Short, Sullivan, & Feltz, 2005). As such, recruiting is key to the development of highly efficacious teams. Recruiting highly skilled players will boost the team's overall ability, thus enhancing CE. However, in addition to recruiting star players, it is also important to recruit for effort and select "team players" who will work hard to ensure the team's goals and potential are accomplished. As the adage goes, "hard work can beat talent," and that is why more-skilled teams can be beaten by less-skilled teams (Feltz, Short, & Sullivan, 2008).

It is important to highlight that persistence toward a collective goal will enhance a team's CE, because successful performance requires long-term commitment, and more efficacious teams will strive for longer toward their goals (Feltz & Öncü, 2014). Furthermore, preparation of training sessions oriented to the mastering of new skills and team plays is crucial to the development of CE in teams. Preparation decreases anxiety, while mastery experiences instill confidence at both the individual- and the team-level of analysis (Feltz et al., 2008). Furthermore, as extant research on efficacy beliefs and deliberate practice in sports has shown (see Ericsson, Hoffman, Kozbelt, & Williams, 2018; Feltz et al., 2008), training sessions should be supported by specific feedback from knowledgeable coaches and other role models. High-efficacy coaches usually offer more instructional feedback and positive reinforcement than low-efficacy coaches and tend to exhibit leadership styles that are preferred by performers (Feltz et al., 2008).

The development of a task-oriented rather than an ego-oriented performance climate is also essential to the development of efficacy beliefs. In other words, a performance climate wherein preparation, effort, and persistence are reinforced will promote the enhancement of self, collective, and relational efficacy beliefs (Feltz et al., 2008). In contrast, an ego-oriented climate wherein winning is everything has been linked to negative psychobiosocial states in both individual and team sport settings (Duda, 2013). Promoting the development of peer-leaders within the team is another important step in the development of a positive performance climate and will help to boost performers' CE as well as positively influence other team processes, including CO, TMM, and CD. Peer-leaders are a major source of confidence in team settings because they model confidence and help fellow teammates to interpret their psychobiosocial states as positive and functional rather than negative and dysfunctional to performance (Cotterill & Fransen, 2016).

Overall, coaches and practitioners should keep in mind that CE is linked to other team processes, akin to TDT tenets and the overarching applied psychology notion that team processes share a many-to-many basis relationship. To aid the practitioner, a summary of intervention strategies and their expected outcomes on CE and all other team processes covered in this section is presented in Table 7.1. Notably, some coaches and practitioners might be better at developing cohesion, whereas others might be more effective at developing TMM and CD, or at enhancing teammates' CE beliefs. However, over-emphasis on one team process will lead to dysfunction rather than optimal functioning, whereas systemic interventions simultaneously targeting all of these team processes will render better team outcomes. To this point, experimental trials testing the feasibility and impact of team-level interventions anchored on TDT tenets is one of many open research avenues in group dynamics in sport, exercise, and performance psychology.

Future research

To advance research on the nomological network linking several team processes and outcomes, scholars must test alternative equivalent and non-equivalent models of team dynamics. While research thus far suggests the structural model proposed in TDT is the best fit model, alternative models might exist in the natural world. Similar to chemical reactions and language, wherein molecules and words can be arranged in endless ways (i.e., "the infinite use of finite means"), the linkage among CO, TMM, CD, and CE might vary depending on the task and performance context. In addition to cross-correlational research on the entire nomological network proposed in TDT, experimental research testing specific input-output relations is also welcomed. For instance, interventions targeting the linkage between CO and TMM or between TMM and CD are welcomed to test TDT by the parts rather than by the whole and to advance evidence-based practice guidelines on team-level interventions.

TABLE 7.1 Summary of Intervention Strategies and Expected Primary Outcome

Intervention Strategy	*Expected Primary Outcome*	
	Increase	*Decrease*
Develop multiple peer-leaders within the team	CO, TMM and CD, CE	
Develop contingency plans to address worse-case scenarios	TMM and CD	
Develop a task-oriented performance climate	CE	Negative affect and Burnout
Establish clear social and task goals	CO	Social cliques
Establish clear individual roles and team norms	CO	Social loafing
Encourage open and positive communication through verbal and non-verbal means	CO, TMM and CD, CE	
Encourage teammates to think aloud to explain their decisions to their fellow teammates	TMM and CD	
Propose problem-solving activities that require inductive, deductive, and abductive thinking	TMM and CD	
Propose cross-training, role-play, and video-analysis training	TMM and CD	
Provide positive and instructional feedback	TMM and CD, CE	
Recruit individuals with different skill sets	TMM and CD	Groupthink
Recruit skilled players to enhance the teams overall skill level	CE	
Recruit hardworking players to enhance the teams overall effort and persistence level	CE	

Exploring the influence of different individuals' characteristics and contextual characteristics on the linkage among CO, TMM, CD, CE, and team outcomes through multilevel modelling is important given that individuals are nested within teams which are bounded to a given performance milieu. The study of how leadership influences the nomological network proposed in TDT is particularly warranted, as leadership is central to the science of working teams.

Furthermore, longitudinal studies using advanced multivariate statistics can add insights into whether high- and low-performing teams develop differently over time. Similar to how elite performers show different developmental trajectories than their less accomplished counterparts, team processes might develop differently in "expert teams." Different teams might progress differently through the so-called forming, storming, norming, and performing stages (Tuckman, 1965), and learning about the trajectories of high-performing teams might generate best-practice guidelines. On this front, multi-method studies on whether CO, TMM, CD, and CE are integral to the umbrella construct of team resilience are warranted.

Finally, psychophysiological research should be conducted to identify the peripheral and central physiological markers of CO, TMM, CD, and CE. For instance, high- and low-level of psychophysiological synchrony and neural activation might predict or reflect cohesiveness, shared and complementary mental states, joint action, and group-level confidence in social settings. Research on multiperson physiological monitoring and hyperbrains is a ripe area for research, with methodological paradigms in music, cooperative juggling, and gestural imitation being available in the literature.

Concluding summary

In this chapter, I provided a brief overview of TDT, which purports that CO is the first team process to emerge because a group of individuals only becomes a team once they have set shared goals together. Furthermore, I suggested that once CO is established, other key team processes influence one another, akin to the notion of reciprocal determinism in applied social psychology. Accordingly, practitioners should ensure that quality goals are set and that all correlates of cohesion are fostered in the early stages of team development. After that, practitioners should target multiple team processes simultaneously as, for instance, enhancing TMM influences CE and vice-versa. I have also suggested that practitioners should understand the sub-dimensions of CO, TMM, and CE if they are to develop high-performing teams so as to increase social and task bonds; shared and complementary mental models; and mastery experiences, effort, preparation, and persistence within a team. Overall, the goal of TDT is to help practitioners to develop systemic applied interventions to aid team development and functioning in sports and beyond, as well as to stimulate research toward the development of a general theory of team dynamics in sport, exercise, and performance psychology.

References

Bandura, A. (1997). *Self-efficacy: The exercise of control*. New York, NY: W. H. Freeman.

Bosselut, G., McLaren, C. D., Eys, M. A., & Heuzé, J. P. (2012). Reciprocity of the relationship between role ambiguity and group cohesion in youth interdependent sport. *Psychology of Sport and Exercise*, *13*, 341–348. doi:10.1016/j.psychsport.2011.09.002

Boulton, L., & Cole, J. (2016). Adaptive flexibility: Examining the role of expertise in the decision making of authorized firearms officers during armed confrontation [Special issue]. *Journal of Cognitive Engineering and Decision Making*, 291–308. doi:10.1177/1555343416646684

Carron, A. V. (1982). Cohesiveness in sport groups: Interpretations and considerations. *Journal of Sport Psychology*, *4*, 123–138. doi:10.1123/jsp.4.2.123

Carron, A. V., & Eys, M. A. (2012). *Group dynamics in sport* (4th ed.). Morgantown, WV: Fitness Information Technology.

Carron, A. V., & Hausenblas, H. A. (1998). *Group dynamics in sport* (2nd ed.). Morgantown, WV: Fitness Information Technology.

Carron, A. V., & Spink, K. S. (1993). Team building in an exercise setting. *The Sport Psychologist*, 7, 8–18. doi:10.1123/tsp.7.1.8

Carron, A. V., Widmeyer, W. N., & Brawley, L. R. (1985). The development of an instrument to assess cohesion in sport teams: The group environment questionnaire. *Journal of Sport Psychology*, 7, 244–266. doi:10.1123/jsp.7.3.244

Cashmore, E. (2006). *Sport and exercise psychology: The key concepts*. New York, NY: Routledge.

Cotterill, S. T., & Fransen, K. (2016). Athlete leadership in sport teams: Current understanding and future directions. *International Review of Sport and Exercise Psychology, 9*, 116–133. doi:10.1080/1750984X.2015.1124443

Duda, J. L. (2013). The conceptual and empirical foundations of Empowering Coaching™: Setting the stage for the PAPA project. *International Journal of Sport and Exercise Psychology, 11*, 311–318. doi:10.1080/1612197X.2013.839414

Dumas, G., Nadel, J., Soussignan, R., Martinerie, J., & Garnero, L. (2010). Inter-brain synchronization during social interaction. *PLoS ONE, 5*, e121166. doi:10.1371/journal.pone.0012166

Eccles, D. W., & Tran, K. B. (2012). Getting them on the same page: Strategies for enhancing coordination and communication in sports teams. *Journal of Sport Psychology in Action, 3*, 30–40. doi:10.1080/21520704.2011.649229

Ericsson, K. A., Hoffman, R. R., Kozbelt, A., & Williams, A. M. (Eds.). (2018). *The Cambridge handbook of expertise and expert performance*. Cambridge, UK: Cambridge University Press.

Feltz, D. L., & Öncü, E. (2014). Self-confidence and self-efficacy. In A. G. Papaioannou & D. Hackfort (Eds.), *Routledge companion to sport and exercise psychology: Global perspectives and fundamental concepts* (pp. 417–419). New York, NY: Routledge.

Feltz, D. L., Short, S. E., & Sullivan, P. J. (2008). *Self-efficacy in sport*. Champaign, IL: Human Kinetics.

Filho, E. (2015). "Team chemistry" through chemistry lenses: Interdisciplinary science or a metaphorical conundrum? *Frontiers in Psychology, 6*, e38. doi:10.3389/fpsyg.2015.00038

Filho, E. (2019). Team dynamics theory: Nomological network among cohesion, team mental models, coordination, and collective efficacy. *Sport Sciences for Health, 15*, 1–20. doi:10.1007/s11332-018-0519-1

Filho, E., Bertollo, M., Tamburro, G., Schinaia, L., Chatel-Goldman, J., di Fronso, S., … & Comani, S. (2016). Hyperbrain features of team mental models within a juggling paradigm: A proof of concept. *PeerJ, 4*, e2457. doi:10.7717/peerj.2457

Filho, E., & Rettig, J. (2018a). Team coordination in high-risk circus acrobatics. *Interaction Studies, 19*, 500–519. doi:10.1075/is.16035.fil

Filho, E., & Rettig, J. (2018b). The road to victory in the UEFA women's Champions League: A multi-level analysis of successful coaches, teams, and countries. *Psychology of Sport and Exercise, 39*, 132–146. doi:10.1016/j.psychsport.2018.07.012

Filho, E., & Tenenbaum, G. (2012). Team mental models in sports: An overview. In R. Schinke (Ed.), *Athletic insight's writings in sport psychology* (pp. 329–342). Hauppauge, NY: Nova Science Publishers.

Filho, E., & Tenenbaum, G. (2020). Team mental models: Taxonomy, theory, and applied implications. In G. Tenenbaum, & R. C. Eklund (Eds.), *Handbook of sport psychology* (4th ed., pp. 611–631). Hoboken, NJ: Wiley.

Filho, E., Tenenbaum, G., & Yang, Y. (2015). Cohesion, team mental models, and collective efficacy: Towards an integrated framework of team dynamics in sport. *Journal of Sports Sciences, 33*, 641–653. doi:10.1080/02640414.2014.957714

Gorman, J. C. (2014). Team coordination and dynamics: Two central issues. *Current Directions in Psychological Science, 23*, 355–360. doi:10.1177/0963721414545215

Johnson-Laird, P. N. (2010). Mental models and human reasoning. *Proceedings of the National Academy of Sciences of the United States of America, 107*, 18243–18250. doi:10.1073/pnas.1012933107

Leo, F. M., González-Ponce, I., García-Calvo, T., Sánchez-Oliva, D., & Filho, E. (2019). The relationship among cohesion, transactive memory systems, and collective efficacy in professional soccer teams: A multilevel structural equation analysis. *Group Dynamics: Theory, Research, and Practice, 23*, 44–56. doi:10.1037/gdn0000097

Leo, F. M., González-Ponce, I., Sánchez-Miguel, P. A., Ivarsson, A., & García-Calvo, T. (2015). Role ambiguity, role conflict, team conflict, cohesion and collective efficacy in sport teams: A multilevel analysis. *Psychology of Sport and Exercise, 20*, 60–66. doi:10.1016/j.psychsport.2015.04.009

Mohammed, S., Ferzandi, L., & Hamilton, K. (2010). Metaphor no more: A 15-year review of the team mental model construct. *Journal of Management, 36*, 876–910. doi:10.1177/0149206309356804

Mohammed, S., Hamilton, K., Sánchez-Manzanares, M., & Rico, R. (2017). Team cognition: Team mental models and situation awareness. In E. Salas, R. Rico, & J. Passmore (Eds.), *The psychology of team working and collaborative processes* (pp. 369–392). Hoboken, NJ: Wiley Blackwell.

Pescosolido, A. T., & Saavedra, R. (2012). Cohesion and sports teams: A review. *Small Group Research, 43*, 744–758. doi:10.1177/1046496412465020

Romyn, D. J., & Kebbell, M. R. (2018). Mock terrorists' decisions concerning use of the internet for target selection: A red-team approach. *Psychology, Crime and Law, 24*, 589–602. doi:10.1080/1068316X.2017.1396332

Sänger, J., Müller, V., & Lindenberger, U. (2012). Intra- and interbrain synchronization and network properties when playing guitar in duets. *Frontiers in Human Neuroscience, 6*, 1–19. doi:10.3389/fnhum.2012.00312

Shamsie, J., & Mannor, M. J. (2013). Looking inside the dream team: Probing into the contributions of tacit knowledge as an organizational resource. *Organization Science, 24*, 513–529. doi:10.1287/orsc.1120.0741

Short, S. E., Sullivan, P., & Feltz, D. L. (2005). Development and preliminary validation of the collective efficacy questionnaire for sports. *Measurement in Physical Education and Exercise Science, 9*, 181–202. doi:10.1207/s15327841mpee0903_3

Tuckman, B. (1965). Developmental sequence in small groups. *Psychological Bulletin, 63*, 384–399. doi:10.1037/h0022100

Westli, H., Johnsen, B., Eid, J., Rasten, I., & Brattebø, G. (2010). Teamwork skills, shared mental models, and performance in simulated trauma teams: An independent group design. *Scandinavian Journal of Trauma, Resuscitation and Emergency Medicine, 18*, 1–8. doi:10.1186/1757-7241-18-47

8

CULTURAL CODES PROVIDE NOVEL STRATEGIES FOR MENTAL TRAINING

Yang Ge and Liwei Zhang

"Mental training" is an umbrella term for multiple techniques and methods, including imagery, pre-performance routines, relaxation, and self-talk, that sport psychology researchers and practitioners use to help athletes achieve optimal performance in high-pressure contexts. Traditionally, mental training techniques are regarded as a means to improve mental abilities for athletes, in a similar way that physical training techniques improve physical abilities. By enhancing cognitive and self-control ability, or formulating adaptive thinking and behaviors, mental advantages for sport performance can be developed. For example, sport psychologists use relaxation technique to help athletes regulate arousal level (e.g., Kellmann, Pelka, & Beckmann, 2018) or use mindfulness meditation to strengthen athletes' self-regulation capacities (e.g., Slagter, Davidson, & Lutz, 2011). In recent decades, mindfulness approaches have become popular among sport psychologists and have been adopted by researchers and practitioners around the world (e.g., Gross et al., 2018; Henriksen, Diment, Hansen, & Larsen, 2016; Zhang et al., 2016). For example, Gardner and Moore (2012) developed a Mindfulness-Acceptance-Commitment (MAC) model to help athletes reduce behavioral issues and emotional distress, and to enhance athletic performance.

Mindfulness training protocols successfully integrate Eastern philosophy and Buddhist practices into a Western theoretical framework (Gardner & Moore, 2012; Zhang et al., 2016). Although mindfulness programs have been shown to be effective for performance enhancement, Marks (2008) claimed that Western athletes, coaches, and sport psychologists have had an ambivalent relationship with mindfulness, because it does not originate from a Western religious or cultural background. Thus, contextualizing sociocultural differences and including multicultural perspectives in applied sport psychology work is advantageous for engaging in more comprehensive and ethical practices (Ryba, Stambulova, Si, & Schinke, 2013).

Cultural competency

As one of the largest industries in the world, sport provides a global stage for athletes and sport professionals to exchange their talents and knowledge. The International Society of Sport Psychology has published several position stands calling for researchers and practitioners to become more culturally competent by gaining greater awareness of the sociocultural aspects of sport participants and their career development (e.g., Ryba et al., 2013). The term "cultural competence" refers to the ability to recognize participants, clients, and self as cultural beings who perceive and understand the world in different ways, with the focus not only on athlete performance and development but also on their safety and well-being (Ryba et al., 2013). This long-term cultural void in sport psychology has been criticized by researchers over many decades (e.g., Duda & Allison, 1990). As Gill (2001) stated, "We can only make important contributions to the real world of developing sport and exercise participants when we incorporate gender and cultural analyses" (p. 497). Fisher, Butryn, and Roper (2005) argued for integrating cultural studies perspectives into sport psychology, including re-examining how existing cultural norms and practices affect athletes' daily lives and well-being.

Responding to these calls, researchers have brought fresh insights to investigate the socio-psychological issues in sport. For instance, Kavoura, Ryba, and Chroni (2015) explored the construction of athletic identity of Greek female judokas who competed in a traditional masculine sport and lived in a patriarchal society. They identified gender oppression of the female judokas in negotiating the conflicting social expectations of being both females and judokas, which presented distinctive challenges for female athletes compared to male athletes. Carless and Douglas (2013) explored the narratives of young athletes, revealing that cultural pressures toward a strong and exclusive athletic identity that prioritizes performance outcomes over other life matters can lead to mental health issues for athletes. For researchers in the cultural studies area, cultural factors are not merely independent variables defining group membership but also more fundamental and related to basic psychological processes of perception, cognition, intellectual functioning, value acquisition, identity, and social interaction (McGannon & Smith, 2015).

To respond to this perceived cultural void, a new genre referred to as cultural sport psychology (CSP; Schinke & Hanrahan, 2009) has been increasingly promoted. We briefly outline the propositions and existing findings related to CSP below and then offer Chinese sport psychology practice as an example to illustrate how the intersecting sport system and the cultural narratives create particular challenges and strengths for Chinese athletes (Ge et al., 2019; Si, Duan, Li, Zhang, & Su, 2015).

Cultural sport psychology

Schinke and colleagues raised the important question: "Is it possible that diversity in locations and people affect applied techniques, delivery of service, and methods of inquiry?" (Schinke, Michel, Danielson, Gauthier, & Pickard, 2005, p. 1). Following discussion of conducting reflexive research and practice at the level of societies and communities (Ryba & Wright, 2005), CSP was defined to reflect unique aspirations and needs stemming from race, ethnicity, gender, and geography, among other considerations.

The rationale for CSP was unfolded as "exploration of the unique point of view of cultural community members and the psychological and performance implications that result from the cultural standpoints" (Blodgett, Schinke, McGannon, & Fisher, 2014, p. 2), wherein marginalized topics and cultural identities are especially relevant. CSP researchers address the power and privilege issues perpetuated in and through the practices of the domain, to encourage practitioners to challenge the taken-for-granted assumptions and practices, built on a white, positivistic epistemology (see Butryn, 2010), and to make sport and exercise psychology professionals rethink research and practice through a culturally reflexive lens (Blodgett et al., 2014). Milestone publications of CSP include the textbooks *Cultural Sport Psychology* (Schinke & Hanrahan, 2009), *The Cultural Turn in Sport Psychology* (Ryba, Schinke, & Tenenbaum, 2010), and *The Psychology of Sub-Culture in Sport and Physical Activity* (Schinke & McGannon, 2014).

As an emerging area, CSP has been increasingly accepted by researchers and practitioners. For example, Schinke and colleagues (2006) chronicled the relocation experience of Canadian Aboriginal athletes who moved to white mainstream society to pursue sporting success. Within these relocation stories, unique cross-cultural challenges and identity conflicts of aboriginal athletes were identified that would never be experienced by athletes and researchers who were born in mainstream North America. Stambulova and Ryba (2014), in exploring athletes' career development paths across countries, suggested researchers and practitioners be more proactive in anticipating and matching changes in the modern sport contexts. They adopted the cultural praxis paradigm (i.e., blending theories, research, applied work, and social change together; Ryba & Wright, 2005) to encourage researchers to investigate career assistance. They broadened the landscape of traditional sport psychology work through a holistic lifespan and ecological perspective toward athletes: being reflexive and situated in relevant sociocultural and historical contexts; attending to the multifaceted lived experiences in sport and beyond; and facilitating collaboration between practitioners, researchers, and athletes. These outlooks encouraged sport psychologists to focus on the issues of marginalization, representation, and social justice (Stambulova & Ryba, 2014).

Ryba and colleagues (2013) further promoted the view that athletes are holistic cultural beings who are constructed and also actively construct the sociocultural contexts in which they are embedded, which might also stimulate evolutions within mental training projects. To respond to the call for culturally competent research and practice, we present the example of mental training and sport psychology practices embedded in a Chinese cultural background. Through our discussions, we share the Chinese philosophy of being, which may offer a new lens for other sport psychologists to work with athletes and stimulate further discovery of mental training strategies.

Delivering sport psychology services in Chinese cultural contexts

The Chinese sport system is prominent in terms of major games performance outcomes. China produced its first world champion, in Rong Guotuan, a table tennis player, in 1959. By the end of 2018, Chinese athletes had collectively won 240 Olympic titles and broken over 1,273 world records. These outstanding achievements not only reflect the talent and dedication of athletes and coaches but also reinforce the success of what is termed the Whole-Nation Chinese sport system. Si and colleagues (2015) explored the unique characteristics of the Chinese sport system, Chinese culture, and their intersection with Chinese elite athletes' psychological manifestations. They identified the country's collectivist national culture and authoritative social order, as central elements of the Chinese sport system.

Building on this, Ge and colleagues (2019) characterized the Chinese Whole-Nation system as having three key features: (a) centralized structure, (b) medal orientation, and (c) semi-closed environment. The centralized structure represents the hierarchical power relationships among athletes, coaches, and administrators. In contrast to athletes taking the major responsibility for their own sport career in Western sport systems, Chinese athletes are fully taken care of by the Whole-Nation system. Thus, the power is centered on the national sport organization and its representative officers, as they own the authority to allocate resources and budget. Moreover, according to the traditions of "honoring the teacher and respecting his teaching," coaches and officials naturally possess a higher power than athletes. For Chinese athletes, fitting into this power relationship is critical for their success. The second characteristic of the Whole-Nation system is the strong medal orientation, which is common to many competitive sport teams across the world. However, in China, the pressure to win gold medals is especially fierce and extends beyond athletes, to encompass coaches and administrators. Medals are a key indicator in their performance assessment. Therefore, winning medals in international competition is the central mission for the whole sport department. Since the Beijing Olympic Games in 2008, public attention in China toward winning medals has declined and the medal orientation has weakened accordingly. The third characteristic, semi-closed environment, is reflected in the fact that most Chinese provincial or national athletes, coaches, and sport professionals commit to full-time training. They live in residences together, in restricted access areas. As athletes are seen as precious national resources, this semi-closed management is to guarantee their training participation, nutritional needs, and doping control.

Si et al. (2015) identified two key psychological challenges for Chinese athletes and coaches: (a) Chinese athletes often experience extreme distress following poor performance and find it hard to shake off negative feelings, and (b) the relationship-oriented cultural values mean that interpersonal conflicts among athletes, coaches, and officials tend to negatively influence athletes' sport performance. Both of these issues relate to the collectivist culture, whereby Chinese athletes carry the burden of high internal and external expectations of good results in important competitions. Due to the strong relationship-oriented cultural values, athletes may experience unbearable external pressures from significant others, especially their coaches and family. For example, Liu, Zhang, and Ge (2019) reported suicide ideation among Chinese elite athletes, presenting the story of a male athlete contemplating suicide after his female coach was crying beside him because he lost in a competition. This collectivist culture and values lead to a closer psychological connection among people, which shapes the way that Chinese people see and interact with the outside world. Accordingly, Chinese sport psychologists generate multiple culturally meaningful strategies, some of which are described below, to assist athletes to adapt to the sport system, pursue sport excellence, and maintain good mental health. The second author has worked with Chinese professional athletes and national teams for more than 20 years. In the next section, we present three key cultural concepts and practices that he and his team have used to assist Chinese Olympic athletes to fit into the national sport context.

Sacrifice

China is dominated by a collectivist culture, which values the morality and practices of sacrificing personal welfare to fulfil collective interests. Different from the self-hood discourses in Western individualist culture, such as self-autonomy, self-efficacy and self-awareness, in this collectivist culture, people are more connected and less differentiated from each other. "People are motivated to find a way to fit in with relevant others, to fulfil and create obligation, and in general to become part of various interpersonal relationships" (Matsumoto, 1999, p. 290). Accordingly, sacrifice is conceptualized as a significant noble virtue in the cultural value system, whereas emphasizing personal needs and self-efforts while ignoring collective needs would be interpreted as being selfish or having a moral defect, likely leading to being excluded and rejected from social groups.

Sacrifice is closely related to patriotic affection, dedication, and submission. For Chinese athletes and coaches, the pride of devoting themselves to achieve glory for the nation is deeply rooted. Competing on the international stage, patriotic affection serves one of the strongest psychological drives for Chinese athletes and coaches to gain the best result. Moreover, pursuing success for the nation also releases some social pressures and assists athletes to avoid self-centered thinking. In Chinese culture, striving for personal success has a complicated meaning. There is a proverb that "the nail that sticks up get pounded down," which indicates the cultural norms of valuing teamwork, avoiding self-expression, and remaining modest. This tradition is in stark contrast with Western values that encourage personal expressions of individuality. To address this contradiction, patriotic motivation shifts the meaning of striving for personal success to gaining national pride, which releases the social pressure of pursuing personal success and reinforces patriotic identities.

Sacrificing personal welfare for collective interests is the priority for athletes and coaches who live in the Whole-Nation system. In the collectivist culture, personal value is imbedded in collective interests. On most occasions, social needs and values are important determinants of individuals' decisions about their life path, from selecting a career to choosing a life partner. As they are trained and supported by the Whole-Nation system, athletes have highlighted the obligation for them to achieve success for the nation (Ge et al., 2019). The patriotic identity and dedicated practice help athletes gain credit and maintain positive interpersonal relationships with their coaches and officers in the higher positions of the system. Thus, sport psychologists who work within the Chinese sport system need to understand and respect sacrifice as a key cultural value and expectation.

Jingjie

Chinese sport psychologists commonly agree that mental training is a progressive process from the application of specific mental skills training to the enhancement of one's overall mentality, referred to as *Jingjie* in Chinese. *Jingjie* is a somewhat spiritual concept, representing the notion that an individual has achieved a perfect existential status, being conscientious, selfless, responsible, and beloved in dealing with hardships and the ever-changing world (not dissimilar to Maslow's notion of self-actualization being at the top of a hierarchy of needs; see Figure 8.1).

In Chinese philosophy, learning how to fit into the social and natural environments and to reach a status of coexisting harmoniously is an enduring theme. To achieve this status, Zhang and Zhang (2011b) proposed eight dichotic relationships to help athletes navigate self-imposed and environmentally imposed demands: tension vs. calm; simple vs. complicated; fighting spirit vs. quiet mentality; confident vs. modest; physical training vs. mental training; internal focus vs. external focus; pay vs. gain; and short-term goal vs. long-term goal. These dyads could be represented in the Tai chi symbol (Figure 8.2), where athletes shift their identities within these seemingly opposite states. For example, during competitions an athlete will need a fighting spirit in difficult moments when behind in the game, but in a critical moment such as the final shot he/she needs

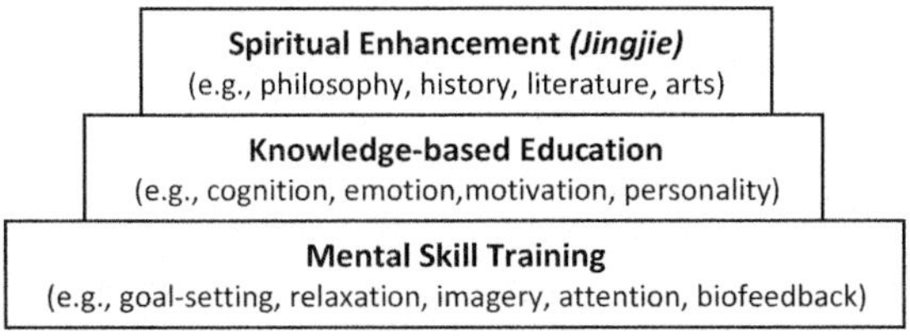

FIGURE 8.1 The athletes' psychological development system (Zhang & Zhang, 2011a).

FIGURE 8.2 Tai chi symbol.

to regulate emotions and stay calm. Another example is related to the pair of simple vs. complicated. During training and preparation, athletes should show close attention to detail, whereas in competition, especially in critical moments, athletes need simplicity in the form of a clear mind to facilitate a quick decision and execution. By negotiating the meaning of these relationships, athletes seek to develop a comprehensive and flexible understanding of how to deal with the multiple issues and demands in sport.

The enhancement of *Jingjie* helps athletes comprehensively understand the intricate relationships between themselves and the external world. Such understanding can be transformed into strategies for athletes when facing high pressure and ever-changing sport contexts, helping them to gain better self-control and to make wise decisions. In preparing for the 2012 London Olympics, the sport psychologists for the Chinese trampoline team designed a series of psychological activities, including psychology seminars and posters, planetarium visit, and speech contest, to prepare athletes mentally. The topics of these activities ranged from the basic psychological knowledge and skills (e.g., how to cultivate confidence; how to use the dual system of self-control) to Chinese philosophy and spiritual life (e.g., inner peace; Chinese history and literature). All of these interventions were directed to achieving mental balance and a state of clarity (complete immersion in the present task and eradication of unnecessary thoughts), peacefulness (feeling calm and prepared for the upcoming challenges), and having a flexible mind (understanding and accepting all the transformations of the internal and external worlds and responding to them naturally) (Zhang, 2012, 2017).

Inner peace

Self-control is presented as a core of mental training in Chinese sport psychology. In the intense and unpredictable world of competition, the biggest challenge for athletes is to control their own thoughts, emotions, and body, to focus on the task at hand. In traditional Chinese values, one of the major competencies for competitors remains *inner peace*, which means maintaining the status quo in a transforming environment, which can also be understood as staying calm, controlled, and disciplined in the face of an opponent.

Inner peace (or *Pingchangxin* in Chinese) is a spiritual and philosophical ideology in Chinese culture. Its core idea is to conform to nature, have no evaluation of good and evil, and maintain a peaceful mind in moments of adversity and frustration, in order to reach the realm of freedom. It is the ideal status of self-control, which is characterized as handling complicated matters with ease and maintaining body-mind balance (Zhang, 2017; Zhang & Zhang, 2011b). To reach the status of a balanced and peaceful mind, reflective activities and contemplation are highly valued in Chinese traditional practices. The embodied experience of these mindfulness practices helps athletes to focus their attention on the inner mind, transforming this inner power into self-control in navigating the outside world. Through persistent practice, the connection of mind and body is strengthened, so that athletes gain the confidence to control themselves in high-pressure environments (Zhang & Li, 2019).

Chinese calligraphy is one of the cultural practices that we used in mental training projects. Chinese calligraphy is a form of aesthetically pleasing writing or the artistic expression of Chinese words with ink and water on silk or paper by different sizes brushes. Distinguishing the features of calligraphy includes an emphasis on motion charged with dynamic life. According to Stanley-Baker (2010), "Calligraphy is sheer life experienced through energy in motion that is registered as traces on silk or paper, with time and rhythm in shifting space its main ingredients" (p. 8). Kao et al. (2014) supported the effectiveness of Chinese calligraphy handwriting in stimulating cognitive activation, physiological slowdown, emotional stability, and perceptual sharpening. Participants successfully used calligraphy to adjust attention and reduce stress, producing similar effects to meditation. Calligraphy practices require delicate motor movement of the wrist, which can improve fine motor movements (Sun & Zhang, 2014).

The second author has used calligraphy practice as one of the mental training techniques to help the national trampoline team, national freestyle aerial team, and a windsurfing athlete to prepare for the Olympic Games. Feedback from the athletes varied. Some athletes spoke highly of calligraphy practice, expressing the view that it not only helped them acquire a peaceful mind but also reinforced the collectivist esteem of being Chinese. However, the windsurfing athlete reported only moderate support for calligraphy practice (Zhang & Li, 2017). Athletes may need extensive time to understand the meaning of Chinese philosophy embedded in calligraphy practice, which is quite different from their daily body movement training. These different evaluations of mental training effectiveness also remind us that, for individual athletes, centralizing their own needs and interests before implementing mental training techniques is important.

Conclusion: moving to culturally competent mental training practice

Part of the rationale for CSP is that the current sport psychology domain is permeated with Eurocentric ideologies and assumptions, which privileges certain identities and their way of knowing, such as white, male, heterosexual, and middle class while marginalizing other identities. Furthermore, traditional sport psychology practices consider athletes and exercisers as "universal" beings and stereotype them based on their multifaceted social identities, such as gender, ethnicity, sexual orientation, and social class, which leads to simplification of problems and potential discrimination. Ryba et al. (2013) conceptualized culturally competent sport psychology practices as (a) recognizing hidden ethnocentric philosophical assumptions that permeate mainstream sport psychology, (b) regarding differences among social group members as socially constructed and as relational and fluid rather than inherent and fixed, and (c) focusing on the meaning instead of the cause of cross-cultural and cultural issues. Following these principles, researchers and professionals should recognize that sport and physical activities are cultural products, where problems and issues that athletes encounter are also social and organizational dysfunctions. Thus, in designing high-quality and ethical mental training programs, sport psychology researchers and practitioners should strengthen awareness of their own cultural backgrounds, increase understanding of other worldviews, and use culturally appropriate communication and intervention methods (Ryba et al., 2013).

Culturally competent mental training practices represent a holistic view of athletes. Traditional sport psychology tends to focus on the performance aspects of athletes, while ignoring other aspects of their lives. The performance-centered narratives in sport psychology, which emphasized dedication, masculinity, toughness, and competition, jeopardizes athletes' well-being and long-term development (Carless & Douglas, 2013). Wylleman, Alfermann, and Lavallee (2004) suggested a holistic, life-span developmental perspective to understand athletes' transitions in their athletic careers as well as in other domains of the their lives, including the changes they encounter at a psychological level (from adolescence into young adulthood), a psychosocial level (development of temporary or stable relationships with a partner), and at the academic or vocational level (transiting into higher education or into a professional occupation). Henriksen, Stambulova, and Roessler (2010) advocated for a holistic ecological approach to investigate the environment in which athletes develop, analyzing family, peers, schools, cultures, organization, sport system, team history, and other contextual factors that contribute to athletes' successes in career transitions. Miller and Kerr (2002) stated, "Performance excellence is attained only through optimal personal development" (p. 141). Through a comprehensive understanding of athletes' lives and the sociocultural contexts, researchers and practitioners move from the mechanical view of mental process to focusing on the overall development of athletes.

References

Blodgett, A. T., Schinke, R. J., McGannon, K. R., & Fisher, L. A. (2014). Cultural sport psychology research: Conceptions, evolutions, and forecasts. *International Review of Sport and Exercise Psychology, 8*, 24–43. doi:10.1080/1750984X.2014.942345

Butryn, T. M. (2010). Interrogating whiteness in sport psychology. In T. V. Ryba, R. J. Schinke, & G. Tenenbaum (Eds.), *The cultural turn in sport psychology* (pp. 127–152). Morgantown, WV: Fitness Information Technology.

Carless, D., & Douglas, K. (2013). Living, resisting, and playing the part of athlete: Narrative tensions in elite sport. *Psychology of Sport and Exercise, 14*, 701–708. Retrieved from http://eprints.leedsbeckett.ac.uk

Duda, J. L., & Allison, M. T. (1990). Cross-cultural analysis in exercise and sport psychology: A void in the field. *Journal of Sport & Exercise Psychology, 12*, 114–131. doi:10.1123/jsep.12.2.114

Fisher, L. A., Butryn, T. M., & Roper, E. A. (2005). Diversifying (and politicizing) sport psychology through cultural studies: A promising perspective revisited. *Athletic Insight, 7*, 23–35. Retrieved from https://www.athleticinsight.com/Vol7Iss3/DiversifyPDF.pdf

Gano-Overway, L. A., & Duda, J. L. (1999). Interrelationships between expressive individualism and other achievement goal orientations among African and European American athletes. *Journal of Black Psychology, 25*, 544–563. doi:10.1177/0095798499025004005

Gardner, F. L., & Moore, Z. E. (2012). Mindfulness and acceptance models in sport psychology: A decade of basic and applied scientific advancements. *Canadian Psychology, 53*, 309. doi:10.1037/a0030220

Ge, Y., Schinke, R., Dong, D., Lu, C., Si, G., & Oghene, O. (2019). Working with Chinese Olympic athletes in their national sport system: From the conceptual to a proposed research–practice integration. *International Journal of Sport and Exercise Psychology, 17*, 5–17. doi:10.1080/1612197x.2016.1164227

Gill, D. L. (2001). In search of feminist sport psychology: Then, now, and always. *The Sport Psychologist, 15*, 363–449. doi:10.1123/tsp.15.4.363

Gross, M., Moore, Z. E., Gardner, F. L., Wolanin, A. T., Pess, R., & Marks, D. R. (2018). An empirical examination comparing the mindfulness-acceptance-commitment approach and psychological skills training for the mental health and sport performance of female student athletes. *International Journal of Sport and Exercise Psychology, 16*, 431–451. doi:10.1080/1612197X.2016.1250802

Henriksen, K., Hansen, J., Diment, G., & Larsen, C. H. (2016). Using acceptance commitment training in a team sport leading up to, during and following the 2014 Winter Olympic Games. In G. Cremades, & L. S. Tashman (Eds.), *Global practices and training in applied sport, exercise, and performance psychology: A case study approach* (pp. 69–78). New York, NY: Routledge.

Henriksen, K., Stambulova, N., & Roessler, K. K. (2010). Holistic approach to athletic talent development environments: A successful sailing milieu. *Psychology of Sport and Exercise, 11*, 212–222. doi:10.1016/j.psychsport.2009.10.005

Kao, H. S., Zhu, L., Chao, A. A., Chen, H. Y., Liu, I. C., & Zhang, M. (2014). Calligraphy and meditation for stress reduction: An experimental comparison. *Psychology Research and Behaviour Management, 7*, 47–52. doi:10.2147/PRBM.S55743

Kavoura, A., Ryba, T. V., & Chroni, S. (2015). Negotiating female judoka identities in Greece: A Foucauldian discourse analysis. *Psychology of Sport and Exercise, 17*, 88–98. doi:10.1016/j.psychsport.2014.09.011

Kellmann, M., Pelka, M., & Beckmann, J. (2018). Psychological relaxation techniques to enhance recovery in sports. In M. Kellmann, M. Pelka, & J. Beckmann (Eds.), *Sport, recovery and performance: Interdisciplinary insights* (pp. 247–259). Abingdon, UK: Routledge.

Liu, J., Zhang, L., & Ge, Y. (2019). *The suicidal ideation of Chinese elite athletes.* Unpublished manuscript, Beijing Sport University, China.

Marks, D. R. (2008). The Buddha's extra scoop: Neural correlates of mindfulness and clinical sport psychology. *Journal of Clinical Sport Psychology, 2*, 216–241.

Matsumoto, D. (1999). Culture and self: An empirical assessment of Markus and Kitayam's theory of independent and interdependent self-construals. *Asian Journal of Social Psychology, 2*, 289–310. Retrieved from http://www.davidmatsumoto.com/content/1999%20Culture%20and%20Self.pdf

McGannon, K. R., & Smith, B. (2015). Centralizing culture in cultural sport psychology research: The potential of narrative inquiry and discursive psychology. *Psychology of Sport and Exercise, 17*, 79–87. doi:10.1016/j.psychsport.2014.07.010

Miller, P. S., & Kerr, G. A. (2002). Conceptualizing excellence: Past, present, and future. *Journal of Applied Sport Psychology, 14*, 140–153. doi:10.1080/10413200290103464

Peters, H. J., & Williams, J. M. (2009). Rationale for developing a cultural sport psychology. In R. Schinke & S. J. Hanrahan (Eds.), *Cultural sport psychology* (pp. 13–21). Champaign, IL: Human Kinetics.

Ryba, T. V., Schinke, R. J., & Tenenbaum, G. (Eds.) (2010). *The cultural turn in sport psychology.* Morgantown, WV: Fitness Information Technology.

Ryba, T. V., Stambulova, N. B., Si, G., & Schinke, R. J. (2013). ISSP position stand: Culturally competent research and practice in sport and exercise psychology. *International Journal of Sport and Exercise Psychology, 11*, 123–142. doi:10.1080/1612197X.2013.779812

Ryba, T. V., & Wright, H. K. (2005). From mental game to cultural praxis: A cultural studies model's implications for the future of sport psychology. *Quest, 57*, 192–219. doi:10.1080/00336297.2005.10491853

Schinke, R., & Hanrahan, S. J. (Eds.). (2009). *Cultural sport psychology.* Champaign, IL: Human Kinetics.

Schinke, R. J., & McGannon, K. R. (Eds.). (2014). *The psychology of sub-culture in sport and physical activity: Critical perspectives.* New York, NY: Routledge.

Schinke, R. J., Michel, G., Danielson, R., Gauthier, A. P., & Pickard, P. (2005). Introduction to cultural sport psychology: Special edition. *Athletic Insight: The Online Journal of Sport Psychology*, 7(3), 1–6. Retrieved from https://www.academia.edu/18013036/Introduction_to_Cultural_Sport_Psychology_Special_Edition

Si, G., Duan, Y., Li, H. Y., Zhang, C. Q., & Su, N. (2015). The influence of the Chinese sport system and Chinese cultural characteristics on Olympic sport psychology services. *Psychology of Sport and Exercise, 17*, 56–67. doi:10.1016/j.psychsport.2014.08.008

Slagter, H. A., Davidson, R. J., & Lutz, A. (2011). Mental training as a tool in the neuroscientific study of brain and cognitive plasticity. *Frontiers in Human Neuroscience, 5*, 17. doi: 10.3389/fnhum.2011.00017

Stambulova, N. B., & Ryba, T. V. (2014). A critical review of career research and assistance through the cultural lens: Towards cultural praxis of athletes' careers. *International Review of Sport and Exercise Psychology, 7*, 1–17. doi:10.1080/1750984X.2013.851727

Stanley-Baker, J. (2010). Ink painting today. *Centered on Taipei, 10*, 8–11.

Sun G., & Zhang, L. (2014). Calligraphy practice improves stability of fine motor (oral presentation). *Proceedings of the 7th ASPASP International Congress.* Tokyo, Japan:

Asian-South Pacific Association of Sport Psychology, Japanese Society of Sport Psychology.
Wylleman, P., Alfermann, D., & Lavallee, D. (2004). Career transitions in sport: European perspectives. *Psychology of Sport and Exercise, 5*, 7–20. doi:10.1016/S1469-0292(02)00049-3
Zhang, C. Q., Si, G., Duan, Y., Lyu, Y., Keatley, D. A., & Chan, D. K. (2016). The effects of mindfulness training on beginners' skill acquisition in dart throwing: A randomized controlled trial. *Psychology of Sport and Exercise, 22*, 279–285. doi:10.1016/j.psychsport.2015.09.005.
Zhang, K., & Zhang, L. (2011a). Doctrine and method: What Chinese culture can contribute to athletes' psychological training and consultation. *Journal of Tianjin University of Sport, 26*, 196–199. (in Chinese). doi:10.3969/j.issn.1005-0000.2011.03.003
Zhang, L., & Zhang, K. (2011b). Dialectics for self-control: Approaches to help athlete cope with eight relationships. *Journal of Tianjin University of Sport, 26*(3), 185–190. (in Chinese). doi:10.3969/j.issn.1005-0000.2011.03.001
Zhang, L. (2012, October). The psychological preparation of Chinese athletes for London Olympic games. In Z. X. Mao (Ed.), *In 2012 Olympic psychological service for Chinese athletes*. Symposium conducted at the meeting of the Beijing Sports University, Beijing, China (in Chinese).
Zhang, L. (2017). Is a peaceful mind a winning mind? Comment on Hardy et al. (2017). *Progress in Brain Research, 232*, 187–190.
Zhang, L., & Li, M. (2017). You don't know when and how mental training will make a difference: A surprise from a windsurfing athlete in Rio OG. In G. Si, J. Cruz, & J. C. Jaenes (Eds.), *Sport psychology: Linking theory to practice: Proceedings of the XIV ISSP World Congress of Sport Psychology* (p. 18). Sevilla, Spain: International Society of Sport Psychology.
Zhang, L., & Li, M. (2019). In pursuit of excellence: Skill oriented and spirit oriented mental training of an Olympic athlete. *Journal of Capital University of Physical Education and Sports, 31*, 110–114 (in Chinese).

SECTION 2

Technological advancements

9

SOCIAL MEDIA AND SPORT PSYCHOLOGY PRACTICE

Stewart T. Cotterill

Social media and sport psychology practice

The past 20 years have seen significant advances in technology that have transformed the world in previously unimaginable ways. The profession of sport psychology has not been immune to these changes, and there are increasing demands on practitioners to communicate with their clients utilizing social media platforms, including Facebook, Instagram, and Twitter. There has also been a significant increase in the use of video conference and communication platforms, such as FaceTime, Skype, and Zoom, as well as integrated online client booking and management platforms (e.g., SimplyBook, 10to8). The potential to be continuously "connected" with friends, family, peers, and clients is unprecedented, with geography no longer presenting a realistic barrier (Cotterill, 2019a).

For sport psychology practitioners there has been a resulting increase in the demands for communication with their athletes, players, teams, squads, colleagues, and employers using social media platforms. There has also been a significant increase in the use of video communication platforms (e.g., Skype, FaceTime, Facebook Messenger). Tools such as Twitter have also become increasingly important for sharing scholarly and professional information (Verhagen, Bower, & Khan, 2014), although from a professional perspective, there can be issues with this easy access to information as these sources do not undergo any quality control (MacNamara & Collins, 2015). There is also evidence that most conversations on social media are no longer simply text-based but involve images or video (Cotterill, 2019a).

Key questions for sport psychology consultants include: How to use the technology? What platforms to use? Ethical questions about whether you should correspond with athletes under the age of 18? Should you share photos and videos? Can you separate your professional and private versions of you?

How accessible should you be? What impact is social media and digital technology having on the communication expectations of clients? In addition, there is also the issue of the impact of social media on athlete performance, with research suggesting that engagement with social media prior to performance can influence performance outcomes (Miah, 2012).

In this chapter, I will explore the challenges and opportunities that novel technological tools and social media present to sport psychology practitioners and how advances in software and hardware can be utilized by practitioners to maximize behavior change and performance. I will also discuss the professional, ethical, and moral challenges that these new platforms can present to sport psychology practitioners and the importance of effectively managing your online footprint.

Social media

Social media is a form of communication that uses mobile and web-based technologies to create highly interactive platforms via which individuals and communities share, co-create, and modify user-generated content (Kietzmann, Hermkens, McCarthy, & Silvestre, 2011). The term "social media" encompasses not just social networking sites, such as Facebook, LinkedIn, and WhatsApp, but also video- and photo-sharing sites, such as YouTube, Instagram, Snapchat, and Flickr; micro-blogging applications, such as Twitter; aggregator sites, such as Digg; and even virtual worlds (Cotterill, 2019a). Social media are inherently designed to facilitate human connections and have been conceptualized as "architected by design to readily support participation, peer-to-peer conversation, collaboration and community" (Meraz, 2009, p. 682).

For professional athletes, social media can be a tool through which they can break news, manage their brand, and interact with fans and followers (Sanderson, 2011). One major implication of social media is that material can be transmitted to a very wide audience without the express consent or knowledge of the originator. This means that errors of judgment now have the potential to have a far greater reach than was previously the case. This fact led Kietzmann and colleagues (2011) to reflect that "social media introduce substantial and pervasive changes to communication between organizations, communities, and individuals" (p. 250).

Data from the most recent Global Web Index (2019) makes for interesting reading. Ninety-eight percent of all digital consumers have at least one social media account. Social networking also forms the largest percentage (32%) of online time with online television (14%) accounting for the next largest allocation. Since the 2012 Global Web Index, there has been a significant increase in the number of social media/messaging accounts that individuals have. In 2012 the average was three, increasing to an average of eight in 2016.

Outside of China, Facebook is the top network in terms of membership (85%) and contributions (40%), but YouTube generates the greatest number of visitors (86%). Among messaging services, Facebook Messenger (72%) is the largest, with

WhatsApp (66%) in second place. Twitter is slightly more popular than Instagram in terms of visitors, though Instagram is the service of choice for 16–24-year-olds. The average time spent online is 2 hours and 22 minutes per day, but this increases to 3 hours and 1 minute for 16–24-year-olds (Global Web Index, 2019).

There are also differences in the demographics of users of the different social media platforms. There is an older demographic on Facebook and LinkedIn, with younger users preferring Snapchat, Tumblr, Vine, and Instagram. These data and trends underline the recognition that the use of social media, and mobile technology to access it, is significant and continuing to grow quickly. Interestingly, while the main motivations for using social media are to stay in touch, or remain up-to-date with news; in the 16–24 age group, the two most popular motives are to fill up spare time and to find funny or entertaining content (Global Web Index, 2019).

Online communications are increasingly becoming more mobile and instantaneous. For example, Kemp (2015) reported that mobile devices accounted for 38% of overall online traffic. Data for 2015 also highlights that around 30% of the world population had at least one active social media account (Kemp, 2015); and approximately 1.65 billion people access these applications through mobile devices (Córdova, 2016).

Types of social media

There are many different formats, platforms, and applications that offer a social media function, although these can broadly be combined under the following headings: blogging, social networks, messaging services, team messaging tools, podcasting, video calling/conferencing, and video-sharing sites.

Blogging

Blogs

Web logs, or "blogs," are frequently updated websites where content (e.g., text, pictures, audio, and video) is posted and displayed in reverse chronological order. These updates work in a similar way to opinion columns written in newspapers and magazines. There is also the option on these websites for readers of the blog to make comments on the information posted and to engage in discussions with both the author and other interested parties. Blogging can offer a strong platform from which to communicate ideas, experiences, commentaries, recommendations, and opinions. These blogs also offer a way to communicate with a large and specialized audience from a local to a national, and even a global level. Examples of sport and exercise psychology blogs include: Believe-Perform (believeperform.com/), Peak Performance Sports (peaksports.com/sports-psychology-blog/), and the Association of Applied Sport Psychology blog (appliedsportpsych.org/blog/).

Vlogs

A video blog, or video log, usually shortened to vlog, is a form of blog for which the medium is video – that is, a form of web television. The term "vlog" is also used by video streamers who don't use a blog but post scheduled updates via other means, like YouTube.

Twitter

Twitter is an online social media networking site. Individuals or companies can set up a profile page and then put out short messages, called "tweets," of up to 140 characters long (referred to as microblogging). Individuals can also add photos to tweets or links to webpages and videos. You can then opt to "follow" other people's tweets so that their updates appear on your timeline (effectively, the homepage that shows all the recent tweets of those you follow). Twitter can be a great tool for sharing ideas, keeping up-to-date with literature, learning from colleagues, disseminating your own research, and getting real-time feedback (Mills, 2013).

The "impact" aspect of Twitter can be quantified via three measures: (1) in-degree influence (number of followers), which indicates the size of your audience; (2) retweet influence (the number of retweets containing your name), which indicates your ability to generate content with "pass-on" value; and (3) mention retweet (the number of mentions containing your name), which indicates your ability to engage others in a conversation (Cha, Haddadi, Benevenuto, & Gummadi, 2010).

However, Twitter also has it downsides. It is a public forum, and as a result, athletes and professionals who are tweeting are not only representing themselves but also their clubs, teams, organizations, and sponsors. This increased personal exposure comes with an added responsibility of appropriate tweeting that athletes and consultants do not always get right. There have been a number of famous examples of Twitter blunders. For example, Australian rugby union star Israel Folau was sacked by Rugby Australia in May 2019 following a homophobic social media post on Instagram. Also, Greek pole vaulter Paraskevi Papachristou was banned from competing at the 2012 Olympic Games after posting a racist tweet, supposedly as a joke, about Africans in Greece. The importance of carefully considering what you say on social media and how it will be perceived has been emphasized as a key aspect of impression management (Cotterill, 2019a).

Social networks

Facebook

Facebook is the largest platform globally with almost 98% of all digital users having an account (Global Web Index, 2019). Facebook is a social networking website where individuals, companies, and organizations can set up profile pages;

individuals can "add friends," while companies can gain "likes" for photos or ideas. Similar to LinkedIn, specific user groups can also be set up. Setting up "invite only" user groups can be especially useful when working with younger athletes at a club due to their high degree of interaction with social media. However, caution should be applied, especially when working with younger athletes, as being "friends" with children may not be professionally appropriate, as discussed later in the chapter.

LinkedIn

LinkedIn is a professional networking site offering individuals the opportunity to set up a profile page, which is equivalent to an online curriculum vitae (CV) or resumé. Additionally, there is the opportunity for people to create professional networking groups. These groups are often by invite only and can only be joined if approved by the group organizer. LinkedIn is used increasingly for advertising jobs and opportunities that relate to the information on your profile. The online presentation of information resembles a formatted CV containing only the most relevant facts on education, current and past positions, as well as previous experience.

Flickr

Flickr is an image and video-hosting website and web services suite. As well as being a popular site for sharing and embedding personal photographs, and as an online community, the service is also widely used by bloggers to host images that are then embedded in blogs and on social media. Users create a free account and upload their own photos and videos to share with friends and followers online. What sets Flickr apart from other popular photo-sharing apps like Facebook and Instagram is that it is a photo-centric platform developed for professional photographers and photography enthusiasts to show off their work while enjoying the work of others.

Messaging services

Text (SMS)

Text messaging, sending short written messages between electronic devices such as mobile telephones, is a quick and simple way to communicate and has overtaken telephone calls as the preferred mode of communication for under 25s (OFCOM, 2012). Texting can be a useful way of staying in touch with clients you know well and especially useful as a "checking in" or monitoring method (Cotterill & Symes, 2014). There are issues, though, with this type of instant written communication; in particular, trying to convey the relevant paralinguistic interpretation of the words used can be difficult. Paralanguage relates to non-spoken elements of communication that are crucial to interpreting the meaning of the language used, such as facial expressions and body language. To address this shortcoming of texting, a system of in-message symbols has developed. Originally, these symbols used letters to denote a face :-) or used an abbreviation to indicate a behavioral reaction (e.g., LOL – laugh out loud). In more recent years, these simple strategies have been replaced with an ever-increasing range of Emojis – images used to convey meaning and emotion in written communication.

WhatsApp

WhatsApp is a free, cross-platform messaging app for smartphones used to exchange text, images, video, and audio messages. A key feature of WhatsApp is that users can set up "groups" that enable secure communication between designated individuals. The security (encryption) features of WhatsApp also mean that it is one of the more secure forms of online communication.

It is popular with teenagers because of features like group chatting, voice messages, and location sharing. The user base has gone beyond 1.5 billion people in 2018 and is still growing (99Firms.com, 2019). Similar to text messaging, WhatsApp offers sport psychology practitioners the ability to set up training groups to communicate directly with all group members with a single message, rather than sending individual text messages (Cotterill & Symes, 2014).

Instagram

Instagram is an online photo/video-sharing platform where users can upload and share high-quality images and other visual resources on various social network sites. It provides users an instantaneous way to capture and share their life moments with friends through pictures and videos. Since its launch in October 2010, it has attracted more than 1 billion active monthly users, with Instagram usage doubling between 2016 and 2018, and 95 million posts made every day (Smith, 2019). In addition to its photo capturing and manipulation functions, Instagram also provides similar social connectivity to Twitter that allows a user to follow any number of other users, called "friends." On Instagram by default, images and videos are public, which means they are visible to anyone using the Instagram app or Instagram website. Users consume photos and videos mostly by viewing a core page showing a "stream" of the latest photos and videos from their connections, listed in reverse chronological order. Users can also rate favorites or comment on posts. Such actions will appear in referenced user's "Updates" page so that users can keep track of "likes" and comments about their posts (Cotterill, 2019a).

Team messaging tools

A number of tools have been developed to foster better communication between athletes, consultants, and parents/guardians. Examples include TeamPages

(teampages.com), Takkle, MySportsSite, and Elliston Sport. These tools offer SMS services to connect with a specific user group to provide instant information on changes to games or training, to post-training schedules, and to share photos and videos.

Podcasting

Podcasts are a way to produce and distribute materials on any topic. A podcast is typically an episodic series of audio, radio, or video downloaded to a computer or mobile device. A great advantage of a podcast is that it can be downloaded to portable devices such as MP3/4 players, tablets, laptops, and smart phones. As a result, this broadcast information is easy to listen to "on the go" (e.g., in the car, on the bus, walking to college). Podcasts have also become increasingly important in formal educational settings (Harris & Park, 2008), as another medium through which information can be consumed. More and more educational providers are producing lectures and other learning episodes as podcasts and vodcasts (video podcasts). Podcasts can be accessed from a wide range of sources, but the Apple iTunes online store currently has the largest selection. Examples of sport psychology-focused podcasts include: Dr Patrick Cohn's sport psychology podcast (peaksports.com), BelievePerform's extensive list of invited podcasts (believeperform.com), and Dan Abraham's *The Psych Show* (danabrahams.com).

Video calling and conferencing

Skype, FaceTime, Facebook Messenger, and Zoom

These formats facilitate face-to-face communication across an internet connection. An obvious advantage is the opportunity for a consultant to be able to provide continued support without having to be in the same place at the same time as the client, although Cotterill (2012) argues that moving away from face-to-face interactions can compromise the quality of the explicit and implicit communication that takes place.

Skype is one of the most established video conferencing and communication tools. Specifically, it provides voice and video calls between computers, tablets, smart phones, games consoles, and smart TVs. Skype also has a messaging service for users. Skype was first released in 2003 and was acquired by eBay in 2005, then by Microsoft in 2011.

FaceTime is another video communication product, launched in 2010, that is preinstalled on all Apple products (computers, tablets, and smart phones). FaceTime offers a video conferencing/calling alternative for Apple customers.

Facebook Messenger is an instant messaging service through which users can send messages, photos, files, and videos. The service also supports voice and video calling. Originally part of the main Facebook site, Messenger was separated out in 2014 with over 1.2 billion recorded users by April 2017 (Constine, 2017).

Zoom is a web and video conferencing platform using Cloud-based solutions. The company was founded in 2011. A key feature of the Zoom platform is that it can host video conferences with up to 500 participants.

Video-sharing sites

YouTube

YouTube is a free video-sharing website that makes it easy to watch and share online videos. Individuals can create and upload their own videos to share with others. Originally launched in 2005, YouTube is now one of the most popular sites on the Web, with visitors watching around 6 billion hours of video every month. YouTube comes close to Facebook in terms of the number of active users (Córdova, 2016). Cooper (2013) also reported that in the United States, YouTube has higher audience levels than any television or cable channel among the 18–34-year-old demographic.

Social media and athlete performance

There is an increasing interest in the impact of social media on athlete performance. For example, after the 2012 London Olympic Games a number of British coaches and officials believed that social networking sites distracted some athletes, which may have led to substandard performances (Miah, 2012). More recently, Encel, Mesagno, and Brown (2017) explored Facebook use and the relationship to performance in a group of 298 male and female athletes. Results highlighted that 31.9% of athletes used Facebook during a competition and 68.1% had accessed Facebook within two hours prior to competition. The time spent on Facebook prior to competition was significantly (and positively) correlated with the concentration disruption component of sport anxiety. This finding is a concern, as when concentration disruption occurs prior to, or during competition, the effectiveness of an athlete's mental preparation may decline (Baker, Côté, & Hawes, 2000). One of the reasons for this engagement prior to competition might be a "fear of missing out" (referred to as FOMO) from push notifications, a desire to stay connected with other individuals continually (Przybylski, Murayama, DeHaan, & Gladwell, 2013). This perspective suggests that the solution might not be as simple as banning access to social media prior to performance.

Also, athletes are now controlling their own narratives through Twitter, Instagram, and Facebook. Much of the research on social media and athletes to date has focused on its marketing advantages. Indeed, athletes have been encouraged to engage more with fans. However, an increasing number of studies suggest that media exposure can be damaging. Indeed, athletes competing at the 1996 Olympic Summer Games in Atlanta and 1998 Olympic Winter Games in Nagano identified media as a factor that negatively impacted their performance (Forrester, 2018). If an athlete receives positive feedback, their self-efficacy can be elevated. If they receive negative commentary, their self-belief can be compromised. This means that fans and those trolling social network sites have the power to influence the mental state of an athlete.

Professional, ethical, and moral considerations

Digital footprint

An individual's digital footprint refers to the information and data they generate, through purposive action or passive recording, when they go online (Thatcher, 2014). This digital footprint relates to the sites you visit, the comments you make, and the videos/images you post. Digital footprints are becoming increasingly important to employers who are using them as a means of verifying identity and the perceived suitability of candidates for positions within organizations (Benson & Filippaios, 2010). One solution to this challenge would be to limit the extent of your digital footprint, although recent research suggests that a lack of a digital footprint for some professions can be as damaging as one badly managed (Buchanan, Southgate, Smith, Murray, & Noble, 2017). This is especially true for professions where often the first step in finding a consultant is an online search for information. A particular concern here relates to younger demographic groups. Children and teenagers are building a much larger and more diverse digital identity than any other group in history as they are "online" from a much younger age than any preceding demographic group. As a result, sport psychologists working with this age group should ideally be able to advise regarding the potential consequences of their digital footprint.

Privacy and ethical issues

Many social media users are unaware of the extent of their digital footprint and the security of their personal information. Many users are unaware of privacy settings, and how to ensure that their private posts and networks remain relatively private. This lack of privacy makes it easy for a diverse range of individuals with differing motives to access information. As previous highlighted, Instagram is an example where the default setting is for public access to all of an individual's information and posts. In support of this point, Thompson and colleagues (2008) in a survey of medical students reported that only around 30% had activated privacy settings on their Facebook accounts. This is concerning for this group as the practice of "googling" individuals has become increasingly mainstream (Cotterill, 2019a), and search engines such as Google are increasingly likely to "pick up" all of the publicly available online information relating to an individual, regardless of when it was posted. It is also important to recognize that the action of joining another person's network gives them full access to your own network, allowing them to view all personal interactions. Also, privacy settings can be complex and may change without warning.

Implications for applied practice

Communities of practice

As mentioned previously, some social media platforms are often used to form in-professional groups. These sharing groups reflect Lave and Wenger's (1991) concept of learning within "Communities of Practice." Wenger, McDermott, and Snyder (2002) proposed that communities of practice share common elements, including: a domain of knowledge, a community of people, and shared practices (Cassidy, Jones, & Potrac, 2004). In providing a sport-specific definition, Culver and Trudel (2006) suggested that a community of practice is a "group of people who share a common concern, set of problems, or a passion about a topic, and who deepen their knowledge and expertise in this area by interacting on an on-going basis" (p. 98). Social networking sites (e.g., Facebook) and group messaging services (e.g., WhatsApp) could help to facilitate the social interactions through which this social learning can take place. Social media and networking offers the opportunity for communities of practice to include the "right" group of individuals. Technology also can enable communities of practice to span the globe with near instant communication possible much of the time.

Guidance on social media interactions and online activity

A lack of awareness of the opportunities and risks that social media presents to both sport psychology consultants and clients have resulted in a number of organizations seeking to provide greater guidance. The International Society for Sport Psychology (ISSP) published guidance relating to online interactions as part of the *ISSP Position Stand on the Use of the Internet in Sport Psychology* (Watson, Tenenbaum, Lidor, & Alfermann, 2001). The authors highlighted a need for guidelines to underpin practice relating to confidentiality, record keeping and electronic communications, transfer and sharing of client information, and boundaries of competence.

Professional body guidance for psychologists

The British Psychological Society (BPS) Division of Clinical Psychology has produced a guide, titled *e-Professionalism: Guidance on the Use of Social Media by Clinical Psychologists*. In the guide, summary recommendations include:

- Social media offers significant opportunities but also challenges relating to professional boundaries.
- Psychologists should not transmit any service user identifiable information via social media without explicit permission from the service user to publish the material online.
- Psychologists should be aware that standards of personal conduct apply to use of social media and should always consider the appropriateness of material submitted to social media; they are strongly advised to use (and monitor and

update regularly) privacy settings to restrict access to social media which contains personal material.

- If psychologists interact with service users via social media they should communicate clearly with regard to the nature of the relationship. Interaction with current or former service users via social media in a personal/social capacity should only be undertaken with caution and after careful consideration of the relevant professional and ethical issues.
- Interactions between colleagues within professional and educational settings can also raise issues and dilemmas particularly where there are power imbalances and an evaluative component.
- Whilst conducting research using social media has many advantages and is to be welcomed, there are some practical and ethical issues that can arise, which may require advice from more experienced colleagues.

Lannin and Scott (2014), writing for the American Psychological Association (APA) magazine *Monitor on Psychology*, made the following "best practice" suggestions:

- To manage boundaries online, and in particular to set appropriate boundaries with clients to avoid conflict of interest.
- To develop online technological competence, and in particular to develop an understanding of social media.
- Reduce liability risk online, and in particular intentional or inadvertent disclosure of confidential information.

Guidance for coaches

Cotterill (2019a) developed social media guidance for sports coaches that suggested a range of basic steps to help protect themselves, their clients, and the information that they generate. These steps focused on privacy, digital footprint, sharing professional information, consuming online information, and integrating your digital footprint.

Privacy

First and foremost, it is important to appreciate that often information is not truly private, and there are different levels of privacy. A useful starting point is to check the privacy settings on any account that is set up. Also, think about what you say and what you post (comments, pictures, and videos). Remember, messages can be shared beyond your "group" over which you have no control.

Digital footprint

Similar to the previous recommendation, think about the photos you take and the websites you visit. Images files such as pictures and videos are particularly important. This is true for images of yourself and what you do, but also of others as well. Think about whether the images and videos you share of the organizations you work for or the teams you work with (crucially if they are under the age of 18, but also for adults) are embarrassing to you or to them, or may be in breach of contractual arrangements.

Sharing professional information

Online environments present another method to communicate with other professionals. Options include WhatsApp, LinkedIn, Facebook Messenger, as well as some sport or organization-specific platforms. While social media is also an option, this form of messaging is less secure. Most social media platforms give you the option to delete or block individual users, which might be a more effective way to deal with antagonistic situations rather than having an online argument.

Consuming online information

The internet provides access to a diverse range of sources. The volume of video in particular is staggeringly high through a platform such as YouTube. As a result, the potential to access great practical tips, drills, and consultancy advice is unprecedented. When accessing some of this information, though, always keep in mind the question "what is the source of this information?" Do you view the publisher as being respectable and expert in terms of the content? You always need to evaluate the authenticity of the information and its source.

Integrating your digital footprint

Developing a good online profile does not need to be difficult. You can populate multiple social media platforms with the same social media content. For example, if you post information to Instagram, you can also set the account up so the same information is automatically posted on Facebook, Twitter, and LinkedIn. This can help you to communicate information to different audiences quickly and effectively. Again, YouTube can offer easy to follow "how to" videos, showing you how to link these different accounts.

Future research

There is currently a lack of understanding of social media use by sport psychology practitioners and the associated challenges they might face. This, in turn, makes it very difficult to understand the developmental needs of individual consultants. Inevitably, the challenges of social media are not the same across all sports and for all consultants, with specific challenges being more prominent in some sports, at some levels, and varying according to the client group (Cotterill, 2019a). As a result, future research is needed to better understand the social media habits and requirements of sport psychologists, and the knowledge, skills, and expertise that should be embedded in professional training and continued professional development (CPD) provision within the profession. Indeed, more broadly, there are unanswered questions regarding the effectiveness of the online environment for psychological service provision (Cotterill, 2019b).

References

99Firms.com. (2019). *WhatsApp 2019: Stats and facts.* Retrieved from https://99firms.com/blog/whatsapp-statistics/

Baker, J., Côté, J., & Hawes, R. (2000). The relationship between coaching behaviours and sport anxiety in athletes. *Journal of Science and Medicine in Sport, 3*, 110–119. doi:10.1016/S1440-2440(00)80073-0

Benson, V., & Filippaios, F. (2010). Effects of digital footprint on career management: Evidence from social media in business education. In: M. D. Lytras, P. Ordonez De Pablos, A., Ziderman, Lytras, M. D., Ordonez De Pablos, P., Ziderman, A., Roulstone, A., Maurer, H., & Imber, J. J. (Eds.), *Knowledge management, information systems, e-learning, and sustainability* (pp. 480–486). Berlin, Germany: Springer.

Buchanan, R., Southgate, E., Smith, S. P., Murray, T., & Noble, B. (2017). Post no photos, leave no trace: Children's digital footprint management strategies. *E–learning and Digital Media, 14*, 275–290. doi:10.1177/2042753017751711

Cassidy, T., Jones, R., & Potrac, P. (2004). *Understanding sports coaching: The social, cultural and pedagogical foundations of coaching practice.* Abingdon, UK: Routledge.

Cha, M., Haddadi, H., Benevenuto, F., & Gummadi, K.P. (2010). Measuring user influence in Twitter: The million follower fallacy. *Proceedings of the Fourth International Conference on Weblogs and Social Media* (pp. 10–17). Washington, DC. Retrieved from https://homepages.dcc.ufmg.br/~fabricio/download/icwsm2010_cha.pdf

Constine, J. (2017). Facebook Messenger hits 1.2 billion monthly users, up from 1 billion in July. *Tech Crunch.* Retrieved from https://techcrunch.com/2-17/04/12/Messenger

Cooper, B. (2013). *Social media statistics.* Retrieved from https://www.slideshare.net/strutta/top-social-media-stats-for-2013

Córdova, M. (2016). Social media, learning, networks and promotion opportunities for tennis coaches. *ITF Coaching and Sport Science Review, 68*, 5–7.

Cotterill, S. T. (2012). *Team psychology in sports: Theory and practice.* Abingdon, UK: Routledge.

Cotterill, S. T. (2019a). Communicating with athletes: The influence of social media. In R. Thelwell & M. Dicks (Eds.), *Professional advances in sports coaching* (pp. 318–335). Abingdon, UK: Routledge.

Cotterill, S. T. (2019b). Social media use and perceptions of sport psychology practitioners. *Proceedings of the British Psychological Society Division of Sport and Exercise Sciences Annual Conference.* Birmingham, UK: British Psychological Society.

Cotterill, S. T., & Symes, R. (2014). Integrating social media and new technologies into your practice as a sport psychology consultant. *Sport and Exercise Psychology Review, 10*, 55–64.

Culver, D. & Trudel, P. (2006). Cultivating coaches' communities of practice: Developing the potential for learning through interactions. In R. Jones (Ed.), *The sports coach as educator: Reconceptualising sports coaching* (pp. 97–112). London, UK: Routledge.

Encel, K., Mesagno, C., & Brown, H. (2017). Facebook use and its relationship with sport anxiety. *Journal of Sports Sciences, 35*, 756–761. doi:10.1080/02640414.2016.1186817

Forrester, N. W. (2018). The selfie Olympics: What's the impact of social media on performance? *The Conversation*. Retrieved from https://theconversation.com/the-selfie-olympics-whats-the-impact-of-social-media-on-performance-92273

Global Web Index. (2019). *Social: Flagship report. Global web index*. Retrieved from https://www.globalwebindex.com/2019-consumer-trends

Harris, H. & Park, S. (2008). Educational usages of podcasting. *British Journal of Educational Technology, 39*, 548–551. doi:10.1111/j.1467–8535.2007.00788.x

Kemp, S. (2015). *Digital, social and mobile worldwide in 2015*. Retrieved from https://wearesocial.com/uk/special-reports/digital-social-mobile-worldwide-2015

Kietzmann, J. H., Hermkens, K., McCarthy, I. P., & Silvestre, B. S. (2011). Social media? Get serious! Understanding the functional building blocks of social media. *Business Horizons, 54*, 241–251. doi:10.1016/j.bushor.2011.01.005

Lannin, D. G., & Scott, N. A. (2014, February). Best practices for an online world. *Monitor on Psychology*, 57–61. Retrieved from http://www.apamonitor-digital.org/apamonitor/201402/MobilePagedReplica.action?pm=2&folio=62

Lave, J., & Wenger, E. (1991). *Situated learning: Legitimate peripheral participation*. Cambridge, UK: Cambridge University Press.

MacNamara, A., & Collins, D. (2015). Twitterati and paperati – evidence versus popular opinion in science communication. *British Journal of Sports Medicine, 49*, 1227–1228. doi:10.1136/bjsports-2015-094884

Meraz, S. (2009). Is there an elite hold? Traditional media and social media agenda setting influence in blog networks. *Journal of Computer-Mediated Communication, 14*, 682–707. doi:10.1111/j.1083-6101.2009.01458.x

Miah, P. A. (2012, August 9). *Viewpoint: London 2012, a social media Olympics to remember*. London, UK: British Broadcasting Corporation.

Mills, J. (2013). Why should sport and exercise scientists use Twitter and what should they use it for? *The Sport & Exercise Scientist, 37*, 24.

OFCOM. (2012). *Communications market report*. Retrieved from http://stakeholders.ofcom.org.uk/binaries/research/cmr/cmr12/CMR_UK_2012.pdf

Przybylski, A., Murayama, K., DeHaan, C., & Gladwell, V. (2013). Motivational, emotional, and behavioural correlates of fear of missing out. *Computers in Human Behavior, 29*, 1841–1848. doi:10.1016/j.chb.2013.02.014

Sanderson, J. (2011). To tweet or not to tweet: Exploring division 1 athletic departments' social media policies. *International Journal of Sport Communication, 4*, 492–513. doi:10.1123/ijsc.4.4.492

Smith, K. (2019). *49 incredible Instagram statistics*. Retrieved from https://www.brandwatch.com/blog/instagram–stats/

Thatcher, J. (2014). Living on fumes: Digital footprints, data fumes, and the limitations of spatial big data. *International Journal of Communication, 8*, 1765–1783. doi:1932-8036/20140005

Thompson, L. A., Dawson, K., Fredig, R., Boyer, J., Coutts, J., & Pardice Black, N. (2008). The intersection of online social networking with medical professionalism. *Journal of General Internal Medicine, 23*, 954–957. doi:10.1007/s11606-008-0538-8

Verhagen, E., Bower, C., & Khan, K. M. (2014). How BJSM embraces the power of social media to disseminate research. *British Journal of Sports Medicine, 48*, 680–681. doi:10.1136/bjsports–2013–092780

Watson, J. C., Tenenbaum, G., Lidor, R., & Alfermann, D. (2001). ISSP position stand on the use of the internet in sport psychology. *International Journal of Sport Psychology, 32*, 207–220. doi:10.1080/1612197X.2017.1295557

Wenger, E., McDermott, R. & Snyder, W. (2002). *Cultivating communities of practice: A guide to managing knowledge*. Cambridge, MA: Harvard University Press.

10

MOBILE TECHNOLOGIES AND PERCEPTUAL-COGNITIVE TRAINING

Itay Basevitch, Nataniel Boiangin, and Camilo Sáenz-Moncaleano

In sport, the ability to make an optimal decision during a game is a key component of expertise. Furthermore, during the decision-making process, skills, such as anticipating an opponent's action accurately and quickly, and generating relevant options, are necessary to achieve successful performance. Research examining methods of training these perceptual-cognitive skills has used gaze behavior data from experts to instruct novices when and where to look for cues. Additionally, video-based technology using the occlusion paradigm has been adapted to train players' decision-making skills. With the advancement of mobile technology and, especially, laptops, handheld and tablet devices, coaches and players are now able to (a) receive feedback immediately during games or practices and (b) individualize training based on the needs of the players. Companies such as EyeGym, CogniSens, IntelliGym, and gameSense have developed technology to monitor and train perceptual-cognitive skills in various sports, including, baseball, ice hockey, American football, and soccer. However, to take advantage of these technological advancements, more research is needed to establish the validity and reliability of training methods and technologies, and to examine the transferability of the skills to natural environments.

Mobile technologies and perceptual-cognitive training

Technology is a key component in the quest for optimizing human performance (Filho & Tenenbaum, 2018; Schack, Bertollo, Koester, Maycock, & Essig, 2014). In elite sports, coaches and athletes spend countless hours training to improve, win, and break records. With the advancement of technology, especially with the introduction of handheld and mobile devices (e.g., smart phones, tablets, notebooks), technology has become accessible to both elite and recreational athletes and can be used continuously at various times and places. A developing aspect of human performance that has benefited from the advancement of technology is the area of perception and cognition in sports (Craig, 2013).

For example, video-based, virtual reality, and eye tracking technology have advanced the domain and increased knowledge and understanding of the mechanisms that lead to expert performance (Kredel, Vater, Klostermann, & Hossner, 2017; Panchuk, Vine, & Vickers, 2015; Vignais, Kulpa, Brault, Presse, & Bideau, 2015). The ability to read the game and make optimal decisions is an integral component in achieving expertise in team sports. Specifically, gaze behavior, anticipation, option generation, optimization and response selection, and pattern recognition and recall are essential perceptual-cognitive skills that differentiate between high- and low-level athletes (Mann, Williams, Ward, & Janelle, 2007). Advanced technology in the domain has allowed researchers and practitioners to measure and train these skills, leading to improved performance (Hadlow, Panchuk, Mann, Portus, & Abernethy, 2018; Ward, Suss, & Basevitch, 2009). However, application of research findings and the integration of technology systematically and in everyday training is lacking, and further collaborations and efforts are needed to advance the domain (Causer, Janelle, Vickers, & Williams, 2012).

Perceptual-cognitive processes and skills

To perform at the highest level, players need to consistently make optimal decisions. In Tenenbaum's (2003) model, an information-processing perspective is used to explain the processes involved in decision-making. The model is similar to an earlier human performance model (Marteniuk, 1976), wherein the environment serves as the source of information, the action as the output factor, while the perceptual (e.g., gaze behavior) and cognitive (e.g., anticipation) systems serve as the main processors of information and initiate the decision-making command. In the models, these processes interact (and overlap), leading to an eventual decision (and evaluation of the decision) and outcome. Noteworthy, the various components involved in the decision-making process (e.g., gaze behavior, anticipation, option generation, and option selection) have been studied separately to understand their specific roles (Mann et al., 2007), and together to understand their interaction and the dynamic and ecological nature of decision-making, taking into account task constraints and affordances (Araujo, Davids, & Hristovski, 2006).

Some of the main processes involved in decision-making that have been studied extensively are (a) gaze behavior and cue utilization (Sáenz-Moncaleano, Basevitch, & Tenenbaum, 2018); (b) pattern recognition and recall (Gorman, Abernethy, & Farrow, 2013); (c) anticipation (Williams, Ward, Knowles, & Smeeton, 2002); and (d) choosing the best option and making a decision (Raab & Johnson, 2007). These cognitive processes are emphasized herein because they link with the training and technology developed in the domain (Broadbent, Causer, Williams, & Ford, 2015), which is covered later in the chapter.

The body of literature in the perceptual-cognitive domain indicates that *when* and *where* a player looks to extract information from the environment is essential for anticipating what will happen (Mann et al., 2007). Previous studies have indicated that high-level players compared to lower-level players (a) generally use fewer fixations for longer durations but more importantly have the flexibility to adjust their gaze behavior based on the task and situational demands (Mann et al., 2007); (b) fixate on different areas at different temporal points to extract cues needed to predict actions (Panchuk & Vickers, 2006); and (c) have longer quiet-eye periods (i.e., the time between the last fixation and movement initiation) (Lebeau et al., 2016).

Another advantage that high-level players have is the ability to recognize and recall patterns (e.g., in soccer the position of teammates and opponent players) better than lower-level players (Gorman, Abernethy, & Farrow, 2012). The efficient gaze behaviors and memory advantages allow more experienced players to predict what is going to occur next (i.e., anticipate) more accurately and more quickly (Mann et al., 2007), and choose the optimal decision, leading to a successful outcome (Raab & Johnson, 2007; Ward, Ericsson, & Williams, 2013). Although numerous studies have examined these processes to understand and measure their underpinning mechanisms, relatively little research has been conducted to train and improve athletes' perceptual-cognitive skills (Williams & Ward, 2007).

Methods of training perceptual-cognitive skills

Research examining the benefits of training perceptual-cognitive skills started in the 1960s (e.g., Haskins, 1965). However, only recently, with the use of innovative technology, research has expanded in the domain and focused on training skills such as anticipation and cue utilization leading to successful performance (Causer et al., 2012). The results of these studies have generally been positive and support the notion that perceptual-cognitive skills can be trained (Hadlow et al., 2018). Two main research directions that align well with the advancement of technology have developed (Causer et al., 2012).

The first research direction is supported by the advancement of video-based technology and the occlusion paradigm (Jones & Miles, 1978). Specifically, in the temporal occlusion paradigm a video of a developing play (using various presentation formats such as large screens, 3D technology, and virtual reality) is stopped at different temporal points (e.g., 120ms pre, 0ms, and 120ms after foot contact in a developing play in soccer; see Ward et al., 2013). In the spatial occlusion paradigm different parts of the environment are occluded during the developing play (e.g., kicking leg, supporting leg, head of a penalty taker in soccer). In both paradigms, players are asked to anticipate (predict what will happen next), generate options (which options are plausible), and/or make a decision (which option will lead to the best outcome). The speed and accuracy of the responses are recorded (using a variety of response methods such as verbal, written, or full body movement) which provide information on crucial temporal points and spatial cues needed to anticipate, generate options, and make optimal decisions, in addition to identifying expert-novice differences (Müller & Abernethy, 2012).

The second research direction is based on eye tracking technology, allowing researchers to monitor, record, and analyze eye fixations during task performance (Kredel et al., 2017). Eye-trackers are similar to eyeglasses but have high-frequency cameras mounted on the frames that record the environment (in front of the person) and the pupil. The information from these cameras is processed, and using advanced algorithms, fixations are identified. Fixation frequencies and durations related to areas of interest (e.g., head, leg, ball, goal) can be calculated and measured, in addition to the timing and order of the fixations and the quiet eye period.

Training protocols aimed at improving perceptual-cognitive skills have used both eye tracking and video-based technologies to measure and improve these skills. For example, Williams and colleagues (2002) trained recreational tennis players to anticipate tennis serves (study 2). Based on gaze behavior data from skilled tennis players (study 1), one training group received specific instructions on the important cues to look at (i.e., explicit instructions) and another group was directed to focus on general important areas (i.e., guided discovery). Both groups were trained using the temporal occlusion paradigm and were asked to verbally report where they anticipated the serve would land, receiving feedback after their response. Results indicated that the training groups improved their ability to anticipate the serve location quickly and accurately compared to the placebo (who viewed a technical instructional video) and control groups in both video and field-based settings. Noteworthy, the training groups received only 45 minutes of training in each setting (video and field based) totaling 90 minutes of intervention.

Anticipation training has also been examined in handball, particularly players' ability to predict attacking shots on goal (Abernethy, Schorer, Jackson, & Hagemann, 2012). Using the temporal occlusion paradigm (336 trials), novice goalkeepers were divided into four groups of anticipation training: explicit learning, verbal cueing, color cueing, and implicit learning. Results indicated that all the training groups, except for the color cueing group, improved their anticipation skills, compared to the control and placebo groups (viewed tapes of a recorded match).

In one of the first studies that adapted quiet-eye training using eye tracking technology, basketball free throw shooting percentage was examined over a period of two seasons (Harle & Vickers, 2001). One team received quiet-eye training, by watching a video that compared each player's own gaze behavior to an elite player. Two other teams received no training, but free throw accuracy statistics were collected. The team that received the training improved their free throw percentage by approximately 23%, while the other two teams improved by less than 10%. Furthermore, the training team lengthened their quiet-eye duration during free throws and this increase was associated with more successful free throw shots. Quiet-eye duration was not measured for the other two teams.

Thus, it is not possible to conclude that the change in gaze behavior led to the improvement in free throw shooting.

Mobile technologies used to train perceptual-cognitive skills

Mobile technologies aimed at improving perceptual-cognitive skills align on a continuum of two dimensions: (a) specificity, from general to domain specific, and (b) functionality, from higher (e.g., decision-making) to lower (e.g., visual) - order skills (Figure 10.1; see Appelbaum & Erickson, 2018; Fadde & Zaichkowsky, 2019; Hadlow et al., 2018). Importantly, the dimension of functionality is similar to the processes described in the decision-making model presented earlier in the chapter (Tenenbaum, 2003), starting from the process of looking for environmental information using the visual system (visual cues and gaze behavior) to processing and interpreting visual cues to meaningful information (option generation and decision-making). The specificity dimension is important as research has indicated that training that is specific to the task (representative) is more effective in transferring the skills to the real-world environment, which is ultimately the main purpose of the technologies (Rosalie & Müller, 2012).

We provide examples from technologies that fall into various points of the general-specific domain, and the lower-higher-order functionality factors of the model (Figure 10.1). These technologies also align to the perceptual-cognitive skills mentioned earlier in the chapter. Information about the applications, usage,

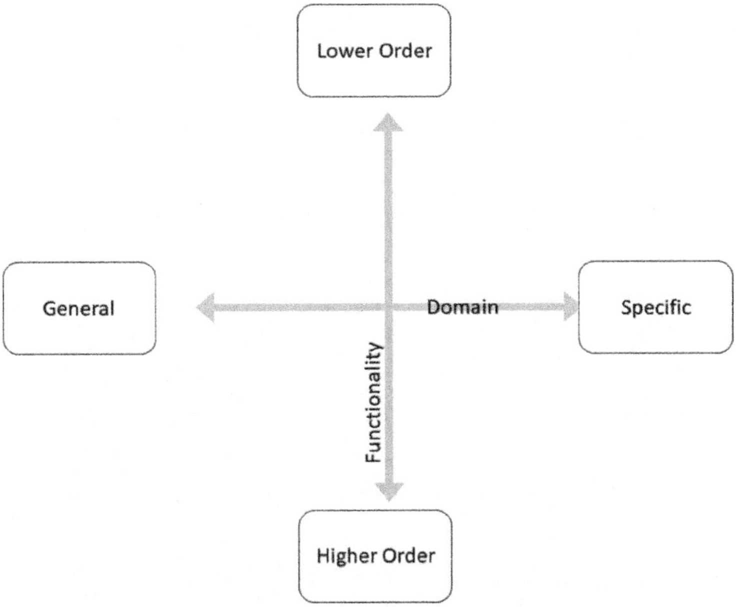

FIGURE 10.1 A schema of categorizing mobile technologies developed for training skills related to perceptual-cognitive processes.

training recommendations, and transferability to representative and real-world tasks are presented for each technology.

EyeGym is an example of a training tool that targets general and lower-level perceptual and cognitive skills. In the past couple of years, EyeGym has gathered much media attention (e.g., https://edition.cnn.com/2017/11/08/golf/sherylle-calder-eye-doctor-england-rugby/index.html) as many elite sport teams (e.g., England Rugby and Australia Cricket) and professional athletes (e.g., Kenny Stills an American Football player) have been using the technology and testify to its usefulness. EyeGym is a web-based software that can be operated on desktops, laptops, and tablets (while it can be used with mobile phones, it is not recommended because of the screen size). The software helps train visual skills such as eye jumps, scanning, and peripheral awareness using various game type applications (see Figure 10.2 for an example screen shot). It is geared toward athletes, scholars, and business professionals to advance basic visual skills and possibly transfer them to other domain-specific perceptual-cognitive skills, such as decision-making and anticipation (EyeGym, 2019). In general, the company states that training 5–30 minutes, 3–4 times a week is the preferred scheduling, with results being seen in the field after a few weeks to a few months. Research examining the effectiveness of the software is limited to previous versions of the software, unpublished research, and to vision training in general. Most of the support comes from anecdotal evidence and success stories linked to the usage of the software. Other similar visual training applications include Ultimeyes and Vizual Edge (for a review on the effectiveness of these mobile training technologies and others, see Appelbaum & Erickson, 2018).

NeuroTracker is another technology used to train visual skills (e.g., awareness), in addition to cognitive skills such as attention and memory (Hadlow et al., 2018). The software is a 3D multiple-target tracking task, where players track several numbered balls highlighted at the start of the trial while they move around the 3D virtual space and bounce back from the sides (see Figure 10.3). When the movement stops, players click on the tracked balls. The number of balls and their movement speed is adjusted as players progress. The tracking task is suggested to

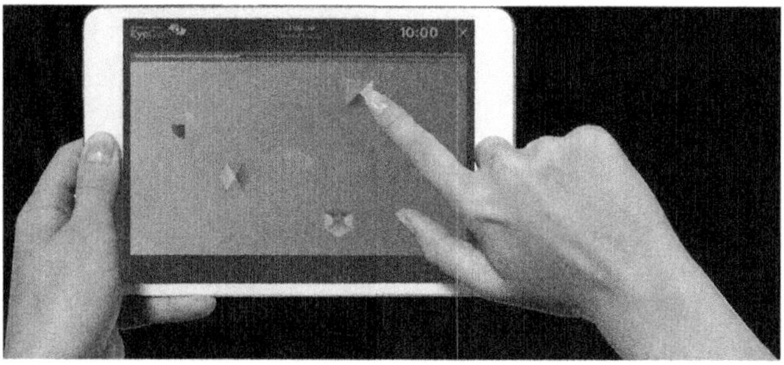

FIGURE 10.2 An example of an EyeGym screen capture of a training application. The user clicks on the keyboard as fast as possible when the orange object appears.

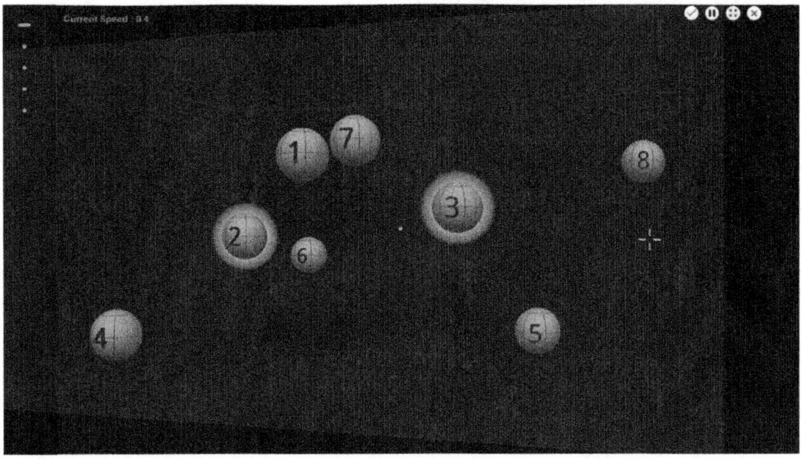

FIGURE 10.3 A screen capture of NeuroTracker by CogniSens.

simulate similar scenarios in team sports in which players need to track movements of other teammates and opponent players simultaneously (NeuroTracker, 2009). The technology runs on desktops, laptops, and notebooks, and 3D glasses are required. Training recommendations stated by the company are no more than three sessions per day, every other day (around 18 minutes per week). The manufacturer asserts that players will see improvements after accumulating 1.5–3 hours of training (NeuroTracker, 2009). Several elite sport teams (e.g., Manchester United, Vancouver Canucks, and Oakland A's) and players (e.g., Matt Ryan, quarterback for the Atlanta Falcons, and Stephen Curry, point guard for the Golden State Warriors) use NeuroTracker to improve on-field skills, and the application has gained media attention from major outlets such as Sports Illustrated, Fox News, and NBC Sports (e.g., https://www.cbsnews.com/news/super-bowl-falcons-quarterback-matt-ryan-brain-cognitive-training/). Research examining the effectiveness of the technology has found improvements that transferred to general cognitive functions, such as attention, inhibition, and working memory (Parsons et al., 2016), and specific perceptual-cognitive skills, such as decision-making (Romeas, Guldner, & Faubert, 2016; for a review of research related to NeuroTracker and a similar product Neurotrainer, see Appelbaum & Erickson, 2018; Harris, Wilson, & Vine, 2018). However, most of the research has been conducted by people involved in the company and more independent research is needed.

IntelliGym is another interesting software, which currently has specific platforms for hockey and soccer. In the application, players are in control of a "spaceship" among friendly and opponent spaceships and need to pass and shoot an object around and to target areas (see Figure 10.4). The company suggests that training on the application improves pattern recognition, anticipation, and decision-making skills, and suggests training twice a week, 15–30 minutes per

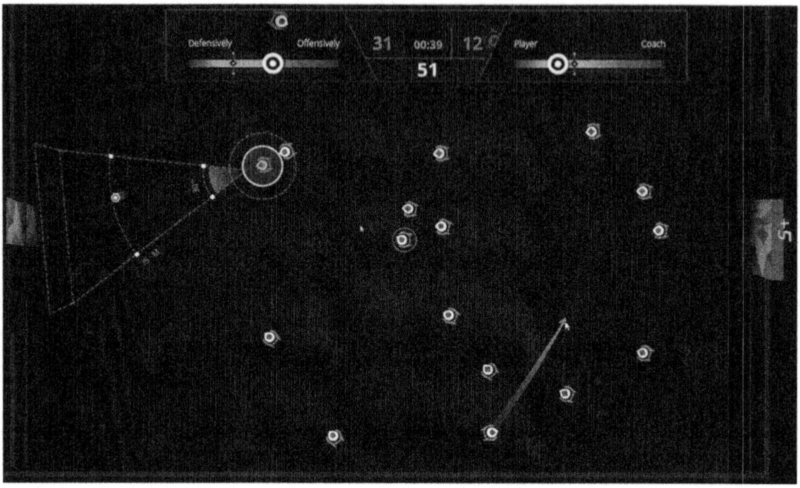

FIGURE 10.4 An image of the soccer version of IntelliGym (The Soccer IntelliGym, 2019).

session, with improvements seen after around 20 sessions (The Soccer IntelliGym, 2019). The application works on Windows and Apple computers/laptops but currently does not run on tablets or mobile phones. IntellyGym is used by soccer clubs such as PSV Eindhoven and Red Bull Salzburg and hockey teams such as the USA under-17 team. There has been scarce research examining the transfer of the skills to representative and real-world tasks. Two studies that examined transfer to representative tasks indicated that IntelliGym training improved soccer performance; specifically (a) players trained using the IntelliGym application were more likely to score higher on a soccer-specific, decision-making task (small-moderate effect, $r = .38$; Schul & Memmert, 2017) and (b) the IntelliGym training group improved on-field soccer performance by 27% more than the control group (Savelsbergh, 2017).

A more cognitive- and domain-specific application for baseball and softball batters is gameSense. It uses a similar paradigm to temporal occlusion and helps train anticipation of pitches from a batter's perspective (see Figure 10.5). Recorded clips of pitchers are shown to players and occluded after ball release. Players click as quickly as possible on the correct pitch type (e.g., fastball or curveball) and identify whether the pitch is a strike or ball (i.e., pitch recognition). In about 25 minutes players can view around 1,000 pitches of different varieties. The software can be used on computers, laptops, tablets, and mobile phones. The app is used by several professional and college teams such as the Arizona Diamond Backs, Cincinnati Reds, and Ohio State University. Although, there does not seem to be any specific research examining the effectiveness of gameSense, previous research on anticipation training suggests that the transfer to the field is possible (Fadde, 2006; Williams et al., 2002). There are similar applications

FIGURE 10.5 An image of the softball version of gameSense (gameSense Sports, n.d.).

designed to train domain-specific perceptual-cognitive skills, such as Axon sports, Eon Sports, StriVR, Beyond Sports, and Trinity VR (for a review see Appelbaum & Erickson, 2018; Fadde & Zaichkowsky, 2019).

Summary, limitations, and future directions

The advancement of research in the area of perceptual-cognitive skills and of the technology in the domain has developed in parallel. The numerous review articles in the area in just the past couple of years testify to the importance and excitement surrounding the domain (e.g., Appelbaum & Erickson, 2018; Hadlow et al., 2018; Harris et al., 2018; Fadde & Zaichkowsky, 2019). Previous research has provided information on several levels: namely, (a) understanding – of the perceptual-cognitive processes and their underlying mechanisms, (b) measurement – developing tools that can measure, assess, and monitor perceptual-cognitive skills, and (c) training – providing support that these skills can be trained with a variety of methods and technologies. Additionally, innovative technologies that are geared to train a spectrum of perceptual-cognitive skills have developed and are becoming more mobile, user-friendly, and advanced. These are very important and promising developments in the domain. However, several issues remain in the form of limitations and gaps that need to be addressed so that every athlete, coach, and team can make use of perceptual-cognitive training technologies systematically and as part of the regular training schedule, similar to gym workouts.

The main concern with mobile training technologies is the transferability to domain-specific, representative, and real-world tasks (Broadbent et al., 2015). Three factors should be considered: (a) the skill that is trained needs to correspond with the transfer target skill, (b) the technology task needs to be similar to the transfer target task, and (c) the interaction with the technology needs to be similar to the real-world environment (e.g., stimuli and response; see Hadlow et al., 2019). Additionally, research examining the effectiveness of training technology should be much more rigorous (e.g., include placebo and control groups), systematic (e.g., examine a variety of training protocols) and, importantly, independent of the technology company (Harris et al., 2019).

Another main concern is the paucity of research and technology geared toward the team setting (and not the individual). Shared mental modules and team decision-making is an emerging topic in the domain (Gershgoren et al., 2016; Filho, Gershgoren, Basevitch, & Tenenbaum, 2014). Innovative technology that can help train a team to work more efficiently with optimal coordination and understanding is warranted. Furthermore, use of current knowledge from the research domain needs to be adapted to technological developments. For example, gaze behavior is a mechanism that links with players' anticipation and decision-making skills (Panchuk et al., 2015). Thus, technology that corrects gaze behavior based on successful and elite players' gaze behavior could help improve decision-making skills and performance. This could be done with an advanced eye tracking device, coupled with virtual reality that provides feedback (and evaluates) gaze behavior live during performance. Finally, to address these concerns, move the field forward, and continue advancing mobile training technology, stronger collaborations among researchers, practitioners (e.g., players, coaches, and applied sport psychologists), and technology companies is required.

References

Abernethy, B., Schorer, J., Jackson, R. C., & Hagemann, N. (2012). Perceptual training methods compared: The relative efficacy of different approaches to enhancing sport-specific anticipation. *Journal of Experimental Psychology: Applied, 18*, 143–153. doi:10.1037/a0028452

Appelbaum, L. G., & Erickson, G. (2018). Sports vision training: A review of the state-of-the-art in digital training techniques. *International Review of Sport and Exercise Psychology, 11*, 160–189. doi:10.1080/1750984X.2016.1266376

Araujo, D., Davids, K., & Hristovski, R. (2006). The ecological dynamics of decision-making in sport. *Psychology of Sport and Exercise, 7*, 653–676. doi:10.1016/j.psychsport.2006.07.002

Broadbent, D. P., Causer, J., Williams, A. M., & Ford, P. R. (2015). Perceptual-cognitive skill training and its transfer to expert performance in the field: Future research directions. *European Journal of Sport Science, 15*, 322–331. doi:10.1080/17461391.2014.957727

Causer, J., Janelle, C. M., Vickers, J. N., & Williams, A. M. (2012). Perceptual expertise: What can be trained? In N. J. Hodges & A. M. Williams (Eds.), *Skill acquisition in sport: Research, theory and practice* (pp. 306–324). New York, NY: Routledge.

Craig, C. (2013). Understanding perception and action in sport: How can virtual reality technology help? *Sports Technology, 6*, 161–169. doi:10.1080/19346182.2013.855224

EyeGym. (2019). EyeGym. Retrieved from http://www.eyegym.com

Fadde, P. J. (2006). Interactive video training of perceptual decision-making in the sport of baseball. *Technology, Instruction, Cognition and Learning, 4*, 265–285.

Fadde, P. J., & Zaichkowsky, L. (2019). Training perceptual-cognitive skills in sports using technology. *Journal of Sport Psychology in Action*, 1–10. doi:10.1080/21520704.2018.1509162

Filho, E. S., Gershgoren, L., Basevitch, I., & Tenenbaum, G. (2014). Profile of high-performing college soccer teams: An exploratory multi-level analysis. *Psychology of Sport and Exercise*, *15*, 559–568. doi:10.1016/j.psychsport.2014.05.008

Filho, E., & Tenenbaum, G. (2018). Advanced technological trends in exercise psychology. In S. Razon, & M. Sachs (Eds.), *Applied exercise psychology: The challenging journey from motivation to adherence* (pp. 111–121). New York, NY: Routledge.

gameSense Sports. (n.d.). gameSense Sports. Retrieved from https://www.gamesensesports.com/

Gershgoren, L., Basevitch, I., Filho, E., Gershgoren, A., Brill, Y. S., Schinke, R. J., & Tenenbaum, G. (2016). Expertise in soccer teams: A thematic inquiry into the role of shared mental models within team chemistry. *Psychology of Sport and Exercise*, *24*, 128–139. doi:10.1016/j.psychsport.2015.12.002

Gorman, A. D., Abernethy, B., & Farrow, D. (2012). Classical pattern recall tests and the prospective nature of expert performance. *The Quarterly Journal of Experimental Psychology*, *65*, 1151–1160. doi:10.1080/17470218.2011.644306

Gorman, A. D., Abernethy, B., & Farrow, D. (2013). Is the relationship between pattern recall and decision-making influenced by anticipatory recall? *The Quarterly Journal of Experimental Psychology*, *66*, 2219–2236. doi:10.1080/17470218.2013.777083

Hadlow, S. M., Panchuk, D., Mann, D. L., Portus, M. R., & Abernethy, B. (2018). Modified perceptual training in sport: A new classification framework. *Journal of Science and Medicine in Sport*, *21*, 950–958. doi:10.1016/j.jsams.2018.01.011

Harle, S. K., & Vickers, J. N. (2001). Training quiet eye improves accuracy in the basketball free throw. *The Sport Psychologist*, *15*, 289–305. doi:10.1123/tsp.15.3.289

Harris, D., Wilson, M. R., & Vine, S. J. (2018). A systematic review of commercial cognitive training devices: Implications for use in sport. *Frontiers in Psychology*, *9*, e709. doi:10.3389/fpsyg.2018.00709

Haskins, M. J. (1965). Development of a response-recognition training film in tennis. *Perceptual and Motor Skills*, *21*, 207–211. doi:10.2466/pms.1965.21.1.207

Jones, C. M., & Miles, T. R. (1978). Use of advance cues in predicting the flight of a lawn tennis ball. *Journal of Human Movement Studies*, *4*, 231–235.

Kredel, R., Vater, C., Klostermann, A., & Hossner, E. J. (2017). Eye-tracking technology and the dynamics of natural gaze behavior in sports: A systematic review of 40 years of research. *Frontiers in Psychology*, *8*, e1845. doi:10.3389/fpsyg.2017.01845

Lebeau, J. C., Liu, S., Sáenz-Moncaleano, C., Sanduvete-Chaves, S., Chacón-Moscoso, S., Becker, B. J., & Tenenbaum, G. (2016). Quiet eye and performance in sport: A meta-analysis. *Journal of Sport & Exercise Psychology*, *38*, 441–457. doi:10.1123/jsep.2015-0123

Mann, D. Y., Williams, A., Ward, P., & Janelle, C. M. (2007). Perceptual-cognitive expertise in sport: A meta-analysis. *Journal of Sport & Exercise Psychology*, *29*, 457–478. doi:10.1123/jsep.29.4.457

Marteniuk, R. (1976). *Information processing in motor skills*. New York, NY: Holt, Rinehart & Winston.

Müller, S., & Abernethy, B. (2012). Expert anticipatory skill in striking sports: A review and a model. *Research Quarterly for Exercise and Sport*, *83*, 175–187. doi:10.1080/02701367.2012.10599848

NeuroTracker. (2009). NeuroTracker professional. Retrieved from https://neurotracker.net/performance/.

Panchuk, D., & Vickers, J. N. (2006). Gaze behaviors of goaltenders under spatial-temporal constraints. *Human Movement Science, 25*, 733–752. doi:10.1016/j.humov.2006.07.001

Panchuk, D., Vine, S., & Vickers, J. N. (2015). Eye tracking methods in sport expertise. In N. J. Baker & D. Farrow (Eds.), *Routledge handbook of sport expertise* (pp. 202–213). New York, NY: Routledge.

Parsons, B., Magill, T., Boucher, A., Zhang, M., Zogbo, K., Bérubé, S., … & Faubert, J. (2016). Enhancing cognitive function using perceptual-cognitive training. *Clinical EEG and Neuroscience, 47*, 37–47. doi:10.1177/1550059414563746

Raab, M., & Johnson, J. G. (2007). Expertise-based differences in search and option generation strategies. *Journal of Experimental Psychology: Applied, 13*, 158–170. doi:10.1037/1076-898x.13.3.158

Roelands, B., & De Pauw, K (2019). Technological impact on human performance. *International Journal of Sports Physiology and Performance, 14*, 1. doi:10.1123/ijspp.2018-0941

Romeas, T., Guldner, A., & Faubert, J. (2016). 3D-multiple object tracking training task improves passing decision-making accuracy in soccer players. *Psychology of Sport and Exercise, 22*, 1–9. doi:10.1016/j.psychsport.2015.06.002

Rosalie, S. M., & Müller, S. (2012). A model for the transfer of perceptual-motor skill learning in human behaviors. *Research Quarterly for Exercise and Sport, 83*, 413–421. doi:10.1080/02701367.2012.10599876

Sáenz-Moncaleano, C., Basevitch, I., & Tenenbaum, G. (2018). Gaze behaviors during serve returns in tennis: A comparison between intermediate- and high-skill players. *Journal of Sport & Exercise Psychology, 40*, 49–59. doi:10.1123/jsep.2017-0253

Savelsbergh, G. J. P. (2017). Football IntelliGym efficacy analysis: PSV Eindhoven and AZ Alkmaar football academies. *Zenodo.* doi:10.5281/zenodo.268696

Schack, T., Bertollo, M., Koester, D., Maycock, J., & Essig, K. (2014). Technological advancements in sport psychology. In A. G. Papaioannou & D. Hackfort (Eds.), *Routledge companion to sport and exercise psychology* (pp. 953–965). London, UK: Routledge.

Schul, K., & Memmert, D. (2017). Evaluating cognitive training system for football players. *Zenodo.* doi:10.5281/zenodo.835432

Tenenbaum, G. (2003). An integrated approach to decision making. In J. L. Starkes, & K. A. Ericsson (Eds.), *Expert performance in sport: Advances in research on sport expertise* (pp. 191–218). Champaign, IL: Human Kinetics.

The Soccer IntelliGym. (2019). The Soccer IntellyGym. Retrieved from https://football.intelligym.com/product/

Vignais, N., Kulpa, R., Brault, S., Presse, D., & Bideau, B. (2015). Which technology to investigate visual perception in sport: Video vs. virtual reality. *Human Movement Science, 39*, 12–26. doi:10.1016/j.humov.2014.10.006

Ward, P., Ericsson, K. A., & Williams, A. M. (2013). Complex perceptual cognitive expertise in a simulated task environment. *Journal of Cognitive Engineering and Decision Making, 7*, 231–254. doi:10.1177/1555343412461254

Ward, P., Suss, J., & Basevitch, I. (2009). Expertise and expert performance-based training (ExPerT) in complex domains. *Technology, Instruction, Cognition and Learning, 7*, 121–145.

Williams, A. M., & Ward, P. (2007). Perceptual-cognitive expertise in sport: Exploring new horizons. In G. Tenenbaum & R. Eklund (Eds.), *Handbook of sport psychology* (pp. 203–223). New York, NY: Wiley.

Williams, A. M., Ward, P., Knowles, J. M., & Smeeton, N. J. (2002). Anticipation skill in a real-world task: Measurement, training, and transfer in tennis. *Journal of Experimental Psychology: Applied, 8*, 259–270. doi:10.1037/1076-898x.8.4.259

11

EYE TRACKING AND CARDIOVASCULAR MEASUREMENT TO ASSESS AND IMPROVE SPORTING PERFORMANCE

Emily M. Crowe, Mark R. Wilson, David J. Harris, and Samuel J. Vine

One of the difficulties of working in applied sports psychology is the lack of objective data to help understand the psychological components of an athlete's performance (Watson & Coker-Cranney, 2018). This may be one of the primary explanations for the disparity between how important coaches and athletes report psychological elements of elite performance to be and how much they invest in tracking and supporting such elements (Pain & Harwood, 2004). In this chapter, we discuss two objective psychophysiological measures that provide valuable insight into the psychology of performing under pressure in elite sports and can address the need for objective data to support athlete performance. Both measures – eye tracking and cardiovascular reactivity – have considerable evidence underpinning their efficacy in research environments (e.g., Kredel, Vater, Klostermann, & Hossner, 2017; Moore, Vine, Wilson, & Freeman, 2012). We discuss some practical issues that require consideration when using such measures in applied sports settings and report a case study. Combining these measures enables an in-depth and objective investigation into the complex interplay between visuomotor and physiological factors in the sporting environment.

Eye tracking

In dynamic and unpredictable sporting arenas, athletes must be able to identify and process only the most important visual information to support successful decision-making and motor actions (Mann, Williams, Ward, & Janelle, 2007). It is therefore unsurprising that mobile eye trackers have frequently been applied in sporting environments to understand the perceptual and attentional mechanisms that underpin sporting expertise (see Moran, Campbell, & Ranieri, 2018 for a review). Identifying the optimal gaze behaviour for a given skill serves as a conceptual tool for applied work because such models can be used to train athletes to adopt optimal gaze behaviours and detect deviations from expert gaze behaviour to help troubleshoot any problems.

One particular gaze strategy termed the 'quiet eye' (QE; Vickers, 1996) has been identified in many sports and is proposed to reflect a critical period of cognitive processing during which task-relevant environmental cues are processed, and motor plans are coordinated (Vickers, 2007). An earlier QE onset (i.e., the starting point of this gaze strategy) and longer QE duration have been consistently observed in expert athletes and prior to successful outcomes (see Lebeau et al., 2016, for a meta-analysis and review). This finding has led to the effective introduction of QE training interventions, which utilise eye tracking to improve athletes' performance by providing feedback about their gaze behaviour in relation to an expert model (e.g., Harle & Vickers, 2001; Lebeau et al., 2016; Vine, Moore, & Wilson, 2011).

A key characteristic of elite athletes is that they must maintain this control of attention in pressurised and fatiguing environments (Wilson, 2012). Another common application of eye tracking in sport is, therefore, to investigate how gaze behaviour, such as the QE, changes when an athlete feels anxious or fatigued. The QE reflects goal-directed control of attention, something which elite athletes must maintain in pressurised and fatiguing environments to avoid performance breakdowns (Wilson, 2012). QE durations have been shown to decrease under pressure (e.g., Causer, Holmes, Smith, & Williams, 2011; Vine, Moore, & Wilson, 2013) and physiological fatigue (Wilson, Webb, Wylie, & Vine, 2018), with subsequent detrimental effects on performance. Such research highlights the efficacy of using eye tracking as an objective index of psychological processes, which are determinants of performance outcomes yet are inaccessible through athlete reports or coach observations.

Cardiovascular measures of stress

The sporting arena provides a perfect environment in which to explore the effects of pressure on performance: some athletes rise to this challenge, while others collapse. These diverging outcomes may be driven by different evaluations and responses to the stressful stimulus. The biopsychosocial model of challenge and threat (BPSM; Blascovich, 2008) is a theoretical framework that explains how individuals respond differently to pressure. Under pressure, individuals evaluate the demands of (e.g., task difficulty) and resources available (e.g., skill level) to complete a task. When perceived resources outweigh or are equal to perceived demands, a challenge state is experienced, whereas when demands outweigh resources, a threat state is experienced. This cognitive evaluation has effects on the physiological stress response, resulting in distinct cardiovascular profiles which can be used as objective indices of challenge and threat states (Seery, 2011).

As challenge states are associated with better performance outcomes than threat states (see Hase, O'Brien, Moore, & Freeman, 2018 for a review), cardiovascular measures can be utilised to predict subsequent performance. Importantly, athletes can be trained to make more productive appraisals, either by positively reinterpreting heightened arousal as beneficial for performance or by developing their coping resources to counteract particularly threatening stimuli (Moore, Vine, Wilson, & Freeman, 2015).

To summarise, the assessment of the objective, psychophysiological measures we have highlighted – both eye tracking and cardiovascular – has two main benefits for the applied practitioner working alongside coaches and technical support staff:

1 They provide insights into the current mental state of the athlete and can be used to predict how performance will be influenced under pressure.
2 They can be used directly to support targeted biofeedback training to improve performance under pressure.

However, as with all psychophysiological measurements, there are a number of practical considerations to note before deciding whether to adopt them in applied practice.

Eye tracking in practice

Current mobile eye tracking devices consist of glasses with miniature cameras mounted on the frames to record an individual's eye movements during the performance of 'real-world' motor skills (see Panchuk, Vine, & Vickers, 2015). To simultaneously capture the visual environment in front of individuals and localise their gaze in that field of view, a scene camera is mounted on the front of the glasses. Infra-red light is directed towards the eye to illuminate the pupil, which causes reflections from the cornea that are used to determine the position of the eye relative to the visual scene (Duchowski, 2007).

Prior to data collection, a calibration procedure is performed in which individuals are asked to focus on a series of pre-defined locations to determine where their eyes are in relation to the environment. Practitioners can then view an individual's current gaze location overlaid onto the scene, either in vivo as the skill is being performed or retrospectively after the skill has been completed, and data have been downloaded. Specific measures (e.g., QE or percentage of time fixating certain areas of interest) are then calculated via post-hoc analysis of the video footage.

Cardiovascular measures in practice

Impedance cardiography is commonly used to index cardiovascular reactivity in the challenge and threat literature (e.g., Brimmell, Parker, Wilson, Vine, & Moore, 2019). This non-invasive technique measures beat-to-beat changes in the electrical conductivity of the thorax via electrodes (Newman & Callister, 1999). Cardiac output (CO) is the amount of blood flow that is ejected from the heart per minute and indicates sympathetic-adrenomedullary (SAM) activation, leading to the release of adrenaline and a subsequent increase in cardiac activity. Both challenge and threat states are characterised by an increase in CO. Threat states are also characterised by hypothalamic-pituitary-adrenocortical axis (HPA) activation, leading to the release of cortisol, which dampens the effect of SAM activation, thus reducing cardiac activity and limiting dilation of the blood vessels. A challenge state is therefore characterised by relatively higher CO than a threat state. Total peripheral resistance (TPR) is the net dilation versus constriction of the vasculature and is also calculated based on CO and HR estimated from the impedance cardiograph. Generally, a challenge-threat index (CTI) is calculated by converting each participant's CO and TPR reactivity values into z-scores and summing them such that a large CTI value corresponds with a cardiovascular response more akin to a challenge state (Seery, Weisbuch, & Blascovich, 2009). Importantly, these variables are not measured directly and are estimated based on arterial pressure and electrical signals from the heart.

Data collection issues

Using eye tracking and impedance cardiography in naturalistic sporting environments often requires a trade-off between assessing the skill in the most ecologically valid way and reliably capturing the data. In this section, we outline some challenges faced when using these measurement techniques in sport.

Calibration

Calibration refers to the process in which the eye tracker determines where a participant is looking in relation to the visual environment. This process is extremely important because the quality and accuracy of the subsequent data collection is largely dependent on the accuracy of calibration (Duchowski, 2007). Due to the variety in eye trackers, there are limited standard operating procedures regarding the evaluation of calibration, when to re-calibrate, and when or how to correct calibration problems post-hoc. Current best practice is therefore to follow the guidelines for the eye tracker being used. Another consideration is that, while calibration could be perfect, individuals can use their peripheral vision, which is not recorded from the eye tracker, to successfully execute the task. For example Croft, Button, and Dicks (2010) reported that some cricket batsmen rarely foveated the ball but were still successful at executing the task. Consequently, while eye tracking provides a window into how foveal vision is being used during a sporting task it cannot measure the use of peripheral vision or covert attention.

Sporting environments

To obtain the most realistic data, researchers want to test athletes in dynamic and naturalistic situations that closely mimic the complexity of the sporting arena. However, movement and sweating of athletes can be problematic for accurate data collection. Eye tracking glasses can move and electrodes from the impedance cardiograph can become displaced, which results in inaccurate or missing data. Researchers often fail to consider these periods of missing data in their analysis, leading to potentially inaccurate conclusions being drawn. Importantly, cardiovascular variables relating to challenge and threat must be taken *prior to performance* whilst athletes are seated, so as not to be confounded by activity level. Hence the CTI is not appropriate as an online measure for active sporting tasks and may not be capturing the indices of psychological pressure as they are happening. More specifically for eye tracking methods, changes in light conditions should be considered. Sunlight can interfere with the corneal reflection utilised to track the eye, which can contribute to inaccurate data (Discombe & Cotterill, 2015). Such issues can be overcome by anticipating them prior to data collection and developing modified protocols.

Processing data

The data collected from eye trackers and impedance cardiography require extensive pre-processing to enable the extraction of meaningful information from very rich data sets. Given that the scene is constantly changing in real-world settings, automatic processing of eye movements (as used for computer-based tasks) is usually not possible. Instead, videos are extracted and analysed on a frame-by-frame basis, which can be time-consuming and is somewhat subjective (Venker et al., 2020). Consequently, assessments of inter-rater reliability are considered good practice. At each frame, researchers can extract the location of gaze relative to the scene, which can be interpreted (spatially and temporally) to allow for the identification of different gaze behaviours (e.g., fixations, saccades, and smooth pursuits; see Discombe & Cotterill, 2015).

Often researchers will identify regions of interest (ROIs) and record when and how frequently gaze is located in such regions throughout a given time period, or the order in which these ROIs are viewed to gain insight into what information individuals prioritise to make decisions (e.g., Moore, Harris, Sharpe, Vine, & Wilson, 2020). For other tasks, we may be interested in where gaze is located before a critical movement to understand how vision supports movement planning or control. This vision-in-action approach (Vickers, 2007) requires a video showing the motor behaviour (often a side-on view of the performer) to be synchronised with the gaze behaviour video for further analysis of QE variables. In both cases, there might be certain points during the video that are more revealing than others, and it is up to the practitioner to ascertain these most meaningful time points through some form of task analysis. Since this processing and data extraction is subjective, this should be done via discussions with the athletes and coaches to determine the crucial components of data for further analysis or processing.

Practitioners have control over several parameters when using impedance cardiography that will influence subsequent processing. When faced with a large data set, practitioners must decide which time points are most important and how to pre-process the data (e.g., filtering) because cardiovascular data are typically quite noisy (i.e., accompanied by meaningless information). In addition, there is commonly missing data from such measures so analysis plans should be pre-determined and clearly specify how to deal with periods of missing cardiovascular data (e.g., exclusion, interpolation).

Athlete engagement

A critical aspect of utilising evidence-based practice within sports is that the coaches, athletes, and support staff must engage in the process and see potential value. Therefore, prior to the development of any protocols, it is important to engage in extensive discussions with athletes and coaches to involve them in the planning process and understand the relevance from their perspective. Developing a language that both coaches and athletes can understand is essential in the feedback stage of applied work. Using videos to clearly illustrate how an athlete's behaviour changes during different components of a project and audio feedback with graphs depicting the data enables them to fully understand the results of project. Moreover, engaging with athletes can be fruitful in identifying subsequent projects to further explore how performance can be enhanced.

Using eye tracking and cardiovascular measurements in the sporting arena

Despite a wealth of experimental research aiming to disentangle the relationship between emotional states, gaze behaviour, and expertise, there has been limited use of these tools by practitioners working directly with athletes. The case study below highlights the use of eye tracking and impedance cardiography for objective measurement of psychological aspects of performance in an applied sporting setting. We highlight the benefits of utilising these tools to provide coaches and athletes with reliable insights into an athlete's psychological state (see Panchuk et al., 2015). Case studies are an effective way to obtain a large amount of data on a particular athlete that can then be evaluated collaboratively between coach and athlete to help improve performance (Anderson, Mahoney, Miles, & Robinson, 2002).

The following section details a case study from the combined run-shoot event of modern pentathlon. In this final event of the competition, athletes complete four laser shoots (each requiring five successful target hits) and four 800-metre runs. There is a staggered start, with the individual with the most cumulative points prior to this event (i.e., from the swim, dressage, and fencing) starting a given time before their competitors; therefore, the first athlete to finish the combined run-shoot wins the overall event. As modern pentathlon is a multi-event sport, athletes are extremely fatigued by the fifth event, which can result in pressure-induced breakdowns in decision-making and attentional control. Indeed, Bertollo, Saltarelli, and Robazza (2009) interviewed 14 elite modern pentathletes who reported difficulties they experienced during competition, including dysfunctional body symptoms (e.g., muscle tension, fatigue), attentional difficulties (e.g., focussing difficulties, thinking about execution), and coping problems (e.g., loss of control, coping under pressure). This study highlights the emotional and cognitive experiences of modern pentathletes both before and during competition. Eye tracking and impedance cardiography might provide individual insights into the effects of fatigue and psychological pressure on performance, and provide data to support targeted feedback and interventions to improve athletes' performance under pressure.

Case study: developing a visuomotor model of shooting in the combined event

Aims

Athletes commonly compete in pressurised and fatiguing environments. This case study explored how visuomotor control and performance were affected when modern pentathletes completed a run-laser shoot task under a combination of these factors. We aimed to identify the conditions each athlete found most challenging and suggest training practices to facilitate optimal visuomotor control and performance.

Data collection

Twelve athletes completed a combined run-laser shoot task under four conditions: a matrix of low and high pressure and low and high fatigue (see Figure 11.1). We manipulated fatigue by modifying the pace at which athletes completed an 800-metre run prior to the execution of the shooting task. We introduced psychological pressure via instructions designed to induce social-evaluative threat. Specifically, in the low-pressure conditions athletes were told that we were calibrating the equipment and checking that data were being accurately recorded. In the high-pressure trials, athletes were told they were in a competition against each other and that the data were being recorded for a documentary. Both subjective and objective indices revealed that the pressure manipulations were successful. Impedance cardiography measures were collected prior to the run-shoot task, and shooting performance metrics and eye tracking data were collected during the task. Cardiovascular variables were combined into a CTI (see Seery, 2011) to gain insight into each athlete's response to the pressurised situation.

Results and conclusions

Data from the baseline condition (i.e., low pressure, low fatigue) enabled the development of a model of visuomotor control in laser shooting (Figure 11.2). This model was generated to provide a 'point of reference' demonstrating the most optimal visuomotor strategy for athletes. On arrival at the shooting gates,

Condition 1	Condition 2
Low Pressure, Low Fatigue	Low Pressure, High Fatigue
Condition 3	**Condition 4**
High Pressure, Low Fatigue	High Pressure, High Fatigue

FIGURE 11.1 Matrix of the four environmental conditions for the run-laser shoot task.

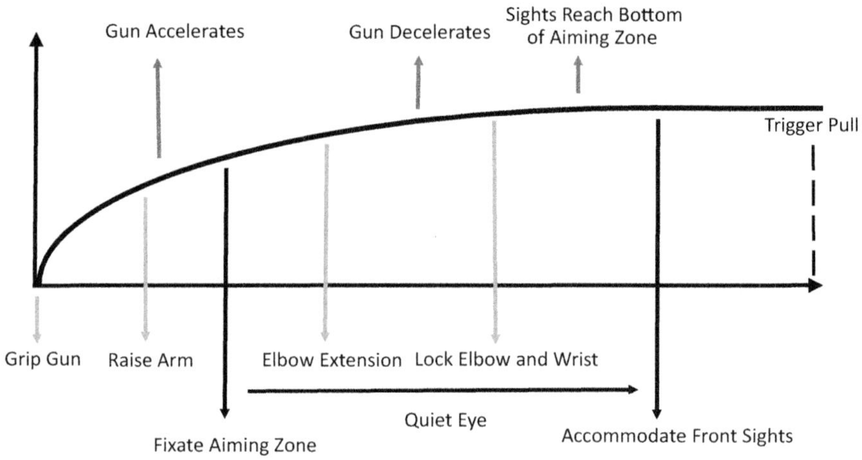

FIGURE 11.2 Schematic diagram of the model of visuomotor control in laser shooting.

athletes grip the gun and raise the arm towards the target. On the first shoot of a series, during this gun acceleration, they fixate the aiming zone, which defines the start of the QE period. During this QE period, athletes' gaze should remain stable on the target whilst they extend and then lock out the elbow and wrist. Athletes then squeeze the trigger, which marks the end of the QE period (i.e., the execution of the critical motor action).

Quiet eye

We first looked for overall trends in the data by considering all athletes together. There was a difference in QE durations across the four conditions, which shows an overall effect of pressure on visuomotor control, but no real effect of fatigue. Specifically, when under high pressure (i.e., Condition 3 and Condition 4) athletes executed a shorter QE for hits compared to low-pressure conditions (see Figure 11.3,

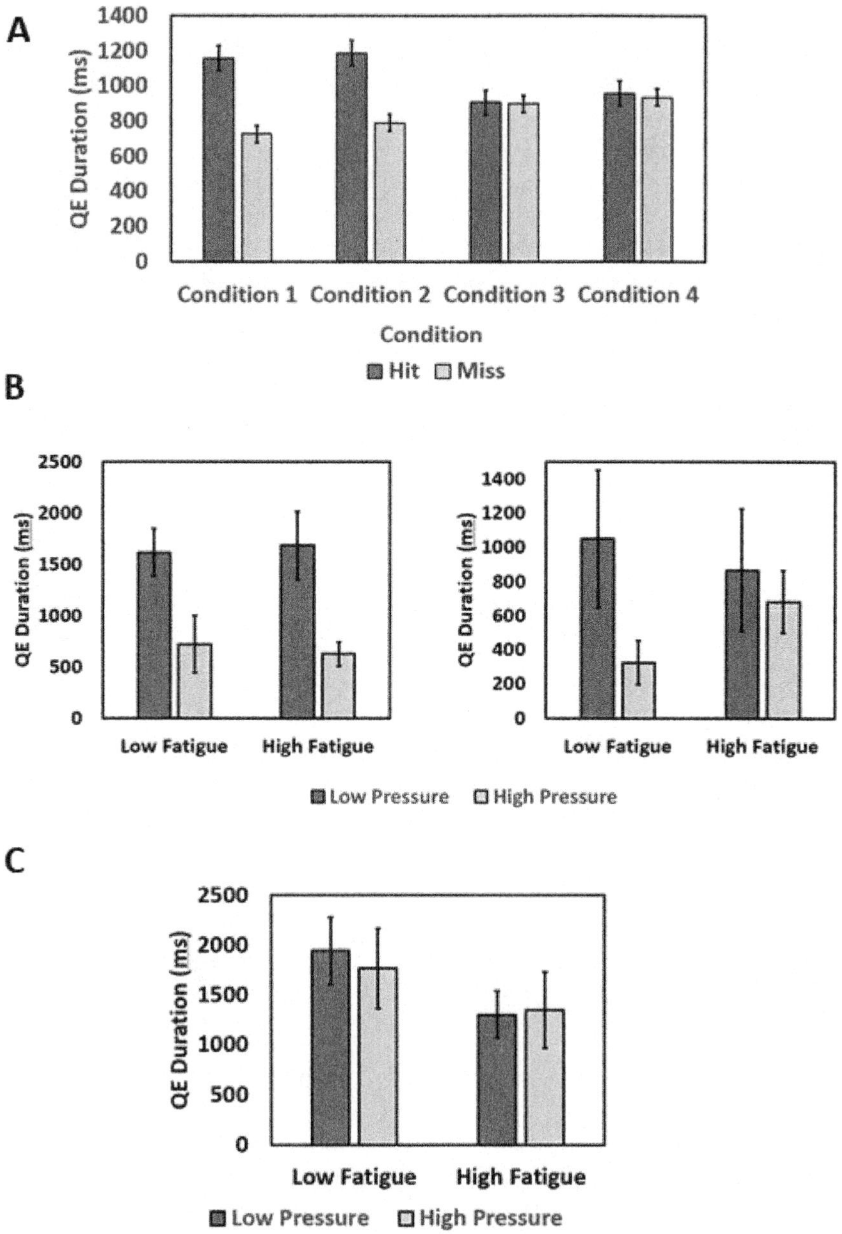

FIGURE 11.3 (A) Hits and misses for all athletes across the four conditions; (B) Individual data for two athletes who displayed shorter QEs in the high-pressure condition; (C) Individual data for one athlete who displayed shorter QEs in the high-fatigue conditions.

Panel A). When averaged across all athletes, poorer performance was also revealed in the high-pressure compared to the low-pressure conditions.[1]

Several theoretical models have been proposed to explain this relationship between anxiety (i.e., an emotional response to pressure) and performance. We drew on the predictions of attentional control theory (Eysenck, Derakshan, Santos, & Calvo, 2007) to suggest that the observed disruptions to QE and performance were likely the result of attentional resources being directed away from task execution and towards distracting stimuli (e.g., worrisome thoughts) as a consequence of feelings of anxiety. We suggest that such disruptions in attentional control are evidence of an inability to maintain the longer QE durations required to ensure 'hits'. In this way, we are able to show the athletes and coaches that our interpretation of their data is supported by theory, which can increase engagement and confidence in the utility of subsequent interventions or training practices.

Since individuals respond differently to fatigue and pressure, each athlete's data were scrutinised independently. Figure 11.3 (Panel B) shows two athletes who demonstrated large reductions in QE from the low- to high-pressure conditions, suggesting they were predominantly affected by pressure. Meanwhile, another athlete displayed reductions in QE from low- to high-fatigue conditions, suggesting that their gaze behaviour was affected by fatigue (Figure 11.3, Panel C). This highlights the differing response of individual athletes and, therefore, the need for bespoke, personalised training programmes to be developed. Specifically, this project enabled us to identify training conditions in which each individual should practice their run-laser shoot to facilitate the development of optimal visuomotor control for competitive situations. Understanding how attentional control changes in different environments using the objective data served as a catalyst for athletes and coaches to develop individualised, evidence-based interventions in preparation for upcoming competition.

Challenge-threat index (CTI)

Cardiovascular markers were also recorded to investigate athletes' physiological response to pressure. Specifically, a CTI was calculated by combining indices of CO and TPR. Figure 11.4 shows that most athletes (7/11) displayed a more threatened (i.e., a more negative CTI value) response following the pressure instructions, indicating that the pressure manipulation was successful and is a suitable protocol that can be applied to other sports. Specifically, in the low-pressure condition, most athletes were in a more challenge state (i.e., a more positive CTI value) where they felt equipped to cope with the demands of the task, whereas after the pressure instructions, most athletes entered a more 'threat' state (i.e., negative value) and evaluated the demands of the task as outweighing their available resources.

We explored the relationship between CTI and performance (i.e., the number of attempts needed to successfully hit five targets in the run-laser

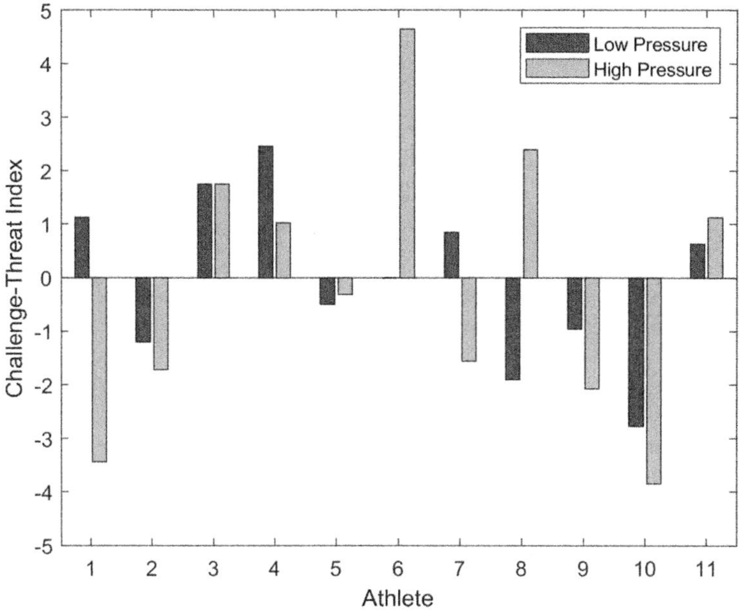

FIGURE 11.4 Challenge-threat index to demonstrate how athletes' physiological responses change under conditions of low and high pressure.

shoot task) to examine the hypothesis that a challenge state typically leads to better performance (Seery, 2011). Again, there were clear individual differences, which further reinforces the need to consider each athlete as an individual instead of exploring group-level data. For example, two athletes became more 'threatened' in the high-pressure condition but experienced different performance consequences. Athlete 1 displayed poorer performance, a result that fits with most research in this area. In contrast, Athlete 2 displayed superior performance despite being more threatened under pressure, which is proposed to reflect this athlete appraising the symptoms of pressure, which are represented in cardiovascular markers (e.g., butterflies, increased heart rate), as facilitative for the sporting task which ultimately led to improved performance (see Figure 11.4).

Feedback is a critical component of applied work. Immediately after each athlete completed the protocol they were debriefed about the aims of the case study. Following data analysis, a group feedback session was held to discuss the efficacy of using these measurement techniques (e.g., how much data was successfully acquired) and an overview of the results at a group level. This also enabled open discussion between athletes, coaches, and other support staff (skill acquisition/performance analysis practitioners) to identify avenues for future exploration. Finally, feedback specific to each athlete (including video feedback) was given to coaches to facilitate the development of training protocols to incorporate these findings into practice.

Conclusions

Eye tracking and impedance cardiography are effective, relatively cheap, and non-invasive techniques that practitioners can use in applied sporting settings to gain valuable insights into an athlete's visuomotor control and cardiovascular reactivity. This chapter outlined the benefits of obtaining objective data that can provide insight into the psychological state of athletes in applied settings. The case study demonstrated the value of using such techniques to collect large volumes of data that enable individualised, in-depth insights into an athlete's performance. We also discussed the challenges of utilising these techniques to highlight factors that require consideration prior to data collection, with a view to supporting practitioners who wish to implement objective measures more effectively in an applied setting.

Acknowledgements

The authors would like to acknowledge Jan Bartu and Chris Price of the Great Britain modern pentathlon team and the English Institute of Sport, respectively. The authors would like to thank all of the athletes who took part in this project.

Note

1 Note that these conclusions were drawn from observation of the descriptive data, and no statistical analyses were performed on the data.

References

Anderson, A. G., Mahoney, C., Miles, A., & Robinson, P. (2002). Evaluating the effectiveness of applied sport psychology practice: Making the case for a case study approach. *The Sport Psychologist, 16*, 432–453.

Bertollo, M., Saltarelli, B., & Robazza, C. (2009). Mental preparation strategies of elite modern pentathletes. *Psychology of Sport and Exercise, 10*, 244–254. doi:10.1016/j.psychsport.2008.09.003

Blascovich, J. (2008). Challenge, threat and health. In J. Y Shah & W. L. Gardner (Eds.), *Handbook of motivation science* (pp. 481–493). New York, NY: Guilford Press.

Brimmell, J., Parker, J., Wilson, M. R., Vine, S. J., & Moore, L. J. (2019). Challenge and threat states, performance, and attentional control during a pressurized soccer penalty task. *Sport, Exercise, and Performance Psychology, 8*, 63–79. doi:10.1037/spy0000147

Causer, J., Holmes, P. S., Smith, N. C., & Williams, A. M. (2011). Anxiety, movement kinematics, and visual attention in elite-level performers. *Emotion, 11*, 595–602. doi:10.1037/a0023225

Croft, J. L., Button, C., & Dicks, M. (2010). Visual strategies of sub-elite cricket batsmen in response to different ball velocities. *Human Movement Science, 29*, 751–763. doi:10.1016/j.humov.2009.10.004

Discombe, R. M., & Cotterill, S. T. (2015). Eye tracking in sport: A guide for new and aspiring researchers. *Sport and Exercise Psychology Review, 11*, 49–58.

Duchowski, A. T. (2007). Eye tracking methodology. *Theory and practice, 328*, 2–3.

Eysenck, M. W., Derakshan, N., Santos, R., & Calvo, M. G. (2007). Anxiety and cognitive performance: Attentional control theory. *Emotion, 7*, 336–353. doi:10.1037/1528-3542.7.2.336

Harle, S. K., & Vickers, J. N. (2001). Training quiet eye improves accuracy in the basketball free throw. *The Sport Psychologist, 15*, 289–305. doi:10.1123/tsp.15.3.289

Hase, A., O'Brien, J., Moore, L. J., & Freeman, P. (2018). The relationship between challenge and threat states and performance: A systematic review. *Sport, Exercise, and Performance Psychology*, 123–144. doi:10.1037/spy0000132

Kredel, R., Vater, C., Klostermann, A., & Hossner, E. J. (2017). Eye tracking technology and the dynamics of natural gaze behavior in sports: A systematic review of 40 years of research. *Frontiers in Psychology, 8*, e1845. doi:10.3389/fpsyg.2017.01845

Lebeau, J. C., Liu, S., Saenz-Moncaleano, C., Sanduvete-Chaves, S., Chacon- Moscoso, S., Becker, B. J., & Tenenbaum, G. (2016). Quiet eye and performance in sport: A meta-analysis. *Journal of Sport & Exercise Psychology, 38*, 441–457. doi:10.1123/jsep.2015-0123

Mann, D. T., Williams, A. M., Ward, P., & Janelle, C. M. (2007). Perceptual-cognitive expertise in sport: A meta-analysis. *Journal of Sport & Exercise Psychology, 29*, 457–478. doi:10.1123/jsep.29.4.457

Moore, L. J., Harris, D. J. Sharpe, B. T., Vine, S. J., & Wilson, M. R. (2019). Perceptual-cognitive expertise when refereeing the scrum in rugby union. *Journal of Sports Sciences, 37*, 1778–1786. doi:10.1080/02640414.2019.1594568

Moore, L. J., Vine, S. J., Wilson, M. R., & Freeman, P. (2012). The effect of challenge and threat states on performance: An examination of potential mechanisms. *Psychophysiology, 49*, 1417–1425. doi:10.1111/j.1469-8986.2012.01449.x

Moore, L. J., Vine, S. J., Wilson, M. R., & Freeman, P. (2015). Reappraising threat: How to optimize performance under pressure. *Journal of Sport & Exercise Psychology, 37*, 339–343. doi:10.1123/jsep.2014-0186

Moran, A., Campbell, M., & Ranieri, D. (2018). Implications of eye tracking technology for applied sport psychology. *Journal of Sport Psychology in Action, 9*, 249–259. doi:10.1080.21520704.2018.1511660

Newman, D. G., & Callister, R. (1999). The non-invasive assessment of stroke volume and cardiac output by impedance cardiography: A review. *Aviation, Space, and Environmental Medicine, 70*, 780–789.

Pain, M. A., & Harwood, C. G. (2004). Knowledge and perceptions of sport psychology within English soccer. *Journal of Sports Sciences, 22*, 813–826. doi:10.1080/02640410410001716670

Panchuk, D., Vine, S., & Vickers, J. N. (2015). Eye tracking methods in sport expertise. In J. Baker & D. Farrow (Eds.), *Routledge Handbook of Sport Expertise* (pp. 202–213). New York, NY: Routledge.

Seery, M. D. (2011). Challenge or threat? Cardiovascular indexes of resilience and vulnerability to potential stress in humans. *Neuroscience & Biobehavioral Reviews, 35*, 1603–1610. doi:10.1016/j.neurobiorev.2011.03.003

Seery, M. D., Weisbuch, M., & Blascovich, J. (2009). Something to gain, something to lose: The cardiovascular consequences of outcome framing. *International Journal of Psychophysiology, 73*, 308–312. doi:10.1016/j.ijpsycho.2009.05.006

Venker, C. E., Pomper, R., Mahr, T., Edwards, J., Saffran, J., & Weismer, S. E. (2020). Comparing Automatic Eye Tracking and Manual Gaze Coding Methods in Young Children with Autism Spectrum Disorder. *Autism Research, 13*, 271-283. doi: 10.1002/aur.2225

Vickers, J. N. (1996). Visual control when aiming at a far target. *Journal of Experimental Psychology: Human Perception and Performance, 22*, 342–354. doi: 10.1177/036354659602406S25

Vickers, J. N. (2007). *Perception, cognition, and decision training: The quiet eye in action.* Champaign, IL: Human Kinetics Publishers.

Vine, S. J., Moore, L. J., & Wilson, M. R. (2011). Quiet eye training facilitates competitive putting performance in elite golfers. *Frontiers in Psychology, 2*, e8. doi:10.3389/fpsyg.2011.00008

Vine, S. J., Moore, L. J., & Wilson, M. R. (2013). Quiet eye and choking: Online control breaks down at the point of performance failure. *Medicine & Science in Sports & Exercise, 45*, 1988–1994. doi:10.1249/MSS.0b013e31829406c7

Watson, J. C., & Coker-Cranney, A. M. (2018) Introduction to the special issue: Using technology in applied sport psychology. *Journal of Sport Psychology in Action, 9*, 213–215. doi:10.1080/21520704.2018.1552446

Wilson, M. R. (2012). Anxiety: Attention, the brain, the body and performance. In S. Murphy (Eds.), *The Oxford handbook of sport and performance psychology* (pp. 173–190). New York, NY: Oxford University Press.

Wilson, M. R., Webb, A., Wylie, L. J., & Vine, S. J. (2018). The quiet eye is sensitive to exercise-induced physiological stress. *Progress in Brain Research, 240*, 35–52. doi:10.1016/bs.pbr.2018.08.008

12

BIOFEEDBACK AND NEUROFEEDBACK FOR MENTAL SKILLS TRAINING IN SPORTS

Ming-Yang Cheng and Tsung-Min Hung

When it is applied in sports, biofeedback training (BFT) is a technique that can enable athletes to modify their psychophysiological behavior by regulating their biological signals (referred to as modalities) in response to real-time feedback, which may result in desirable psychological processes and/or behavioral outcomes, such as improved accuracy in shooting performance. The most common modalities include heart rate variability (HRV), electrodermal activity (EDA), muscle activity (EMG), respiration rate, blood pressure, and neural activity (neurofeedback training, NFT). Electroencephalography (EEG) has been the most commonly applied NFT method for sport performance enhancement. In this chapter, we review the current evidence, provide commentary on the level of evidence, and offer directions for future research.

Theoretical background of biofeedback training

BFT and NFT are designed based on the premise that every physiological change is associated with a parallel change in mental processes and emotional states. According to principles derived from operant learning theory (Skinner, 1963), providing clear feedback acts as positive reinforcement for an athlete. As training progresses, athletes can learn to self-regulate target modalities, which may translate to improved sport performance (Levy & Baldwin, 2019). Hence, BFT and NFT have often been used for psychological skills training in sports (Blumenstein & Orbach, 2018).

Psychological skills training (PST) in sports comprises a variety of psychological methods that aim to promote emotional competence, cognitive abilities, resilience, or mental strength, leading to improved sport performance (Vealey, 2012). PST is especially useful when it is integrated into preperformance psychological preparation routines (Blumenstein & Orbach, 2018). The Wingate five-step approach (W5SA) is one of the most popular periodization approaches that applies BFT as a form of PST. In W5SA, five steps are listed: introduction, identification, simulation, transformation, and realization. Building on the W5SA, Blumenstein and Orbach (2012) proposed the learning-modification-application (LMA) approach. LMA focuses on the specialization of psychological strategies and their application under distractive, stressful conditions.

The integrated psychological skills training program (IPSTP; see Beauchamp, Harvey, & Beauchamp, 2012) is another approach for periodizing BFT, which aims to help athletes realize and monitor their performance states by using BFT. The IPSTP includes seven training phases: orientation and observation, sport analysis, individual or team assessment, concept-utilization, PST intervention strategy, implementation, and evaluation.

Evidence for the effectiveness of biofeedback training in sports

HRV, which provides information regarding the beat-to-beat interval periodicity or time duration between heartbeats, is the most commonly used modality in BFT and is considered to be a safe method applied for performance improvement (Jiménez Morgan & Molina Mora, 2017). HRV has been associated with one's level of anxiety (Goessl, Curtiss, & Hofmann, 2017), which is a core issue in sport performance. The measurement of muscle activity, referred to as EMG, has often been used to assess muscle tension as an indicator of psychological stress (Luijcks et al., 2014). EDA reflects changes in conductivity via sweat gland activity, which is considered an indicator of sympathetic nervous activity (Posada-Quintero et al., 2018). The studies discussed below are summarized in Tables 12.1 and 12.2.

Multimodal biofeedback training for sport performance improvement

The majority of BFT studies have implemented multimodal training, which includes EMG, HRV, EDA, or a combination of these modalities. Benefits of BFT have been reported for swimming performance in pre-elite swimmers (Bar-Eli & Blumenstein, 2004), for serve accuracy in junior elite tennis players (Galloway, 2011), for basketball free-throw performance in intermediate basketball players (Kavussanu, Crews, & Gill, 1998), for short-track speed skating performance in expert speed skaters (Beauchamp et al., 2012), for running performance in college students (Blumenstein et al., 1995), for balance beam performance in college gymnasts (Shaw, Zaichkowsky, & Wilson, 2012), and for improved relaxation in professional athletes of various sports (Pusenjak, Grad, Tusak, Leskovsek, & Schwarzlin, 2015), but benefits have not been reported for injury frequency in elite young football players (Edvardsson, Ivarsson, & Johnson, 2012).

With respect to the quality of the above-mentioned studies, four randomized controlled trials (RCTs; Bar-Eli & Blumenstein, 2004; Blumenstein, Bar-Eli, &

TABLE 12.1 Summary of HRV BFT Findings on Sport Performance Enhancement

Author (Year)	*Design & Participants*	*Control*	*BFT Modality (Type of Feedback)*	*Length of Intervention*	*Verification of Effectiveness*	*Major Weakness*
Prapavessis et al. (1992)	Case study, 1 semiprofessional rifle shooter	Without control group	HR BFT (only 9th & 10th session, audio)	12 sessions (6 weeks)	Performance: Yes Biomarker: Yes	Embedded ECG BFT in part of PST with limited training sessions
Raymond et al. (2005)	RCT, 24 collegiate dancers randomly assigned to three groups	With control group	HRV (Visual)	10 sessions, 20 min (4 weeks)	Performance: Yes Biomarker: No	Lack of biological marker assessments
Paul & Gang (2012)	RCT, 30 collegiate and pre-elite basketball players randomly assigned to three groups	With control group	HRV (Unknown)	10 sessions, 20 min (10 days)	Performance: Yes Biomarker: Yes	Inconsistent training time between HRV group and placebo group
Wakefield & Shipherd (2017)	RCT, 18 college students randomly assigned to three groups	With control group	HRV (Visual)	6 sessions, 10 min (6 weeks)	Performance: Yes Biomarker: No	Short training length per training session No report on the change in biomarkers after HRV BFT
Ortega & Keng (2018)	RCT (matched randomization), 50 intermediate rifle and air-pistol shooters matched assigned to two groups	With control group	HRV (Unknown)	Flexible, 1 to 20 sessions, 60 min (20 days, 4 weeks)	Performance: Yes Biomarker: Yes	Inconsistent training sessions among participants Unclear description of the feedback type and procedures

TABLE 12.2 Summary of Multimodal BFT Findings on Sport Performance Enhancement

Author (Year)	*Design & Participants*	*Control*	*BFT Modality (Type of Feedback)*	*Length of Intervention*	*Verification of Effectiveness*	*Major Weakness*
Blumenstein et al. (1995)	RCT, 39 college students randomly assigned to five groups	With control group	EMG (Visual)	6 session, 20 min	Performance: Yes Biomarker: Yes	Limited sample size for each group
Kavussanu et al. (1998)	RCT, 36 intermediate basketball players randomly assigned to three groups	With control group	EMG BFT EEG, EMG, HR BFT	Unknown	Performance: Yes Biomarker: No	BFT coincided with NFT, leaving unspecific conclusions regarding the training effects
Bar-Eli & Blumenstein (2004)	RCT, 40 pre-elite swimmers randomly assigned to two groups	With control group	HR, EDA, EMG (Auditory)	31 sessions, 35–40 min (10 weeks)	Performance: Yes Biomarker: No	BFT coincided with different modalities
Galloway (2011)	Within subject, six junior national elite tennis players	Without control group	HR, EDA, EMG (Unknown)	5 phases, each phase consist 12 sessions (4 sessions per week)	Performance: Yes Biomarker: Yes	No control group and did not report the BFT training procedures
Beauchamp et al. (2012)	Within subject, 20 expert speed skaters	Without control group	Multiple, depended on the athletes' optimal zone, e.g., HRV, HR, EMG, EDA (Unknown)	6–10 sessions, 45 min (1 per week)	Not assessed	No control group or assessment after BFT.
Edvardsson et al. (2012)	Quasi-experimental design, 27 junior soccer players assigned to two groups	With control group	EDA & HRV (Unknown)	7 sessions (9 weeks)	Performance: Yes Biomarker: No	Nonspecific BFT procedures. No measurements of the biomarker
Shaw et al. (2012)	Within subjects, 11 female college gymnasts	Without control group	HRV (Auditory) Increase SMR Inhibit Theta at Cz	10 sessions, 15 min (2 per week in 5 weeks	Performance: Yes Biomarker: No	Lack of corresponding biological signal comparisons
Pusenjak et al. (2015)	RCT, 39 professional athletes randomly assigned to two groups	With control group	Respiration, HRV, EDA (Unknown)	16 sessions, 60 min (2 per week in 8 weeks)	Performance: No Biomarker: Yes	Nonstructured training protocol

Tenenbaum, 1995; Kavussanu et al., 1998; Pusenjak et al., 2015) and three cohort studies that adopted a one-group, pretest-posttest design (Beauchamp et al., 2012; Galloway, 2011; Shaw et al., 2012) demonstrated positive effects of multimodal BFT on sport performance, whereas one quasi-experimental study (Edvardsson et al., 2012) showed that EDA and HRV were not effective in reducing the occurrence of sports injuries among junior soccer players. The cohort studies permitted limited conclusions due to the lack of a control group and unclear attribution, as two of the three studies did not report the changes to psychophysiological markers following BFT (Beauchamp et al., 2012; Shaw et al., 2012). Viewed collectively, the body of evidence supports the benefits of multimodal BFT on sport performance, given that the findings emanated from both high-quality RCT studies and low-quality cohort designs. The benefits of multimodal BFT were observed among athletes with different levels of expertise, ranging from college students to professional athletes, and different types of sports (e.g., swimming, basketball, and running), which suggests that multimodal BFT is applicable to many types of sport contexts and among athletes with different skill levels. Nevertheless, caution should be exercised when attributing training effects to BFT, given that three studies did not report the concurrent changes in the modalities measured in the athletes (Bar-Eli & Blumenstein, 2004; Kavussanu et al., 1998; Shaw et al., 2012). Furthermore, one study did not assess performance-related measurements during the pretest and posttest (Pusenjak et al., 2015).

Heart rate variability training for sport performance improvement

Positive effects of HRV BFT were demonstrated on dancing performance in collegiate dancers (Raymond, Sajid, Parkinson, & Gruzelier, 2005), basketball technique performance in collegiate and pre-elite basketball players (Paul & Gang, 2012), and performance in intermediate rifle and air-pistol shooters (Ortega & Keng, 2018). For example, the shooting performance of rifle and air-pistol shooters improved after upregulation of HRV to reduce anxiety levels, which was integrated with PST to optimize the self-regulation of performance under pressure (Ortega & Keng, 2018). In contrast, a repetition maximum assessment in one study did not show improvements in a chest press after six sessions of HRV BFT in college students (Wakefield & Shipherd, 2017).

Regarding the quality of the studies, three RCT studies (Ortega & Wang, 2018; Paul & Gang, 2012; Raymond et al., 2005) and one case study (Prapavessis, Grove, McNair, & Cable, 1992) found beneficial effects of HRV BFT on sport performance, whereas one RCT study failed to demonstrate positive effects on chest press performance (Wakefield & Shipherd, 2017). Most of the positive evidence for HRV BFT was provided by studies with RCT designs, and the effects were primarily observed among skilled performers. The only null finding was found among non-skilled college students (Wakefield & Shipherd, 2017). These findings suggest that skill level may moderate the effectiveness of HRV BFT on sport performance enhancement, with athletes at a higher skill level being more likely to benefit from HRV BFT. One can speculate that skilled performers are more sensitive to a subtle change in psychological state compared to their non-skilled counterparts, leading to a better understanding and transfer of control for sport performance.

Neurofeedback training for sport performance improvement

EEG is an effective tool used to assess psychophysiological signals due to its excellent temporal resolution, making it a valuable means of examining mental state variations in response to sport performance. The studies discussed below are summarized in Table 12.3.

EEG markers related to sport performance

Several different EEG markers have been shown to be related to sport performance. The theta frequency band often ranges from 4 to 7 Hz and reflects the learning and memory consolidation processes. The frontal midline theta activity, which has been linked to top-down attention and behavioral monitoring, is thought to originate from the anterior cingulate cortex (ACC; Enriquez-Geppert, Huster, Figge, & Herrmann, 2014), which is responsible for processing awareness and attention and is partially associated with the "default mode network" (Buckner, Andrews-Hanna, & Schacter, 2008).

The alpha frequency band (8–12 Hz) serves as an index to reflect relaxation or cortical inhibition. The alpha frequency band can be further divided into low and high alpha bands. The low alpha band usually ranges from 8 to 10 Hz and has often been associated with general task demands (Cheron et al., 2016). On the other hand, the high alpha band usually ranges from 10 to 12 Hz, reflecting specific attention processing.

The beta frequency band is often referred to as the frequencies from 12.5 to 30 Hz, and it reflects cortical activation and somatosensory information processes (Cheron et al., 2016). Sensorimotor rhythm (SMR), the EEG component that spans the 12–15 Hz range, is inversely related to the activation of the sensorimotor cortex (Sterman, 1996). Reduced activation in the sensorimotor cortex has been considered to be associated with reduced interference in somatosensory processing when an individual is performing a cognitively demanding task (Kober et al., 2015) and in a golf putting task (Cheng, Hung et al., 2015).

Evidence-based EEG NFT studies in sports

The positive effects of EEG NFT on improving sport performance have been observed in a variety of sports, including archery (Landers et al., 1991), basketball (Kavussanu et al., 1998), dancing (Raymond et al., 2005), golf putting (e.g., Arns, Kleinnijenhuis, Fallahpour, & Breteler, 2007; Cheng, Huang et al., 2015),

TABLE 12.3 Summary of EEG NFT Findings on Sport Performance Enhancement

Author (Year)	*Design & Participants*	*Control*	*NFT Modality (Type of Feedback)*	*Length of Intervention*	*Verification of Effectiveness*	*Major Weakness*
Landers et al. (1991)	RCT, 24 pre-elite archers randomly assigned to three groups	With control group	Increased slow potentials at T3 (Visual)	1 session, as long as needed to show shift of slow potential to either T3 (correct feedback) or T4 (incorrect feedback)	Performance: Yes EEG: Yes	Lack of change in slow potentials
Kavussanu et al. (1998)	RCT, 36 intermediate basketball players randomly assigned to three group	With control group	Increasing and decreasing 0.5 Hz–32 Hz power over right and left temporal cortex	Not reported	Performance: Yes EEG: No	Lack of report on EEG signals before and after the training hinders the inference of effects of NFT
Raymond et al. (2005)	RCT, 24 college dancers randomly assigned to three groups	With control group	Alpha over theta or theta over alpha at Pz (Audio)	10 sessions, 20 min (4 weeks)	Performance: Yes EEG: No	No comparison between pre- and posttest on EEG signals
Arns et al. (2008)	Within subject, six experienced golfers (*M* handicap = 12.3)	Without control group	Individualized EEG profile at FPz derived from successful putts in the pretest (Audio)	Three sessions, four series of 80 putts in an ABAB design (no feedback – feedback – no feedback - feedback)	Performance: Yes EEG: Yes	Lack of a post assessment to show the NFT effects
Paul et al. (2012)	Quasi-experimental design, 24 university level archers assigned to two groups with unspecified method	With control group	Increase in SMR (12–15) Hz with decrease (4–7 Hz) at Cz (Audio-visual)	12 sessions, 20 min (3 sessions per week in 4 weeks)	Performance: Yes partially EEG: Yes	Unclear rationale for choosing NFT protocol and unspecified assignment of individuals to the two groups

(*Continued*)

Author (Year)	*Design & Participants*	*Control*	*NFT Modality (Type of Feedback)*	*Length of Intervention*	*Verification of Effectiveness*	*Major Weakness*
Beauchamp et al. (2012)	Within subject, 20 expert skaters	Without control group	Increase in alpha and decrease in beta (Unknown)	6–10 sessions, 45 min (1 session per week)	Performance: No EEG: No	Without pre- and posttest
Faridnia et al. (2012)	RCT, 20 professional swimmers	With control group	First 20 min, increase in beta with decrease in high beta; second 20 min increase in SMR while decrease in theta at C3 and C4 (Visual)	12 sessions, 45 min (3 sessions per week in 4 weeks)	Performance: No EEG: Yes	Unclear rationale for selecting training protocol and without pre and post comparison on performance
Rostami et al. (2012)	Quasi-experimental design, 24 expert shooters	With control group	Increase in SMR and inhibition of high beta at C3 Increase in alpha and theta with inhibition of high beta at Pz (Audio-visual)	15 sessions, 60 min (3 sessions per week for 5 weeks)	Performance: Yes EEG: No	Unspecified participant assignment
Shaw et al. (2012)	Within subjects, 11 female semiprofessional college gymnasts	Without control group	Increase in SMR and decrease in theta at Cz (Audio)	10 sessions, 15 min (2 sessions per week in 5 weeks)	Performance: Yes EEG: Yes	EEG did not show change associated with the NFT at posttest
Strizhkova et al. (2012)	Quasi-experimental design, 28 highly skilled gymnasts	With control group	Increase in alpha at left hemisphere (Unknown)	Not specified	Performance: Yes EEG: Yes	Lack of rationale for training target selection
Sherlin et al. (2013)	Within subject, five professional baseball players	Without control group	Combination of increase and decrease in EEG powers on multiple frequency bands over frontal, central and parietal regions (Audio & visual)	15 sessions, 20–35 min (2–3 sessions per week, in 30 days)	Performance: No EEG: Yes	Limited sample size

Dekker et al. (2014)	Quasi-experimental design, 13 expert gymnasts	With control group	Increase in baseline alpha at C3 and C4 (Audio)	10 sessions, 24 min (5 sessions per week in 2 weeks)	Performance: No EEG: Yes	Lack of performance measurements in pre- and posttest
Gruzelier et al. (2014)	RCT, 64 college students at conservatoire of music and dance randomly assigned to four groups	With control group	Inhibition of alpha with increase in theta at a Pz (Audio)	10 sessions, 20 min (2 sessions per week)	Performance: Yes EEG: Yes	Participants underwent the training simultaneously, which may cause unwanted social comparison
Kao et al. (2014)	Case study, three expert golfers (M handicap = 0)	Without control group	Reduction in pre-putt theta at Fz (Audio & visual)	1 session, approximately 25 min	Performance: Yes EEG: Yes	Limited sample size without placebo counterparts
Cheng et al. (2015)	RCT, 16 pre-elite golfers (M handicap = 0)	With control group	Increase in pre-putt SMR at Cz (Audio)	8 sessions, 30-45 min (1 to 2 sessions per week in 5 weeks)	Performance: Yes EEG: Yes	Relatively small sample size
Ring et al. (2015)	RCT, 24 recreational golfers (M handicap = 23) randomly assigned to two groups	With control group	Reduction in pre-putt theta and high-alpha at Fz (Audio, no feedback when threshold met)	3 sessions on separate, 60 min	Performance: Yes EEG: Yes	Possible confounding by placebo effect
Sherlin et al. (2015)	RCT, 16 division 1 collegiate golfers randomly assigned to two groups	With control group	Not specified (Audio & visual)	Ranging from 16 - 22 sessions, 20 min (at least 1 session per week, in 15 weeks)	Performance: Yes EEG: No	Ambiguous NFT protocol with varied training length
Maszczyk et al. (2018)	RCT, 18 unknown level of judokas randomly assigned to two groups	With control group	Increase in 14–19 Hz with inhibition of 3–8 Hz at O1 and O2 (Audio & visual)	10 sessions, 25 min (5 weeks)	Performance: Yes EEG: Yes	Unclear rationale for selecting training protocol and limited information provided on the analysis of performance and EEG data

gymnastics (e.g., Maszczyk et al., 2018; Shaw et al., 2012), judo (Maszczyk et al., 2018), and shooting (Rostami, Sadeghi, Karami, Abadi, & Salamati, 2012). For example, Rostami et al. (2012) found that expert shooters improved their performance after 15 sessions of NFT by increasing alpha (8–12 Hz) and theta (4–8 Hz) activity while inhibiting high beta (20–30 Hz) activity at the Pz electrode. Furthermore, eight sessions of upregulating SMR NFT resulted in improved golf putting performance in skilled golfers (Cheng, Huang, et al., 2015), suggesting that reducing cognitive load by minimizing the processing demands of irrelevant information in the sensorimotor cortex is beneficial for psychomotor performance (Cheng et al., 2017).

Several studies did not find EEG NFT to be effective for improving sport performance (Dekker, Van den Berg, Denissen, Sitskoorn, & van Boxtel, 2014; Gruzelier, Thompson, Redding, Brandt, & Steffert, 2014; Paul, Ganesan, Sandhu, & Simon, 2012; Ring, Cooke, Kavussanu, McIntyre, & Masters, 2015; Sherlin, Larson, & Sherlin, 2013). For example, EEG NFT for inhibiting alpha activity while increasing theta activity did not improve dancing performance (Gruzelier et al., 2014). A lack of an effect of NFT has also been reported in a study in which golfers practiced inhibiting high alpha and theta activity at the Fz site (Ring et al., 2015).

As for the level of evidence, positive results were demonstrated in six RCT studies (Cheng, Huang et al., 2015; Faridnia, Shojaei, & Rahimi, 2012; Landers et al., 1991; Maszczyk et al., 2018; Raymond et al., 2005; Sherlin, Ford, Baker, & Troesch , 2015), six cohort studies (Arns et al., 2008; Beauchamp et al., 2012; Paul et al., 2012; Rostami et al., 2012; Shaw et al., 2012; Strizhkova, Cherapkina, & Strizhkova, 2012), and one case study (Kao, Huang, & Hung, 2014). For the null findings, four were RCT studies (Faridnia et al., 2012; Gruzelier et al., 2014; Kavussanu et al., 1998; Ring et al., 2015), and one used a quasi-experimental design (Paul et al., 2012). These studies adopted different training protocols in various sport contexts.

In summary, the evidence regarding the effectiveness of EEG NFT for enhancing sport performance is equivocal. Although a large number of high-quality studies using RCT designs demonstrated a positive effect of EEG NFT on sport performance, a small number of RCT studies failed to show effects. This equivocality may be due to variations in the training target selected and/or the training duration (Hung & Cheng, 2018; Mirifar, Beckmann, & Ehrlenspiel, 2017). A data-driven approach for selecting training targets is recommended for future studies because this approach provides higher ecological validity (Cooke et al., 2018).

Limitations and future directions of biofeedback and neurofeedback training in sports

Greater clarity is required regarding the principles for effective BFT/NFT protocols and the underlying mechanisms for enhancing sport performance. First, a standardized training protocol should be established (Hung & Cheng, 2018), and the protocol can include but should not be limited to the provision of standardized instructions, the implementation of structured pre-post investigations, and the elucidation of the rationale for target selection (Cooke et al., 2018). Second, it is important to establish an effective training duration, including the number of training sessions and the duration of each training session, for both immediate and long-term effects. Third, integrating BFT and NFT with preperformance routines is recommended because skilled performers are highly specialized in cortical activations, as reflected by distinct patterns observed during the preperformance stage (Hatfield, 2018). Similarly, developing customized BFT/NFT for elite athletes is recommended (Cheng, Huang et al., 2015) in light of the results of an fMRI study showing that brain activity is significantly reduced in Neymar's brain compared to the brains of other professional footballers during the ankle rotation task (Naito & Hirose, 2014). Future studies should consider the periodization of psychological preparation to structure and tailor the BFT/NFT for preperformance routines (Blumenstein & Orbach, 2018) or as part of a mindfulness program (Khazan, 2019) for athletes with different skill levels. Fourth, applying BFT/NFT for the assessment of the effectiveness of PST on stress resistance may provide objective measures with practical implications. Heightened stress has been associated with increased cortical communication between the left temporal region and the premotor cortex in skilled motor performance (Lo, Hatfield, Wu, Chang, & Hung, 2019). BFT/NFT can be used to both assess and assist PST in reducing these interferences.

Summary

Although some evidence supports the effectiveness of BFT/NFT in improving sport performance, the evidence is generally inconsistent and of mixed quality (Xiang, Hou, Liao, Liao, & Hu, 2018). These inconsistencies may be attributed to the high variability in BFT/NFT protocols, skill levels of participants, and rationales for selecting target modalities. Nevertheless, some studies with rigorous designs have reported positive effects of BFT and NFT. In the future, researchers should investigate this topic by designing studies on PST with standardized protocols and high-quality research designs. In consequence, scientifically rigorous and practically useful BFT/NFT for enhancing sport performance for different types of sports and participants with different skill levels can be feasible.

References

Arns, M., Kleinnijenhuis, M., Fallahpour, K., & Breteler, R. (2007). Golf performance enhancement and real-life neurofeedback training using personalized event-locked EEG profiles. *Journal of Neurotherapy*, *11*, 11–18. doi:10.1080/10874200802149656

Bar-Eli, M., & Blumenstein, B. (2004). Performance enhancement in swimming: The effect of mental training with biofeedback. *Journal of Science and Medicine in Sport*, *7*, 454–464. doi:10.1016/S1440-2440(04)80264-0

Beauchamp, M. K., Harvey, R. H., & Beauchamp, P. H. (2012). An integrated biofeedback and psychological skills training program for Canada's Olympic short-track speedskating team. *Journal of Clinical Sport Psychology, 6*, 67–84. doi:10.1123/jcsp.6.1.67

Blumenstein, B., Bar-Eli, M., Tenenbaum, G., & Bar-Eli, M. (1995). The augmenting role of biofeedback: Effects of autogenic, imagery and music training on physiological indices and athletic performance. *Journal of Sports Sciences, 13*, 343–354. doi:10.1080/02640419508732248

Blumenstein, B., & Orbach, I. (2012). *Psychological skills in sport: Training and application*. Hauppauge, NY: Nova Science.

Blumenstein, B., & Orbach, I. (2018). Periodization of psychological preparation within the training process. *International Journal of Sport and Exercise Psychology 18,* 1–11. doi:10.1080/1612197X.2018.1478872

Buckner, R. L., Andrews-Hanna, J. R., & Schacter, D. L. (2008). The brain's default network. *Annals of the New York Academy of Sciences, 1124*, 1–38. doi:10.1196/annals.1440.011

Cheng, M. Y., Huang, C. J., Chang, Y. K., Koester, D., Schack, T., & Hung, T. M. (2015). Sensorimotor rhythm neurofeedback enhances golf putting performance. *Journal of Sport & Exercise Psychology, 37*, 626–636. doi:10.1123/jsep.2015-0166

Cheng, M. Y., Hung, C. L., Huang, C. J., Chang, Y. K., Lo, L. C., Shen, C., & Hung, T. M. (2015). Expert-novice differences in SMR activity during dart throwing. *Biological Psychology, 110*, 212–218. doi:10.1016/j.biopsycho.2015.08.003

Cheng, M. Y., Wang, K. P., Hung, C. L., Tu, Y. L., Huang, C. J., Koester, D., ... Hung, T. M. (2017). Higher power of sensorimotor rhythm is associated with better performance in skilled air-pistol shooters. *Psychology of Sport and Exercise, 32*, 47–53. doi:10.1016/j.psychsport.2017.05.007

Cheron, G., Petit, G., Cheron, J., Leroy, A., Cebolla, A., Cevallos, C., ... Dan, B. (2016). Brain oscillations in sport: Toward EEG biomarkers of performance. *Frontiers in Psychology, 7*, e246. doi:10.3389/fpsyg.2016.00246

Cooke, A., Bellomo, E., Gallicchio, G., Ring, C., Bellomo, E., Gallicchio, G., & Ring, C. (2018). Neurofeedback research in sport: A critical review of the field. In R. A. Carlstedt (Ed.), *Handbook of sport neuroscience and psychophysiology* (pp. 282–303). New York, NY: Routledge. doi:10.4324/9781315723693-13

Dekker, M. K. J., Van den Berg, B. R., Denissen, A. J. M., Sitskoorn, M. M., & van Boxtel, G. J. M. (2014). Feasibility of eyes open alpha power training for mental enhancement in elite gymnasts. *Journal of Sports Sciences, 32*, 1550–1560. doi:10.1080/02640414.2014.906044

Edvardsson, A., Ivarsson, A., & Johnson, U. (2012). Is a cognitive-behavioural biofeedback intervention useful to reduce injury. *Journal of Sports Science and Medicine 11*, 331–338. Retrieved from http://www.jssm.org

Enriquez-Geppert, S., Huster, R. J., Figge, C., & Herrmann, C. S. (2014). Self-regulation of frontal-midline theta facilitates memory updating and mental set shifting. *Frontiers in Behavioral Neuroscience, 8*, 1–13. doi:10.3389/fnbeh.2014.00420

Faridnia, M., Shojaei, M., & Rahimi, A. (2012). The effect of neurofeedback training on the anxiety of elite female swimmers. *Annals of Biological Research, 3*, 1020–1028. doi:10.22059/japr.2017.61078

Galloway, S. M. (2011). The effect of biofeedback on tennis service accuracy. *International Journal of Sport & Exercise Psychology, 9*, 251–266. doi:10.1080/1612197X.2011.614851

Goessl, V. C., Curtiss, J. E., & Hofmann, S. G. (2017). The effect of heart rate variability biofeedback training on stress and anxiety: A meta-analysis. *Psychological Medicine, 47,* 2578–2586. doi:10.1017/S0033291717001003

Gruzelier, J. H., Thompson, T., Redding, E., Brandt, R., & Steffert, T. (2014). Application of alpha/theta neurofeedback and heart rate variability training to young contemporary dancers: State anxiety and creativity. *International Journal of Psychophysiology, 93,* 105–111. doi:10.1016/j.ijpsycho.2013.05.004

Hatfield, B. D. (2018). Brain dynamics and motor behavior: A case for efficiency and refinement for superior performance. *Kinesiology Review,* 7, 42–50. doi:10.1123/kr.2017-0056

Hung, T. M., & Cheng, M. Y. (2018). Neurofeedback in sport: Theory, methods, research, and efficacy. In Roland A. Carlstedt (Ed.), *Handbook of sport neuroscience and psychophysiology* (pp. 304–319). New York, NY: Routledge. doi:10.4324/9781315723693-14

Jiménez Morgan, S., & Molina Mora, J. A. (2017). Effect of heart rate variability biofeedback on sport performance, a systematic review. *Applied Psychophysiology and Biofeedback, 42,* 235–245. doi:10.1007/s10484-017-9364-2

Kao, S. C., Huang, C. J., & Hung, T. M. (2014). Neurofeedback training reduces frontal midline theta and improves putting performance in expert golfers. *Journal of Applied Sport Psychology, 26,* 271–286. doi:10.1080/10413200.2013.855682

Kavussanu, M., Crews, D., & Gill, D. (1998). The effects of single versus multiple measures of biofeedback on basketball free throw shooting performance. *International Journal of Sport Psychology, 29,* 132–144.

Khazan, I. Z. (2019). *Biofeedback and mindfulness in everyday life.* New York, NY: WW Norton & Company.

Kober, S. E., Witte, M., Stangl, M., Väljamäe, A., Neuper, C., & Wood, G., (2015). Shutting down sensorimotor interference unblocks the networks for stimulus processing: An SMR neurofeedback training study. *Clinical Neurophysiology, 126,* 82–95. doi:10.1016/j.clinph.2014.03.031

Landers, D. M., Petruzzello, S. J., Salazar, W., Crews, D., Kubitz, K. A., Gannon, T. L., & Han, M. (1991). The influence of electrocortical biofeedback on performance in pre-elite archers. *Medicine & Science in Sports & Exercise, 23,* 123–129. doi:10.1249/00005768-199101000-00018

Levy, J. J., & Baldwin, D. R. (2019). Psychophysiology and biofeedback of sport performance. In M. H. Anshel, T. A. Petrie, & J. A. Steinfeldt (Eds.), *APA handbook of sport and exercise psychology* (pp. 745–758). Washington, DC: American Psychological Association. doi:10.1037/0000123-037

Lo, L.-C., Hatfield, B. D., Wu, C.-T., Chang, C.-C., & Hung, T.-M. (2019). Elevated state anxiety alters cerebral cortical dynamics and degrades precision cognitive-motor performance. *Sport, Exercise, and Performance Psychology, 8,* 21–37. doi:10.1037/spy0000155

Luijcks, R., Hermens, H. J., Bodar, L., Vossen, C. J., Van Os, J., & Lousberg, R. (2014). Experimentally induced stress validated by EMG activity. *PLoS ONE, 9,* e95215. doi:10.1371/journal.pone.0095215.g001

Maszczyk, A., Gołaś, A., Pietraszewski, P., Kowalczyk, M., Cięszczyk, P., Kochanowicz, A., ... & Zajac, A. (2018). Neurofeedback for the enhancement of dynamic balance of judokas. *Biology of Sport, 35,* 99–102. doi:10.5114/biolsport.2018.71488

Mirifar, A., Beckmann, J., & Ehrlenspiel, F. (2017). Neurofeedback as supplementary training for optimizing athletes' performance: A systematic review with implications for future research. *Neuroscience and Biobehavioral Reviews, 75,* 419–432. doi:10.1016/j.neubiorev.2017.02.005

Naito, E., & Hirose, S. (2014). Efficient foot motor control by Neymar's brain. *Frontiers in Human Neuroscience, 8*, e594. doi:10.3389/fnhum.2014.00594

Ortega, E., & Keng, J. W. C. (2018). Effectiveness of an integrated mental skills and biofeedback training program on sport shooters. *International Journal of Sport Psychology, 49*, 35–54. doi:10.7352/IJSP2018.49.035

Paul, M., Ganesan, S., Sandhu, J., & Simon, J. (2012). Effect of sensory motor rhythm neurofeedback on psycho-physiological, electro-encephalographic measures and performance of archery players. *Ibnosina Journal of Medicine and Biomedical Sciences, 4*, 32–39. doi:10.4103/1947-489X.210753

Paul, M., & Garg, K. (2012). The effect of heart rate variability biofeedback on performance psychology of basketball players. *Applied Psychophysiology Biofeedback, 37*, 131–144. doi:10.1007/s10484-012-9185-2

Posada-Quintero, H. F., Reljin, N., Mills, C., Mills, I., Florian, J. P., VanHeest, J. L., & Chon, K. H. (2018). Time-varying analysis of electrodermal activity during exercise. *PloS One, 13*, e0198328. doi:10.1371/journal.pone.0198328

Prapavessis, H., Grove, J. R., McNair, P. J., & Cable, N. T. (1992). Self-regulation training, state anxiety, and sport performance: A psychophysiological case study. *The Sport Psychologist, 6*, 213–229. doi:10.1123/tsp.6.3.213

Pusenjak, N., Grad, A., Tusak, M., Leskovsek, M., & Schwarzlin, R. (2015). Can biofeedback training of psychophysiological responses enhance athletes' sport performance? A practitioner's perspective. *Physician and Sportsmedicine, 43*, 287–299. doi: 10.1080/00913847.2015.1069169

Raymond, J., Sajid, I., Parkinson, L. A., & Gruzelier, J. H. (2005). Biofeedback and dance performance: A preliminary investigation. *Applied Psychophysiology Biofeedback, 30*, 65–73. doi:10.1007/s10484-005-2175-x

Ring, C., Cooke, A., Kavussanu, M., McIntyre, D., & Masters, R. (2015). Investigating the efficacy of neurofeedback training for expediting expertise and excellence in sport. *Psychology of Sport and Exercise, 16*, 118–127. doi:10.1016/j.psychsport.2014.08.005

Rostami, R., Sadeghi, H., Karami, K. A., Abadi, M. N., & Salamati, P. (2012). The effects of neurofeedback on the improvement of rifle shooters' performance. *Journal of Neurotherapy, 16*, 264–269. doi:10.1080/10874208.2012.730388

Shaw, L., Zaichkowsky, L., & Wilson, V. (2012). Setting the balance: Using biofeedback and neurofeedback with gymnasts. *Journal of Clinical Sport Psychology, 6*, 47–66. doi:10.1123/jcsp.6.1.47

Sherlin, L. H., Ford, N. C. L., Baker, A. R., & Troesch, J. (2015). Observational report of the effects of performance brain training in collegiate golfers. *Biofeedback, 43*, 64–72. doi:10.5298/1081-5937-43.2.06

Sherlin, L. H., Larson, N. C., & Sherlin, R. M. (2013). Developing a performance brain training™ approach for baseball: A process analysis with descriptive data. *Applied Psychophysiology Biofeedback, 38*(1), 29–44. doi:10.1007/s10484-012-9205-2

Skinner, B. F. (1963). Operant behavior. *American Psychologist, 18*, 503–515. doi:10.1037/h0045185

Sterman, M. B. (1996). Physiological origins and functional correlates of EEG rhythmic activities: Implications for self-regulation. *Biofeedback and Self-Regulation, 21*(1), 3–33. doi:10.1007/BF02214147

Strizhkova, O., Cherapkina, L., & Strizhkova, T. (2012). Neurofeedback course applying of high skilled gymnasts in competitive period. *Journal of Human Sport and Exercise, 7*, 11–14. doi:10.4100/jhse.2012.7.Proc1.21

Vealey, R. S. (2012). Mental skills training in sport. In G. Tenenbaum & R. C. Eklund (Eds.), *Handbook of sport psychology* (pp. 285–309). New York, NY: Routledge. doi:10.1002/9781118270011.ch13

Wakefield, J. C., & Shipherd, A. M. (2017). The effect of biofeedback training on one repetition maximum chest press performance. *International Journal of Exercise Science, 10*, 1105–1115. Retrieved from http://www.intjexersci.com

Xiang, M. Q., Hou, X. H., Liao, B. G., Liao, J. W., & Hu, M. (2018). The effect of neurofeedback training for sport performance in athletes: A meta-analysis. *Psychology of Sport and Exercise, 36*, 114–122. doi:10.1016/j.psychsport.2018.02.004

13

BRAIN STIMULATION TECHNIQUES AND SPORTS PERFORMANCE

Giulia Prete, Maurizio Bertollo, and Luca Tommasi

The continuous effort to enhance personal skills can be defined as the *leitmotiv* for athletes and sportsmen (Kellmann et al., 2018). In the majority of cases, this leads athletes to devote several hours each day to physical training and often to spend time on mental training. A number of new technological tools are now available to further enhance the effects of physical and mental training. The use of these technologies in different sports is a new window for sport psychologists and athletes in a period in which important findings in this field are emerging and evidence of their applied effects is now available (for a review, see Bertollo, Doppelmyr, & Robazza, 2020). In this chapter, we describe the basic functioning of these new techniques, mainly based on safe electrical stimulation of the nervous system. As it will be explained, current research suggests that these technologies could be a viable option to further improve the positive effects of physical and mental training on sport performance.

The birth of brain stimulation techniques: an overview

The use of electrical current to modulate brain activity has a long history (see Guleyupoglu, Schestatsky, Edwards, Fregni, & Bikson, 2013). Following the discovery of bioelectricity by Luigi Galvani (1791) and the invention of the first electrical battery by Alessandro Volta (1800), galvanic (or direct) current had already been applied to the nervous system more than two centuries ago with the aim to mitigate both neurological diseases (i.e., stroke effects; Hellwag & Jacobi, 1802) and psychiatric symptoms (i.e., melancholia; Aldini, 1804). Due to the inconsistent results attributable to the low-intensity electrical stimulation used, however, this kind of treatment was progressively abandoned. In the following century, electrical brain stimulation was resumed with higher intensity stimulation parameters, in the form of electroconvulsive therapy (Priori, 2003). With the use of this therapy, interest in the possible neurophysiological effects of a non-invasive low-intensity brain stimulation expanded greatly. In fact, a number of different methodologies emerged in neurology and psychiatry aimed at treating nervous and mental pathological conditions. In the cognitive neurosciences, different techniques have been developed to address activity modulation, among other potential applications (e.g., enhance mnemonic skills) in healthy individuals (for a review, see Bestmann & Walsh, 2017).

Among these techniques, the best known is transcranial direct current stimulation (tDCS), which consists of a low-intensity electrical stimulation (often applied with an intensity < 2 mA), released by means of at least two electrodes (Figure 13.1) placed over the scalp (bicephalic montage) or over the head and upper body (often on a shoulder). In tDCS, the current flows from one electrode to the other, with a specific polarization: the positive electrode (anode) delivers an excitatory (anodal) stimulation, whereas the negative electrode (cathode) delivers an inhibitory (cathodal) stimulation. In 1980, Merton and Morton, by means of electromyography, measured the motor evoked potentials (MEPs) elicited by tDCS applied over the motor area of healthy individuals, initiating the modern period of non-invasive transcranial electrical stimulation (tES; Merton & Morton, 1980).

In these pioneering applications, however, tES could be painful and lacked spatial resolution, and research subsequently shifted toward transcranial magnetic stimulation (TMS; Barker, Jalinous, & Freeston, 1985). TMS is applied by using

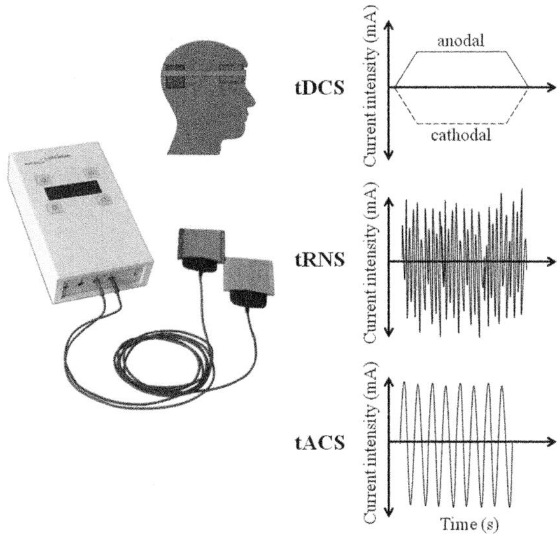

FIGURE 13.1 Example of tES montage on the scalp and transcranial electrical stimulation tool. On the right, tDCS, tRNS, and tACS waveforms are shown.

a coil, and the magnetic field directed by the coil induces an electrical current (Figure 13.2). When a coil is positioned over the scalp, the electrical current flows throughout the scalp and excites (depolarizes) cortical neurons. Compared to tES, TMS has the advantage of a higher spatial resolution, and it can be applied to inhibit or to excite cortical networks, based on the specific set-up used (e.g., single pulse, repetitive TMS, see below).

The vagus nerve stimulation (VNS) technique requires an invasive implantation of an electrical device in the cervical branch of the vagus nerve, and it is mainly used in the treatment of epilepsy (Giordano, Zicca, Barba, Guerrini, & Genitori, 2017). VNS is now applied transcutaneously (tVNS), in a non-invasive manner (Yuan & Silberstein, 2016): a low-intensity current is applied to the vagus nerve, the tenth cranial nerve, on the left ear (Figure 13.3). Importantly, the right ear stimulation is avoided because it contains the efferent vagus fibers to the heart (for a review, see Redgrave et al., 2018).

Among these stimulation techniques, tDCS has become the most popular, as it has been used for longer compared to the others. Different meta-analyses of the effects of tDCS protocols on sport performance have shown contrasting patterns of results. Some have found significant after effects of tDCS on muscle strength (Lattari et al., 2018), whereas other authors have observed a null effect of this technique on isometric, isokinetic, and dynamic strength (Machado et al., 2019) as well as on different indices of performance (Holgado, Vadillo, & Sanabria, 2019).

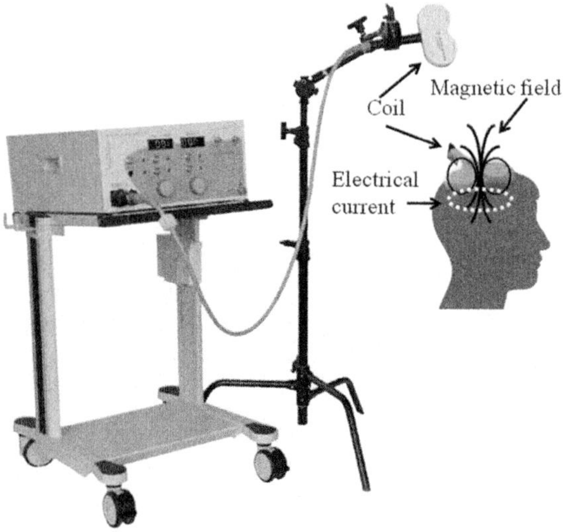

FIGURE 13.2 Left panel: transcranial magnetic stimulation tool; right panel: schematic representation of the magnetic field generated by the coil (black lines) and of the consequent electrical field reaching the brain (white dashed circle).

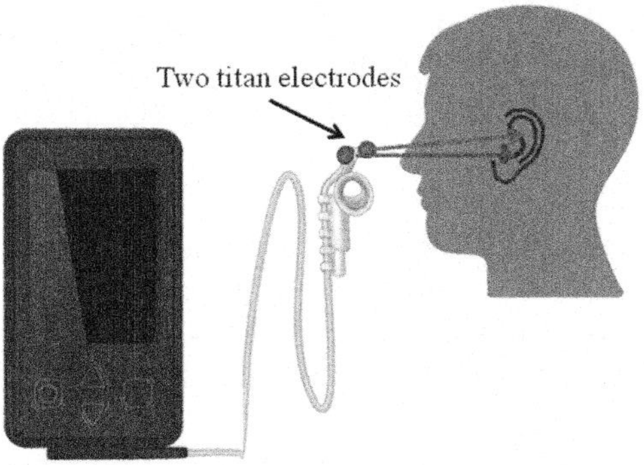

FIGURE 13.3 Left panel: transcranial vagus nerve stimulation (tVNS) tool; right panel: schematic representation of electrodes placement in the ear.

Effects of tDCS on movement and sports performance

At a neuronal level, the functioning of tDCS is based upon the modification of the resting membrane potentials, which can be depolarized (anodal stimulation) or hyperpolarized (cathodal stimulation) at a subthreshold level, inducing a consequent modulation of the spontaneous firing frequency of the cortical neurons (Paulus, Antal, & Nitsche, 2012). This means that the technique is not sufficient to "activate" a cerebral region, but that it modulates the firing activity of regions that are already activated by a given cognitive or motor task (Jackson et al., 2016). Its low spatial resolution has now been overcome by the introduction of high-density tDCS, in which – instead of two large electrodes – a number of small electrodes are placed over the scalp positions corresponding to the cerebral areas to be targeted (Datta et al., 2009). tDCS is often applied at low intensity (0.5–2 mA) for a variable period (5–20 min) and its effects are detectable during the stimulation itself and for minutes after the end of the stimulation, due to its influence on N-methyl-d-aspartate (NMDA) receptors, which in turn lead to neuronal mechanisms similar to those of long-term potentiation (LTP; Liebetanz, Nitsche, Tergau, & Paulus, 2002).

The first evidence of tDCS effects on motor skills was described by Polanía, Nitsche, and Paulus (2011), who applied anodal tDCS over the primary motor cortex (M1) and measured its effects by means of electroencephalography (EEG). The results revealed an increased functional connectivity in motor areas when anodal stimulation was applied during finger movements, with respect to both finger movement alone and tDCS alone. Similar results were then confirmed in stroke patients (Lefebvre et al., 2017), and thus tDCS protocols are currently used for rehabilitation purposes in such a clinical population (e.g., Kang, Summers, & Cauraugh, 2016). Notably, similar effects on functional connectivity induced by anodal tDCS applied over M1 have also been described in a motor imagery task (Baxter, Edelman, Sohrabpour, & He, 2017), confirming the effects of this neuromodulation technique during highly cognitive tasks, and its application to mental skills training.

In addition to its cortical effects, tDCS has also been shown to have behavioral effects. For instance, when applied to M1, tDCS engages a wide cortical network including a series of regions involved in pain control (Tsubokawa, Katayama, Yamamoto, Hirayama, & Koyama, 1991), and therefore tDCS protocols can be useful for the treatment of chronic pain (Baptista et al., 2019). Moreover, tDCS is a valid tool to improve motor learning and motor control as it has been shown to improve performance in a number of different bimanual motor tasks (for a review, see Pixa & Pollok, 2018) as well as to reduce reaction times in a finger tapping paradigm (Zich et al., 2017). Similarly, anodal tDCS on M1 has been shown to improve muscle endurance and decrease muscle fatigue (Cogiamanian, Marceglia, Ardolino, Barbieri, & Priori, 2007), and to increase exercise tolerance in a time-to-exhaustion cycling test (Vitor-Costa et al., 2015), revealing its potential in sports. Furthermore, Arias and colleagues (2016), not only confirmed a reduced sense of fatigue during tDCS but also found that both anodal and cathodal tDCS on M1 reduced reaction times in an arm-reaching task.

tDCS has also been applied over the cerebellum, which is a crucial area for motor regulation and learning. In this regard, it has been shown, for instance, that cerebellar tDCS improves motor learning (Doppelmayr, Pixa, & Steinberg, 2016). It has also been suggested that tDCS improves movement acquisition by decreasing motor error, whereas tDCS applied over M1 increases mnemonic retention of new motor experiences (Ehsani, Bakhtiary, Jaberzadeh, Talimkhani, & Hajihasani, 2016).

Despite differences due to the variability of stimulation parameters, electrode size, and electrode placement, previous research suggests that tDCS leads to electrophysiological and behavioral modifications that benefit performance in a variety of sports, including handball (Hazime et al., 2017), rowing (Liu et al., 2019), taekwondo (Mesquita, Lage, Franchini, Romano-Silva, & Albuquerque, 2019), running (Park, Sung, Kim, Kim, & Han, 2019), and bodybuilding (Kamali et al., 2019), among others (for a review, see Angius, Pascual-Leone, & Santarnecchi, 2018). For example, Hazime and colleagues (2017) measured maximal voluntary isometric contraction of shoulder external and internal rotator muscles in eight handball players, in four different moments: before tDCS, during the stimulation, 30 and 60 minutes after the end of the stimulation. tDCS was applied for 20 minutes at 2 mA of intensity, with the anode placed on M1 and the cathode placed on the contralateral supraorbital region. Results showed that the stimulation enhanced muscle contraction: for internal rotation, an enhancement of contraction was found 60 minutes after tDCS, and for external rotation, the enhancement was found both at 30 and at 60 minutes after the end of the stimulation. Liu et al. (2019) used tDCS to evaluate the prolonged exposition to the stimulation on performance, fatigue perception, and brain activity in a group of professional rowing athletes. In two groups of athletes, they applied tDCS at either 1 mA or 2 mA (between-subjects paradigm) for 20 minutes in each session, for five sessions/week for two consecutive weeks. The main findings of the study were that (a) there were a few differences between the two groups, revealing that 1 mA was enough to modulate both performance and brain activity; (b) no effects were found on perceived fatigue; (c) an enhanced performance was found, as measured by means of lactate threshold power, stamina, and explosive force; and (d) an increased interhemispheric coordination was revealed by means of fMRI.

Different electrical stimulation techniques: tRNS and tACS

In tDCS, current polarity (i.e., anodal and cathodal stimulation) is a crucial parameter, whereas in transcranial random noise stimulation (tRNS) and transcranial alternating current stimulation (tACS), the crucial parameters are frequency range and the specific frequency of the stimulation, which are not polarity dependent (see Paulus et al., 2012). Importantly, the intensity of the stimulation can influence the polarity of tRNS and tACS, with lower intensities (0.4 mA) causing inhibition, and higher intensities (1 mA) inducing excitation (Moliadze, Atalay, Antal, & Paulus, 2012). Specifically, tRNS consists of an alternate current with random frequency (from 0.1 Hz to 640 Hz) and amplitude (see Figure 13.1). In tACS, an oscillating current is applied in the frequency ranges of EEG, and it creates sinusoidal subthreshold modulation of neuronal membrane potentials (see Figure 13.1).

Concerning the motor areas, it has been found that tACS applied at 1–5 kHz on M1 exerts similar effects as anodal tDCS (Chaieb, Antal, & Paulus, 2011), as it interferes with ongoing cortical neurons oscillations. However, reduced MEPs were found when tACS was applied on M1 at 15 Hz (Zaghi et al., 2010), possibly due to an interference of this frequency with spatial and temporal summation of subthreshold potentials. On the other hand, tRNS applied on M1 at full spectrum of frequency (1–640 Hz) has been found to induce a decrement of cortical activity during a finger tapping task (Chaieb et al., 2009).

Despite some evidence suggesting that tRNS would be more efficient compared to the other tES techniques when motor areas are stimulated (Inukai et al., 2016), the majority of applied studies have made use of tDCS, possibly because its mechanisms are better understood. For instance, in a recent study, tACS was applied to the parietal cortex either at 10 Hz or at 20 Hz, and bimanual coordination was evaluated, with the results revealing increased alpha activity in the parietal areas (Berger, Pixa, Steinberg, & Doppelmayr, 2018). On the other hand, a pilot study on a skilled air-pistol shooter (Tommasi et al., 2015) showed that tRNS applied at high frequency (101–640 Hz) on the right parietal and left orbitofrontal cortex improved shooting performance.

It is clear that the effects of tRNS and tACS on sport performance should be explored further. Basic research as well as empirical findings on the effects of tACS on the motor system are promising and warrant further investigation. To date, however, little is known in this field, and any conclusion about their potential application in sports is premature.

Effects of TMS on motor performance

Trancranial magnetic stimulation (TMS) also alters the electrical current, which is induced by means of a magnetic field and ultimately reaches cortical neurons. During TMS, a rapid (around 100–200 μs) and powerful (0.2–4 T) magnetic field is delivered by means of a coil placed on the scalp, which induces a depolarization of the targeted neurons (see Figure 13.2). Regarding TMS, we can refer to two types of stimulation: single-pulse TMS (including paired-pulse TMS, in which two pulses are applied on the same area with a variable inter-stimulus interval) and repetitive TMS (rTMS). Single-pulse TMS is used to interfere with cerebral functioning at a given moment, whereas rTMS is mostly used to generate changes sustained over time (for minutes after the end of the stimulation). When applied over motor areas, TMS induces MEPs visible by means of EEG, but it can also produce an involuntary twitch of the target muscle. The effects induced by TMS can be excitatory or inhibitory depending on stimulation frequency and intensity, as well as the form of the coil used and the configuration of the electrical field generated (see Lefaucheur, 2019).

Compared to tES, TMS has the advantage of a higher spatial resolution insofar that its application on a specific site of the motor areas can stimulate a specific muscular district (Ross, Middleton, Shave, George, & Nowicky, 2007; Sidhu, Bentley, & Carroll, 2009). However, TMS is more expensive, less portable, and requires a precise localization of the target area. As such, TMS is not a "do-it-yourself" tool but requires an equipped laboratory. TMS protocols are widely exploited in the research field but are less frequently used to modulate sport performance with online stimulation.

Relevant to motor performance broadly conceived, TMS research has revealed that motor neuron responses to observation of an action are dependent upon the specific motor requirements of that same action (Behrendt, de Lussanet, Zentgraf, & Zschorlich, 2016; Gangitano, Mottaghy, & Pascual-Leone, 2001), possibly by means of the mirror neuron system (Rizzolatti & Craighero, 2004). In particular, this research field is mostly focused on the role of the motor system in (a) anticipating motor actions in sport-specific domains, (b) detecting the motor system activation itself, often comparing the responses of athletes with those of non-athletes, and (c) evaluating the cortical effects of movement fatigue. Although basic research sheds light on the physiological basis of sport-related performance, further investigations are needed to establish the link between TMS and performance improvement in sports.

A new frontier of electrical neurostimulation in sport: tVNS

In contrast to the neurostimulation techniques described so far, tVNS is applied either on the ear (auricular branch of the vagus nerve, applied by means of a wearable earphone; see Figure 13.3) or on the neck (cervical branch of the vagus nerve), instead of being directly applied on the scalp. Nonetheless, its effects reach a wider cerebral area than cortical neuromodulation due to tES and TMS. The vagus nerve, in fact, also affects subcortical regions, such as the thalamus, hypothalamus, cerebellum, limbic structures, and orbitofrontal cortex (e.g., Chae et al., 2003). The parameters to be set in tVNS are intensity (1–10 mA; adjusted with respect to the individual threshold), frequency (0.5–120 Hz), pulse width (0.1–1 s), and cycles (i.e., duration of the active stimulation and inter-stimulation interval; for a review, see Redgrave et al., 2018). Although the exact mechanisms of action of tVNS are not yet understood, it has been shown that it causes immediate and long-term changes in the cerebral areas reached by the vagus nerve (Kaniusas et al., 2019). The most acknowledged explanation of its effects posits that the nerve stimulation affects the level of norepinephrine concentration, mainly by reaching the *locus coeruleus*, and thus it affects arousal (Aston-Jones & Cohen, 2005) and increases GABA and noradrenaline levels (Keute, Boehere, Ruhnau, Heinze, & Zaehle, 2019). In turn, it is well established that high levels of GABA are related to the reciprocal inhibition of competing responses, possibly leading to the suppression of the "wrong" response in favor of the faster activation of the "correct" one (de la Vega et al., 2014). Based on this rationale, it has been suggested that tVNS could help to enhance motor learning (Stagg, Bachtiar, & Johansen-Berg, 2011). Thus, this technique could be exploited with the aim to improve sport performance in a non-invasive manner (Colzato, 2017).

Effects of neuromodulation on sports performance: an ethical issue

Although the use of neuromodulation techniques is widely considered a clear advancement in clinical practice and research, its application in sport is more controversial. When we speak about neuromodulation protocols used to improve the performance of an athlete, a legitimate question arises: Is there an ethical difference between performance-enhancing drugs and brain stimulation used for performance enhancement? The ethical implication of external aids aimed at improving the performance of an individual has led some authors to introduce a new keyword into the world of amateur and professional athletes: "Neurodoping" (e.g., see Davis, 2013). Neurodoping (or brain-doping), in turn, covers stimulation techniques used to improve the performance measured either at a *given present moment* (e.g., to reduce response times, to increase spatial precision, or reduce the sense of fatigue) or at *a past moment* (i.e., in the learning or training phase). It has been shown, in fact, that neuromodulation protocols improve memory consolidation in the learning phase (e.g., Reis et al., 2009), so that it becomes difficult to detect the possible (current or previous) use of such techniques.

Conclusions

Transcranial and transcutaneous stimulation techniques are increasingly used today, and the interest in their potential benefits has expanded in the past two decades. As discussed, their use in ecologically valid settings remains largely unexplored, but their potential in modifying cerebral, mental, and physical performance is under consideration by clinical, basic, and applied researchers, including sport professionals. All of the methodologies briefly described in this chapter (i.e., tDCS, tRNS, tACS, TMS, and tVNS) are considered harmless and useful to improve cognitive activity or performance. Indeed, their use is accepted by the Food and Drug Administration (the federal U.S. agency, responsible for protecting and promoting public health), and they are not considered "prohibited methods" by the World Anti-Doping Agency (WADA). To this extent, it is important to highlight the ethical issues raised by these new methodologies. If mental training is aimed at improving the mental skills of athletes to enhance their physical performance, is there an ethical difference between mental training, physical exercise, and brain potentiation possibly induced by these techniques? If it is true that their use is not detectable, one should consider that mental training as well as psychotherapy, for instance, are not objectively detectable either. Similarly, the effects of some stimulating substances (e.g., cigarettes, coffee) on the nervous system are well known, although many of them are not considered dangerous nor banned from sport practice (at least up to certain levels). Accordingly, additional research on the ethical implications of neuromodulation techniques is a ripe area of investigation.

To summarize, the neurostimulation techniques can be safe if they are applied at low intensities (< 4 mA) for a duration not longer than one hour/day (see Antal et al., 2017), although their impact depends upon a number of parameters (e.g., dimension and placement of the electrodes, frequency of their application). Given that little evidence is available about neurostimulation techniques applied to sports, it is difficult to suggest specific guidelines for their "correct" use, but we highlight that such techniques should not be administered without expert advice.

References

Aldini, G. (1804). *Essai theorique et experimental sur le galvanisme, 2 vols*. Paris, France: Fournier.

Angius, L., Pascual-Leone, A., & Santarnecchi, E. (2018). Brain stimulation and physical performance. *Progress in Brain Research*, *240*, 317–339. doi:10.1016/bs.pbr.2018.07.010

Antal, A., Alekseichuk, I., Bikson, M., Brockmöller, J., Brunoni, A. R., Chen, R., … & Fregni, F. (2017). Low intensity transcranial electric stimulation: Safety, ethical, legal regulatory and application guidelines. *Clinical Neurophysiology*, *128*, 1774–1809. doi:10.1016/j.clinph.2017.06.001

Arias, P., Corral-Bergantiños, Y., Robles-García, V., Madrid, A., Oliviero, A., & Cudeiro, J. (2016). Bilateral tDCS on primary motor cortex: Effects on fast arm reaching tasks. *PloS One*, *11*, e0160063. doi:10.1371/journal.pone.0160063

Aston-Jones, G., & Cohen, J. D. (2005). An integrative theory of locus coeruleus-norepinephrine function: Adaptive gain and optimal performance. *Annual Review of Neuroscience*, *28*, 403–450. doi:10.1146/annurev.neuro.28.061604.135709

Baptista, A. F., Fernandes, A. M. B., Sá, K. N., Okano, A. H., Brunoni, A. R., Lara-Solares, A., ... & Caparelli-Daquer, E. (2019). Latin American and Caribbean consensus on noninvasive central nervous system neuromodulation for chronic pain management (LAC2-NIN-CP). *Pain Reports, 4*, e692. doi:10.1097/PR9.0000000000000692

Barker, A. T., Jalinous, R., & Freeston, I. L. (1985). Non-invasive magnetic stimulation of human motor cortex. *The Lancet, 325*, 1106–1107. doi:10.1016/S0140-6736(85)92413-4

Baxter, B. S., Edelman, B. J., Sohrabpour, A., & He, B. (2017). Anodal transcranial direct current stimulation increases bilateral directed brain connectivity during motor-imagery based brain-computer interface control. *Frontiers in Neuroscience, 11*, e691. doi:10.3389/fnins.2017.00691

Behrendt, F., de Lussanet, M. H., Zentgraf, K., & Zschorlich, V. R. (2016). Motor-evoked potentials in the lower back are modulated by visual perception of lifted weight. *PloS One, 11*, e0157811. doi:10.1371/journal.pone.0157811

Berger, A., Pixa, N. H., Steinberg, F., & Doppelmayr, M. (2018). Brain oscillatory and hemodynamic activity in a bimanual coordination task following transcranial alternating current stimulation (tACS): A combined EEG-fNIRS study. *Frontiers in Behavioral Neuroscience, 12*, e67. doi:10.3389/fnbeh.2018.00067

Bertollo, M., Doppelmayr, M., & Robazza, C. (2020). Using brain technology in practice. In G. Tenenbaum & R. Eklund (Eds.), *Handbook of sport psychology* (4th ed., pp. 666–693). Hoboken, NJ: Wiley-Blackwell.

Bestmann, S., & Walsh, V. (2017). Transcranial electrical stimulation. *Current Biology, 27*, R1258–R1262. doi:10.1016/j.cub.2017.11.001

Chae, J. H., Nahas, Z., Lomarev, M., Denslow, S., Lorberbaum, J. P., Bohning, D. E., & George, M. S. (2003). A review of functional neuroimaging studies of vagus nerve stimulation (VNS). *Journal of Psychiatric Research, 37*, 443–455. doi:10.1016/s0022-3956(03)00074-8

Chaieb, L., Antal, A., & Paulus, W. (2011). Transcranial alternating current stimulation in the low kHz range increases motor cortex excitability. *Restorative Neurology and Neuroscience, 29*, 167–175. doi:10.3233/RNN-2011-0589

Chaieb, L., Kovacs, G., Cziraki, C., Greenlee, M., Paulus, W., & Antal, A. (2009). Short-duration transcranial random noise stimulation induces blood oxygenation level dependent response attenuation in the human motor cortex. *Experimental Brain Research, 198*, 439–444. doi:10.1007/s00221-009-1938-7

Cogiamanian, F., Marceglia, S. A. R. A., Ardolino, G., Barbieri, S., & Priori, A. (2007). Improved isometric force endurance after transcranial direct current stimulation over the human motor cortical areas. *European Journal of Neuroscience, 26*, 242–249. doi:10.1111/j.1460-9568.2007.05633.x

Colzato, L. S. (Ed.). (2017). *Theory-driven approaches to cognitive enhancement*. New York, NY: Springer.

Datta, A., Bansal, V., Diaz, J., Patel, J., Reato, D., & Bikson, M. (2009). Gyri-precise head model of transcranial direct current stimulation: Improved spatial focality using a ring electrode versus conventional rectangular pad. *Brain Stimulation, 2*, 201–207. doi:10.1016/j.brs.2009.03.005

Davis, N. J. (2013). Neurodoping: Brain stimulation as a performance-enhancing measure. *Sports Medicine, 43*, 649–653. doi:10.1007/s40279-013-0027-z

de la Vega, A., Brown, M. S., Snyder, H. R., Singel, D., Munakata, Y., & Banich, M. T. (2014). Individual differences in the balance of GABA to glutamate in pFC predict the ability to select among competing options. *Journal of Cognitive Neuroscience, 26*, 2490–2502. doi:10.1162/jocn_a_00655

Doppelmayr, M., Pixa, N. H., & Steinberg, F. (2016). Cerebellar, but not motor or parietal, high-density anodal transcranial direct current stimulation facilitates motor adaptation. *Journal of the International Neuropsychological Society, 22*, 928–936. doi:10.1017/S1355617716000345

Ehsani, F., Bakhtiary, A. H., Jaberzadeh, S., Talimkhani, A., & Hajihasani, A. (2016). Differential effects of primary motor cortex and cerebellar transcranial direct current stimulation on motor learning in healthy individuals: A randomized double-blind sham-controlled study. *Neuroscience Research, 112*, 10–19. doi:10.1016/j.neures.2016.06.003

Galvani, L. (1791). *De viribus electricitatis in motu muscolari: Commentarius*. Bononiae: Ex Typographia Instituti Scientiarum.

Gangitano, M., Mottaghy, F. M., & Pascual-Leone, A. (2001). Phase-specific modulation of cortical motor output during movement observation. *Neuroreport, 12*, 1489–1492. doi:10.1097/00001756-200105250-00038

Giordano, F., Zicca, A., Barba, C., Guerrini, R., & Genitori, L. (2017). Vagus nerve stimulation: Surgical technique of implantation and revision and related morbidity. *Epilepsia, 58*, 85–90. doi:10.1111/epi.13678

Guleyupoglu, B., Schestatsky, P., Edwards, D., Fregni, F., & Bikson, M. (2013). Classification of methods in transcranial electrical stimulation (tES) and evolving strategy from historical approaches to contemporary innovations. *Journal of Neuroscience Methods, 219*, 297–311. doi:10.1016/j.jneumeth.2013.07.016.

Hazime, F. A., da Cunha, R. A., Soliaman, R. R., Romancini, A. C. B., de Castro Pochini, A., Ejnisman, B., & Baptista, A. F. (2017). Anodal transcranial direct current stimulation (TDCS) increases isometric strength of shoulder rotators muscles in handball players. *International Journal of Sports Physical Therapy, 12*, 402.

Hellwag, C. F. (1802). *Erfahrungen über die heilkräfte des galvanismus, und betrachtungen über desselben chemische und physiologische wirkungen*. Hamburg, Germany: Friedrich Perthes.

Holgado, D., Vadillo, M. A., & Sanabria, D. (2019). The effects of transcranial direct current stimulation on objective and subjective indexes of exercise performance: A systematic review and meta-analysis. *Brain Stimulation, 12*, 242–250. doi:10.1016/j.brs.2018.12.002

Inukai, Y., Saito, K., Sasaki, R., Tsuiki, S., Miyaguchi, S., Kojima, S., … & Onishi, H. (2016). Comparison of three non-invasive transcranial electrical stimulation methods for increasing cortical excitability. *Frontiers in Human Neuroscience, 10*, e668. doi:10.3389/fnhum.2016.00668

Jackson, M. P., Rahman, A., Lafon, B., Kronberg, G., Ling, D., Parra, L. C., & Bikson, M. (2016). Animal models of transcranial direct current stimulation: Methods and mechanisms. *Clinical Neurophysiology, 127*, 3425–3454. doi:10.1016/j.clinph.2016.08.016

Kamali, A. M., Saadi, Z. K., Yahyavi, S. S., Zarifkar, A., Aligholi, H., & Nami, M. (2019). Transcranial direct current stimulation to enhance athletic performance outcome in experienced bodybuilders. *PloS One, 14*, e0220363. doi:10.1371/journal.pone.0220363

Kang, N., Summers, J. J., & Cauraugh, J. H. (2016). Transcranial direct current stimulation facilitates motor learning post-stroke: A systematic review and meta-analysis. *Journal of Neurology, Neurosurgery, and Psychiatry, 87*, 345–355. doi:10.1136/jnnp-2015-311242

Kaniusas, E., Kampusch, S., Tittgemeyer, M., Panetsos, F., Gines, R. F., Papa, M., … & Samoudi, A. M. (2019). Current directions in the auricular vagus nerve stimulation I – A physiological perspective. *Frontiers in Neuroscience, 13*, e854. doi:10.3389/fnins.2019.00854

Kellmann, M., Bertollo, M., Bosquet, L., Brink, M., Coutts, A. J., Duffield, R., … & Kallus, K. W. (2018). Recovery and performance in sport: Consensus statement. *International Journal of Sports Physiology and Performance, 13*, 240–245. doi:10.1123/ijspp.2017-0759

Keute, M., Boehere, L., Ruhnau, P., Heinze, H. J., & Zaehle, T. (2019). Transcutaneous vagus nerve stimulation (tVNS) and the dynamics of visual bistable perception. *Frontiers in Neuroscience, 13*, e227. doi:10.3389/fnins.2019.00227

Lattari, E., Oliveira, B. R., Júnior, R. S. M., Neto, S. R. M., Oliveira, A. J., Neto, G. A. M., … & Budde, H. (2018). Acute effects of single dose transcranial direct current stimulation on muscle strength: A systematic review and meta-analysis. *PloS One, 13*, e0209513. doi:10.1371/journal.pone.0209513

Lefaucheur, J. P. (2019). Transcranial magnetic stimulation. In K. H. Levin, & Chauvel, P. (Eds.), *Handbook of clinical neurology* (Vol. 160, pp. 559–580). Amsterdam, Holland: Elsevier. doi:10.1016/B978-0-444-64032-1.00037-0

Lefebvre, S., Dricot, L., Laloux, P., Desfontaines, P., Evrard, F., Peeters, A., … & Vandermeeren, Y. (2017). Increased functional connectivity one week after motor learning and tDCS in stroke patients. *Neuroscience, 340*, 424–435. doi:10.1016/j.neuroscience.2016.10.066

Liebetanz, D., Nitsche, M. A., Tergau, F., & Paulus, W. (2002). Pharmacological approach to the mechanisms of transcranial DC-stimulation-induced after-effects of human motor cortex excitability. *Brain, 125*, 2238–2247. doi:10.1093/brain/awf238

Liu, X., Yang, X., Hou, Z., Ma, M., Jiang, W., Wang, C., … & Yuan, Y. (2019). Increased interhemispheric synchrony underlying the improved athletic performance of rowing athletes by transcranial direct current stimulation. *Brain Imaging and Behavior, 13*, 1324–1332. doi:10.1007/s11682-018-9948-3

Machado, D. G. D. S., Unal, G., Andrade, S. M., Moreira, A., Altimari, L. R., Brunoni, A. R., … & Okano, A. H. (2019). Effect of transcranial direct current stimulation on exercise performance: A systematic review and meta-analysis. *Brain Stimulation, 12*, 593–605. doi:10.1016/j.brs.2018.12.227

Merton, P. A., & Morton, H. B. (1980). Stimulation of the cerebral cortex in the intact human subject. *Nature, 285*, 227–227. doi:10.1038/285227a0

Mesquita, P. H. C., Lage, G. M., Franchini, E., Romano-Silva, M. A., & Albuquerque, M. R. (2019). Bi-hemispheric anodal transcranial direct current stimulation worsens taekwondo-related performance. *Human Movement Science, 66*, 578–586. doi:10.1016/j.humov.2019.06.003

Moliadze, V., Atalay, D., Antal, A., & Paulus, W. (2012). Close to threshold transcranial electrical stimulation preferentially activates inhibitory networks before switching to excitation with higher intensities. *Brain Stimulation, 5*, 505–511. doi:10.1016/j.brs.2011.11.004

Park, S. B., Sung, D. J., Kim, B., Kim, S., & Han, J. K. (2019). Transcranial direct current stimulation of motor cortex enhances running performance. *PloS One, 14*, e0211902. doi:10.1371/journal.pone.0211902

Paulus, W., Antal, A., & Nitsche, M. A. (2012). Physiological basis and methodological aspects of transcranial electric stimulation (tDCS, tACS and tRNS). In C. Miniussi, W. Paulus, & P. M. Rossini, (Eds.), *Transcranial brain stimulation* (pp. 93–111). Boca Raton, FL: CRC Press.

Pixa, N. H., & Pollok, B. (2018). Effects of tDCS on bimanual motor skills: A brief review. *Frontiers in Behavioral Neuroscience, 12*, e63. doi:10.3389/fnbeh.2018.00063

Polanía, R., Nitsche, M. A., & Paulus, W. (2011). Modulating functional connectivity patterns and topological functional organization of the human brain with transcranial direct current stimulation. *Human Brain Mapping, 32*, 1236–1249. doi:10.1002/hbm.21104

Priori, A. (2003). Brain polarization in humans: A reappraisal of an old tool for prolonged non-invasive modulation of brain excitability. *Clinical Neurophysiology, 114*, 589–595. doi:10.1016/s1388-2457(02)00437-6

Redgrave, J., Day, D., Leung, H., Laud, P. J., Ali, A., Lindert, R., & Majid, A. (2018). Safety and tolerability of transcutaneous vagus nerve stimulation in humans; a systematic review. *Brain Stimulation, 11*, 1225–1238. doi:10.1016/j.brs.2018.08.010

Reis, J., Schambra, H. M., Cohen, L. G., Buch, E. R., Fritsch, B., Zarahn, E., … & Krakauer, J. W. (2009). Noninvasive cortical stimulation enhances motor skill acquisition over multiple days through an effect on consolidation. *Proceedings of the National Academy of Sciences, 106*, 1590–1595. doi:10.1073/pnas.0805413106

Rizzolatti, G., & Craighero, L. (2004). The mirror-neuron system. *Annual Review of Neuroscience, 27*, 169–192. doi:10.1146/annurev.neuro.27.070203.144230

Ross, E. Z., Middleton, N., Shave, R., George, K., & Nowicky, A. (2007). Corticomotor excitability contributes to neuromuscular fatigue following marathon running in man. *Experimental Physiology, 92*, 417–426. doi:10.1113/expphysiol.2006.035972

Sidhu, S. K., Bentley, D. J., & Carroll, T. J. (2009). Locomotor exercise induces long-lasting impairments in the capacity of the human motor cortex to voluntarily activate knee extensor muscles. *Journal of Applied Physiology, 106*, 556–565. doi:10.1152/japplphysiol.90911.2008

Stagg, C. J., Bachtiar, V., & Johansen-Berg, H. (2011). The role of GABA in human motor learning. *Current Biology, 21*, 480–484. doi:10.1016/j.cub.2011.01.069

Tommasi, V., Prete, G., di Fronso, S., Schinaia, L., Lucafò, C., Tommasi, L., … & Bertollo, M. (2015). The effect of tRNS on performance: A pilot study with a skilled air-pistol shooter. *Biofeedback, 43*, 84–89. doi:10.5298/1081-5937-43.2.02

Tsubokawa, T., Katayama, Y., Yamamoto, T., Hirayama, T., & Koyama, S. (1991). Chronic motor cortex stimulation for the treatment of central pain. In E. R. Hitchcock, G. Broggi, J. Burzaco, J. Martin-Rodriguez, B. A. Meyerson, & S. Tóth (Eds.), *Advances in stereotactic and functional neurosurgery 9. Acta Neurochirurgica Supplementum* (Vol. 52; pp. 137–139). Vienna, Austria: Springer. doi:10.1007/978-3-7091-9160-6_37

Vitor-Costa, M., Okuno, N. M., Bortolotti, H., Bertollo, M., Boggio, P. S., Fregni, F., & Altimari, L. R. (2015). Improving cycling performance: Transcranial direct current stimulation increases time to exhaustion in cycling. *PloS One, 10*, e0144916. doi:10.1371/journal.pone.0144916

Volta, A. (1800). XVII. On the electricity excited by the mere contact of conducting substances of different kinds. In a letter from Mr. Alexander Volta, F. R. S. Professor of Natural Philosophy in the University of Pavia, to the Rt. Hon. Sir Joseph Banks, Bart. K. B. P. R. S. *Philosophical Transactions of the Royal Society of London, 90*, 403–431.

Yuan, H., & Silberstein, S. D. (2016). Vagus nerve and vagus nerve stimulation, a comprehensive review: Part II. *Headache: The Journal of Head and Face Pain, 56*, 259–266. doi:10.1111/head.12650

Zaghi, S., de Freitas Rezende, L., de Oliveira, L. M., El-Nazer, R., Menning, S., Tadini, L., & Fregni, F. (2010). Inhibition of motor cortex excitability with 15 Hz transcranial alternating current stimulation (tACS). *Neuroscience Letters, 479*, 211–214. doi:10.1007/s00429-016-1355-1

Zich, C., Harty, S., Kranczioch, C., Mansfield, K. L., Sella, F., Debener, S., & Kadosh, R. C. (2017). Modulating hemispheric lateralization by brain stimulation yields gain in mental and physical activity. *Scientific Reports, 7*, e13430. doi:10.1038/s41598-017-13795-1

14

VIRTUAL REALITY AND MENTAL TRAINING

Cornelia Frank

The nature of virtual reality

In both research and applied sport settings, Virtual Reality (VR) is a rapidly growing field. VR as a simulation of the real world can be distinguished from augmented realities: On a virtuality continuum (Milgram & Kishino, 1994), VR is at one end with the real world at the other end, whereas augmented reality (AR) lies between the two, a primarily real environment augmented by virtual aspects. Thus, in contrast to AR, VR in the domain of sport is considered "as instances when individuals are engaged in a sport that is represented in a computer-simulated environment which aims to induce a sense of being mentally or physically present and enables interactivity with the environment" (Neumann et al., 2018, p. 185). Immersion is the essential criterion for VR, allowing humans "to participate in the virtual world rather than use it" (Slater & Sanchez-Vives, 2016, p. 3). Although one goal of VR is to simulate reality, VR can be more than a copy of our real world: "the real power of VR is to go beyond what is real, it is more than simulation, it is also creation, allowing us to step out of the bounds of reality and experience paradigms that are otherwise impossible" (Slater & Sanchez-Vives, 2016, p. 2). In the domain of sports, VR allows not only for recreating sports and training environments (e.g., Gray, 2017) but also for creating new experiences (e.g., Hülsmann, Frank, Senna, Ernst, Schack, & Botsch, 2019).

Main components of an interactive VR system

From a minimal point of view, an interactive VR environment is a 3D virtual world displayed by a computer. It entails graphics and a renderer to deliver images to the athlete's eyes, while tracking the athlete's head position and orientation, and allowing him to interact with the system, such as in full-body motion tracking and action displays (Slater & Sanchez-Vives, 2016). The input part of the system conveys information by way of sensors (such as optical motion tracking) and subsequent sensor fusion. A model of the world generates the virtual world and the output part of the system delivers information through a renderer and output devices (such as a display). An interactive VR system thus produces stimuli that let the athlete perceive a virtual world, considers the athlete's actions, and simulates the world as a result of these actions (Miles, Pop, Watt, Lawrence, & John, 2012; for more details on human-centered design, see, Jerald, 2015). Finally, VR systems can furthermore be distinguished according to whether they include avatars that interact with the athlete, such as a virtual mirror image, a virtual coach, a virtual competitor, or a virtual audience (de Kok et al., 2017; Wellner, Sigrist, & Riener, 2010; Wellner, Sigrist, Zitzewitz, Wolf, & Riener, 2010).

The most common immersive VR devices to date are head mounted displays (HMD) or cave automatic virtual environments (CAVE), of which both can create immersion, despite their very different setups. Using an HMD, the athlete wears the device on her/his head and does not see anything of the real world. S/he is fully immersed in a virtual environment that is created directly in front of her/his eyes. Experiencing VR with an HMD thus produces a virtual environment in full size, but without seeing one's own real body as part of this virtual world. In a CAVE, the athlete enters a room onto which the virtual environment is projected and allows the athlete to freely move together with perceiving her/his real body in this environment.

Embodiment in interactive VR

Embodiment in VR refers to the sensations related to having and being inside a body in a virtual environment and to controlling it (Kilteni, Groten, & Slater, 2012). An interactive VR system is not necessarily one that makes the athlete feel like being part of this particular world. To allow the athlete to feel embodied in the VR environment, rather than the laboratory environment, an interactive VR system must be able to effectively substitute the sensory components. According to Slater and Sanchez-Vives (2016), critical factors for effective sensory substitution are a wide field of view to cover the natural field of view of the athlete, stereo projection to create a 3D experience for the athlete, and head tracking to update the virtual world according to the athlete's position and orientation. Furthermore, low latency allows the athlete a nearly real-time experience; a high resolution of displays delivers images of high quality; and a multimodal substitution of senses, if possible, provides the athlete not only with visual but also with auditory or tactile information.

This said, the embodied experience of the athlete in the virtual world depends heavily on the level of immersion and the sensory and motor engagement, which in turn is dependent on the system's technical characteristics (Biocca, 1997). Subjectively, whether or not this results in "a feeling of being there" for the athlete pertains to the notion of presence. Presence relates to the inner experience of the athlete while being in the virtual environment and reflects an illusion of being there, even though one is physically not there (Slater, 2009; Witmer & Singer, 1998). In addition, the sense of agency and body ownership are two of the most critical factors for an embodied interactive experience in VR (Kilteni et al., 2012), as originally conceptualized in the realm of a minimal self by Gallagher (2000). Hence, if an athlete perceives that s/he owns the body s/he is experiencing in VR simulation, and is in control of her/his actions, then the interaction is likely to be an embodied experience and thus a successful one (see Kilteni et al., 2012).

VR and mental training

While VR in sports has been primarily used for leisure and entertainment reasons, researchers and practitioners have started to explore its potential for performance, learning, and coaching across a variety of individual and team sports (for reviews, see Gray, 2019; Miles, Pop, Watt, Lawrence, & John, 2012; Neumann et al., 2018). Research using VR in the area of sport has shown that VR can affect a variety of performance-related factors (e.g., decision-making: Craig, 2013), that it can speed up motor learning (e.g., feedback: Todorov, Shadmehr, & Bizzi, 1997), and that it has the potential to transfer to real sports (e.g., Gray, 2017). The potentials of VR for mental training, however, remain to be explored. During mental training (and in contrast to physical training), psychological techniques are used in a systematic manner to practice and develop psychological skills (e.g., self-confidence or attentional control) in order to improve performance and to succeed in sport (Cox, 2011). Accordingly, mental training includes techniques such as imagery, observation, goal-setting, self-talk, or biofeedback. Virtual training as a controllable simulation of the real world may thus be a valuable adjunct to optimize mental training outcomes. The few studies conducted in the realm of mental training in VR have so far looked at questions relating to anxiety and pressure, attentional focus, biofeedback and breathing, feedback during action observation, and imagery.

Anxiety/pressure

Along the lines of using VR for exposure therapy to treat phobias, Stinson and Bowman (2014) developed a resilience training system for athletes to simulate and practice high-pressure situations. For this purpose, the authors developed a system called Virtual Goalkeeper to practice defending against penalty kicks in a realistic virtual environment. High or low anxiety conditions were introduced by manipulating control, predictability, and feedback. In the high anxiety condition, athletes could not influence the result with their own actions, the start of the penalty kick was delayed, and discouraging messages were displayed after performance. Anxiety was measured using both physiological measures (e.g., heart rate and galvanic skin response) and questionnaires (e.g., Competitive State Anxiety Inventory-2 Revised; Cox, Martens, & Russell, 2003). Results demonstrated that anxiety related to sports can be triggered by a VR system, and thus might be a promising tool for resilience training with athletes.

Focusing on pressure as it relates to competition, Wellner, Sigrist, Zitzewitz et al. (2010) examined rowing performance in three competitive rowers, two recreational rowers, and five non-rowers. Rowing on a virtual river in a rowing simulator with and without an audience standing on both virtual river banks did not lead to any performance differences in their study. Nonetheless, the authors provided valuable insights into the athletes' VR experiences: For instance, 20% of the athletes reported insufficient presence, indicating that they still felt being in the laboratory whilst rowing, and 30% mentioned a lack of realism of the scenario. Among the distracting factors caused by technical problems were a slow-down of the graphics or unrealistic behavior such as unrealistic mechanics of the boat or the oar. The relatively small sample size together with issues of presence and realism may explain the lack of differences in both physiological (e.g., galvanic skin response) and movement variables (e.g., change in stroke rate). Similarly, Wellner, Sigrist, and Riener (2010) investigated the role of a competitor on rowing performance, reporting a trend that a fast competitor led to more changes in biomechanical variables than did a slow competitor. Although these two studies did not reveal any performance differences related to the two pressure situations, they shed light on technical and related psychological issues that may arise in VR studies and that deserve careful consideration.

Attentional focus

In VR research, attentional focus as related to sports has been examined in indoor cycling (Mestre, Ewald, & Maiano, 2011), comparing two VR feedback conditions (with and without a virtual coach) to a no VR feedback condition whilst cycling. In the VR feedback conditions, participants' pedaling speed was used to control the displacement speed of their avatar in VR. Independent of the presence of a coach during feedback, attentional focus was found to be associative for the cycling condition without VR feedback, but dissociative for the cycling condition with VR feedback. This indicates that the mere use of VR may help to shift an internal focus away from somatic cues toward a more external focus of attention.

Breathing and biofeedback

In a single-case study on biofeedback (Lagos et al., 2011), VR was used to practice breathing skills during golf performance and to test the athlete's performance (prior to and after practice) playing nine holes of VR golf. Over the course of 10 weeks, the athlete practiced resonance frequency breathing. This practice included weekly sessions of breathing practice combined with daily practice at home. In addition, the athlete practiced how to transfer the breathing skills to the preparation and execution of golf shots in the VR center during the fourth and seventh week. From this intervention, the authors reported an improvement in golf performance (i.e., 35% reduction of strokes on nine holes of VR golf) together with a reduction in reported anxiety (i.e., 11% for cognitive anxiety and 14% for somatic anxiety as measured by the Competitive State Anxiety Inventory-2; Martens, Burton, Vealey, Bump, & Smith, 1990). Although broad generalizations from this single case study are inevitably limited, this example illustrates how VR can be used in sport psychology interventions.

Feedback during action observation

Using an immersive, low-latency CAVE system, Hülsmann et al. (2019) investigated the impact of observing one's own performance together with a full-body superimposition of a skilled performance while practicing bodyweight squats. For this purpose, novices were asked to perform squat movements in front of a virtual mirror while watching the mirror. Participants either observed their own avatar performing full-body movements or were presented with the movement of a skilled individual superimposed on their own performance, either from a frontal or from a side view. Results showed an advantage for motor performance and cognitive representation of the groups that observed their own avatar performing the squat movements together with the superimposed skilled performance. For the deepest point of the squat, participants who watched from the front adapted their height, while those who watched from the side adapted their backward movement. This indicates that it can be beneficial for novices to observe themselves together with a skilled performance in a virtual mirror during execution and that improvement depends on the VR viewing perspective.

More recently, Frank et al. (2019) investigated the impact of modeling future states of action (i.e., motor imagery during action observation: Frank, Wright, & Holmes, in press) on movement quality, mental representation structure, and self-efficacy of the squat. For this purpose, 3D scans of participants were used to create virtual humans of each participant. While one group practiced the squat by observing and imagining themselves performing a squat they had just executed, another group practiced the squat by observing and imagining themselves performing a squat of a skilled athlete. Findings indicated an advantage of the group practicing a future performance level as compared to the group practicing at their current performance level in terms of motor performance and cognitive representation, suggesting that simultaneous imagery while observing future states of action may help establish cognitive prerequisites that enable better motor performance. These two studies exemplify how VR may be used in the future as an adjunct to observational practice, while its superiority to traditional observational practice remains to be tested.

Imagery

Recently, Ross-Stewart, Price, Jackson, and Hawkins (2018) developed an imagery-assisted VR program to train psychological skills in baseball players.

Arguing that VR may help develop imagery ability in athletes, the authors developed VR footage tailored to each player and let the players watch these replays over the course of three months to rehearse skills and non-skill-specific scenarios. Results indicated an increase in three of five dimensions of the SIAQ (Sport Imagery Ability Questionnaire: Williams & Cumming, 2011) after three months of intervention, and some improvements with regards to strategies used (TOPS: Test of Performance Strategies: Thomas, Murphy, & Hardy, 1999), including a decrease in negative thinking during competition. Despite the lack of a control group, and the lack of interactivity with the VR, the preliminary results of this intervention are promising and provide both detailed information on how to combine imagery and VR as well as anecdotal information from coaches and athletes on their experiences with the program. The imagery-assisted VR program may be of particular interest for practitioners who want to develop programs combining imagery and observation techniques (Frank et al., in press) as it includes a detailed description of the interdisciplinary team and the protocol of the designing, filming, editing, and imagery-assisted VR intervention itself. This study indicates that VR might be a promising tool for mental training (here: imagery) to help develop psychological skills of athletes, and therefore should be investigated further in future research, taking into account recent recommendations on how to design VR research in sport (see below).

The future of VR and mental training

In sports, research on VR is growing (e.g., Neumann et al., 2018), and more and more commercial VR applications are available for sport use (e.g., Appelbaum & Erickson, 2016). As for sports in general, VR offers great opportunities for mental training, as it allows for controlling and manipulating training environments according to the athlete's needs. With the help of VR, researchers and coaches can recreate situations, either for practice purpose (e.g., Lagos, Vaschillo, Vaschillo, Lehrer, Bates, & Pandina, 2011) or to prepare for competition (e.g., Stinson & Bowman, 2014), by adding competitors or audience to the task (e.g., Wellner, Sigrist, & Riener, 2010; Wellner, Sigrist, Zitzewitz et al., 2010). Moreover, in VR, athletes can experience new types of interaction that exceed real-world opportunities, not only in individual sports (e.g., Hülsmann et al., 2019) but also in team sports (Varlet et al., 2013).

So far, VR research in sport psychology, and mental training in particular, has yielded promising results for questions related to anxiety/pressure, attentional focus, relaxation, observation, and imagery, whereas the potential of VR for goal-setting, self-talk, concentration, energizing/psyching up, routines, self-efficacy, or self-confidence remains to be explored. Independent of the particular mental skill to be practiced, future research may focus on whether VR is a valuable adjunct to those techniques, that is, whether mental training with VR is more effective compared to traditional forms of mental training (without VR) and what novel types of interaction we can create when using VR for mental training. For instance, with regard to the critical role of motivational factors prior to competition: Does it make a difference during precompetitive preparation whether an athlete watches a video of her/himself succeeding in a previous competition or whether s/he experiences her/himself winning that competition while being fully immersed? Is it more effective to imagine oneself winning the forthcoming competition or to use VR as an adjunct to immerse oneself into a particular competitive environment and watch oneself succeeding?

Given the current state of research, the benefits of VR for athletes are uncertain and remain to be further explored across different sports. To this end, researchers should rigorously design and report future studies on VR-based mental training alongside recommendations for future VR sport research (Neumann et al., 2018), as well as more general recommendations to maximize reproducibility (Open Science Collaboration, 2017): VR research conducted in the realm of mental training should define and use the term VR accurately, assess and report athlete's VR experience, measure immersion/presence, and provide comprehensive reports of the VR system used, its set-up and procedure.

Whether or not an athlete may profit from using VR (for a recent SWOT-analyses, see Düking, Holmberg, & Sperlich, 2018) depends heavily on the technical requirements of the system. To estimate whether an interactive, immersive VR system is promising for sports and mental training, the following aspects may serve as a guide (Slater & Sanchez-Vives, 2016; Waltemate, Hülsmann, Pfeiffer, Kopp, & Botsch, 2015). First, the field of view must be wide enough to feel present in a given virtual environment rather than restricted by the device. For HMDs, the field of view is determined by the device that is being used. If the device's field of view meets the characteristics of the sports to be trained, then this will allow for presence, and thus for VR-based mental training. Second, the resolution of displays should be high enough to deliver images of high quality to the athlete, with the adequate number of dots per inch depending on the device as well as the purpose and the content of the VR-based mental training. Third, the system should be able to create a 3D experience via stereo projection to promote immersion. Fourth, the system should entail head tracking to track the athlete's position and orientation and to update the virtual world accordingly. Fifth, the system should reliably track and process the athlete's actions to enable continuous interactions during VR-based mental training. Furthermore, while the focus of current VR systems is on the visual sense, multimodal substitution, including auditory or even tactile stimuli, may support realistic sports experiences. Finally, the latency of a system must be low enough to let the athlete experience in real time as latencies higher than 100 ms not only disrupt the virtual experience but also directly affect performance (Waltemate et al., 2016). If those technical requirements are met, then the VR-based mental training is more likely to be successful, and to transfer to sports performance in the real world (Gray, 2017).

Accordingly, it will be essential for future VR-based mental training to provide more specific guidelines on how to build an interactive immersive virtual environment for sports. In addition, it will be important to determine the specific requirements needed for immersive, interactive VR systems as per sports, as some sports may depend on fast rendering (e.g., karate kumite; Zhang et al., 2018) and/or on high-quality images (e.g., interception in baseball; Zaal & Bootsma, 2011). With regard to the mental training itself, it will be crucial to draw on the existing body of research and to further and systematically investigate VR-based mental training in order to evaluate the usefulness of VR as an adjunct for practice and competition. Finally, this will assist the development of guidelines for practitioners on what VR systems to use and how to use VR such that it will be beneficial for mental training. If VR systems for athletes meet the criteria mentioned above, if future research carefully tests the scope and limits of VR, and if VR (that meets the criteria mentioned above) becomes affordable for practitioners, then VR will likely make its way into applied sport psychology.

Conclusions

"In the future, cyberspace will acquire greater prominence thanks to new technologies. These technologies are going to drastically influence the application of psychological training programs" (Dosil, Cremades, & Rivera, 2014, p. 338). Although research on VR is growing, VR has not yet paved its way for being a standard tool in applied sport psychology. Results of VR studies on anxiety/pressure, attentional focus, observation, and imagery indicate that VR may be a valuable way to augment mental training. Future directions of VR for sport psychology and VR-based mental training may include extending VR research to goal-setting, self-talk, and other mental techniques and skills; bringing research from the laboratory to the field; and developing recommendations and guidelines for practitioners. Research questions relating to VR-based mental training are highly interdisciplinary as they relate to the technical requirements of VR systems and to their applicability according to the needs of athletes, teams and their coaches. Accordingly, addressing these questions will require the collaborative effort of research teams, applied practitioners, and hi-tech developers. Collaborative research is warranted to explore the potentials and limits of immersive, interactive VR systems together with related embodied experiences for future VR-based mental training.

References

Appelbaum, L. G., & Erickson, G. (2016). Sports vision training: A review of the state-of-the-art in digital training techniques. *International Review of Sport and Exercise Psychology, 11*, 1–30. doi:10.1080/1750984X.2016.1266376

Biocca, F. (1997). The cyborg's dilemma: Embodiment in virtual environments. *Journal of Computer-Mediated Communication, 3*. doi:10.1111/j.1083-6101.1997.tb00070.x

Cox, R. (2011). *Sport psychology: Concepts and applications*. New York, NY McGraw Hill.

Cox, R., Martens, M., & Russell, W. (2003). Measuring anxiety in athletics: The revised competitive state anxiety inventory-2. *Journal of Sport and Exercise Psychology, 25*, 519–533.

Craig, C. (2013). Understanding perception and action in sport: How can virtual reality technology help? *Sports Technology, 6*, 161–169. doi:10.1080/19346182.2013.855224
de Kok, I., Hülsmann, F., Waltemate, T., Frank, C., Hough, J., Pfeiffer, T., ... & Kopp, S. (2017). *The intelligent coaching space: A demonstration*. doi:10.1007/978-3-319-67401-8_12
Dosil, J., Cremades, J. G., & Rivera, S. (2014). Psychological skills training and programs. In A. G. Papaioannou & D. Hackfort (Eds.), *Routledge companion to sport and exercise psychology* (pp. 327–342). London, UK: Routledge.
Düking, P., Holmberg, H.-C., & Sperlich, B. (2018). The potential usefulness of virtual reality systems for athletes: A short SWOT analysis. *Frontiers in Physiology, 9*, e128. doi:10.3389/fphys.2018.00128
Frank, C., Hülsmann, F., Waltemate, T., Wright, D., Eaves, D., Bruton, A., ... & Schack, T. (2019). Combined action observation and motor imagery in virtual reality. On watching and imagining oneself at a level that one has not yet achieved. *Building the future of sport and exercise psychology*. Abstract book of the 15th European Congress of Sport and Exercise Psychology (p. 19). https://pub.uni-bielefeld.de/record/2933833
Frank, C., Wright, D., & Holmes, P. (in press). Mental simulation and neurocognition: Advances for motor imagery and action observation training in sport. In R. Schinke, & D. Hackfort (Eds.), *Routledge international encyclopedia of sport and exercise psychology*. London, UK: Taylor & Francis.
Gallagher, S. (2000). Philosophical conceptions of the self: Implications for cognitive science. *Trends in Cognitive Science, 4*, 14–21. doi:10.1016/S1364-6613(99)01417-5
Gray, R. (2017). Transfer of training from virtual to real baseball batting. *Frontiers in Psychology, 8*, e2183. doi:10.3389/fpsyg.2017.02183
Gray, R. (2019). Virtual environments and their role in developing perceptual-cognitive skills in sports. In A. M. Williams & R. C. Jackson (Eds.), *Anticipation and decision making in sport* (pp. 342–358). New York, NY: Routledge. doi:10.4324/9781315146270-19
Hülsmann, F., Frank, C., Senna, I. (shared first authorship), Ernst, M. O., Schack, T., & Botsch, M. (2019). Superimposed skilled performance in a virtual mirror improves motor performance and cognitive representation of a full body motor action. *Frontiers in Artificial Intelligence and Robotics, 6*, e43. doi:10.3389/frobt.2019.00043
Jerald, J. (2015). *The VR book: Human-centered design for virtual reality*. New York, NY: ACM Books. doi:10.1145/2792790
Kilteni, K., Groten, R., & Slater, M. (2012). The sense of embodiment in virtual reality. *Presence: Virtual and Augmented Reality, 21*, 373–387. doi:10.1162/PRES_a_00124
Lagos, L., Vaschillo, E., Vaschillo, B., Lehrer, P., Bates, M. & Pandina, R. (2011). Virtual reality-assisted heart rate variability biofeedback as a strategy to improve golf performance: A case study. *Biofeedback, 39*, 15–20. doi:10.5298/1081-5937-39.1.11
Martens, R., Burton, D., Vealey, R., Bump, L., & Smith, D. (1990). Development and validation of the competitive state anxiety inventory-2. In R. Martens, R. Vealey, & D. Burton (Eds.), *Competitive anxiety in sport* (pp. 117–190). Champaign, IL: Human Kinetics.
Mestre, D. R., Ewald, M., & Maiano, C. (2011). Virtual reality and exercise: Behavioral and psychological effect of visual feedback. *Annual Review of Cybertherapy and Telemedicine*, 122–127. doi:10.3233/978-1-60750-766-6-122
Miles H. C., Pop, S. R., Watt, S. J., Lawrence, G. P., & John, N. W. (2012). A review of virtual environments for training in ball sports. *Computers & Graphics, 36*, 714–726. doi:10.1016/j.cag.2012.04.007
Milgram, P., & Kishino, F. (1994). A taxonomy of mixed reality visual displays. *IEICE Transactions on Information and Systems, E77-D*, 1321–1329. doi:10.1.1.102.4646
Neumann, D. L., Moffitt, R. L., Thomas, P. R., Loveday, K., Watling, D. P., Lombard, C. L., Antonova, S., & Tremeer, M. A. (2018). A systematic review of the

application of interactive virtual reality to sport. *Virtual Reality, 22*, 183–198. doi:10.1007/s10055-017-0320-5

Open Science Collaboration. (2017). Maximizing the reproducibility of your research. In S. O. Lilienfeld & I. D. Waldman (Eds.), *Psychological science under scrutiny: Recent challenges and proposed solutions* (pp. 3–21). New York, NY: Wiley.

Ross-Stewart, L., Price, J., Jackson, D., & Hawkins, C. (2018). A preliminary investigation into the use of an imagery assisted virtual reality intervention in sport. *Journal of Sports Science, 6*, 20–30. doi:10.17265/2332-7839/2018.01.003

Slater, M. (2009). Place illusion and plausibility can lead to realistic behaviour in immersive virtual environments. *Philosophical Transactions of the Royal Society, 364*, 3549–3557. doi:10.1098/rstb.2009.0138

Slater, M., & Sanchez-Vives, M. (2016). Enhancing our lives with immersive virtual reality. *Frontiers in Robotics and Artificial Intelligence, 3*, e74. doi:10.3389/frobt.2016.00074

Stinson, C., & Bowman, D. A. (2014). Feasibility of training athletes for high-pressure situations using virtual reality. *IEEE Transactions on Visualization and Computer Graphics, 20*, 606–615. doi:10.1109/TVCG.2014.23

Thomas, P., Murphy, S., & Hardy, L. (1999). Test of performance strategies: Development and preliminary validation of a comprehensive measure of athletes' psychological skills. *Journal of Sport Sciences, 17*, 697–711. doi:10.1080/026404199365560

Todorov, E., Shadmehr, R., & Bizzi, E. (1997). Augmented feedback presented in a virtual environment accelerates learning of a difficult motor task. *Journal of Motor Behavior, 29*, 147–158. doi:10.1080/00222899709600829

Varlet, M., Filippeschi, A., Ben-sadoun, G., Ratto, M., Marin, L., Ruffaldi, E., & Bardy, B. G. (2013). Virtual reality as a tool to learn interpersonal coordination: Example of team rowing. *Presence, 22*, 202–215. doi:10.1162/PRES_a_00151

Waltemate, T., Hülsmann, F., Pfeiffer, T., Kopp, S., & Botsch, M. (2015). Realizing a low-latency virtual reality environment for motor learning. *Proceedings of the 21st ACM Symposium on Virtual Reality Software and Technology*, 139–147. doi:10.1145/2821592.2821607

Waltemate, T., Senna, I., Hülsmann, F., Rohde, M., Kopp, S., Ernst, M., & Botsch, M. (2016). The impact of latency on perceptual judgments and motor performance in closed-loop interaction in virtual reality. *Proceedings of the 22nd ACM Conference on Virtual Reality Software and Technology*, 27–35. doi:10.1145/2993369.2993381

Wellner, M., Sigrist, R., & Riener, R. (2010). Virtual competitors influence rowing. *Presence: Virtual and Augmented Reality, 19*, 313–330. doi:10.1162/PRES_a_00004

Wellner, M., Sigrist, R., von Zitzewitz, J., Wolf, P., & Riener, R. (2010). Does a virtual audience influence rowing? *Journal of Sports Engineering and Technology, 224*, 117–128. doi:10.1243/17543371JSET33

Williams, S., & Cumming, J. (2011). Development and validation of the sport imagery ability questionnaire. *Journal of Sport & Exercise Psychology, 33*, 416–440. doi:10.1123/jsep.33.3.416

Witmer, B. G., & Singer, M. J. (1998). Measuring presence in virtual environments: A presence questionnaire. *Presence: Virtual and Augmented Reality, 7*, 3, 225–240. doi:10.1162/105474698565686

Zaal, F., & Bootsma, R. J. (2011). Virtual reality as a tool for the study of perception-action: The case of running to catch Fly balls. *Presence: Virtual and Augmented Reality, 20*, 93–103. doi:10.1162/pres_a_00037

Zhang, L., Brunnett, G., Petri, K., Danneberg, M., Masik, S., Bandow, N., & Witte, K. (2018). KaraKter: An autonomously interacting Karate Kumite character for VR-based training and research. *Computers & Graphics, 72*, 59–69. doi:10.1016/j.cag.2018.01.008

SECTION 3

Emerging topics and understudied populations

15

SPIRITUALITY IN SPORT PSYCHOLOGY CONSULTING

Maria Luisa M. Guinto

The seeming ephemeral and elusive qualities of spirituality have isolated it from the scientific study of sport psychology for many years. Efforts to integrate spirituality into sport psychology consultations were initially met with resistance as they appeared to cast doubt on the scientific credibility of an emerging discipline (Crust, 2006). It was argued that, contrary to the self-regulation and internal control espoused by sport psychology, spiritual practices relinquished control to forces outside the self. Studies that identified self-belief as the most important feature of mental toughness among high-performing athletes further reinforced the need to promote reliance on psychological and physical resources (e.g., Zeiger & Zeiger, 2018), rather than on external spiritual powers that cannot be measured.

However, studies in the psychology and sociology of sport have provided support for the intersection of spirituality and sports. Drawing from earlier studies on the strong influence of beliefs on cognitions, emotions, and behaviors (e.g., Bandura, 1997), several scholars claimed that spiritual convictions represent a legitimate area of investigation in sports (e.g., Balague, 1999; Nesti, 2011). Among the points raised in defense of the value of spirituality in sports are its contributions to enhancing sport performance and promoting overall well-being (e.g., Joseph, Linley, & Maltby, 2006), offering meaning in adversity such as defeat or injury (e.g., Grindstaff, Wrisberg, & Ross, 2010), and providing coping mechanisms to deal with stress and anxiety (e.g., Watson & Czech, 2005). Moreover, sport psychology professionals argued for the importance of spiritual awareness in sport psychology practice and called for the integration of spirituality in the design and conduct of intervention programs (e.g., Mosley, Frierson, Cheng, & Aoyagi, 2015; Sakar, Hill, & Parker, 2014). Thus, instead of keeping spirituality out of sport psychology consulting, including it as a helpful tool in the development of athletes is encouraged where appropriate (e.g., Balague, 1999; Egli et al., 2014).

Perspectives of spirituality in sport psychology

Traditional views of sport psychology considered the achievement of performance outcomes as the primary objective of interventions, consequently promoting the use of personality assessment and the conduct of mental skills training. However, these views were eventually questioned with the growing awareness of the cost of pursuing performance excellence at the expense of the overall health of the athlete. A gradual shift to a two-pronged objective of enhancing performance excellence while an athlete is engaged in sport as well as personal excellence across the life span has been evident (e.g., Amirault & Orlick, 1999).

One development from this paradigm shift was the promotion of the *athlete-centered model* that acknowledges the advancement of life skills for the intellectual, psychological, emotional, social, and moral growth of the whole person, beyond the athletic identity alone. Originally espoused by Clarke, Smith, and Thibault (1994), this model affirms both performance and personal excellence as equally important developmental outcomes, and that incorporating spirituality is an important move in the holistic service provided by sport psychologists for the individual's overall quality of life (Friesen & Orlick, 2010). In support of this model, Leak and colleagues (2007) asserted that spiritual or self-transcendent strivings were associated with positive emotions, psychological health, sense of meaning and purpose, capacity for intimate and selfless interpersonal relationships, and other-orientedness.

Closely related to this athlete-centered approach is the recognition of spirituality within the growing field of *positive psychology* (Seligman & Csikszentmihalyi, 2000), which focuses on strengths instead of weaknesses, building the good in life instead of fixing the bad, and promoting greatness instead of concentrating solely on the dysfunction of athletes, coaches, and individuals in and outside the domains of sport. The intersection of this positive science with sport psychology promoted interest in factors that enabled sport participants to thrive using their natural strengths to attain overall health and well-being, and draw out the best in themselves. Spirituality is among the factors identified as human strengths and positive psychological attributes (Emmons, 2003) as it offers purpose and meaning to human activities and life. As a result, sport psychology practitioners were encouraged to foster spirituality as a vital attribute to empower athletes to cope with the adversities and pressures of high-performance sport.

Furthermore, the increasing appreciation of cultural diversity in sport over recent decades facilitated the emergence of *cultural sport psychology*, which acknowledged the consideration of race, ethnicity, gender, sexuality, spirituality, and religion in sport psychology (e.g., Ryba, Stambulova, Si, & Schinke, 2013). Given that culture represents deeply held values of a group or society, its profound influence on people must be seriously considered in research and practice among sport participants. Cultural competence and culturally sensitive practice are frequently advocated when working with culturally diverse clients (e.g., Gill & Kamphoff, 2009; Ryba et al., 2013).

Although a growing number of studies have explored the intersection of sport and spirituality, most of these focus on the experiences of Western athletes and coaches (e.g., Grindstaff et al., 2010; Mosley et al., 2015). In keeping with the call for cultural diversity in sport psychology research and practice, I seek to expand the discussion on spirituality in sports from an Asian perspective, examining how Philippine culture underpins the experience of spirituality in sports from an insider's point of view. Moreover, I hope to contribute to the ongoing discussion on the culturally nuanced understanding of spirituality in sports and how this might impact research and practice, particularly with athletes who acknowledge their religious beliefs as vital to their sport performance and overall well-being.

Spirituality in a Philippine context

The Philippines is the most populous Christian society in Asia, the fifth largest Christian country in the world, and the third largest Catholic nation in the world (Philippine Daily Inquirer, 2011). The 2015 Philippine Statistics Yearbook indicates that 90.1% of Filipinos are Christians, including 80.6% Roman Catholics, while the Social Weather Survey (2017) showed that 85% of Filipino respondents said that religion is very important in their lives. The value of being "for God," "pro-God," or "God-oriented," translated in Filipino as *Maka-Diyos*, is considered of primary importance among most Filipinos (Clemente et al., 2008).

Scholars have often conceptualized religion and spirituality as separate and independent constructs (e.g., Hill et al., 2000; Jirásek, 2015), whereas several local studies have emphasized the overlap of religiosity and spirituality in the consciousness of Filipinos; that is, being religious is also understood as being spiritual, and vice versa (e.g., Batara, 2015; Clemente et al., 2008). Filipino spirituality cannot be understood in isolation from religion. As such, to further understand the spirituality of Filipinos, we should focus our attention on understanding their religious beliefs and practices. The conceptual separation between spirituality and religion is not indigenous to Filipinos. As expressed by Yabut (2013), "Both 'spirituality' and 'religion' are borrowed words from the West. Both terms made it complicated, as Westerners understand it. For us, both internal (spiritual) and external (religion) are expressed in 'faith'" (p. 53).

Spirituality among Filipino elite athletes

In this section, I review four qualitative investigations that examined how Filipino athletes make sense of their experience in high-performance sports. I also draw from over 20 years of consulting experience with Filipino athletes to surface insights on the intersection of spirituality and sports. Study 1, entitled *What Makes a Champion: A Narrative Analysis of Filipino Elite Athletes' Storied Lives*, is my doctoral dissertation, which examined the narratives of five Filipino athletes who held world titles during their respective sporting careers (Guinto-Adviento, 2011). Their identities are revealed with their consent. Study 2, entitled *Athlete Engagement: A Qualitative Investigation of the Filipino Athlete*, explored the concept of athlete engagement among ten Filipino athletes competing at the international level (Valbuena, Saunders, Rice, & Aumond, 2014). Study 3 the second section of the book *Boxing in the Philippines: The Fight for Survival* (Orbeta & Guinto-Adviento, 2014), which features an interpretative phenomenological inquiry on the legendary boxer, Manny Pacquiao. Study 4, entitled *A Qualitative Content Analysis of the Bahala na Attitude in Filipino Elite Athletes*, explored the subjective experience of 11 Filipino international athletes (Casuga, Vogel, & Pope-Rhodius, 2017).

Although the four studies had research objectives other than the study of spirituality in sports, they were reviewed for references to spirituality and related concepts such as religion, faith, purpose, fate, destiny, prayer, and God. One of the easiest ways to identify themes is through the repeated or regular occurrence of topics; thus, a less formal variation of the key-word-in-context (KWIC) method was utilized to locate related concepts of spirituality from direct quotes and interpretative statements across the four studies. Using procedures for applied thematic analysis recommended by Guest, MacQueen, and Namey (2012), an academic colleague and I identified three overarching themes: namely, (1) sense of purpose, (2) perspective in victory and defeat, and (3) prayer as expression of faith and managing adversity.

Sense of purpose

This theme refers to the stable and encompassing reason for engaging in sport that goes beyond oneself. In contrast to simple sport objectives, such as achieving a particular standard of performance or winning a game, a sense of purpose is akin to the rudder of a ship that directs the athlete to persist in training and overcome the challenges that come with high-performance sport. Entries that refer to the constant motivation of athletes for engaging in sport, pervasive meaning of their talents and efforts in sports, and the values that guide their sport-related decisions and actions are included in this theme.

The infusion of spirituality in the experience of Filipino elite athletes typically appears in the fundamental belief that their talent is a gift from God, given for a specific purpose beyond the self. In Study 1, for instance, Asia's first chess grandmaster Eugene Torre articulated the use of his God-given talent for the development of young and promising chess players with the potential to be world champions (Guinto-Adviento, 2011).

In Study 2, Valbuena and colleagues (2014) confirmed the experience of *confidence*, *dedication*, *vigor*, and *enthusiasm* as dimensions of athletic engagement. However, *spirituality* surfaced as the fifth dimension of athletic engagement among Filipino athletes that was not found among the comparison groups of New Zealand and Canadian athletes. All 10 interviewees reported that their faith in

God was the foundation of their strong values and purpose in life, and that this helped them through the challenging path to becoming elite athletes.

In Study 3, Manny Pacquiao was most explicit on the purpose of his phenomenal talent in boxing, beyond his primary desire to rescue his family from poverty after his father abandoned them during his youth. Although he had already secured a wealthy life for his immediate family, he aspired for a better life for his countrymen, through his God-given talent in boxing. This compelling life purpose, rooted in his strong relationship with his family, countrymen, and God was evident throughout his narrative (Orbeta & Guinto-Adviento, 2014).

The idea of extraordinary talent in sport as a gift from God has been found among religious athletes in other cultures as well (Balague, 1999; Mosley et al., 2015). However, what is characteristic of Filipino athletes' spirituality is the intertwining of their relationship with God and their relationship with fellowmen. Their acknowledgment of this God-given talent implies that they did nothing to deserve the provision from God and that this cannot be repaid; therefore, they feel obliged to reciprocate by showing generosity to others. The local term for this Filipino social value is *utang ng loob*, translated literally as "debt of one's inner self" but more popularly understood as "debt of gratitude" (Kaut, 1961). Although this value is basically manifested in social interactions involving the reciprocity between the person who helps and the one who is helped, it is likewise demonstrated in how the believer responds to favors received from God. Thus, it makes sense for Filipino athletes to use the fruits of their labor not only for themselves but for the benefit of others, including their extended families, teams, communities, and countrymen.

Perspective in victory and defeat

This theme refers to the viewpoint, outlook, or stance taken by the athlete in relation to success and failure. Elite athletes live with winning and losing, and their perspective on these inevitable experiences in sport allows them to deal with the challenges that accompany high performance. When the stakes are high (i.e., in terms of prize money, national pride, personal status, or endorsements), winning and losing a competition can have an enormous impact on the elite performer. It appears that spirituality provides perspective to Filipino elite athletes. If talent in sport is considered as a gift from God, then victory and defeat take on a significance beyond the self.

In an attempt to explain his record-breaking feats in ten-pin bowling, three-time Guinness world record holder Paeng Nepomuceno attributed his success to God's will in Study 1. However, despite affirming the will of God in both winning and losing, he also recognized the need to do his part through consistent and rigorous training of the body and mind. A firm believer in the saying "God helps those who help themselves," he did not simply leave the outcome of tournaments to divine will but acknowledged his human participation in them as well (Guinto-Adviento, 2011).

Likewise in Study 1, pool's most respected player Efren Reyes revealed his understanding of God's will when he acknowledged winning as a blessing from God. He explained that when God blesses him with a win, he is grateful. However, should God decide to bless his opponent with a win instead, it is not for him to grumble about the loss. Although this statement about God's prerogative to bless him or his opponent with a win may sound simplistic to the outsider, it makes sense for Efren to believe that the God who gave him the talent has the power to decide the outcome of the game. This belief allows him to be more accepting of the highs and lows of the game as natural occurrences in sport and then move on to resume training for future competitions (Guinto-Adviento, 2011).

Similarly, Manny Pacquiao recognized that beyond his hard work in training and competition, God's will prevails. In Study 3, he explained, "God alone decides the final outcome, His will prevails ... only He knows how the fight will go, if you win or lose ..." (Orbeta & Guinto-Adviento, 2014, p. 12). Pacquiao was candid about his hope to win every match, but when asked if he gets anxious before a fight due to mounting expectations of victory, he stated that he trains very hard but once he steps into the ring, he leaves it up to God to decide the outcome.

To the Filipino elite athlete, it appears that belief in God fosters humility in victory and acceptance in defeat. Identifying talent as a gift from God, who ultimately controls the outcome, reminds the winner to be modest in attributing success solely to oneself and the loser to acknowledge a loss without losing oneself. This view also helps the athlete accept defeat minus the potential threat of *hiya*, translated by many as "shame," but more appropriately understood as "sense of propriety" (Pe-Pua & Protacio-Marcelino, 2000, p. 55). Lasquety-Reyes (2016) distinguished two kinds of *hiya* as a form of suffering borne out of shame or embarrassment (i.e., a form of passion) and as an active and sacrificial self-control of individual wants for the sake of others (i.e., a form of virtue). In sport, *hiya* can drive the Filipino athlete to sacrifice a lot for the family, community, team, and country. On the other hand, *hiya* can cause him to suffer when failure to perform as expected is viewed as a form of disgrace to oneself and others. From the lens of spirituality, the Filipino elite athlete may find relief in the assurance that the God who provided the talent in sport as a gift is also in full control of the outcome. As such, all that is required is to sacrificially train oneself in pursuit of excellence in the sport. From the perspective of talent in sport as God's gift and the outcome of sport as God's will, the spiritual Filipino athlete is able to focus on cultivating his talent in training, concentrate on executing his game plan during the fight, with no need to obsess on the result of the game.

Prayer as expression of faith and managing adversity

This theme refers to the spiritual conversations, spoken or in silence, in which athletes engage to acknowledge their faith in God, communicate gratitude, or seek help in times of need before, during, and after competition. The use of prayer for "managing adversity" is deliberate as it acknowledges the necessity of adversity in sport and the ability of athletes to modify and reduce the impact of stress and anxiety by communicating their needs to God. In contrast, prayer as a coping mechanism assumes that athletes have no control over the stress- or anxiety-inducing situation, and all they can do is "cope" with it. Veering away from the need to control the situation, this view of prayer recognizes the predisposition of spiritual athletes to relinquish the obsession to personally control adverse conditions and to allow God to take over the circumstances.

In Study 1, bowler Bong Coo, the most decorated Filipino athlete in the country, narrated how praying the rosary, saying the novena, doing meditation, and engaging in spontaneous prayer helped relieve stress and anxiety during crucial moments in competition. In one tournament where she sustained a knee injury, she narrated how she managed to stay calm and focused on the match through prayers. In another instance, she remembered asking for the intercession of a saint during a major tournament when the odds were against her. In exchange, she promised to wear the medal of the saint and pray the novena in his name. Having won the championship, she kept her promise to wear the medal and prayed the novena for nine days (Guinto-Adviento, 2011).

Also in Study 1, world pool champion Francisco Bustamante recalled a most painful experience at the world nine-ball championship in 2002 when he lost his youngest child to an illness and how his faith in God, openly expressed in prayer, helped him compete in the finals. At that critical moment in his career and family life, Bustamante found strength in his faith and communicated his needs to God in prayer (Guinto-Adviento, 2011).

In Study 3, Casuga and colleagues (2017) explored the subjective experience of *Bahala na* as a culturally normative value. *Bahala na* comes from *Bathala*, the name given to the omnipotent being by the early Filipinos before the Spaniards introduced Catholicism into the country in 1851. Invoking the name of *Bathala* provided courage in times of adversity, allowing believers to take risks with the assurance that *Bathala* will always take care of their needs (Jocano, 1981, p.5). To this day, centuries after the belief in this indigenous deity has given way to institutionalized religion, Filipinos continue to utter *Bahala na* before they proceed with a decision or commit to a course of action in times of uncertainty. Because sport involves many uncertainties, it is not surprising to hear athletes say *Bahala na* when competing, which takes on the dimension of faith when used to draw strength from a benevolent God.

Results from Study 3 (Casuga et al., 2017) revealed that the expression of *Bahala na* was not always used overtly as a religious thought despite its religious roots and associations, although almost half of the participants reported using *Bahala na* as an explicit expression of "faith in the benevolence of God" and "fate." For them, uttering *Bahala na* allowed them to surrender their worries by literally "giving it to God" (p. 8). Three participants reported *Bahala na* as expressing the belief that God could be relied upon to assist in times of great trial, with the qualification that God would only help those who were intently helping themselves. One participant admitted using *Bahala na* for divine assistance during competition, when no one else can help her.

In summary, results from the four studies reveal the undeniable intersection of spirituality and sports in the lives of Filipino elite athletes. More specifically, this intersection is manifested in how spirituality provided the sense of purpose in sport, offered perspective in victory and defeat, and positioned prayer as an expression of faith and for managing adversity.

Implications for sport psychology research

The significance of spirituality in sport has often been overlooked, and in some cases denied its rightful place in sport psychology research for many years. Yet, many sport psychology practitioners recognize the interface of spirituality in sport (e.g., Egli, Fisher, & Gentner, 2014; Mosley et al., 2015). This mismatch between what researchers deem worthy of study and what practitioners encounter in the field is apparent in the limited scholarly attention given to the investigation and application of spirituality in sport psychology consultation.

The study of spirituality in sports is necessarily nested in culture. As evidenced in the four studies on Filipino elite athletes discussed in this chapter, the investigation of spirituality requires the sport psychology researcher to recognize that culture underpins what and how people identify what is meaningful, valuable, and sacred; and how this in turn influences behaviors and practices. However, most of the initiatives on this topic have been conducted and articulated from the lens of Western culture, revealing the underrepresentation of the Eastern view of spirituality in sport. In this chapter, I have provided a nuanced understanding of spirituality in sports from an Asian viewpoint, through the lens of a Filipino and Christian researcher. However, although Christianity is the dominant religion in the Philippines, examination of spirituality in sports among Muslim elite athletes would further enrich the discourse by providing verbal space to the marginalized voice of non-Christians among Filipino elite athletes.

The investigation of spirituality in sports also challenges us to consider interpretative forms of understanding through appropriate qualitative methods that capture a socially constructed and culturally nuanced analysis of the phenomenon. Because spirituality involves what is meaningful and valuable to the person, we need to utilize approaches that unveil the meaning and values of the person. The four qualitative studies reviewed in this chapter represent initiatives in this direction. Although they were not conducted for the primary purpose of examining spirituality in the lives of Filipino elite athletes, the use of narrative inquiry, Scanlan Collaborative Interview Method (SCIM; Lonsdale, Hodge, & Jackson, 2007), interpretative phenomenological analysis, and qualitative content analysis of semi-structured interviews inadvertently allowed the experience of spirituality in sport to emerge. Taking the emic view of how Philippine culture underpins spirituality in sport affirms the importance of language, communication, relational perspectives, cultural practices and meanings, beliefs and values in human development (Ryba et al., 2013).

By amplifying culture in research investigations on spirituality in sport, we stay faithful to the unique internal and external environment of Asian athletes, Filipinos in particular; rather than simply identifying similarities or differences with their Western counterparts. For instance, research on the use of prayer and religious rituals to enhance performance must include the worldview of the athlete from which these religious practices emanate. Reducing them to a set of coping skills and mental strategies limits our perception of the spirituality to overt practices, preventing access to a fuller understanding of the broader cultural framework that provides meaning to such behaviors.

Implications for sport psychology practice

One of the main arguments against the incorporation of spirituality into sport psychology consultation comes from the perception that reliance on supernatural forces diminishes the active role and responsibility of the athlete in determining the outcome of performance (Crust, 2006). As such, sport psychologists are encouraged to focus on working with athletes to strengthen their self-belief, self-regulation, and internal control. However, contrary to this perception, the accounts of the Filipino elite athletes showed how spiritual convictions and religious practices provided psychological resources that promoted a strong sense of purpose in sport as a gift from God, a clear perspective on winning and losing as part of God's will, and harnessing prayer as inner and outer expressions of faith in God that allow them to manage adversity. Instead of relinquishing internal control over their performance, the athletes were able to let go of the fixation to control the outcome of game because of their belief in a God who gifted them with talent in sport and whose will is to bless them in multiple ways aside from simply winning games. In the process, they are able to focus on developing their skill in training, concentrate on performing important tasks in competition, and recover from adversities that come with sport, such as defeat, injury, or lack of adequate support and resources.

In order to provide practical considerations for sport psychology consultants who may encounter athletes who profess their faith in Christianity, Egli and Fischer (2017) proposed the incorporation of spirituality in four areas: (i) education, (ii) intake interview, (iii) mental skills training, and (iv) collaboration and referral. A review of their recommendations reveals that most of the points they raised also apply to practitioners working with athletes who profess spiritual beliefs other than Christianity. First, they challenged sport psychology professionals to educate themselves by seeking out appropriate theoretical frameworks when working with athletes who profess their spiritual beliefs, practice reflexivity, and continue or begin including spirituality in sport psychology training programs. Second, they proposed the inclusion of questions related to an athlete's or coach's faith, religion, or spirituality in the intake interview to assess their preference to include or exclude these components in their consulting relationship. Third, they suggested the integration of spirituality into mental skills training by using the language of individual athletes and coaches with whom they work, and gradually incorporating their spiritual beliefs and religious practices into the training. Fourth, they encouraged sport psychology professionals to collaborate with other helping professionals who specialize in providing spiritual mentoring or guidance in sport, such as pastors and chaplains.

The accounts shared by the Filipino elite athletes in this chapter reveal how spirituality infused their sport experience, even before any formal incorporation of their religious beliefs and practices in their training and competition. In a way, this simplifies the work of the sport psychology consultant, who wishes to utilize existing beliefs and practices into the consulting relationship. On the other hand, the consultant must also assess how such beliefs and practices facilitate or hinder sport performance. Although spirituality has been found to provide purpose, perspective, and prayer as reservoirs of meaningful attributions and psychospiritual resources, it can also hinder personal growth and well-being when it promotes guilt, shame, and anxiety. For instance, if the athlete believes that defeat is a punishment from God, then this may result in negative views of oneself; blaming of others; or alienation from God, who is now considered punitive. Ultimately, the goal of integrating spirituality into sport participation and performance is to help athletes flourish as individuals.

Conclusion

This chapter featured the integration of spirituality in sport psychology research and practice in the context of Filipino culture. Additionally, it highlighted the need for a nuanced understanding of spirituality in sport to affirm cultural sensitivity in the consulting relationship. The integration of spirituality in sport is recognized as a complex phenomenon that requires sensitivity to the unique circumstances of every athlete, and thus no generalization of the espoused principles to all Filipino elite athletes is claimed. Nonetheless, I hope this chapter provides insights about spirituality in sports and provokes questions that will enliven the discourse within the discipline of sport psychology.

References

Amirault, K., & Orlick, T. (1999). Finding balance within excellence. *Journal of Excellence*, *2*, 37–52.

Balague, G. (1999). Understanding identity, value, and meaning when working with elite athletes. *The Sport Psychologist*, *13*, 89–98. doi:10.1123/tsp.13.1.89

Bandura, A. (1997). *Self-efficacy: The exercise of control*. New York, NY: W. H. Freeman. doi:10.5860/choice.35-1826

Batara, J. B. L. (2015). Overlap of religiosity and spirituality among Filipinos and its implications towards religious prosociality. *International Journal of Research Studies in Psychology*, *4*, 3–21. doi:10.5964/ejop.v12i4.1170

Casuga, S. M., Vogel, E. B., & Pope-Rhodius, A. (2017). A qualitative content analysis of the *Bahala na* attitude in Filipino elite athletes. *International Journal of Sport Psychology, 48*, 419–434. doi:10.7352/IJSP.2017.48.419

Clarke, H., Smith, D., & Thibault, G. (1994). *Athlete-centred sport: Annex to the national planning framework for sport.* Ottawa, Canada: Canadian Sport Policy Steering Committee. Retrieved from https://athletescan.com/sites/default/files/images/athlete-centred-sport-discussion-paper.pdf

Clemente, J. A., Belleza, D., Catibog, E. V. D., Laguerta, J., Solis, G., & Yu, A. (2008). A look into the value system of Filipino adolescents. *Philippine Journal of Psychology, 41*, 1–32.

Crust, L. (2006). Challenging the "myth" of a spiritual dimension in sport. *Athletic Insight, 8*, 17–31. Retrieved from http://www.athleticinsight.com/Vol8Iss2/Spiritual.htm

Egli, T. J., Czech, D. R., Shaver, G., Todd, S. Y., Gentner, N., & Biber, D. D. (2014). The experience of Christian prayer in coaching: A qualitative investigation. *Journal of Psychology and Christianity, 33*, 45–57.

Egli, T. J., & Fisher, L. A. (2017). Christianity and sport psychology: One aspect of cultural competence. *Journal of the Christian Society for Kinesiology, Leisure and Sport Studies, 4*, 19–27.

Egli, T. J., Fisher, L. A., & Gentner, N. (2014). AASP-certified consultants' experiences of spirituality within sport psychology consultation. *The Sport Psychologist, 4*, 394–405. doi:10.1123/tsp.2013-0082

Emmons, R. A. (2003). Personal goals, life meaning, and virtue: Wellsprings of a positive life. In C. L. M. Keyes, & J. Haidt (Eds.), *Flourishing: Positive psychology and the life well-lived* (pp. 105–128). Washington, DC: American Psychological Association. doi:10.1037/10594-005

Friesen, A., & Orlick, T. (2010). A qualitative analysis of holistic sport psychology consultants' professional philosophies. *The Sport Psychologist, 24*, 227–244. doi:10.1123/tsp.24.2.227

Gill, D. L., & Kampoff, C. S. (2009). Cultural diversity in applied sport psychology. In R. J. Schinke, & S. J. Hanrahan (Eds.), *Cultural sport psychology* (pp. 45–56). Champaign, IL: Human Kinetics.

Grindstaff, J. S., Wrisberg, C. A., & Ross, J. R. (2010). Collegiate athletes' experience of the meaning of sport injury: A phenomenological investigation. *Perspectives in Public Health, 130*, 127–135. doi:10.1177/1757913909360459

Guest, G., MacQueen, K. M., & Namey, E. E. (2012). Introduction to applied thematic analysis. In G. Guest, K. M. MacQueen, & E. E. Namey (Eds.), *Applied thematic analysis* (pp. 3–20). Thousand Oaks, CA: Sage. doi:10.4135/9781483384436

Guinto-Adviento, M. L. (2011). *What makes a champion: A narrative analysis of Filipino elite athletes' storied lives.* Unpublished doctoral dissertation, Ateneo de Manila University, Philippines. doi:10.13140/RG.2.2.34276.01922

Hill, P. C., Pargament, K. I., Hood, R. W. Jr., McCullough, M. E., Swyers, J. P., Larson, D. B., & Zinnbauer, B. J. (2000). Conceptualizing religion and spirituality: Points of commonality, points of departure. *Journal for the Theory of Social Behavior, 30*, 51–77, doi:10.1111/1468-5914.00119

Jirásek, I. (2015) Religion, spirituality, and sport: From religio athletae toward spiritus athletae. *Quest, 67*, 290–299. doi:10.1080/00336297.2015.1048373

Jocano, F.L. (1981). *Folk Christianity: A preliminary study of conversion and patterning of Christian experience in the Philippines.* Quezon City, Philippines: Trinity Research Institute.

Joseph, S., Linley, P. A., & Maltby, J. (2006). Positive psychology, religion and spirituality. *Mental Health, Religion & Culture, 9*, 209–212. doi:10.1080/13694670600615227

Kaut, C. R. (1961). *Utang–na–loob*: A system of contractual obligation. *Southwestern Journal of Anthropology, 17*, 256–272.

Lasquety-Reyes, J. (2016). In defense of hiya as a Filipino virtue. *Asian Philosophy, 26*, 66–78. doi:10.1080/09552367.2015.1136203

Leak, G. C., DeNeve, K. M., & Greteman, A. J. (2007). The relationship between spirituality assessed through self– transcendent goal strivings, and positive psychological attributes. *Social Scientific Study of Religion, 18*, 263–279. doi:10.1163/ej.9789004158511.i-301.102

Lonsdale, C., Hodge, K., & Jackson, S. A. (2007). Athlete engagement: II. Development and initial validation of the Athlete Engagement Questionnaire. *International Journal of Sport Psychology, 38*, 471–492.

Mosley, M. J., Frierson, D. J., Cheng, Y., & Aoyagi, M. W. (2015). Spirituality and sport: Consulting the Christian athlete. *The Sport Psychologist, 29*, 371–386. doi:10.1123/tsp.2013–0123

Nesti, M. (2011). Phenomenology and sports psychology: Back to the things themselves! *Sport, Ethics and Philosophy, 5*, 285–296. doi:10.1080/17511321.2011.602582

Orbeta, N. & Guinto-Adviento, M. L. (2014). Boxing in the Philippines: The fight for survival. In P. C. Terry, L. Zhang, Y. Kim, T. Morris, & S. Hanrahan (Eds.), *Secrets of Asian sport psychology*, 1–23. doi:10.1080/1359813042000314781

Pe-Pua, R., & Protacio-Marcelino, E. A. (2000). Sikolohiyang Pilipino (Filipino psychology): A legacy of Virgilio G. Enriquez. *Asian Journal of Social Psychology, 3*, 49–71, doi:10.1111/1467–839X.00054

Philippine Daily Inquirer. (2011). *Philippines still top Christian country in Asia, 5th in world*. Retrieved from https://globalnation.inquirer.net/21233/philippines–still–top–christian–country–in–asia–5th–in–world#ixzz5sLDjNoOU

Ryba, T. V., Stambulova, N. B., Si, G., & Schinke, R. J. (2013). ISSP position stand: Culturally competent research and practice in sport and exercise psychology. *International Journal of Sport and Exercise Psychology, 11*, 1–20. doi:10.1080/1612197X.2013.779812

Sarkar, M., Hill, D. M., & Parker, A. (2014). Working with religious and spiritual athletes: Ethical considerations for sport psychologists. *Psychology of Sport and Exercise, 15*, 580–587. doi:10.1016/j.psychsport.2014.05.006

Seligman, M. E. P., & Csikszentmihalyi, M. (2000). Positive psychology: An introduction. *American Psychologist, 55*, 5–14. doi:10.1037/0003-066X.55.1.5

Social Weather Survey. (2017). *First quarter 2017 social weather survey*. Retrieved from https://www.sws.org.ph/swsmain/artcldisppage/?artcsyscode=ART-20170413105521

Valbuena, M. J. D., Sauders, J., Rice, V., & Aumond, E. (2014). Athlete engagement: A qualitative investigation of the Filipino athlete. *Silliman Journal, 55*, 116–146.

Watson, N. J., & Czech, D. C. (2005). The use of prayer in sport: Implications for sport psychology consulting. *Athletic Insight, 7*, 26–35. Retrieved from http://www.athleticinsight.com/Vol7Iss4/PrayerinSports.htm

Yabut, H. J. (2013). Isang paglinaw sa mga paniniwala at pagpapakahulugan sa ispirituwalidad at relihiyon ng mga Pilipino. *Diwa e-Journal, 1*, 43–60.

Zeiger J. S., & Zeiger, R. S. (2018). Mental toughness latent profiles in endurance athletes. *PLoS ONE, 13*, e0193071. doi:10.1371/journal.pone.0193071

16

MINORITIES

Stephanie J. Hanrahan

When I was invited to write this chapter on minorities, my first thought was why was a White person being asked to write a chapter on this topic? I do have some experience being the only White person, or one of a few White people, in my work in Latin America, Africa, and Cleveland, Ohio, as well as my work with Indigenous youth in Australia and Hawaii. In fact, I'm writing this chapter while working at the National Sports Institute in Papua New Guinea, where I am the only White person staying at the Institute. My experiences of being in the minority, however, are different to the experiences of people of color being the minority within a White majority. Through no effort or intent on my part, I experience White privilege (more on that later). My next thought was why have I assumed that "minority" refers to race. Again, I'm in the majority by being heterosexual. Perhaps I'm a minority when it comes to hair color (blond)? Although I've had nine knee surgeries (the last two being total knee replacements), I still consider myself to be able bodied – so I am also not part of the minority group of people with disabilities (covered in another chapter within this text). Over four months I corresponded with a Black sport psychologist, hoping to have this person as a co-author (or maybe even the first author), in my mind bringing legitimacy to this chapter. Work, responsibilities, and life got in the way, so I am afraid that readers are stuck with an author from the mainstream writing this chapter on minorities.

What are minorities?

A minority is the smaller number of a part, especially a number or part representing less than half the whole. A minority can also relate to the state or period of being under the age of full legal responsibility. Given the separate chapter on youth in this book, I have not included age as a component of this chapter. For the purposes of this chapter, minority will refer to a category of people who experience relative disadvantage compared to members of a dominant social group – usually members of small (relative to the whole) groups of people within a community or country who differ from the main population in features such as race, ethnicity, religion, or language.

Wagley and Harris (1958) suggested five characteristics that distinguish minority groups: (a) unequal treatment and relatively less power over their lives compared to the majority, (b) distinguishing cultural or physical traits like language or skin color, (c) involuntary membership in the group, (d) awareness of subordination, and (e) a high rate of in-group marriage. When Wagley and Harris wrote this article in 1958, more than 90% of people disapproved of interracial marriages (Gallup Organization, 2007). By 2007, less than 20% disapproved of interracial marriages (Gallup Organization, 2007). Assuming that trend has continued, it is likely safe to say that the fifth characteristic listed by Wagley and Harris carries less weight than it did 60 years ago. Nevertheless, it is worth people in the majority noting the involuntary membership and awareness of subordination of people in minority groups. Many people may only think of minorities in terms of distinguishing characteristics and unequal treatment or power.

White privilege

As mentioned above, White people experience privilege just because of the color of their skin. McIntosh (1988) provided 46 examples of unearned advantages that pervade social inequities, including:

- I can go shopping alone most of the time, fairly well assured that I will not be followed or harassed by store detectives.
- I can turn on the television or open to the front page of the paper and see people of my race widely and positively represented.
- When I am told about our national heritage or about "civilization," I am shown that people of my color made it what it is.
- If a traffic cop pulls me over or if my tax return is audited, I can be sure I haven't been singled out because of my race.
- I can go home from most meetings of organizations I belong to feeling somewhat tied in, rather than isolated, out of place, outnumbered, unheard, held at a distance, or feared.
- I can take a job with an affirmative action employer without having my co-workers on the job suspect that I got it because of my race.

White privilege in sport can include people not questioning how I became involved in a particular sport (e.g., swimming, ice hockey), having performance success attributed to my skill or hard work instead of my genes, and having the majority of research in sport sciences (including sport psychology) being conducted by people who likely have similar cultural backgrounds to me.

Holm, Rowe Gorosh, Brady, and White-Perkins (2017) developed exercises to increase health workers' awareness of privilege in their lives and work, and to improve their understanding of the effect of privilege on their own and others' lived experiences. The exercises involved employees determining whether or not 22 statements similar to those listed above were true for them, sharing how many of the 22 statements applied to them, and then having small group discussions highlighting differences between participants. The facilitator concluded by defining privilege as "unearned advantages that one might take for granted while simultaneously not recognizing that others lack them" (Holm et al., 2017, p. 362). Encouragingly, in anonymous evaluations, many participants indicated that participating in the exercises led to not only increased awareness of privilege but the new recognition of their obligation to address the effects of privilege on the quality of health care (Holm et al., 2017). Perhaps similar activities could be used effectively in sport, not only with sport psychologists but also with coaches and other support staff.

Stigmatization and stagnation

Stigmatization is the action of describing or regarding someone or something as worthy of disgrace or great disapproval. Stagnation is the lack of activity, growth, or development. These two terms are related because stigmatization can lead to stagnation (Dahal, 2018). For example, if there is a stigma against Black athletes competing in ice hockey, then there will be a stagnation in the participation rates of Blacks in ice hockey. Similarly, the stigmatization (and denial) of mental illness in athletes can lead to a stagnation in service provision addressing mental health issues in athletes (Schwenk, 2000). Likewise, there may be a stigma against athletes seeking sport psychology services, which may limit the growth and development of the field of sport psychology. Martin (2005) reported that younger athletes, male athletes, and athletes from contact sports may stigmatize the seeking of sport psychology services. Changing language (e.g., from "sport psychology and counselling" services to "performance enhancement" services) might help some athletes to be open to seeking sport psychology services (Martin, 2005). Frustratingly, however, adopting this course of action, although potentially diminishing the stigma of seeing a sport psychologist, might at the same time reinforce the stigma associated with mental illness.

As an example of how complex this area can be, the stigma associated with seeing a sport psychologist is influenced not only by gender, age, and type of sport, but also by culture. Ong and Harwood (2018) found that Western athletes (mostly British and White) held less stigma toward sport psychology consulting and less preference for a consultant of the same race or culture compared to Eastern athletes (mostly Chinese Singaporeans). Western sport psychologists should therefore be aware that athletes from (at least some) Eastern cultures might find seeking help from them to be in conflict with their Eastern cultural belief systems and be aware of the level of resistance these athletes might have to psychological interventions (Ong & Harwood, 2018).

Systematic oppression

Systematic oppression, or oppression by institution, is when the laws of a society or organization create unequal treatment of a specific social identity group or groups or people. In the sport and exercise literature there are examples of oppression related to disability (e.g., Smith, Bundon, & Best, 2016), fatness (e.g., Ebbeck & Austin, 2017), religion (e.g., Toffoletti & Palmer, 2015), culture (e.g., Blodgett, Schinke, McGannon, & Fisher, 2015), gender (e.g., Burke, 2014), sexual orientation (e.g., Anderson, Magrath, & Bullingham, 2016), and race (e.g., Hylton, 2015).

It is not clear whether sport is a cause or a possible solution to systematic oppression. Donald Lee, a lawyer and partner in a sports management firm, has argued that the National Collegiate Athletic Association (NCAA) is racist. The NCAA brings in billions of dollars each year, primarily from television contracts, making primarily White administrators and coaches rich on the backs of unpaid, primarily Black, athletes (Lee, 2016). Kareem Abdul-Jabbar (former National Basketball Association star), however, has argued that "sport is one of the few areas in which Americans of all races can talk to each other" (Abdul-Jabbar, 2018).

In the context of this book, the question is whether sport psychologists should be apolitical and focus only on performance enhancement or if the field of sport psychology is a microcosm of society with similar inequitable power structures that should be actively addressed by those within the profession. At the very least I believe as practitioners we should be purposeful (i.e., aware and considerate) in our use of language. Toni Morrison, a Nobel Prize winner, noted, "[Oppressive] language does more than represent violence, it is violence; does more than represent the limits of knowledge, it limits knowledge" (https://www.nobelprize.org/nobel_prizes/literature/laureates/1993/morrison-lecture.html). When talking to male athletes, should sport psychologists consciously avoid referring to wives and girlfriends (assuming heterosexuality) and use gender-neutral terms, such as "partners"? Should we comment when a coach or athlete says a male athlete is running, throwing, or playing "like a girl"? What if a swimmer with a lower leg amputation refers to herself as "The Crip"? Although as sport psychologists we will not eliminate oppression, we can ensure that we do not blindly support (often through inaction) the unequal treatment of individuals or groups.

Benefits of cultural competence and diversity

Individuals from linguistically and culturally diverse backgrounds are less likely to seek psychological support or treatment than the mainstream population (Gainsbury, 2017). In addition, when they do seek help, the treatment outcomes for people from ethnic minorities are worse than for White clients (Huey, Tilley,

Jones, & Smith, 2014). The good news is that minority clients who work with practitioners who have received cultural sensitivity training stay in treatment longer, report greater satisfaction (Wade & Bernstein, 1991), and experience significantly greater reduction in symptoms compared to those who received usual care (Ngo et al., 2009). The Association of Applied Sport Psychology requirement for individuals to complete a course on diversity (or equivalent) before becoming a Certified Mental Performance Consultant is a step in the right direction. Other professional organizations have also recognized the importance of culture. The International Society of Sport Psychology (ISSP) has outlined the skills associated with cultural competence (Ryba, Stambulova, Si, & Schinke, 2013) and, along with the European Federation of Sport Psychology (FEPSAC), is adding requirements for cultural competence to its certified practitioner processes (Schinke et al., 2018).

Diversity and inclusion are human rights issues, but diversity is more than just "the right thing to do." Diversity can enhance performance. In terms of fitness, doing the same training over and over leads to plateaus. Diversifying exercises or training has fitness benefits (American College of Sports Medicine, 2018). The same is true for sport and performance – diversity can enhance performance. Ostergaard, Timmermans, and Kristinsson (2011) found a positive relationship in organizations between a culture open to diversity and innovative performance. Employee diversity within organizations was found to be positively related to the likelihood of introducing innovation. Perhaps the field of sport psychology will become more innovative as it becomes more diverse.

Models of cultural competence

Cultural competence is frequently defined as "a set of consistent behaviours, attitudes and policies that enable a system, agency or individual to work within a cross-cultural context or situation effectively" (National Health and Medical Research Council, 2006; Watt, Abbott, & Reath, 2016). The content and scope of cultural competency curriculum frameworks and models, however, vary considerably (Betancourt, 2003; Watt et al., 2016). There is general agreement that elements of cultural competence include knowledge, awareness/attitudes, and behaviors/skills (Watt et al., 2016). Knowledge includes understanding of client and community context, cultural protocols, socio-political and environmental determinants of well-being and performance, and culturally relevant guidelines and community resources. Attitudes relate to critical awareness of culture and inequities, respect for cultural differences, cultural self-reflection, and motivation to learn about culture. Skills include cross-cultural communication, advocacy and action, and client-centered skills.

Given the diverse elements that make up cultural competence, it should not be viewed as a dichotomous variable with practitioners being either culturally competent or culturally incompetent. As described in previous sport psychology publications about culture (e.g., Hanrahan, 2015), Wells (2000) depicted a six-stage model of cultural development with three cognitive stages and three affective stages. The cognitive stages are experienced first and involve gaining knowledge about culture and its expressions. The affective stages involve application of knowledge gained in the cognitive phases and emphasize attitudinal and behavioral change. The affective phase requires actual engagement with people from diverse cultures; simply reading about culture or attending lectures on the topic will not develop the affective stages. In the first stage, cultural incompetence, there is no awareness of the cultural implications of behavior. In the second stage, cultural knowledge, the process of learning the elements of cultures and their roles that shape and define behavior takes place. The final cognitive stage, cultural awareness, involves recognizing and understanding the cultural implications of behavior.

Cultural sensitivity, the first affective stage, involves the integration of cultural knowledge and awareness into individual and institutional behaviors. Cultural competence, the second affective stage, encompasses routine application of culturally appropriate interventions and practices. The final stage, cultural proficiency, is the integration of cultural competence into practice, teaching, and research as well as extension of cultural competence into the organizational culture. Two guiding principles for developing cultural awareness and competence are: (a) maintaining a wide, objective, and open attitude toward individuals and their cultures (avoiding using one's own culture as a yardstick against which other cultural practices are compared and judged; Wells, 2000), and (b) using cultural information as a point of departure rather than the final destination, which is stereotyping that does not allow for individual differences (Lee & Hanrahan, 2020). For example, upon learning that a new client is originally from China, cultural information (e.g., China tends to be a collectivistic culture where people act in the interests of the group rather than of themselves) can provide a starting point for the practitioner. Because of individual differences, however, the practitioner should be aware that the athlete might have collectivistic tendencies but should not assume the client is definitely collectivistic.

Importance of cultural competence in sport (does it really matter?)

Sporting clients who work with culturally competent practitioners experience satisfaction and tend to adopt effective coping strategies (Schinke, McGannon, Parham, & Lane, 2012). Cultural insensitivity experienced by clients has been reported to be related to social isolation (Smith, 2013), reduced performance (Blodgett, Schinke, Smith, Peltier, & Pheasant, 2011), and a drop-off in participation (McGannon & Schinke, 2013). If sport psychology practitioners as a whole become more culturally sensitive and competent, then there should be corresponding benefits to sports participation, performance, and well-being.

Culturally competent practitioners or culturally targeted interventions?

Most of the publications related to culturally competent practice in sport psychology have focused on the practitioners, not the selected interventions (Hacker & Mann, 2017). The usual suggestions are for practitioners to engage in self-reflection (Hanrahan, 2011; Terry, 2009) and cultural reflexivity (Ryba et al., 2013; Schinke et al., 2012). In the past, I have stuck to the term "reflection" rather than "reflexivity" because reflexivity is a form of reflection, and I believe it is not a term clearly understood by the majority of readers. Technically, reflection is a subject–object association, and reflexivity is a subject–object–subject relation, or what has been characterized as a "bending-back" (Alexander, 2017). Whatever term is used, the idea is for practitioners to consider their own cultural backgrounds; the cultural backgrounds of their clients; and how the two may influence the relationships between clients and practitioners, behaviors, and performances. Ideally, engaging in cultural reflection/reflexivity can lead to culturally sensitive interventions (Hacker & Mann, 2017; Ryba et al., 2013).

Culturally competent practitioners engage in context-driven practice, often meaning that culturally appropriate interventions emerge from the context, instead of pre-determining a particular course of action. As a field, sport psychology has few (if any) culturally targeted interventions, unless one includes interventions that simply have included language translations, as done in many studies of cultural adaptations of interventions in clinical psychology (Nagayama Hall, Ibaraki, Huang, Marti, & Stice, 2016). An example of translating the language of a sport psychology intervention is Bernier, Thienot, Codron, and Fournier (2009), who created a French mindfulness and acceptance program using acceptance and commitment therapy tools developed by Hayes and Strosahl (2004). If additional cultural adaptations were made to the intervention, they were not specifically mentioned in the study. Culturally competent professionals recognize that therapeutic relationships are influenced by the cultural beliefs and values of both practitioners and clients. Simply translating the language of intervention programs may not be sufficient to create culturally targeted interventions. See Table 16.1 for a list of suggestions for culturally competent practice.

There is so much we don't know (need for future research)

Huey et al. (2014) stressed that psychology researchers need to compare culturally tailored treatments to generic treatments in randomized controlled trials, with both treatments having the same core content, being of similar length and intensity, differing only in the absence or inclusion of key cultural features. If a culturally tailored treatment results in significantly greater engagement, symptom reduction, or improved well-being compared to a generic treatment, then it could be concluded that it is the cultural features that accounted for the difference. This suggestion for randomized controlled trials, although scientifically

TABLE 16.1 Suggestions for Culturally Competent Practice

- Learn a few words of the client's language. Even just knowing how to say "hello" and "thank you" shows the practitioner has taken an interest in them and their culture.
- Observe cultural norms such as dress, eye contact, food, way of eating, and social hierarchies.
- Try to learn about the culture of the client ahead of time while keeping in mind the information is just a starting point, not an absolute description of the client.
- When working in another culture, dress to fit local expectations.
- Ask questions. Many athletes enjoy speaking to someone with a genuine interest in their culture.
- Avoid making assumptions.
- Take advantage of opportunities to work with people from other cultures.
- Reflect on one's own culturally constituted beliefs, values, and behaviors.
- Try to be aware of potential differences in power and privilege.
- Look for commonalities among people and cultures, while respecting cultural differences.
- Consider clients' views of their issues, perceived causes, and methods of coping.

sound, may be unrealistic. As argued above, culturally competent practitioners engage in context-driven practice, allowing the specific context to determine the course of action. The adaptation of interventions to individual clients (a requisite of being a culturally competent practitioner) is not possible in the proposed testing of culturally tailored treatments.

Another factor that makes the testing of culturally tailored interventions challenging is that people are not from a single culture – we are all influenced by multiple cultural factors (e.g., ethnicity, race, religion, education, sexual orientations, socio-economic status, gender, (dis)ability). In the area of sport, there are also differences in level (e.g., recreational, college, international, professional), type (e.g., team, individual, contact, non-contact), as well as specific sport subcultures (e.g., surfing versus figure skating). If researchers compare the effects of an intervention on Black versus White athletes, other aspects of culture could confound and confuse results. Simple cross-cultural studies tend to make the erroneous assumption that all people of one culture are the same, which is patently not true. Considering only the building blocks of DNA (excluding the effects of socialization), there is greater genetic variance within racial groups than there is between them (American Anthropological Association, 1998).

In addition, if the focus is only on the content of the treatment, the influence of the practitioner is ignored. It is well established that practitioners play an extremely important role in the alliance-outcome relationship (e.g., Del Re, Flückiger, Horvath, Symonds, & Wampold, 2012). What is not well understood is how practitioners contribute to the relationship. If researchers only focus on testing culturally adapted specific interventions or treatments, excluding the influence of the cultural awareness or sensitivity of the practitioners, best practice for people of diverse cultures will not be determined. It is likely if a person receives a "culturally tailored treatment" from a culturally insensitive person, the outcome could be sub-optimal.

I'm not suggesting that randomized controlled trials will not provide useful information that can be used to help sport psychologists work effectively with minority clients, but that additional forms of research are also needed. Some possibilities include learning about culturally relevant risk factors, running focus groups with representatives of the culture of interest, and trying to determine differences between practitioners in terms of how they (do or don't) work effectively with minority clients.

One thing that all sport psychology researchers can do is clearly describe the participants in their studies. Participant descriptions should include information about ethnicity and/or race, sexual orientation, gender identity, socio-economic status, immigrant status, language preferences, and disability status (American Psychological Association, 2010), not just age and sex, as typically reported in most sport psychology journals. As a field we need to move past the false assumption that results obtained from primarily White, middle class, English speaking male athletes are equally true for the rest of the world.

References

Abdul-Jabbar, K. (2018, August 29). Kareem Abdul Jabbar: What sports have taught me about race in America. *The Guardian*. Retrieved from https://www.theguardian.com/sport/2018/aug/28/notes-from-an-ungrateful-athlete-why-race-and-sports-matter-in-america

Alexander, P. A. (2017). Reflection and reflexivity in practice versus in theory: Challenges of conceptualization, complexity, and competence. *Educational Psychologist, 52*, 307–314. doi:10.1080/00461520.2017.1350181

American Anthropological Association. (1998, May 17). *Statement on "Race."* Retrieved from http://www.aaanet.org/stmts/racepp.htm

American College of Sports Medicine. (2018). *ACSM's guidelines for exercise testing and prescription* (10th ed.). Philadelphia, PA: Wolters Kluwer.

American Psychological Association. (2010). *Publication manual* (6th ed.). Washington, DC: Author.

Anderson, E., Magrath, R., & Bullingham,R. (2016). *Out in sport: The experiences of openly gay and lesbian athlete in competitive sport*. London, UK: Routledge.

Bernier, M., Thienot, E., Codron, R., & Fournier, J. F. (2009). Mindfulness and acceptance approaches in sport performance. *Journal of Clinical Sports Psychology, 4*, 320–333.

Betancourt, J. (2003). Cross-cultural medical education: Conceptual approaches and frameworks for evaluation. *Academic Medicine, 78*, 560–569.

Blodgett, A., Schinke, R. J., Smith, B., Peltier, D., & Pheasant, C. (2011). Exploring vignettes as a narrative strategy for co-producing the research voices of aboriginal community members. *Qualitative Inquiry, 17*, 522–533. doi:10.1177/107780041140988

Blodgett, A. T., Schinke, R. J., McGannon, K. R., & Fisher, L. A. (2015). Cultural sport psychology research: Conceptions, evolutions, and forecasts. *International Review of Sport and Exercise Psychology, 8*, 24–43. doi:10.1080/1750984X.2014.942345

Burke, M. (2014). Women's standpoints and internalism in sport. *Journal of the Philosophy of Sport, 41*, 39–52. doi:10.1080/00948705.2013.858399

Dahal, A. (2018). An appalling scenario growing corruption and its obnoxious impacts on public lives – with special reference of South-Asian stigma. *International Journal of Social Science Studies, 6*(5), 74–85. doi:10.11114/ijsss.v6i5.3237

Del Re, A. C., Flückiger, C., Horvath, A. O., Symonds, D., & Wampold, B. E. (2012). Therapist effects in the therapeutic alliance-outcome relationship: A restricted-maximum likelihood meta-analysis. *Clinical Psychology Review, 32*, 642–649. doi:10.1016/j.cpr.2012.07.002

Ebbeck, V., & Austin, S. (2017). Burning off fat oppression: Self-compassion exercises for personal trainers. *Fat Studies: An Interdisciplinary Journal of Body Weight and Society, 7*, 81–92. doi:10.1080/21604851.2017.1360670

Gainsbury, S. M. (2017). Cultural competence in the treatment of addiction: Theory, practice and evidence. *Clinical Psychology and Psychotherapy, 24*, 987–1001.

Gallup Organization. (2007). *The* Gallup poll *briefing*. Washington, DC: Author.

Hacker, C. M. & Mann, M. E. (2017). Talking across the divide: Reflections and recommendations for context-driven, cultural sport psychology. *Journal of Sport Psychology in Action, 8*, 76–86. doi:10.1080/21520704.2017.1287144

Hanrahan, S. J. (2011). Sport psychology services are multi-cultural encounters: Differences as strengths in therapeutic relationships. In D. Gilbourne & M. Andersen (Eds.), *Critical essays in applied sport psychology* (pp. 145–156). Champaign, IL: Human Kinetics.

Hanrahan, S. J. (2015). Running across borders: Cross-cultural exercise psychology. In M. Anderson & S. J. Hanrahan (Eds.), *Doing exercise psychology* (pp. 33–45). Champaign, IL: Human Kinetics.

Hayes, S. C., & Strosahl, K. D. (2004). *A practical guide to acceptance and commitment therapy*. New York, NY: Springer.

Holm, A. L., Rowe Gorosh, M., Brady, M., & White-Perkins, D. (2017). Recognizing privilege and bias: An interactive exercise to expand health care providers' personal awareness. *Academic Medicine, 92*, 360–364. doi:10.1097/ACM.0000000000001290

Huey, S. J., Tilley, J. L., Jones, E. O., & Smith, C. A. (2014). The contribution of cultural competences to evidence-based care for ethnically diverse populations. *Annual Review of Clinical Psychology, 10*, 305–338.

Hylton, K. (2015). 'Race' talk! Tensions and contradictions in sport and PE. *Physical Education and Sport Pedagogy, 5*, 503–516. doi:10.1080/17408989.2015.1043253

Lee, D. H. (2016, January 8). College sports exploits unpaid black athletes. But they could force a change. *Washington Post*. Retrieved from https://www.washingtonpost.com/posteverything/wp/2016/01/08/college-sports-exploits-unpaid-black-athletes-but-they-could-force-a-change/?noredirect=on&utm_term=.7af32deffcdb

Lee, S.-M., & Hanrahan, S. J. (2020). Power and privilege. In D. Hackfort & R. Schinke (Eds.), *International encyclopedia of sport psychology* (pp. 507–523). London, UK: Routledge.

Martin, S. B. (2005). High school and college athletes' attitudes toward sport psychology consulting. *Journal of Applied Sport Psychology, 17*, 127–139. doi:10.1080/10413200590932434

McGannon, K. R., & Schinke, R. J. (2013). "My first choice is to work out at work; then I don't feel bad about my kids": A discursive psychological analysis of motherhood and physical activity participation. *Psychology of Sport and Exercise, 14*, 179–188. doi:10.1016/j.psychsport.2012.10.001

McIntosh, P. (1988). *White privilege and male privilege: A personal account of coming to see correspondences through work in women's studies*. Wellesley, MA: Wellesley College, Center for Research on Women. Retrieved from http://www.collegeart.org/pdf/diversity/white-privilege-and-male-privilege.pdf

Nagayama Hall, G. C., Ibaraki, A. Y., Huang, E. R., Marti, C. N., & Stice, E. (2016). A meta-analysis of cultural adaptations of psychological interventions. *Behavior Therapy, 47*, 993–1014. doi:10.1016/j.beth.2016.09.005

National Health and Medical Research Council. (2006). *Cultural competency in health: A guide for policy, partnerships and participation*. Canberra, ACT: Commonwealth of Australia.

Ngo, V. K., Awarnow, J. R., Lange, J., Jaycox, L. H., Rea, M. M., Landon, C., … & Miranda, J. (2009). Outcomes for youths from racial-ethnic minority groups in a quality improvement intervention for depression treatment. *Psychiatric Services, 60*, 1357–1364. doi:10.1176/ps.2009.60.10.1357

Ong, N. C. H., & Harwood, C. (2018). Attitudes toward sport psychology consulting in athletes: The role of culture and personality. *Sport, Exercise, and Performance Psychology*, 7, 46–59. doi:10.1037/spy0000103

Ostergaard, C. R., Timmermans, B., & Kristinsson, K. (2011). Does a different view create something new? The effect of employee diversity on innovation. *Research Policy, 40*, 500–509. doi:10.1016/j.respol.2010.11.004

Ryba, T. V., Stambulova, N. B., Si, G., & Schinke, R. J. (2013). ISSP position stand: Culturally competent research and practice in sport and exercise psychology. *International Journal of Sport and Exercise Psychology, 11*, 123–142. doi:10.1080/1612197X.2013.779812

Schinke, R. J., McGannon, K. R., Parham, W. D., & Lane, A. M. (2012). Toward cultural praxis and cultural sensitivity: Strategies for self-reflexive sport psychology practice. *Quest, 64*, 34–46. doi:10.1080/00336297.2012.653264

Schinke, R. J., Si, G., Zhang, L., Elbe, A.-M., Watson, J., Harwood, C., & Terry, P. C. (2018). A joint position stand of the ISSP, FEPSAC, ASPASP, and AASP on professional accreditation. *Psychology of Sport and Exercise, 38*, 107–115. doi:10.1016/j.psychsport.2018.06.005

Schwenk, T. L. (2000). The stigmatisation and denial of mental illness in athletes. *British Journal of Sports Medicine, 34*, 4–5. doi:10.1136/bjsm.34.1.4

Smith, B. (2013). Sporting spinal cord injuries, social relations, and rehabilitation narratives: An ethnographic creative non-fiction of becoming disabled through sport. *Sociology of Sport Journal, 30*, 132–152. doi:10.1123/ssj.30.2.132

Smith, B., Bundon, A., & Best, M. (2016). Disability sport and activist identities: A qualitative study of narratives of activism among elite athletes with impairment. *Psychology of Sport and Exercise, 26*, 139–148. doi:10.1016/j.psychsport.2016.07.003

Terry, P. C. (2009). Strategies for reflective sport psychology practice. In R. J. Schinke & S. J. Hanrahan (Eds.). *Cultural sport psychology* (pp. 79–89). Champaign, IL: Human Kinetics.

Toffoletti, K., & Palmer, C. (2015). New approaches for studies of Muslim women and sport. *International Review for the Sociology of Sport, 52*, 146–163. doi:10.1177/1012690215589326

Wade, P., & Bernstein, B. L. (1991). Cultural sensitivity training and counselor's race: Effects on black female clients' perceptions and attrition. *Journal of Counselling Psychology, 38*, 9–15.

Wagley, C., & Harris, M. (1958). *Minorities in the new world: Six case studies*. New York, NY: Columbia University Press.

Watt, K., Abbott, P., & Reath, J. (2016). Developing cultural competence in general practitioners: An integrative review of the literature. *BMC Family Practice, 17*, 158. doi:10.1186/s12875-016-0560-6

Wells, M. I. (2000). Beyond cultural competence: A model for individual and institutional cultural development. *Journal of Community Health Nursing, 17*, 189–199.

17

PSYCHOLOGICAL INTERVENTIONS WITH PARALYMPIC ATHLETES

Michelle D. Guerrero, Jeffrey J. Martin, and Eva Prokesova

Introduction

The purpose of this chapter is to summarize the literature on mental skills and athletes with disabilities and offer specific suggestions for applied practitioners working in the field. We have divided this chapter into three sections. In the first section, we provide information designed to help sport psychologists work with athletes with disabilities and focus specifically on the sport psychologist-athlete relationship. We argue that the context for such interactions should fall within a personal developmental model of consulting that revolves around foundation qualities, psychological methods and skills, and facilitative and debilitative factors (see Figure 17.1). Foundation qualities include non-sport-specific factors like global self-esteem and how such factors can enhance (i.e., strong self-esteem) or hinder (i.e., weak self-esteem) adaptive sport behaviors such as effective training. Psychological methods refer to practices like goal setting that can enhance a psychological skill such as the ability to concentrate. Finally, the personal developmental model recognizes that factors outside the sport experience (e.g., sound sleep patterns, good nutrition) can facilitate performance, whereas other factors unique to disability sport (e.g., discrimination, chronic pain) can be debilitating to training and performance. Readers interested in learning more about the model should consult additional work by Martin (1999, 2012, 2017a). It should be noted that sport psychologists can also work effectively with coaches and sport personnel in addition to athletes (Katz, 2007; Larson, 2014; Lundqvist, Ståhl, Kenttä, & Thulin, 2018). Because building an accepting, trusting, and respectful relationship between the sport psychologist and athlete is fundamental to the success of the mental skills program, in the second section, we discuss general considerations (e.g., implementation and delivery) when working with athletes with disabilities and briefly highlight existing applied work within this area.

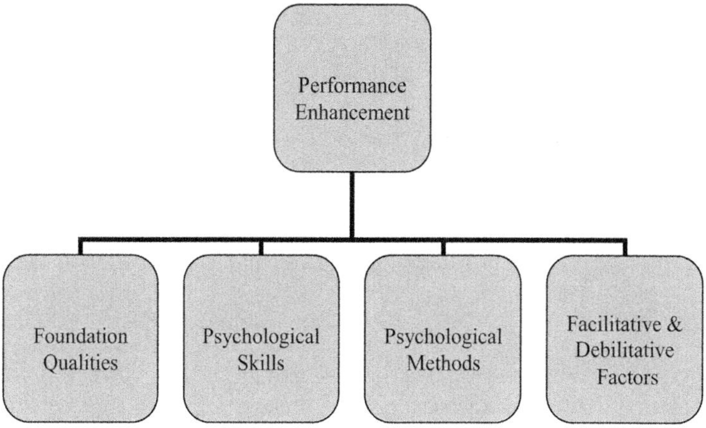

FIGURE 17.1 Personal development model (Martin, 1999).

In the final section, we present and discuss two psychological interventions – mindfulness and gratitude – and argue their usefulness for athletes with disabilities. We conclude the chapter by presenting potential future avenues for sport psychologists and researchers to explore.

Mental skills consulting with athletes with disabilities

Prior to consulting

Before working with athletes with disabilities, sport psychologists should first reflect on their own beliefs about disability and learn about disability sport in four ways. First, receiving some formal and informal mentoring from experienced practitioners can help prepare sport psychologists to work with athletes with disabilities (Katz, 2007). Second, more and more publications about applied work with athletes with disabilities are being produced and sport psychologists are urged to read that body of work (e.g., Hanrahan, 1996; Katz, 2009; Martin, 2011, 2012, 2015). Third, like many athletes, athletes with disabilities feel affirmed and proud when offered praise for significant athletic achievements, such as winning a Paralympic medal or setting a personal best record. However, when they are viewed as heroic and praised for performing everyday mundane life activities (e.g., shopping), they often feel discomfort and annoyance (Martin, 2019). Although such praise is often well intentioned, it conveys a subtler message, often called the *Supercrip* stereotype, that to live with a disability is a tragic experience, requiring athletes to possess daily doses of courage to "overcome" their disability. Most people, including athletes with disabilities, have good and bad days, and their lives are often filled with joy and meaning. Sport psychologists are not immune to the socialization processes that paint people with disabilities as heroic and having a disability as tragic. Hence, sport psychologists should examine their own beliefs about what it means to have a disability and monitor how they interact with their clients to determine if their language also reinforces a tragedy model of disability. Such self-examination can help sport psychologists avoid inadvertently endorsing a Supercrip stereotype. Fourth, many people (including disability sport coaches) have expressed views that disability sport is a second-class sport and less important than able-bodied sport (Radtke & Doll-Tepper, 2014). Again, sport psychologists should engage in some serious introspection and determine if they also make such value judgments.

When consulting

In this section, we discuss three factors that are unique to athletes with disabilities and have the potential to influence the work of sport psychologists. While it may seem obvious, sport psychologists should strive to understand their athlete's impairment. Sport psychologists should talk to their athletes about what it is like to live with a disability and how it affects their ability to train well, compete, and live an athletic lifestyle. Consistent with a personal developmental model, experiences outside of sport clearly influence training and competition. Empathic sport psychologists understand their athletes' sport because it helps them be effective and enhances their credibility. When working with athletes with disabilities, sport psychologists have the additional challenge of understanding their athletes' impairment.

Classification

In disability sport athletes are "classified" or graded based on their ability to perform various physical tests (Tweedy & Vanlandewijck, 2011). This results in athletes with different disabilities competing against each other in the same classification. Although the classification system is somewhat controversial, it is a hallmark of the disability sport experience and can often be a stressful experience. Many times athletes are given short notice of their classification appointment and at other times have to wait many hours. While both factors lead to stress the biggest stressor is the knowledge that athletes can be reclassified and possibly compete against athletes with a less severe level of impairment who can perform better. Athletes may also attempt to cheat (known as sandbagging) in order to get classified at a level lower than their true capabilities resulting in performing against inferior competition. The classification procedure is unique to disability sport and is a potential stressor that sport psychologists may be required to help their clients manage (Martin, 2016; Martin, 2017b).

Motivation

Although athletes with and without disabilities are often very similar in their sport motivations (e.g., to perform well, to win) some athletes with disabilities have multi-faceted motivations that go beyond sport. Sport is often used as a mechanism to be viewed as normal and even beyond normal. Adjusting to a recent acquired impairment, fighting discrimination and marginalization, and promoting the broader disability cause and the disability sport movement are all motivations not typically seen in able-bodied athletes. For example, elite athletes with disabilities can develop identities as athletic activists and political activists (Smith, Bundon, & Best, 2016). Sport psychologists who help athletes explore and understand their motivations can help athletes develop a more meaningful sport career (Martin, 2017b).

Injury and pain

Relative to able-bodied athletes, athletes with disabilities lose more training time due to injury. The International Paralympic Committee (IPC) tracks injuries at the Paralympics and found that in 2012 the injury rate was 17.8 injuries per 100 athletes. In contrast the Olympic injury rate was about 13 injuries per 100 athletes (Willick et al., 2013). In addition to injuries, athletes with disabilities often deal with chronic pain and sport psychologists may be called upon to help athletes develop pain management strategies. Additionally, helping athletes distinguish among pain from their disability, pain from a secondary condition (e.g., shoulder tendonitis), pain as a sign of a potential injury, and fatigue-related pain is important. Failure to understand such differences may lead to injury if trying to train through pain or losing important fitness by unnecessarily ceasing training (Martin, 2017b).

Psychological skill training with athletes with a disability

Psychological skills training (PST) is defined as "the systematic and consistent practice of mental or psychological skills for the purpose of enhancing performance, increasing enjoyment, or achieving greater sport and physical activity self-satisfaction" (Weinberg & Gould, 2011, p. 250). The rationale for PST is based on an assumption that an athlete's negative thoughts, emotions, and bodily sensations can hinder peak performance and that mental strategies can be used to enhance optimal performance (Hays, 1995). PST programs typically include cognitive and behavioral techniques such as self-talk, imagery, arousal regulation, relaxation, and goal setting, and more recently mental toughness training (e.g., Gucciardi, Gordon, & Dimmock, 2009). Oftentimes, PST programs are multi-modal, meaning that multiple techniques are taught to and utilized by the athlete.

Applied work within disability sport has focused primarily on practical considerations when delivering PST programs to athletes with disabilities (Hanrahan, 1998; Katz, 2009; Larsen, 2014). The process of delivery for many cognitive and behavioral strategies will be generally identical for athletes with and without disabilities, especially for athletes with intellectual, sensory, or physical impairments (Hanrahan, 1998, 2015). However, making modifications to the delivery of strategies may be necessary for some athletes. For example, transferring a written imagery script to an audio recording or to Braille when consulting with a blind athlete; using visuals, speaking clearly, and avoiding mumbling when working with a deaf or hearing-impaired athlete; skipping the tension phase of a progressive muscular relaxation session when working with athletes with cerebral palsy to avoid potential muscle spasms (Hanrahan, 1998). Furthermore, sport psychology consultants should be mindful that athletes with disabilities might face specific sport- and nonsport-related challenges and barriers compared to able-bodied athletes (de Bressy de Guast, Golby, Van Wersch, & d'Arripe-Longueville, 2013). Some challenges might be related to the disability category (Martin, 1999), impairment onset (Asken, 1991), socialization into sport (Williams & Taylor, 1994), accessibility of training and competition facilities (Campbell & Jones, 2002), or functional classification (Wu & Williams, 2001). Thus, such challenges may need to be considered when designing and implementing PST programs. Overall, the PST programs should be designed, accommodated, and applied in correspondence with the individual needs of the particular athlete (Lim, Jang, O'Sullivan, & Oh, 2018).

Athletes and coaches of high-performance disability sports value the use of mental skills (Martin, 2012; Ponnusamy, Guerrero, & Martin, 2018). Yet compared to research with able-bodied athletes, few PST interventions have been conducted with athletes with disabilities. There is, however, growing research showing that PST is applicable and useful to athletes with disabilities. PST programs have been conducted with athletes with visual impairments (Hanrahan, 1996; Hanrahan, Grove, & Lockwood, 1990) and athletes with spinal cord injury and amputations (de Bressy de Guast et al. 2013; Hanrahan, 1995; Lim et al. 2018). In most of these studies, the PST program followed a multi-modal format. For example, Lim et al.'s (2018) PST program comprised self-talk, imagery, cognitive reconstructing, and routine, while de Bressy de Guast et al.'s (2013) program included strategies such as imagery, relaxation, injury management, and confidence building. Outcomes of previous studies supported the notion that PST is applicable and useful to athletes with disabilities.

More attention of experts in sport psychology was gradually given to area of high-performance disability sport, especially the Paralympic Games. The Paralympics belongs to the highest level of competition in disability sport, which can cause athletes to experience increased levels of perceived challenge and stress (Martin, 2012). Some studies have focused on the uniqueness of the Paralympic games, where additional perceived stressors can be involved – increased media attention, transfers on and off the plane, long flights, toilet accessibility during the flight, transfers from the Paralympic village, functional classification of Paralympic athletes before the competition, testing for performance-enhancing drugs when urinating via catheter (Martin, 2012), application of sport psychology tools, and working with sport psychology consultants in preparation for the competition (e.g., Blumenstein & Orbach, 2015; Lim et al., 2018; Lundqvist et al., 2018).

Mindfulness and gratitude as potential psychological interventions

In this section, we elaborate on mindfulness and gratitude as two new potential approaches to psychological skill development. Both positive psychology approaches have shown promise in able-bodied sport but have yet to be examined in disability sport. We hope their inclusion here will stimulate research in this area.

Mindfulness

> Yesterday is a memory. Tomorrow is the unknown. And now, is the knowing.
>
> —*The Buddha*

Mindfulness is both a process (mindful practice) and an outcome (mindful awareness; Shapiro & Carlson, 2017). Mindful practice is the systematic practice of intentionally attending in an open, discerning way, which involves both knowing and shaping the mind. Mindful awareness is referred to as an abiding presence or awareness, stemming from a deep knowing that manifests as freedom of mind. Considering these aspects together, the construct of mindfulness is described as the awareness that emerges through intentionally attending in an open, caring, and nonjudgmental way. When individuals are mindfully aware, they respond to all life experiences, regardless of nature (positive, negative, or neutral), in an open, receptive manner; they accept what is right in front of them; they are freed from the desire to grasp, to change things, or to frame things in a particular way. At the deepest level, mindfulness is about freedom: freedom from reflexive patterns; freedom from reactivity; and, ultimately, freedom from suffering. Some believe that mindfulness is a naturally occurring trait, suggesting that all people have a certain level of mindful awareness that occurs without knowledge or practice of the skill. However, one's trait level of mindfulness can be cultivated through informal (e.g., mindful eating, mindful driving) and formal (e.g., body scan meditation, sitting meditation) practices.

Mindfulness-based interventions have been conducted with various populations, ranging from people with chronic pain to cancer to those with cardiovascular disease (see Shapiro & Carlson, 2017 for a review). Such interventions have led to symptom reduction and improvements in emotional functioning (Shapiro & Carlson, 2017). This is not entirely surprising given that mindfulness has been identified as a potential buffer between pain experiences and the outcome. In fact, a bulk of mindfulness-based intervention research has been conducted with patients with cancer and pain conditions (e.g., chronic pain, low back pain, fibromyalgia; see Carlson, 2012 for a review). Results of these interventions suggest benefits of practicing mindfulness, such as improvements in pain perception, psychological distress, emotional states, perceptions of hope, and quality of life. Some mindfulness-based interventions have been carried out with people with physical disabilities, albeit not within a sport context. Effects of an eight-week, internet-delivered mindfulness training intervention for people with spinal cord injuries showed greater improvements in symptoms of depression and anxiety, pain catastrophizing, and specific facets of mindfulness for those participating in the mindfulness-based intervention compared to those receiving psychoeducation training (control group; Hearn & Finlay, 2018).

A well-argued mechanism responsible for the transformational effects of mindfulness is captured in the term "reperceiving," which can be described as a shift in perspective (Shapiro & Carlson, 2017). Instead of being immersed in one's own narrative or life story, reperceiving allows the individual to stand back and witness it. Reperceiving is the hallmark of mindfulness practice; it increases capacity for objectivity in relationship to one's internal and external experiences. Reperceiving is seen as a meta-mechanism, comprising four additional mechanisms: (1) self-regulation; (2) values clarification; (3) cognitive, emotional, and behavioral flexibility, and (4) exposure. For instance, the process underpinning the exposure mechanism is that when people purposely and repeatedly observe or witness their own negative emotions, thoughts, and body sensations, they become less fearful, overwhelmed, or frightened by these states. Baer (2003) offered an example of the exposure mechanism with chronic pain patients:

> Prolonged exposure to the sensations of chronic pain, in the absence of catastrophic consequences, might lead to desensitization, with a reduction over time in the emotional responses elicited by the pain sensations. Thus the practice of mindfulness skills could lead to the ability to experience pain sensations without excessive reactivity.
>
> *(p. 128)*

Other mechanisms have been proposed such as the self-awareness, self-regulation, and self-transcendence model, mindfulness-to-meaning theory, and the Buddhist psychological model (see Shaprio & Carlson, 2017). Each model proposes different hypotheses, though all include an underlying component of reappraisal and complement the reperceiving model.

Research examining the effectiveness of mindfulness-based interventions is growing, albeit with able-bodied athletes (Goodman, Kashdan, Mallard, & Schumann, 2014; Gross et al., 2018). Gross et al. (2018) examined the effects of a mindfulness-acceptance-commitment (MAC) intervention compared to traditional PST on the mental health and sport performance of female student athletes. Athletes in the MAC intervention followed the manualized protocol by Gardner and Moore (2007), which included seven modules: (1) psychoeducation; (2) mindfulness and cognitive defusion; (3) values and values-driven behavior; (4) acceptance; (5) commitment; (6) skill consolidation and poise (which combines mindfulness, acceptance, and commitment); and (7) maintaining and enhancing mindfulness, acceptance, and commitment. Athletes in the MAC intervention also completed the Brief Centring Exercise (Eifert & Forsyth, 2005) and several other experiential exercises. In comparison, athletes in the PST intervention followed the manualized protocol by Suinn (1986), which included seven strategies: relaxation training, stress management, positive thought control, self-regulation, mental rehearsal, concentration, and energy control. Results showed that athletes in the MAC intervention, compared to those in the PST intervention, reported reduced psychological, emotional, and behavioral concerns, and enhanced sport performance (via coach ratings). It is reasonable to assume that similar benefits would also be documented in a sample of athletes with disabilities.

Gratitude

Gratitude is foundational to well-being. It can take many different forms and can be understood as a state, trait, a mood, or an emotion (McCullough, Emmons, & Tsang, 2002). Trait gratitude is defined as "a generalized tendency to recognize and respond with grateful emotion to the role of other people's benevolence in the positive experiences and outcomes that one obtains" (McCullough et al., 2002, p. 112), whereas state gratitude is described as feeling grateful, appreciative, and thankful during a particular moment (Emmons & Mishra, 2011). Both state and dispositional gratitude has been shown to enhance overall psychological, social, and physical well-being, and dispositional gratitude has been linked with lower negative affect and problematic functioning (see Emmons & Mishra, 2011 for a review). Such benefits have been documented in diverse samples, including patients with neuromuscular disease, college students, early adolescents, and older adults (Emmons & McCullough, 2003; Froh, Sefick, & Emmons, 2008; Killen & Macaskill, 2015).

Based on the broaden-and-build theory of positive emotions (Fredrickson, 2001), positive emotions – joy, interest, contentment, pride, and love – are believed to broaden temporary thought-action repertoires that then build various enduring personal resources (i.e., social, psychological, physical, intellectual), whereas negative emotions narrow attention. People experiencing positive emotions show patterns of thoughts that are flexible, creative, and integrative; show an increased preference for variety; and accept a wider collection of behavioral options (see Isen, 2001 for a review). Like other positive emotions, gratitude broadens and builds (Chen, 2018). Expressing gratitude can prompt people to focus on the benefits in life and on the benevolence of others (broadening), which can lead to an accumulation of social resources (building).

Other potential mechanisms responsible for why gratitude promotes well-being have been hypothesized. One hypothesis is that gratitude promotes well-being by facilitating effective coping skills for dealing with adversity. Gratitude has been linked with distinct coping styles of seeking social support, positive reframing, approach-oriented problem solving, and active coping (Wood, Joseph, & Linley, 2007). In a study involving undergraduate women with trauma history, post-trauma gratitude had the strongest association with emotional growth, and was negatively linked with post-traumatic stress disorder (Vernon, Dillon, & Steiner, 2009). Another hypothesis is that expressing gratitude promotes physical health. Participants of gratitude interventions have reported reduced bodily complaints and increased sleep duration and quality (Emmons & McCullough, 2003). Additional experimental research has shown that gratitude increases parasympathetic myocardial control (McCraty & Childre, 2004).

Limitations and conclusions

Psychological preparation is an important component for success in disability sport. However, applied disability sport research suffers from several weaknesses. First, there is still an unsatisfactory number of instruments that have shown they can produce valid and reliable scores to evaluate athletes' psychological skills (Bastos, Corredeira, Probst, & Fonseca, 2012). Using appropriate assessments of psychological skills is crucial in order to evaluate the level and use of such skills, to target specific skills, and to monitor improvements and outcomes in psychological training. On a similar note, there is a lack of psychological tests and instruments translated into sign language or any other suitable form for athletes with hearing impairment (Clark & Sachs, 1991). Second, experimental studies in disability sport often suffer from small sample sizes, lack of randomization, and use of non-specific control groups (Blumenstein & Orbach, 2015; Lim et al., 2018; Martin, 2008). Despite these limitations, applied research on disability sport continues to grow, and therefore, we are hopeful that many of these limitations will be addressed in future research. We hope that the information outlined in this chapter informs readers of important considerations when working with and designing PST programs for athletes with disabilities. Further, by introducing the psychological approaches of mindfulness and gratitude we hope that researchers are curious to explore and discover their benefits within the population of athletes with disabilities.

Summary

Sport psychologists working with all athletes discover the idiosyncratic strengths and weaknesses they possess. Athletes vary tremendously based on their personality, sport, family experiences, and a host of other untold influences and decisions that shape who they are. Hence, despite the above observations about common experiences faced by athletes with disabilities (i.e., classification, motivation, injury, and pain), sport psychologists are advised to treat each athlete they work with as a unique individual. Moreover, there are many things to consider when designing, implementing, and delivering PST programs to athletes with disabilities. Underpinning all these considerations, the sport psychologist must remember one core principle: athletes with disabilities are *athletes*, and therefore the basic tenets of a PST still apply to this population (Hanrahan, 1998). While mindfulness and gratitude originated from the positive psychology literature, the applicability of these approaches in disability sport appears promising. Consider, for example, a former able-bodied athlete who has acquired a permanent physical disability. Initially this athlete may have a difficult time coping with several life-altering changes, pain, or redeveloping an athletic identity. Based on the empirical evidence presented above, practicing mindfulness and expressing gratitude might help reduce pain symptoms and negative affective states (e.g., depression, anxiety, fear, anger), and improve overall well-being. Although we are unaware of any research showing that these psychological approaches directly improve performance, it is evident that mindfulness and gratitude contribute to the development of optimal functioning and well-being – aspects equally important to athletic performance.

References

Asken, M. J. (1991). The challenge of the physically challenged: Delivering sport psychology services to physically disabled athletes. *The Sport Psychologist, 5*, 370–381.

Baer, R. A. (2003). Mindfulness training as a clinical intervention: A conceptual and empirical review. *Clinical Psychology: Science and Practice, 10*, 125–143. doi:10.1093/clipsy.bpg015

Bastos, T. L., Corredeira, R., Probst, M., & Fonseca, A. M. (2012). Preliminary analysis of the psychometric properties of the Portuguese version of the test of performance strategies (TOPS) in athletes with disabilities. *European Journal of Adapted Physical Activity, 5*, 7–22. doi:10.5507/euj.2012.006

Blumenstein, B., & Orbach, I. (2015). Psychological preparation for Paralympic athletes: A preliminary study. *Adapted Physical Activity Quarterly, 32*, 241–255. doi:10.1123/APAQ.2014-0235

Campbell, E., & Jones, G. (2002). Sources of stress experienced by elite male wheelchair basketball players. *Adapted Physical Activity Quarterly, 19*, 82–99. doi:10.1123/apaq.19.1.82

Chen, L. H. (2018). Gratitude and athletes' well-being. In A. Brady & B. Grenville-Cleave (Eds.), *Positive psychology in sport and physical activity: An introduction* (pp. 129–139). New York, NY: Routledge.

Clark, R. A., & Sachs, M. L. (1991). Challenges and opportunities in psychological skills training in deaf athletes. *The Sport Psychologist, 5*, 392–398.

de Bressy de Guast, V., Golby, J., Van Wersch, A., & d'Arripe–Longueville, F. (2013). Psychological skills training of an elite wheelchair water-skiing athlete: A single-case study. *Adapted Physical Activity Quarterly*, 30, 351–372. doi:10.1123/apaq.30.4.351

Eifert, G. H., & Forsyth, J. P. (2005). *Acceptance and commitment therapy for anxiety disorders*. Oakland, CA: New Harbinger.

Emmons, R. A., & McCullough, M. E. (2003). Counting blessings versus burdens: An experimental investigation of gratitude and subjective well-being in daily life. *Journal of Personality and Social Psychology, 84*, 377–389. doi:10.1037/0022-3514.84.2.377

Emmons, R. A., & Mishra, A. (2011). Why gratitude enhances well-being: What we know, what we need to know. In K. M. Sheldon, T. B. Kashdan, & M. Steger (Eds.), *Designing positive psychology: Taking stock and moving forward* (pp. 248–262). New York, NY: Oxford University Press.

Fredrickson, B. L. (2001). The role of positive emotions in positive psychology: The broaden- and-build theory of positive emotions. *American Psychologist, 56*, 218–226. doi:10.1037/0003-066X.56.3.218

Froh, J. J., Sefick, W. J., & Emmons, R. A. (2008). Counting blessings in early adolescents: An experimental study of gratitude and subjective well-being. *Journal of School Psychology, 46*, 213–233. doi:10.1016/j.jsp.2007.03.005

Gardner, F. L., & Moore, Z. E. (2007). *The psychology of human performance: The mindfulness-acceptance-commitment approach*. New York, NY: Springer.

Goodman, F. R., Kashdan, T. B., Mallard, T. T., & Schumann, M. (2014). A brief mindfulness and yoga intervention with an entire NCAA division I athletic team: An initial investigation. *Psychology of Consciousness: Theory, Research, and Practice, 1*, 339–356. doi:10.1037/cns0000022

Gross, M., Moore, Z. E., Gardner, F. L., Wolanin, A. T., Pess, R., & Marks, D. R. (2018). An empirical examination comparing the mindfulness-acceptance-commitment approach and psychological skills training for the mental health and sport performance of female student athletes. *International Journal of Sport and Exercise Psychology, 16*, 431–451. doi:10.1080/1612197X.2016.1250802

Gucciardi, D. F., Gordon, S., & Dimmock, J. A. (2009). Evaluation of a mental toughness training program for youth-aged Australian footballers: I. A quantitative analysis. *Journal of Applied Sport Psychology, 21*, 307–323. doi:10.1080/10413200903026066

Hanrahan, S. J. (1995). Psychological skills training for competitive wheelchair and amputee athletes. *Australian Psychologist, 30*, 96–101. doi:10.1080/00050069508258911

Hanrahan, S. J. (1996). *Mental skills training for blind and visually impaired athletes*. Belconnen, ACT: Australian Sports Commission.

Hanrahan, S. J. (1998). Practical considerations for working with athletes with disabilities. *The Sport Psychologist, 12*, 346–357. doi:10.1123/tsp.12.3.346

Hanrahan, S. J., Grove, J. R., & Lockwood, R. J. (1990). Psychological skills training for the blind athlete: A pilot program. *Adapted Physical Activity Quarterly, 7*, 143–155.

Hays, K. F. (1995). Putting sport psychology into (your) practice. *Professional Psychology: Research and Practice, 26*, 33–40. doi:10.1037/0735-7028.26.1.33

Hearn, J. H., & Finlay, K. A. (2018). Internet-delivered mindfulness for people with depression and chronic pain following spinal cord injury: A randomized, controlled feasibility trial. *Spinal Cord, 56*, 750–761. doi:10.1038/s41393-018-0090-2

Isen, A. M. (2001). An influence of positive affect on decision making in complex situations: Theoretical issues with practical implications. *Journal of Consumer Psychology, 11*, 75–85. doi:10.1207/S15327663JCP1102_01

Katz, J. (2007). Reflections on the Paralympic HQ psychology service: Athens 2004. *Sport & Exercise Psychology Review, 2*, 25–28.

Katz, J. (2009) Role development and delivery of sport psychology at the Paralympic Games. In B. Hemmings & T. Holder (Eds.), *Applied sport psychology: A case based approach* (pp. 181–203). Chichester, UK: Wiley-Blackwell.

Killen, A., & Macaskill, A. (2015). Using a gratitude intervention to enhance well-being in older adults. *Journal of Happiness Studies, 16*, 947–964.

Larson, C. H. (2014). Preparing for the European championships: A six-step intervention program in disability sports. *Journal of Sport Psychology in Action, 5*, 186–197. doi:10.1080/21520704.2014.971989

Lim, T. H., Jang, C. Y., O'Sullivan, D., & Oh, H. (2018). Applications of psychological skills training for Paralympic table tennis athletes. *Journal of Exercise Rehabilitation, 14*, 367–374. doi:10.12965/jer.1836198.099

Lundqvist, C., Ståhl, L., Kenttä, G., & Thulin, U. (2018). Evaluation of a mindfulness intervention for Paralympic leaders prior to the Paralympic Games. *International Journal of Sports Science & Coaching, 13*, 62–71. doi:10.1177/1747954117746495

Martin, J. J. (1999). A personal development model of sport psychology for athletes with disabilities. *Journal of Applied Sport Psychology, 11*, 181–193. doi:10.1080/10413209908404199

Martin, J. J. (2008). Multidimensional self-efficacy and affect in wheelchair basketball players. *Adapted Physical Activity Quarterly, 25*, 275–288. doi:10.1123/apaq.25.4.275

Martin, J. J. (2012). Psychological perspectives on athletes with disabilities. In S. Mellalieu & S. Hanton (Eds.), *Professional practice issues in sport psychology: Critical reviews* (pp. 54–78). New York, NY: Routledge.

Martin, J. J. (2015). Determinants of elite disability sport performance. *Kinesiology Review, 4*, 91–98. doi:10.1123/kr.2014-0082

Martin, J. J. (2016). The psychology of Paralympians and mental preparation. In Y. C. Vanlandewijck, & W. R. Thompson (Eds.), *Training and coaching the Paralympic athlete* (pp. 96–107). London, UK: Wiley.

Martin, J. J. (2017a). Psychological considerations for Paralympic athletes. In E.O. Acevedo (Ed.), *Oxford encyclopedia of sport, exercise, and performance psychology*. New York, NY: Oxford University Press.

Martin, J. J. (2017b). *Handbook of disability sport and exercise psychology*. New York, NY: Oxford University Press.

Martin, J. (2019). Mastery and belonging or inspiration porn and bullying: Youth sport special populations. *Kinesiology Review, 8*, 195–203. doi:10.1123/kr.2019-0013

McCraty, R., & Childre, D. (2004). The grateful heart: The psychophysiology of appreciation. In R. A. Emmons & M. E. McCullough (Eds.), *The psychology of gratitude* (pp. 230–255). New York, NY: Oxford University Press.

McCullough, M. E., Emmons, R. A., & Tsang, J.-A. (2002). The grateful disposition: A conceptual and empirical topography. *Journal of Personality and Social Psychology, 82*, 112–127. doi:10.1037//0022-3514.82.1.112

Ponnusamy, V., Guerrero, M. D., & Martin, J. J. (2018). Perceived importance of selected psychological strategies among elite Malaysian athletes. *Journal of Clinical Sport Psychology, 12*, 129–143.

Radtke, S., & Doll-Tepper, G. (2014). *A cross-cultural comparison of talent identification and development in Paralympic sports: Perceptions and opinions of athletes, coaches and officials*. Berlin, Germany: SportVerlag.

Shapiro, S. L., & Carlson, L. E. (2017). *The art and science of mindfulness: Integrating mindfulness into psychology and the helping professionals*. Washington, DC: American Psychological Association.

Smith, B., Bundon, A., & Best, M. (2016). Disability sport and activist identities: A qualitative study of narratives of activism among elite athletes with impairment. *Psychology of Sport & Exercise, 26*, 139–148. doi:10.1016/j.psychsport.2016.07.003

Suinn, R. M. (1986). *Seven steps to peak performance: The mental training manual for athletes*. Lewistown, NY: Hans Huber.

Tweedy, S. M., & Vanlandewijck, Y. C. (2011). International Paralympic Committee position stand—background and scientific principles of classification in Paralympic sport. *British Journal of Sports Medicine, 45*, 259–269. doi:10.1136/bjsm.2009.065060

Vernon, L. L., Dillon, J. M., & Steiner, A. R. W. (2009). Proactive coping, gratitude, and posttraumatic stress disorder in college women. *Anxiety, Stress, & Coping, 22*, 117–127. doi:10.1080/10615800802203751

Weinberg, R. S., & Gould, D. (2011). *Foundations of sport and exercise psychology* (5th ed.). Champaign. IL: Human Kinetics.

Williams, T., & Taylor, D. (1994). Socialization, subculture, and wheelchair sport: The influence of peers in wheelchair racing. *Adapted Physical Activity Quarterly, 11*, 416–428. doi:10.1123/apaq.11.4.416

Willick, S. E., Webborn, N., Emery, C., Blauwet, C. A., Pit-Grosheide, P., Stomphorst, J., … & Derman, W. (2013). The epidemiology of injuries at the London 2012 Paralympic Games. *British Journal of Sports Medicine, 47*, 426–432. doi:10.1136/bjsports-2013-092374

Wood, A. M., Joseph, S., & Linley, P. A. (2007). Coping style as a psychological resource of grateful people. *Journal of Social & Clinical Psychology, 26*, 1076–1093. doi:10.1521/jscp.2007.26.9.1076

Wu, S. K., & Williams, T. (2001). Factors influencing sport participation among athletes with spinal cord injury. *Medicine & Science in Sports & Exercise, 33*, 177–182. doi:10.1097/00005768-200102000-00001

18

INNOVATIONS IN MENTAL SKILLS TRAINING FOR YOUNG ATHLETES

Paul McCarthy and Bryan McCann

Tom Gregory's memoir – *A Boy In The Water* – invites us inside the world of an 11-year-old boy who swam the English Channel on September 6, 1988. The crossing involved 12 hours of swimming to cover the 32 miles from Wissant Bay in Northern France to Folkestone Harbour in England. A remarkable feat built on a young boy's motivation and his inspirational coach. Tom became the youngest swimmer ever to complete this extraordinary endurance feat. This astonishing endeavor materialized not only because of his effort but also owing to the support of his sister, parents, and peers among others, which underlines the lattice of interconnected relations helping young athletes to flourish (MacNamara & Collins, 2013). Tom's memoir reveals an embroidery of strategies to cope with aversive challenges and thrive through uncertainty.

The demands of youth sport require child and adolescent athletes to manage various stressors, including training, injury, coping with losses, physical and psychosocial development, selection and deselection; although not alone because youth sport participation is buttressed by parents, peers, coaches, and, depending on the level of competition, sport science support staff (Larsen, Alfermann, & Christensen, 2012). We see young athletes display passion, ambition, discipline, trust, and respect – values that steady the boat when the sea of sporting life is rough – but we do not know what mental skills training (MST) best develops these values among young athletes. Extrapolating from Weinberg and Gould's (2007, p. 250) definition of MST – "the systematic and consistent practice of mental or psychological skills for the purpose of enhancing performance, increasing enjoyment, or achieving greater sport and physical activity self-satisfaction" – the emphasis on MST stretches beyond performance toward psychological well-being. Yet before we jump in as psychologists or mental skills coaches, we need to acknowledge that just because a young athlete presents with various levels of stress, it does not mean they need treatment, and having models (e.g., CBT, person-centered therapy) available does not mean we should use them (Andersen, 2009). We need to understand how MST fits with the support a young athlete needs (Visek, Harris, & Blom, 2009) and how we tailor MST as sport psychologists and coaches (Dohme, Bloom, Piggott, & Backhouse, 2019; Henriksen, Larsen, Storm, & Ryon, 2014) when invited to help.

In this chapter, we explore the content of MST, whether MST works, and the case for MST in youth sport, especially how sport psychologists work with youth athletes by adjusting to their physical, social, emotional, and psychological needs. Drawing from a cognitive-behavior therapy (CBT) orientation, we examine the educational base to open our work with young athletes and how we progress toward engaging with young athletes one-to-one and serving alongside parents, coaches, and siblings.

What is mental skills training?

MST involves learning and applying cognitive-behavioral techniques to assess, check, and manage thoughts, feelings, and behaviors for performance success and psychological well-being (Sharp, Woodcock, Holland, Cumming, & Duda, 2013; Vealey, 1988). MST programs include various psychological skills and techniques (e.g., goal-setting, self-talk, imagery, and relaxation). Although the efficacy of MST packages on performance correlates is documented (Brown & Fletcher, 2017; Foster, Maynard, Butt, & Hays, 2016), the effectiveness of MST as a package (i.e., how they work in practice) is less researched compared with its individual components (e.g., goal-setting, self-talk). We are just establishing how MST works best for young athletes (Dohme, Backhouse, Piggott, & Morgan, 2017; Foster et al., 2016; Sharp et al., 2013) because we already know that MST plays a crucial role in elite athletic performance (Dohme et al., 2019; Gould & Maynard, 2009; Hardy et al., 2017) and in developing talent (MacNamara, Button, & Collins, 2010; MacNamara & Collins, 2013). This lineage underlines how well-developed mental skills help young athletes cope with the challenges and stressors inherent in sport, and maintain their long-term involvement (Gould & Carson, 2008; Henriksen, Stambulova, & Roessler, 2010).

Vealey (1988, 2007) differentiated between psychological skills and psychological techniques. Psychological skills regulate an athlete's behavior to meet the demands of a specific sport, and athletes develop these capacities or abilities to undertake a task (Birrer, Rothlin, & Morgan, 2012). These skills include attention, arousal regulation, motor control, motivation, perceptual cognitive functions, self-skills (e.g., self-awareness, self-efficacy, self-worth, self-confidence), plus personal development, life, coping, communication, leadership, and recovery skills (Birrer et al., 2012). These psychological skills reflect expected outcomes (e.g., improved attentional focus, increased self-confidence) and psychological techniques present a way to achieve these outcomes. A technique improves the skill, and the skill helps the athlete to manage the task at hand. Cultivating psychological skills depends on the four basic psychological techniques of imagery, goal-setting, self-talk, and physical relaxation techniques used in sport psychology interventions (Vealey, 2007). Sport psychologists often deliver these four basic psychological techniques as a multimodal MST package.

Many sport psychologists, coaches, and administrators wish to know whether MST benefits performance and the collective research suggests that it does (Brown & Fletcher, 2017). To explain, psychologists categorize interventions as biopsychosocial with a focus on improving performance and psychological well-being. Brown and Fletcher's (2017) meta-analysis showed that psychological and psychosocial interventions have a moderate positive effect on sport performance with the effects lasting at least a month post-intervention. We need to consider these results carefully because formal evaluations do not sensitively and comprehensively assess the work of sport psychologists (Martindale & Collins 2007). Assessment tools available to measure the effectiveness of MST interventions are often atheoretical with limited precision to assess change over time in target skills within a MST program (Murphy & Tammen, 1998).

MST interventions typically come from CBT (see Meichenbaum, 1985), with researchers adapting them to sport performance issues and other performance domains (e.g., Gould, 2002; Noh, Morris, & Andersen, 2007). Although research contributions have grown, there is still limited research exploring MST among children and adolescents in sport (Henriksen et al., 2014). According to Foster et al. (2016), MST research among children and adolescents falls into three main categories: effectiveness (Tremayne & Newbery, 2005), MST models when engaging with children and adolescents (Visek et al., 2009), and guidelines to adapt to the child or adolescent athlete (Orlick & McCaffrey, 1991; Sharp et al., 2013; Weiss, 1991).

Foster et al. (2016) examined the delivery of MST to youngsters among 12 experienced sport psychology consultants from the United Kingdom. Two key findings emerged. First, although the sport psychology consultants adjusted the content and form of delivery of MST when supporting children and adolescents, changes were not based on developmental theories in psychology. Second, the adjustments to content and delivery were social (e.g., establishing rapport), cognitive (e.g., modifying language), and humanistic (e.g., using self-discovery). Taken together, working with child and adolescent athletes requires knowledge and understanding of cognitive, social, emotional, intellectual, and physical development, and the ability to translate this knowledge and understanding into useful applied practice (Weiss, 2011). With many children and adolescents growing up within talent development squads, it is axiomatic that our research in this field informs MST at this level (Dohme et al., 2017).

Young athletes' psychological needs and adjustments in MST

Young athletes present a broader range of developmental variability compared with adults (Visek, Harris, & Blom, 2013). This variability encourages more developmental and gender-specific biopsychosocial adaptations to work with young athletes. We consider children from mid-childhood (aged six years) to mid-adolescence (aged 17 years) within the athletic context. The challenge for sport psychologists is to match the services they offer to the needs of the client(s) before them, yet we remain uncertain about these needs because the research base is limited (Dohme et al., 2019). Tailoring the services delivered means adjusting to language, session time, and verifying that the client understands and can do what is requested as homework. For instance, completing a thought record sheet or identifying troubling emotions is work best undertaken during the consultation time to allow the child to learn and gain confidence to complete their subsequent homework tasks (Beck, 2011).

Relaxation, goal-setting, self-talk, imagery, and concentration or focus are skills adapted to sport from CBT. These skills offer several benefits to young athletes. To begin, relaxing under the strain of performance demands is a cornerstone in sport and performance psychology. Many athletes seek to reduce worries and muscular tension to perform their skills. Techniques for relaxation include progressive muscular relaxation, autogenic training, Benson's relaxation response, diaphragmatic breathing, and mindfulness. The goal of these techniques is to reduce sympathetic nervous system activation and increase parasympathetic nervous system activation. These adjustments allow more fluid movement and save energy to sustain performance.

Relaxation combines well with other psychological skills (e.g., self-talk, attention) because athletes can focus on their breathing to release them from unhelpful thinking, which reduces the cognitive elements of anxiety. A young golfer, for example, standing over her tee shot can focus on the target and count from one to five as she breathes in. When she returns her eyes to the ball, she can breathe out as she counts from five to one before beginning her swing. This simple cognitive task of counting allows her to think helpfully (i.e., mindful task) and combines with an external focus of attention (i.e., the target and ball) and breathing rhythmically.

Self-talk counteracts or reframes unhelpful thinking and reinforces helpful thinking (Mace, 1990). One element of self-talk is cognitive restructuring, which is a skill best grasped when young to subdue the inner critic and destructive monologues that precipitate and perpetuate under the pressure of performance (MacNamara & Collins, 2013). We can encourage young athletes to present stories from new perspectives. For instance, we could ask, "How might a kind friend talk about you as a swimmer?" or "How might a good coach explain what happened in your last game?"

Mental imagery is the ability to simulate in the mind information not being perceived by the senses (Kremer, Moran, Walker, & Craig, 2012). For young athletes, "seeing," "hearing," and "feeling" things in their imagination is exciting and practical because they can learn and augment motor skills, promote injury recovery, and prepare for challenging environments (Fortes et al., 2018). Mental practice is using mental imagery to rehearse actions without engaging in the physical movements. Finally, concentration is an attentional process to focus on the task at hand while ignoring distractions. Anecdotal, descriptive, and experimental evidence supports the claim of this vital mental skill for successful sport performances (Kremer et al., 2012).

The amassed research supports the benefits of these mental skills to improve performance and well-being (Dohme et al., 2019). We are enriching our understanding about what young athletes need, when, where, and from whom. In CBT, young athletes can assume ownership of their mental fitness by planning and reviewing training and competitions in a notebook. They can set and review goals, set aside time for imagery practice, and blend their array of mental skills (e.g., relaxation and self-talk) into their practice and competition plans. In this way, mental skills are integrated, reinforced, refined, and developed.

How can sport psychologists work best with young athletes?

Foster et al. (2016) presented a comprehensive model of social, cognitive, and humanistic factors to adjust content and delivery of MST. Their modifications included matching interventions to ability, developing rapport, fun, simplicity, and incorporating MST into physical practice. The broad range of factors suggested a holistic approach to working with young athletes rather than narrow, undifferentiated performance enhancement. The sport psychologists' adjustments were not based on their knowledge of developmental theories in psychology but ad hoc changes according to the audience based on an empathic understanding of maturational level, cognitive, and social abilities.

We have several other examples of MST programs for youth athletes (e.g., Fournier, Calmels, Durand-Bush, & Salmela, 2005; Gucciardi, Gordon, & Dimmock, 2009a, 2009b). For instance, Gucciardi et al. (2009a) compared a traditional MST program with one focusing on developing mental toughness with three teams of under-15 Australian football players. Both programs were equally effective in developing athletes' mental toughness. Fournier et al. (2005) examined the effectiveness of a ten-month MST program on the performance of ten nationally ranked female gymnasts (M_{age} = 12 yr.). They focused on developing self-talk, relaxation, goal-setting, focusing, and visualization skills in 25 half-hour sessions. The athletes' performance on the vault, bar, beam, and floor improved during the MST program.

There is sufficient evidence to suggest that MST benefits young athletes' mental and technical development, but these mental skills should be woven within the philosophical approach adopted in coaching and participation at this level. Miller and Kerr's (2002) athlete-centered model of consultancy emphasized physical, social, emotional, and intellectual development from which performance excellence can emerge but with a concomitant understanding of the developmental needs of young athletes. In practice, personal excellence could cultivate performance excellence when coaches and sport psychologists reduce the verbal complexity of instructions, choose fewer goals, and deliver short training sessions (Tremayne, 1995). The limited exposure of young athletes to MST offers a clean slate for sport psychologists to deliver such training to receptive participants (Harwood, 2008, Martin et al., 2001)

Alternative approaches to performance restoration and optimization

Mental skills form part of the cycle of professional practice with a strong emphasis on learning, practicing, reflecting, and refining these skills to suit the presenting issues (Hays, 2009; Kremer & Moran, 2013; Moran & Toner, 2017). In CBT practice, for example, we see a typical cycle of assessment, case formulation, intervention, and evaluation. CBT emerges from several basic principles. First, it requires a sound therapeutic alliance between the psychologist and client based on warmth, empathy, caring, genuineness, and competence. Second, psychologists focus on the present circumstances and formulate the client's problems as they evolve with treatment. Third, clients collaborate with the psychologist to solve the presenting issues, with the client becoming their own psychologist. Finally, sessions are structured and time limited. Clients identify, test, and respond to their dysfunctional thoughts and beliefs and use various techniques to change thoughts, feelings, and behavior.

These basic principles apply to all clients (Beck, 2011). When we work with young athletes we will typically meet the client in a consulting room because CBT varies according to individual client needs, number and extent of their issues, developmental and intellectual level, gender, and cultural background. From the young client's perspective, treatment depends on developing a strong therapeutic bond, goals, motivation to change, experiences, and preferences for treatment, among other factors. At a practical level, the client and the psychologist develop the therapeutic relationship, plan treatment and structure sessions, identify and respond to dysfunctional cognitions, highlight the positive, and accelerate cognitive and behavioral change between sessions with homework (Beck, 2011). Cognitive therapy is based on a model hypothesizing that emotions, behaviors, and physiology are influenced by perceptions of events – not the events themselves. Our work focuses on construing the event. For example, waiting at the start line of a cross-country race will present varied emotional and behavioral responses to this same event based on what is going through the child's head. Together, the young athlete and sport psychologist collaborate to understand what this event means to this athlete.

Restoring and optimizing performance in almost any field (e.g., sport, education, business) involves at least two people collaborating to help one person improve performance. The working alliance between the sport psychologist and young athlete can be tense, awkward, clumsy, elegant, and life-changing (Andersen, 2009). The role of the sport psychologist is one of support, with the athlete establishing and playing the central role in the consultation. Often sport psychologists adopt a directive (e.g., CBT) or non-directive (e.g., person-centered therapy) model of treatment, shaping the collaboration through assessment, formulation, intervention, and evaluation.

A word of caution emerges from the literature in counselling and psychotherapy when we consider therapeutic change. What accounts for the changes clients make in their lives when they work with a psychologist? Debate thrives on the comparative efficacy of various therapies, but in reality, there is little difference in efficacy among them (Luborsky et al., 2000). If slight differences exist among therapies, then the non-specific factors (e.g., quality of relationship) matter. "Lambert's pie" (Assay & Lambert, 1999) estimates that 85% of the change a client experiences in therapy comes from non-specific factors (i.e., client factors, relationship variables, and expectancy/hope), and only 15% of the variance in therapeutic outcomes is attributable to the psychologist's specific techniques or models.

When we consider these findings from counselling and psychotherapy, it seems worthwhile to put MST in context. The specific mental skills and techniques that comprise MST form part of the therapeutic process, but, by the above estimates, they are lower in the hierarchy of influence. The relationship between the sport psychologist and the young athlete depends on both the content (i.e., what the young athlete is bringing to the interaction – their thoughts, feelings, behaviors, and experiences) and the process (i.e., the dynamics of the relationship). The *what* (i.e., what is the client saying verbally and non-verbally?) and the *how* (i.e., how is the sport psychologist working with the young athlete and what is happening between them) themes feature prominently in the working alliance. Beutler and Castonguay (2006) reported that the key principles of change for clients with particular forms of distress were developing a strong therapeutic alliance, challenging cognitive appraisals, and self-disclosing. In short, in terms of importance, the relationship comes first, then the techniques, strategies, and skills.

Applied research directions

There are several avenues for applied research on MST among young athletes. First, we need to explore the efficacy of MST among young athletes, addressing the benefits that psychological support can provide and how they are achieved most effectively. MST forms part of the psychoeducation process but is also part of the intervention process within a CBT program. The British Psychological Society's (2017) practice guidelines present the cycle of professional practice with four key ethical values – respect, competence, responsibility, and integrity – and five core skills: assessment and establishment of agreements with the client, formulation of the client needs and problems, intervention or implementation of solutions, evaluation of outcomes, and communication through reporting and reflecting on outcomes.

It is conceivable within sport and exercise contexts that the role of the intervention (i.e., implementation of solutions) supersedes the other core skills because young athletes confront many challenges (e.g., feeling anxious) and coaches often seek immediate "change" for their young athletes. The reflective accounts of sport psychologists working with young athletes offer possibilities to build a strong therapeutic relationship and help young athletes to help themselves. For example, Foster et al. (2016) suggested role modelling and comparative narratives help young athletes to communicate effectively in consultancy and Howells (2016) proposed using simple, individualized, enthusiastic, and patient delivery using practical examples, and incorporating technological aids where appropriate.

With the right support, coaches can play a crucial role in developing mental skills among young athletes. Gould, Damarjian, Medbery, and Lauer (1999) reported junior tennis coaches held a basic understanding of MST techniques but did not use these techniques with their athletes because they lacked the process knowledge to include them in practice. Similar findings emerged among the coaches in Sharp et al.'s (2013) qualitative investigation of the effectiveness of an MST program for youth athletes. In sum, MST sessions ought to meet the coaches' needs to feel secure if they are speaking and sharing mental skills within sessions. The practical application of MST in simple, hands-on activities and their systematic development is necessary (Gould et al., 1999; Pain & Harwood, 2008; Sharp et al., 2013). To echo Vealey's (1988) comments, education is the foundation phase, and sport psychologists must help consumers to implement techniques, but they need not attempt this education alone.

A thread running through the research relates to understanding how receptive young athletes are to MST. For instance, Sharp et al.'s (2013) study among athletes and coaches suggested that their MST program improved athletes' skills, knowledge and techniques, aided team cohesion, and developed openness, honesty and self-regulation. Wrisberg, Simpson, Loberg, Withycombe, and Reed (2009) examined student-athletes' receptivity to MST delivered by sport psychology consultants. Females were more open than males, and athletes with experience of consulting were more receptive than those with no prior experience. Those with highly effective consulting experience were more receptive than those with less effective experience. We need to know how MST is best organized, taught, delivered, and followed up on. MST programs might be best delivered individually (Gordin & Henschen, 1989) or collectively (Sharp et al., 2013), but issues of long-term adherence (Bull, 1991), individually tailored programs (Weinberg & Williams, 2015), and variability in the athlete-practitioner relationship (Sharp & Hodge, 2014; Wrisberg et al., 2009) severely restrict the guidance for sport psychologists working with young athletes.

Sport psychologists aim to educate, model, and train young athletes to maximize motivation and self-regulate through behavior change. Dohme et al. (2019) suggested that researchers could study the expediency of behavior change theories to increase athletes' effective use of psychological skills and characteristics. They recommended Michie, van Stralen, and West's (2011) COM-B model, which comprises four components – capability, opportunity, motivation, and behaviors – with the first three components shaping an individual's intention to engage in behaviors. Motivation to engage in a behavior (e.g., using mental skills) depends upon opportunity (i.e., factors outside the young athlete's control that prompt or make the behavior possible) and capability (i.e., the knowledge, skills, psychological and physical capacity) to participate in the behavior. The COM-B has not been considered or evaluated in the youth athlete development literature but holds potential.

Conclusion

The accumulating research supports MST programs as an indispensable and meaningful investment among young athletes (Dohme et al., 2019). Sport psychologists commonly report using mental skills in their work with young athletes and adapt as best they can to their varying needs. While psychological skills relate to skills of the mind, psychological characteristics relate to qualities of the mind (Kent, 2006). Both psychological skills and psychological characteristics can be strengthened through systematic development and training (MacNamara & Collins, 2011), but the relationship with the sport psychologist is the foundation for this development.

References

Andersen, M. B. (2009). The "canon" of psychological skills training for enhancing performance. In K. F. Hays (Ed.), Performance psychology in action: A casebook for working with athletes, performing artists, business leaders, and professionals in high-risk occupations (pp. 11–34). Washington, DC: American Psychological Association. doi:10.1037/11876-001

Asay, T. P., & Lambert, M. J. (1999). The empirical case for the common factors in therapy: Quantitative findings. In M. Hubble, B. L. Duncan, & S. D. Miller (Eds.), *The heart and soul of change: What works in therapy* (pp. 33–55). Washington, DC: American Psychological Association.

Beck, A. T. (1987). Cognitive approaches to panic disorder: Theory and therapy. In S. Rachman & J. Maser (Eds.), *Panic: Psychological perspectives* (pp. 91–109). Hillsdale, NJ: Erlbaum.

Beck, J. S. (2011). *Cognitive behavior therapy: Basics and beyond* (2nd ed.). New York, NY: Guilford Press.

Beutler, L. E., & Castonguay, L. G. (2006). The task force on empirically based principles of change. In L. G. Castonguay & L. E. Beutler (Eds.), *Principles of therapeutic change that work* (pp. 3–10). New York, NY: Oxford University Press.

Birrer, D., Rothlin, P., & Morgan, G. (2012). Mindfulness to enhance athletic performance: Theoretical considerations and possible impact mechanisms. *Mindfulness, 3*, 235–246. doi:10.1007/s12671-012-0109-2

Brown, D. J., & Fletcher, D. (2017). Effects of psychological and psychosocial interventions on sport performance: A meta-analysis. *Sports Medicine, 47*, 77–99. doi: 10.1007/s40279-016-0552-7

British Psychological Society. (2017). *Practice guidelines*. Retrieved from https://www.bps.org.uk/article-types/guidelines

Bull, S. J. (1991). Personal and situational influences on adherence to mental skills training. *Journal of Sport & Exercise Psychology, 13*, 121–132. doi:10.1123/jsep.13.2.121

Dohme, L.-C., Backhouse, S., Piggott, D., & Morgan, G. (2017). Categorizing and defining popular psychological terms used within the youth athlete talent development literature: A systematic review. *International Review of Sport and Exercise Psychology, 10*(1), 134–163. doi:10.1080/ 1750984X.2016.1185451

Dohme, L.-C., Bloom, G. A., Piggott, D., & Backhouse, S. (2019). Development, implementation and evaluation of an athlete-informed mental skills training program for elite youth tennis players. *Journal of Applied Sport Psychology*, 1–21. doi:10.1080/10413200.2019.1573204

Fortes, L. S., Freitas-Junior, C. J., Paes, P. P., Vieira, L. F., Nascimento-Junior, J. R. A., Araujo Lima-Junior, D. R. A., & Ferreira, M. E. C. (2018). Effect of an eight-week imagery training programme on passing decision-making of young volleyball players. *International Journal of Sport and Exercise Psychology, 6*, 1–9. doi:10.1080/1612197X.2018.1462229

Foster, D., Maynard, I., Butt, J., & Hays, K. (2016). Delivery of psychological skills training to youngsters. *Journal of Applied Sport Psychology, 28*, 62–77. doi:10.1080/10413200.2015.1063097

Fournier, M., Calmels, C., Durand-Bush, N., & Salmela, J.H. (2005). Effects of a season-long PST program on gymnastic performance and on psychological skill development. *International Journal of Sport and Exercise Psychology, 3*, 59–78. doi:10.1080/1612197X.2005.9671758

Gordin, R. D., & Henschen, K. P. (1989). Preparing the USA women's artistic gymnastics team for the 1988 Olympics: A multimodel approach. *The Sport Psychologist, 3*, 366–373. doi:10.1123/tsp.3.4.366

Gould, D. (2002). Moving beyond the psychology of athletic excellence [Special issue]. *Journal of Applied Sport Psychology, 14*, 247–248. doi:10.1080/10413200290103536

Gould, D., & Carson, S. (2008). Life skills development through sport: Current status and future directions. *International Review of Sport and Exercise Psychology, 1*, 58–78. doi:10.1080/17509840701834573

Gould, D., & Maynard, I. (2009). Psychological preparation for the Olympic Games. *Journal of Sports Sciences, 27*, 1393–1408. doi:10.1080/02640410903081845

Gould, D., Medbery, R., Damarjian, N., & Lauer, L. (1999). A survey of mental skills training knowledge, opinions, and practices of junior tennis coaches. Journal of Applied Sport Psychology, 11, 28–50. doi:10.1080/10413209908402949

Gucciardi, D. F., Gordon, S., & Dimmock, J. A. (2009a). Evaluation of a mental toughness training program for youth-aged Australian footballers: I. A quantitative analysis. *Journal of Applied Sport Psychology, 21*, 307–323 doi:10.1080/10413200903026066

Gucciardi, D. F., Gordon, S., & Dimmock, J. A. (2009b). Evaluation of a mental toughness training program for youth-aged Australian footballers: II. A qualitative analysis. *Journal of Applied Sport Psychology, 21*, 324–339. doi:10.1080/10413200903026074

Hardy, L., Barlow, M., Evans, L., Rees, T., Woodman, T., & Warr, C. (2017). Great British medallists: Psychosocial biographies of super-elite and elite athletes from Olympic sports. *Progress in Brain Research, 232*, 1–119. doi:10.1016/bs.pbr.2017.03.004

Harwood, C. (2008). Developmental consulting in a professional football academy: The 5Cs coaching efficacy program. *The Sport Psychologist, 22*, 109–133. doi:10.1123/tsp.22.1.109

Hays, K. F. (Ed.). (2009). *Performance psychology in action: A casebook for working with athletes, performing artists, business leaders, and professionals in high-risk occupations*. Washington, DC: American Psychological Association.

Henriksen, K., Larsen, C. H., Storm, L. K., & Ryom, K. (2014). Sport psychology interventions with young athletes: The perspective of the sport psychology practitioner. *Journal of Clinical Sport Psychology, 8*, 245–260. doi:10.1123/jcsp.2014-0033

Henriksen, K., Stambulova, N., & Roessler, K. K. (2010). Holistic approach to talent development environments: A successful sailing milieu. *Psychology of Sport and Exercise, 11*, 212–222. doi:10.1016/j.psychsport.2009.10.005

Howells, K. (2016). Butterflies, magic carpets, and scary wild animals: An intervention with a young gymnast. *Case Studies in Sport and Exercise Psychology, 1*, 26–37. doi:10.1123/cssep.2016-0006

Kent, M. (2006). *The Oxford dictionary of sports science and medicine* (3rd ed.). Oxford, UK: Oxford University Press.

Kremer, J., & Moran, A. P. (2013). *Pure sport: Practical sport psychology* (2nd ed.). London, UK: Routledge.

Kremer, J., Moran, A., Walker, G., & Craig, C. (2012). *Key concepts in sport psychology.* London, UK: Sage.

Larsen, C., Alfermann, D., & Christensen, M. K. (2012). Psychological skills in a youth soccer academy: A holistic ecological perspective. *Sport Science Review, 11*, 51–74. doi:10.2478/v10237- 012-0010-x

Luborsky, L., Rosenthal, R., Diguer, L., Andrusyna, T. P., Berman, J. S., Levitt, J. T., … & Krause, E. D. (2002). The Dodo bird verdict is alive and well – mostly. *Clinical Psychology: Science and Practice, 9*, 2–12. doi: 10.1093/clipsy.9.1.2

Mace, R. (1990). Cognitive behavioral interventions in sport. In J. G. Jones & L. Hardy (Eds.), *Stress and performance in sport* (pp. 203–230). Chichester, UK: Wiley.

MacNamara, A., Button, A., & Collins, D. (2010). The role of psychological characteristics in facilitating the pathway to elite performance Part 2: Examining environmental and stage-related differences in skills and behaviours. *The Sport Psychologist, 24*, 74–96. doi:10.1123/tsp.24.1.74

MacNamara, A., & Collins, D. (2011). Development and initial validation of the psychological characteristics of developing excellence questionnaire. *Journal of Sports Sciences, 29*, 1273–1286. doi:10.1080/02640414.2011.589468

MacNamara, A., & Collins, D. (2013). Do mental skills make champions? Examining the discriminant function of the psychological characteristics of developing excellence questionnaire. *Journal of Sports Sciences, 31*, 736–744. doi:10.1080/02640414.2012.747692

Martin, S. B., Akers, A., Jackson, A. W., Wrisberg, C. A., Nelson, L., Leslie, P. J., & Larson, L. (2001). Male and female athletes' and nonathletes' expectations about sport psychology consulting. *Journal of Applied Sport Psychology, 13*, 18–39. doi:10.1080/10413200109339002

Martindale, A., & Collins, D. (2007). Enhancing the evaluation of effectiveness with professional judgement and decision making. *The Sport Psychologist, 21*, 458–474. doi:10.1123/tsp.21.4.458

Meichenbaum, D. (1985). *Stress inoculation training.* New York, NY: Pergamon Press.

Michie, S., van Stralen, M. M., & West, R. (2011). The behaviour change wheel: A new method for characterising and designing behaviour change interventions. *Implementation Science, 6*, e42. doi:10.1186/1748-5908-6-42

Miller, P. S., & Kerr, G. A. (2002). Conceptualising excellence: Past, present, and future. *Journal of Applied Sport Psychology, 14*, 140–155. doi:10.1080/10413200290103464

Moran, A. P., & Toner, J. (2017). *A critical introduction to sport psychology* (3rd ed.). London, UK: Routledge.

Murphy, S., & Tammen, V. (1998). In search of psychological skills. In J. L. Duda (Ed.), *Advances in sport and exercise psychology measurement* (pp. 195–209). Morgantown, WV: Fitness Information Technology.

Noh, Y. E., Morris, T., & Andersen, M. B. (2007). Psychological intervention for injury reduction in ballet dancers. *Research in Sports Medicine: An International Journal, 15*, 13–32. doi:10.1080/15438620600987064

Orlick, T., & McCaffrey, N. (1991). Mental training with children for sport and life. *The Sport Psychologist, 5*, 322–334. doi:10.1123/tsp.5.4.322

Pain, M. A., & Harwood, C. (2004). Knowledge and perceptions of sport psychology within English soccer. *Journal of Sports Sciences, 22*, 813–826 doi:10.1080/02640410 410001716670

Sharp, L., & Hodge, K. (2014). Sport psychology consulting effectiveness: The athlete's perspective. *International Journal of Sport and Exercise Psychology, 12*, 91–105. doi:10.1080/1612197X.2013. 804285

Sharp, L., Woodcock, C., Holland, M. J. G., Cumming, J., & Duda, J. L. (2013). A qualitative evaluation of the effectiveness of a mental skills training program for youth athletes. *The Sport Psychologist, 27*, 219–232. doi:10.1123/tsp.27.3.219

Tremayne, P. (1995). Children and sport psychology. In T. Morris & J. Summers (Eds.), *Sport psychology: Theories, applications and issues* (pp. 516–537). New York, NY: Wiley.

Tremayne, P., & Newbery, G. (2005). Mental skill training program for children. In D. Hackfort, R. Lidor, & J. Duda (Eds.), *Handbook of research in applied sport psychology* (pp. 93–106). Morgantown, WV: Fitness Information Technology.

Vealey, R. (1988). Future directions in psychological skills training. *The Sport Psychologist, 2*, 318–336.

Vealey, S. R. (2007). Mental skills training in sport. In G. Tenenbaum, R. Eklund, & R. Singer (Eds.), *Handbook of sport psychology* (3rd ed., pp. 285–309). Hoboken, NJ: Wiley.

Visek, A. J., Harris, B. S., & Blom, L. C. (2009). Doing sport psychology: A youth sport consulting model for practitioners. *The Sport Psychologist, 23*, 271–291.

Visek, A. L., Harris, B. S., & Blom, L. C. (2013). Mental training with youth sport teams: Developmental considerations and best practice recommendations. *Journal of Sport Psychology in Action, 4*, 45–55. doi:10.1080/21520704.2012.733910

Weinberg, R. S., & Gould D. (2007). *Foundations of sport and exercise psychology* (4th ed.). Champaign, IL: Human Kinetics.

Weinberg, R. S., & Williams, J. M. (2015). Integrating and implementing a psychological skills training program. In J. Williams & V. Krane (Eds.), *Applied sport psychology: Personal growth to peak performance* (pp. 329–358). New York, NY: McGraw Hill.

Weiss, M. R. (1991). Psychological skill development in children and adolescents. *The Sport Psychologist, 5*, 335–354. doi:10.1123/tsp.5.4.335

Weiss, M. R. (2011). Teach the children well: A holistic approach to developing psychosocial and behavioural competencies through physical education. *Quest, 6*, 55–65. doi: 10.1080/00336297.2011.10483663

Wrisberg, C., Simpson, D., Loberg, L., Withycombe, J., & Reed, A. (2009). NCAA division 1 student-athletes' receptivity to mental skills training by sport psychology consultants. *The Sport Psychologist, 23*, 470–486. doi:10.1123/tsp.23.4.470

19

CONTEMPORARY APPROACHES TO SPORT LEADERSHIP

Megan E. Gilchrist and Clifford J. Mallett

Leadership is a critical group process necessary for team functioning and success. Team success has been attributed, in part, to effective leadership from coaches, athletes, and management staff (Fletcher & Arnold, 2011; Morgan, Fletcher, & Sarkar, 2015). In our own work with high performance teams, leadership is a consistent area for improvement with coaches and athletes. We have come to realize, however, that improving the leadership capabilities of others is a challenging and, at times, elusive task; therefore, as we will discuss shortly, we view leadership as a *wicked problem*.

Broadly speaking, leadership is defined as "a process whereby an individual influences a group [or team] of individuals to achieve a common goal" (Northouse, 2010, p. 3). Thus, leadership involves a process of influence, bounded within a group that is working toward a common goal (Northouse, 2010). Extending Northouse's definition in several important ways, leadership does not reside within an individual; instead, it exists within the interdependent relationships between leaders and followers within a team (Haslam, Reicher, & Platow, 2011). Additionally, anyone can (theoretically) be a leader (Northouse, 2010). Although appointed leaders (e.g., coach, captain) are formally responsible for leadership tasks, influential group members may emerge as informal leaders (Loughead & Hardy, 2005). Concomitantly, simply appointing individuals to leadership positions does not guarantee their effectiveness as leaders (Fransen, Vanbeselaere, De Cuyper, Vande Broek, & Boen, 2014).

When it comes to understanding leadership and developing leadership in sport, the social identity approach to leadership (Haslam et al., 2011) offers a promising line of inquiry to inform practice. From a social identity perspective, when considering leadership, the significance of the group cannot be overstated. It is an individual's ability to think in terms of "we" and not "I" that allows for the existence of leadership because without the presence of a group to lead, leadership is not possible (Haslam et al., 2011). For leaders to be effective, they must first understand the group (i.e., its values, norms, relevant sub-groups), then represent the group, and finally bring to life the goals and values that are important to the group. Effective leadership is therefore embedded within and inseparable from the group, and the context in which that group exists (Haslam et al., 2011).

Leadership research is extensive, which is largely due to the perceived importance and centrality of leadership to team functioning (see Haslam et al., 2011; Northouse, 2010). According to Jones (2002) "effective leadership is the lifeblood of both sport and business organisations" (p. 273). It is noteworthy that leadership is a complex interpersonal process influenced by various social, political, and cultural forces (e.g., Cruickshank, Collins, & Minten, 2013; Haslam et al., 2011). Despite the critical importance of leadership, based on our experiences with high-performance teams, effective leadership is often elusive and poorly understood and enacted; consequently, we classify it here as a wicked problem (Rittel & Webber, 1973; Vaughan, Mallett, Davids, Potrac, & López-Felip, 2019).

Wicked problems are problems or challenges that are highly complex, difficult to define, and inseparable from the context in which they exist (Rittel & Webber, 1973). Due to this inseparability, wicked problems are also unique. Although leadership issues might exist in teams, the underlying reasons for and emergence of these issues are likely to differ depending on the team, its culture, and its context. Every problem is a symptom of another problem (Rittel & Webber, 1973). For example, poor team leadership might reflect the pressures associated with not performing in an industry obsessed by winning that, in turn, is driven by the increasingly commercialized and globalized nature of high-performance sport. Considering athlete leadership, the divide in the playing group may be representative of deeper team culture issues, which are further underpinned by the performance-driven nature of high-performance sport as a result of the commercialization of sport more broadly.

When it comes to "solving" wicked problems, potential solutions are good-bad rather than true-false; there is no perfect answer and our judgments of these solutions may differ depending on our beliefs and values (Rittel & Webber, 1973). Any potential solutions that are implemented also cause a ripple effect. For instance, by appointing certain players as leaders, a strategy that is often successful (e.g., Hodge, Henry, & Smith, 2014), inevitably others in the group are excluded as leaders, which may create a divide within the playing group (Cole & Martin, 2018). Thus, potential solutions can lead to unintended consequences. Acknowledging leadership as a wicked problem recognizes the difficulty associated with understanding leadership within a team and acknowledges varied solutions (e.g., diverse perspectives regarding leadership development; Duguay, Loughead, & Munroe-Chandler, 2016; Slater & Barker, 2018) and their unintended consequences that may arise.

Given the solution to leadership challenges rests in how well the problem is defined, this needs to be the first port of call. However, "one of the most intractable problems is that of defining problems...and of locating problems...In turn, and equally intractable, is the problem of identifying the actions that might effectively narrow the gap between what-is and what-ought-to-be" (Rittel & Webber, p. 159). Therefore, understanding the team and potential challenges is critical to shaping and developing leadership capability.

The remainder of this chapter will focus on three key considerations of leadership. First, we will discuss the importance of leaderful teams, where there is leadership across different levels and individuals. Second, we identify the importance of followers. Typically, leadership development, as the name suggests, focuses on leaders. Without followers, leadership is not possible. Third, high-performance sport is a volatile and results-driven context, which may promote the use of less desirable leadership behaviors. Although effective leaders are often lauded as transformational, there are times where transformational leadership appears to be ineffective. Prior to addressing these considerations, we provide a brief overview of coaches and athletes as leaders.

Coach as leader

Coaches engage in diverse and myriad leadership behaviors on a daily basis to intentionally influence followers. These behaviors include the recruitment and selection of team members (e.g., athletes and support staff/assistant coaches; Molan, Matthews, & Arnold, 2016); task-related behaviors, such as instruction and feedback; as well as relational behaviors such as social support (Loughead & Hardy, 2005). Ultimately, coaches are required to create a training and competition environment conducive to superior performance. Thus, coaches occupy an inherently influential position. As a result, their power is derived from the position rather than any individual characteristics and the coach is a "hierarchically recognised position of authority" (Wilson, 2017, p. 154). This is not surprising given the responsibility and accountability of the team's performance ultimately lies with the coach (Gammelsæter, 2013) and the coach's ability to influence key performance dimensions, such as motivation (Gillet, Vallerand, Amoura, & Baldes, 2010) and cohesion (Price & Weiss, 2013). As a result, leadership is inherent in the coaching role.

Coaches are leaders in their own right; critically, they are also charged with developing and promoting leadership in other areas of the organization (e.g., among athletes and assistant coaches; Hodge et al., 2014; Manz, Pearce, Mott, Henson, & Sims Jr., 2013). Coaches, however, do not always have the requisite knowledge or skills to develop the leadership capacities of themselves and others. When this is the case, coaches often seek external support (Cruickshank & Collins, 2013) in an attempt to develop leadership within their team.

Athlete as leader

Increasingly, the importance of effective athlete leaders is recognized as a critical contributor of team success. Similar to coaches as leaders, athletes engage in diverse leadership roles that are different yet complementary to coaches' leadership behaviors (Loughead & Hardy, 2005). Athlete leaders are often the bridge between the coach and the team, engage in more democratic and supportive behaviors when compared to coaches, and are responsible for on-field decision-making (Cotterill & Cheetham, 2017; Loughead & Hardy, 2005). Although leadership is part of a coach's job description, leadership for athletes means engaging in tasks above and beyond their playing role, for which they are often not appropriately prepared (Cotterill & Cheetham, 2017).

Athlete leaders face unique challenges. Although leadership is inherent within a coach's position, athlete leadership represents an additional job for the athlete while, simultaneously, maintaining their on-field performance. Captains carry extra pressure for team performance (Camiré, 2016). Separating playing form from leadership duties is a key consideration for athlete leaders (Cotterill, Cheetham, & Fransen, 2019). When athlete leaders are not playing well, their leadership credibility may be called into question by others, and the leaders themselves may feel fraudulent. For a professional ice hockey captain, speaking up in the locker room was difficult when he was not performing on the ice (Camiré, 2016). Leadership can, for some athletes, be a burden and it appears as though playing well earns athlete leaders the right to "lead."

Another challenging aspect for athlete leaders is the regularity and consistency with which they need to act as leaders. Athlete leadership includes on- and off-field tasks and responsibilities within and external to the team (Camiré, 2016; Cotterill & Cheetham, 2017). For example, athlete leaders are required to make on-field decisions, motivate players, engage with fans, and regularly speak with the media. Additionally, a large component of athlete leadership appears to be leading by example, including on-field and off-field behaviors, such as turning up early, driving team standards, and superior performance (Camiré, 2016; Cotterill & Cheetham, 2017). Within elite and professional teams, such behaviors are designed to facilitate performance and create a culture of excellence (Cruickshank et al., 2013; Hodge et al., 2014). There seems little respite for athlete leaders and limited opportunities to turn off (Smith, Arnold, & Thelwell, 2017). Leadership also encompasses athletes' discretionary time (Smith et al., 2017). By engaging in and embodying their team's standards of excellence, athlete leaders often have to make decisions regarding alcohol, recovery, and nutrition on a consistent and ongoing basis. For athlete leaders, this leadership role can be a 24/7 job above and beyond their playing role.

Leaderful teams

Promoting effective leadership within teams often means distributing leadership across multiple people. Distributing leadership allows individuals to work to their strengths and minimizes leadership voids if any one leader is unavailable (Manz et al., 2013). When it comes to leadership, there is strength in numbers. Leadership can be shared across various individuals and groups. For instance, coaches can share duties, coaches also rely on athletes to contribute to leadership, and leadership can be distributed across different athletes. Leaderful teams, therefore, are teams where leadership is effectively shared within and across coaches and athletes.

Athlete leadership roles are diverse; therefore, having a single captain may mean there are leadership voids within the team. For example, the captain may be an effective on-field leader, but not great at creating a strong team atmosphere off the field. To reduce the burden on any single player, formalizing an athlete leadership group provides athletes (and coaches) with clarity regarding athlete leadership roles. Captains lean on other senior players for leadership support (Cotterill & Cheetham, 2017). In doing so, it relieves some of the pressures on the captain and simultaneously provides leadership experience to other teammates (Camiré, 2016). Recently, Fransen et al. (2017) used social network analysis (discussed later in the chapter) to identify that the team with the highest quality of shared athlete leadership was associated with positive indicators of team functioning and performance.

Shared leadership is also beneficial among coaches. Coaches rarely work in isolation, particularly at the elite level. Therefore, head coaches are responsible for overseeing a cohesive coaching group where all coaches, to varying degrees, have their own styles, roles, and responsibilities (Fletcher & Streeter, 2016; Molan et al., 2016). Coaches have different strengths that, together, may provide a more well-rounded, complementary coaching group. For instance, Molan et al. (2016) reported that assistant coaches have closer day-to-day relationships with athletes than the head coach. Illustrating a shared structure among coaches, Graham Henry, the head coach of the New Zealand All Blacks stated,

> Although I was called head coach, and they were called assistant coaches… we're all on the same level, and I always conducted it that way. …Because the more ownership you can give these guys… the better they're gonna feel… and that's why they're gonna coach well.
>
> *(Hodge et al., 2014, p. 69)*

The relationship between coaches and athlete leaders is critical to leadership effectiveness and team functioning (Cotterill et al., 2019; Webster, Hardy, & Hardy, 2017). Athlete leaders are a conduit between coaches and the wider team; coaches rely on athlete leaders to reinforce and clarify their messages with the team (Carson & Walsh, 2018) and athlete leaders are the voice of the team to the coaches (Cotterill et al., 2019). When this relationship between the coaches and athlete leaders is strained, it might become a source of stress for the athlete leaders (Smith et al., 2017) and can result in ambiguity and confusion for the team (Webster et al., 2017).

In this section, we have argued that effective leadership is more often than not shared within and across coaches and athletes. This leadership, however, is not typically distributed evenly across these individuals; nor is it realistic (nor ideal) for all team members to be leaders. Shared leadership does not result in leaders abdicating responsibility (Manz et al., 2013). As a result, shared leadership, in the sporting sense, is not entirely horizontal; there remains a (somewhat) vertical leadership structure where single individuals (e.g., the head coach and, to a lesser degree, the captain) are responsible for key decisions. There is a distribution but not a release of power and influence. This distribution of power is evident at the coach and captain level. Just as the head coach needs to lead the coaches and the team, the captain needs to lead the player leadership group and the players.

To illustrate this point, in their work on serial winning coaches, Mallett and Lara-Bercial (2016) referred to these coaches as "benevolent dictators" (p. 305). These coaches considered others' perspectives and collaborated with athletes but, ultimately, were responsible for decision-making, which was, at times, unpopular among athletes. It is the coach who has the last word (Camiré, 2016). Similarly, in their discussion of culture change within a professional rugby union team, Cruickshank et al. (2013) identified that coaches shaped the environment in such a way that players were provided with a degree of autonomy and self-regulation, yet responses and behaviors were shaped by coaches in such a way as to elicit desired and appropriate outcomes, which were ultimately designed to "minimise the likelihood of potentially dangerous swings in control" (p. 285). Finally, in their description of the horizontal coaching structure and player leadership group within the New Zealand All Blacks, Hodge et al. (2014) acknowledged it was Graham Henry, the head coach, who proposed this distribution of influence and power.

The implicit assumption regarding leaderful teams is there are multiple competent leaders within the team; however, this is not always the case. When team members have limited leadership knowledge, ability, or skill, shared leadership is unlikely to facilitate team functioning (Conger & Pearce, 2003). Coaches may need to consider other potential situations where shared leadership may not be appropriate. For instance, Morgan et al. (2015) reported that transformational leadership from the coach was the dominant leadership approach in the early stages of the England Rugby Team's victorious 2003 World Cup campaign that, over time, shifted to a more shared approach. Shared leadership takes time to learn and implement. Shared leadership in and of itself is not a silver bullet; instead shared leadership is a tool used by leaders (i.e., the head coach) in certain situations to help the team achieve a common goal (Locke, 2003).

Engendering followership

Often, we attach too much focus to the leaders: what leaders do (Bucci, Bloom, Loughead, & Caron, 2012), the challenges leaders experience (Cotterill & Cheetham, 2017), and developing leadership capabilities (Duguay et al., 2016). However, leaders are only leading if people are following; quite simply, if there are no followers, there are no leaders (Haslam et al., 2011). Followers in this context are "people who are influenced in ways that motivate them to actively contribute to collective goals" (Steffens, Haslam, Jetten, & Mols, 2018, p. 26). Although, at times, followership is associated with negative connotations (e.g., followers are sheep; Steffens et al., 2018), followers are critical, active contributors to team processes and performance and their presence allows leadership to exist. The emphasis on leaders, therefore, needs to be about engaging followers and facilitating the leader-follower relationship to put the group in the best position possible to achieve their goals. To engage followers, leaders must foster a shared group identity because, referring back to an earlier point, without a group, there is no one to lead (Haslam et al., 2011).

Critically, leaders must understand the group they are seeking to lead. According to Haslam et al. (2011), "*it is impossible to lead a group unless one first understands the nature of the group that is to be led*" (p. 207; emphasis in original). Understanding the group includes its values, norms, attitudes, and behaviors. There are different ways coaches and athlete leaders can understand the group including, activities such as personal disclosure mutual sharing (PDMS), where individuals share previously untold stories related to their sporting/team involvement and their personal life (Slater, Evans, & Turner, 2015). More recently, social identity mapping (see Cruwys et al., 2016; Haslam et al., 2017; Slater & Barker, 2018) has been posited as a technique whereby individuals identify relevant sub-groups within their team and the relationships that exist between these groups. Moreover, creating team covenants or shared values statements (Henriksen, 2015) provides team members with an understanding of what is important and why.

Once the team has identified what is important to them and why (e.g., relevant sub-groups, values), leaders and other group members should reflect these qualities in their day-to-day behaviors. Identifying key components (e.g., sub-groups, values) is relatively "easy" for team members to address. Teams typically work through exercises in small groups to arrive at a coherent picture for the team. What is significantly more challenging, however, is translating these values into lived reality (Henriksen, 2015). Leadership, therefore, moves beyond understanding the group and additionally encompasses the translation of values on a piece of paper into structures and behaviors that are lived on a consistent basis. Team members, with an emphasis on leaders, need to engage in behaviors that support their espoused values. In a sporting environment, points of consideration include: on- and off-field behaviors, rewards and sanctions for behaviors and attitudes that support/do not support what is important to "us," and the tangible structures and strategies that can be implemented to help reinforce who we are.

To reiterate a point we made earlier, coaches may not have comprehensive knowledge of leadership and leadership development, yet they are important stakeholders when working with teams to develop leadership capacity. Therefore, careful consideration should be given to the level of involvement from the coach during these processes. It is important for the coach to be aware of the program of leadership development and be part of the process rather than a passive bystander. If leadership effectiveness rests on leaders understanding and embodying what is important to the group, this also includes the coaches. Moreover, coaches have more regular contact with athletes and support staff, and are, therefore, in a stronger position (in terms of frequency and influence) to reinforce key messages. The coach should champion the program among the team. Over-involvement has the potential to become problematic because it may hinder the leadership development and capability of athletes (e.g., athletes may not respond openly or honestly in the presence of their coach). The coach's presence may, at times, stifle the athlete voice or promote athletes to respond to questions or activities in ways that they believe the coach wants. Therefore, support of rather than total participation in the program of leadership development seems more preferable.

The concept and act of followership is also important for aspiring leaders. Recent research has shown that, in a military setting, cadets who identified as followers (i.e., individuals who believed the task was more important than getting their own way; those who work hard for other people's ideas) were more likely to be perceived as leaders by their peers than those cadets who self-identified as leaders (Peters & Haslam, 2018). For aspiring leaders, it is therefore important to be group-oriented and work hard for the group. Doing your job well is the first step to becoming a leader.

Interestingly, in this same study, commanders had different perspectives of leaders compared with the cadets (Peters & Haslam, 2018). For the commanders, those cadets who self-identified as leaders were more likely to be perceived as leaders. Applying that logic to a sport setting, it is important for coaches to understand athletes' perspectives on not only what is important to the team but also which athletes are perceived to be the most influential leaders. Coaches and athletes may have different perspectives regarding who are the "best" leaders (Fransen et al., 2014). This can become problematic because those athletes designated to lead might not be influential among the very people they are expected to lead, creating an ineffective leadership structure. The athlete voice is, therefore, critical to the creation of values and behaviors that are important to the team and underpin effective leadership, and to understand athletes' perspectives when it comes to appointing leaders within the team.

A technique that has been useful in understanding athletes' perspectives of influential athlete leaders within the team is social network analysis (SNA; Fransen et al., 2014). Athletes are asked to judge their teammates' leadership abilities, which provides coaches with invaluable insight into influential athletes within the team. This information can be used to guide the selection of formal athlete leaders.

So far, this section has focused on athletes as followers in the traditional view of leaders leading "down"; yet, leadership is multidirectional and leaders also need to lead up (e.g., athletes leading coaches; coaches leading board members), sideways (e.g., athletes leading fellow athlete leaders; coaches leading coaches), and out (e.g., external stakeholders such as the media and fans). The key with leading in different directions is that there needs to be alignment in communication and behaviors that reinforce the values and identities that are important to the team.

Are leadership behaviors always "desirable?"

Until this point in the chapter, leadership and leadership behaviors have been discussed in a positive way. Leaders steer the direction of the group, engage in on- and off-field decision-making, and foster an environment conducive to high performance. Sport, however, is a highly political, socially complex, ruthless and volatile, performance-driven environment (e.g., Cruickshank & Collins, 2015; Cruickshank et al., 2013), which lends itself to leaders engaging in less than desirable leadership behaviors. These behaviors include, but are not limited to, Machiavellianism, self-promoting behaviors, deceit, and cold-blooded ruthlessness (e.g., Arnold, Fletcher, & Hobson, 2018; Cruickshank & Collins, 2015). Although common sense may suggest that these leadership behaviors are counterproductive, researchers have reported that, in certain circumstances, these less desirable (from a moral and ethical standpoint) behaviors may, in fact, contribute to success from the athletes' (Arnold et al., 2018) and leaders' (Cruickshank & Collins, 2015) perspectives.

Although these behaviors may contribute to success in the normative sense, research has also shown that from a psychological and well-being perspective, these types of behaviors are potentially damaging (Arnold et al., 2018). Recently, there has been increased interest in and concern about athletes' psychological health and well-being, particularly in high-performance sport (Henriksen et al., 2019). Although these less desirable leadership behaviors can potentially result in success, coaches need to be acutely aware of the effects on athletes' (and other coaches and support staff) health and well-being, which is often not the case.

It is a potentially dangerous assertion that coaches *need* to engage in these negative behaviors. The positive outcomes (e.g., motivation, resilience, learning, and awareness) identified by Arnold et al. (2018) can all be attained through more positive means. For instance, there is extensive research to suggest that psychological need-supportive coaching behaviors and transformational leadership are associated with not only superior performance but also positive individual outcomes for athletes within the high-performance domain (e.g., Morgan et al., 2015). Additionally, referring back to the concept of benevolent dictator (Mallett & Lara-Bercial, 2016), perhaps less desirable behaviors need to be underpinned by a strong sense of care, support, and trust in order to ensure their success.

Summary

At the beginning of this chapter, we posited that leadership was a wicked problem. Indeed, there is no magic solution to leadership; nor is there one "right way" to develop leadership. There is also no endpoint when it comes to leadership in either the short-term (e.g., clocking off at the end of the day) or long-term (e.g., as long as teams exist, leadership is necessary). In our work with high-performance sports teams, effective leadership has, at times, remained elusive and, in other instances, taken years to evolve.

Based on the ideas raised in this chapter, we leave the reader with some guiding principles for consideration:

1 When it comes to leadership, the importance of the context cannot be overstated. When wanting to develop leaders, take time to understand the context, including the values and standards of the team; leadership, for example, will "look" different in cricket compared with Australian rules football.
2 To improve the quality and quantity of leaders within your team, it is necessary to build the capabilities of others. Team members (e.g., athletes, assistant coaches) need to be given opportunities to engage in leadership tasks and reflect on their experiences in order to learn and improve.
3 Leadership is an extra challenge for coaches and athletes who are, at times, not fully prepared for the additional responsibility. Leadership (and followership) requires time and investment of resources that can be draining. Leadership is often shared in teams between coaches and players, and it is important that all concerned are clear on how that collaboration works and who makes what decisions.
4 Building on the previous point, sharing leadership tasks and responsibilities can reduce the burden on any one individual; however, leaders (e.g., player leadership group) need to know how to lead together. Leadership is not just about *my* leadership capabilities but about *our* leadership capabilities. Within-leadership group functioning is a critical component to leadership effectiveness; therefore, working on group processes (e.g., communication) with the collective leaders is important.

References

Arnold, R., Fletcher, D., & Hobson, J. A. (2018). Performance leadership and management in elite sport: A black and white issue or different shades of grey? *Journal of Sport Management, 32*, 452–463. doi:10.1123/jsm.2017-0296

Bucci, J., Bloom, G. A., Loughead, T. M., & Caron, J. G. (2012). Ice hockey coaches' perceptions of athlete leadership. *Journal of Applied Sport Psychology, 24*, 243–259. doi: 10.1080/10413200.2011.636416

Camiré, M. (2016). Benefits, pressures, and challenges of leadership and captaincy in the National Hockey League. *Journal of Clinical Sport Psychology, 10*, 118–136. doi:10.1123/jcsp.2015-0033

Carson, F., & Walsh, J. (2018). Every day's a new day: A captain's reflection on a losing season. *Sports, 6*(4), 1–10. doi:10.3390/sports6040115

Cole, J., & Martin, A. J. (2018). Developing a winning sport team culture: Organizational culture in theory and practice. *Sport in Society, 21*, 1204–1222. doi:10.1080/17430437.2018.1442197

Conger, J. A., & Pearce, C. L. (2003). A landscape of opportunities: Future research and shared leadership. In C. L. Pearce & J. A. Conger (Eds.), *Shared leadership: Reframing the hows and whys of leadership* (pp. 285–304). Thousand Oaks, CA: Sage.

Cotterill, S., & Cheetham, R. (2017). The experience of captaincy in professional sport: The case of elite professional rugby. *European Journal of Sport Science, 17*, 215–221. doi: 10.1080/17461391.2016.1245788

Cotterill, S., Cheetham, R., & Fransen, K. (2019). Professional rugby coaches' perceptions of the role of the team captain. *The Sport Psychologist*, Advance online publication. doi:10.1123/tsp.2018-0094

Cruickshank, A., & Collins, D. (2013). Culture change in elite sport performance teams: Outlining an important and unique construct. *Sport and Exercise Psychology Review, 9*(2), 6–21. Retrieved from https://www.bps.org.uk/publications/sport-and-exercise-psychology-review

Cruickshank, A., & Collins, D. (2015). Illuminating and applying "the dark side": Insights from elite team leaders. *Journal of Applied Sport Psychology, 27*, 249–267. doi:10.1080/10413200.2014.982771

Cruickshank, A., Collins, D., & Minten, S. (2013). Culture change in a professional sports team: Shaping environmental contexts and regulating power. *International Journal of Sports Science and Coaching, 8*, 319–326. doi:10.1260/1747-9541.8.2.319

Cruwys, T., Steffens, N. K., Haslam, S. A., Haslam, C., Jetten, J., & Dingle, G. A. (2016). Social identity mapping: A procedure for visual representation and assessment of subjective multiple group memberships. *British Journal of Social Psychology, 55*, 613–642. doi:10.1111/bjso.12155

Duguay, A. M., Loughead, T. M., & Munroe-Chandler, K. J. (2016). The development, implementation, and evaluation of an athlete leadership development program with female varsity athletes. *The Sport Psychologist, 30*, 154–166. doi:10.1123/tsp.2015-0050

Fletcher, D., & Arnold, R. (2011). A qualitative study of performance leadership and management in elite sport. *Journal of Applied Sport Psychology, 23*, 223–242. doi:10.1080/10413200.2011.559184

Fletcher, D., & Streeter, A. (2016). A case study analysis of a high performance environment in elite swimming. *Journal of Change Management, 16*, 123–141. doi:10.1080/14697017.2015.1128470

Fransen, K., Haslam, S. A., Mallett, C. J., Steffens, N. K., Peters, K., & Boen, F. (2017). Is perceived athlete leadership quality related to team effectiveness? A comparison of three professional sports teams. *Journal of Science and Medicine in Sport, 20*, 800–806. doi:10.1016/j.jsams.2016.11.024

Fransen, K., Vanbeselaere, N., De Cuyper, B., Vande Broek, G., & Boen, F. (2014). The myth of the team captain as principal leader: Extending the athlete leadership classification within sport teams *Journal of Sports Sciences, 32*, 1389–1397. doi:10.1080/02640414.2014.891291

Gammelsæter, H. (2013). Leader succession and effectiveness in team sport. A critical review of the coach succession literature. *Sport, Business and Management: An International Journal, 3*, 285–296. doi:10.1108/SBM-06-2013-0015

Gillet, N., Vallerand, R. J., Amoura, S., & Baldes, B. (2010). Influence of coaches' autonomy support on athletes' motivation and sport performance: A test of the hierarchical model of intrinsic and extrinsic motivation. *Psychology of Sport & Exercise, 11*, 155–161. doi: 10.1016/j.psychsport.2009.10.004

Haslam, S. A., Reicher, S., & Platow, M. J. (2011). *The new psychology of leadership: Identity, influence and power.* East Sussex, England: Psychology Press.

Haslam, S. A., Steffens, N. K., Peters, K., Boyce, R. A., Mallett, C. J., & Fransen, K. (2017). A social identity approach to leadership development: The 5R program. *Journal of Personnel Psychology, 16*, 113–124. doi:10.1027/1866-5888/a000176

Henriksen, K. (2015). Developing a high-performance culture: A sport psychology intervention from an ecological perspective in elite orienteering. *Journal of Sport Psychology in Action, 6*, 141–153. doi:10.1080/21520704.2015.1084961

Henriksen, K., Schinke, R., Moesch, K., McCann, S., Parham, W. D., Larsen, C. H., & Terry, P. (2019). Consensus statement on improving the mental health of high performance athletes. *International Journal of Sport and Exercise Psychology*. doi:10.1080/1612197X.2019.1570473

Hodge, K., Henry, G., & Smith, W. (2014). A case study of excellence in elite sport: Motivational climate in a world champion team. *The Sport Psychologist, 28*, 60–74. doi:10.1123/tsp.2013-0037

Jones, G. (2002). Performance excellence: A personal perspective on the link between business and sport. *Journal of Applied Sport Psychology, 14*, 268–281. doi:10.1080/10413200290103554

Locke, E. A. (2003). Leadership: Starting at the top. In C. L. Pearce & J. A. Conger (Eds.), *Shared leadership: Reframing the hows and whys of leadership* (pp. 271–284). Thousand Oaks, CA: Sage.

Loughead, T. M., & Hardy, J. (2005). An examination of coach and peer leader behaviors in sport. *Psychology of Sport and Exercise, 6*, 303–312. doi:10.1016/j.psychsport.2004.02.001

Mallett, C. J., & Lara-Bercial, S. (2016). Serial winning coaches: People, vision and environment. In M. Raab, P. Wylleman, R. Seiler, A. Elbe, & A. Hatzigeorgiadis (Eds.), *Sport and exercise psychology research* (pp. 289–322). London, UK: Academic Press.

Manz, C. C., Pearce, C. L., Mott, J. W., Henson, Z., & Sims Jr., H. P. (2013). Don't take the lead…share the lead: Surprising leadership lessons from big time college sports. *Organizational Dynamics, 42*, 54–60. doi:10.1016/j.orgdyn.2012.12.007

Molan, C., Matthews, J., & Arnold, R. (2016). Leadership off the pitch: The role of the manager in semi-professional football. *European Sport Management Quarterly, 16*, 274–291. doi:10.1080/16184742.2016.1164211

Morgan, P. B. C., Fletcher, D., & Sarkar, M. (2015). Understanding team resilience in the world's best athletes: A case study of a rugby union World Cup winning team. *Psychology of Sport and Exercise, 16*, 91–100. doi:10.1016/j.psychsport.2014.08.007

Northouse, P. G. (2010). *Leadership: Theory & practice* (5th ed.). Thousand Oaks, CA: Sage.

Peters, K., & Haslam, S. A. (2018). I follow, therefore I lead: A longitudinal study of leader and follower identity and leadership in the marines. *British Journal of Psychology, 109*, 708–723. doi:10.1111/bjop.12312

Price, M. S., & Weiss, M. R. (2013). Relationships among coach leadership, peer leadership, and adolescent athletes' psychosocial and team outcomes: A test of transformational leadership theory. *Journal of Applied Sport Psychology, 25*, 265–279. doi:10.1080/10413200.2012.725703

Rittel, H. W. J., & Webber, M. M. (1973). Dilemmas in a general theory of planning. *Policy Sciences, 4*, 155–169. doi:10.1007/BF01405730

Slater, M. J., & Barker, J. B. (2018). Doing social identity leadership: Exploring the efficacy of an identity leadership intervention on perceived leadership and mobilization in elite disability soccer. *Journal of Applied Sport Psychology, 31*, 65–86. doi:10.1080/10413200.2017.1410255

Slater, M. J., Evans, A. L., & Turner, M. J. (2015). Implementing a social identity approach for effective change management. *Journal of Change Management, 16*, 18–37. doi:10.1080/14697017.2015.1103774

Smith, M. J., Arnold, R., & Thelwell, R. C. (2017). "There's no place to hide": Exploring the stressors encountered by elite cricket captains. *Journal of Applied Sport Psychology, 30*, 150–170. doi:10.1080/10413200.2017.1349845

Steffens, N. K., Haslam, S. A., Jetten, J., & Mols, F. (2018). Our followers are lions, theirs are sheep: How social identity shapes theories about followership and social influence. *Political Psychology, 39*, 23–42. doi:10.1111/pops.12387

Vaughan, J., Mallett, C. J., Davids, K., Potrac, P., & López-Felip, M. A. (2019). Developing creativity to enhance human potential in sport and life: A wicked transdisciplinary challenge. *Frontiers in Psychology,* Advance online publication. doi:10.339/fpsyg.2019.02090

Webster, L. V., Hardy, J., & Hardy, L. (2017). Big hitters: Important factors characterizing team effectiveness in professional cricket. *Frontiers in Psychology, 8*, 1140. doi:10.3389/fpsyg.2017.01140

Wilson, N. (2017). Developing distributed leadership: Leadership emergence in a sporting context. In C. Ilie & S. Schnurr (Eds.), *Challenging leadership stereotypes through discourse* (pp. 147–170). Singapore: Springer.

20

REFEREES

Developmental, performance, and training considerations

Roy David Samuel

Referees are an integral and important part of the sport environment, being those who oversee the game rules, facilitating fairness and sportive behavior. Moreover, referees are performers on their own merit; they are required to cope with various demands on and off the field, pertaining to performance (e.g., fitness, decision-making, game management), career development (e.g., motivation, career transitions, and change-events), and work-life balance. Due to the breadth of the refereeing topic, a focus is given in this chapter to soccer and basketball refereeing. Assuming a holistic perspective, the motivational and developmental aspects of referees' careers are initially discussed. Then, aspects pertaining to referee training, including psychological skill training and mental preparation for matches, are deliberated. Next, performance considerations are presented, focusing on decision-making, game management, the human-technology interface, and match evaluation. Finally, future avenues for research, training, and applied practice are presented.

According to the *Dictionary of Sport and Exercise Science* (2006), a referee is "an official who oversees the play in a sport or game, judges whether the rules are being followed, and penalizes fouls or infringements" (p. 175). As such, referees are an integral and important part of the sport environment. They often attract scrutiny from the other sport participants (e.g., players, coaches, fans, media) and rarely receive credit or support for their endeavors. MacMahon and Plessner (2008) identified three categories of referees, based on their movement demands, number of observed cues, and the amount of interaction with athletes. *Interactors* (e.g., soccer, basketball, handball referees) have high physical movement demands and numerous environmental cues to process. *Sport monitors* (e.g., gymnastics, volleyball referees) have low-to-medium physical movement and interaction demands, yet relatively numerous environmental cues to process. Finally, *reactors* (e.g., tennis line judges) have low movement and interaction demands, and relatively few cues to monitor. Naturally, more research attention has been given to major sports' officiating, such as soccer (association football) and basketball. For example, a review of the existing soccer refereeing research between the years 1988 and 2016 identified 267 articles, mainly focusing on decision-making aspects, injuries, organizational issues, psychology, physiology, and referee development (Pina, Passos, Araújo, & Maynard, 2018).

Acknowledging the important role of referees, researchers have begun in recent years to consider them as performers on their own merit (Dosseville & Laborde, 2015; MacMahon et al., 2014). Referees have unique motivation (Philippe, Vallerand, Andrianarisoa, & Brunel, 2009) and career processes (Samuel, Galily, & Tenenbaum, 2017), demanding physical standards (Weston, 2015), visual and cognitive requirements (Helsen & Bultynck, 2004; Spitz, Put, Wagemans, Williams, & Helsen, 2018), emotional coping demands (Wolfson & Neave, 2007), and game management expectations (Samuel, 2015). The various dimensions associated with the interactor refereeing role, from a holistic approach, are shown in Figure 20.1. The first level reflects referees' motives and passions as well as their psychological core (i.e., values, interests, beliefs, and personality traits). Without a strong inclination toward refereeing, it is very difficult to persevere, as this occupation can be discouraging in terms of financial rewards or public appreciation. To develop a meaningful refereeing career, referees must effectively cope with various career demands and transitions, develop their skills and fitness through deliberate practice, and engage in psychological skill training, as can be seen in the second level of Figure 20.1. They also need a chance to pursue excellence in a system which does not always allow this. There are several influencing factors which might facilitate or debilitate referees' career development, such as external support resources and work-life balance. Finally, as shown in level three of Figure 20.1, a referee's main task is to perform well, by incorporating adequate decision-making with proper game management. In recent years, the human-technology interface has also become an important aspect of refereeing performance. There are several influencing factors related to refereeing performance, such as match preparation, teamwork, personal characteristics, and performance evaluation. Moreover, we should acknowledge that all three levels tend to influence each other. For example, referees who are undermotivated or do not possess a certain psychological core (e.g., trait self-control) might not aspire to develop a refereeing career by investing the needed effort to reach excellence. Similarly, if a referee does not perform well, the chances of experiencing a long-term and successful career are also diminished.

Motivation and career development

Motives for refereeing

In general, referees report intrinsic motives for refereeing (Hancock, Dawson, & Auger, 2015; Livingston et al., 2017; MacMahon et al., 2014). For example, in

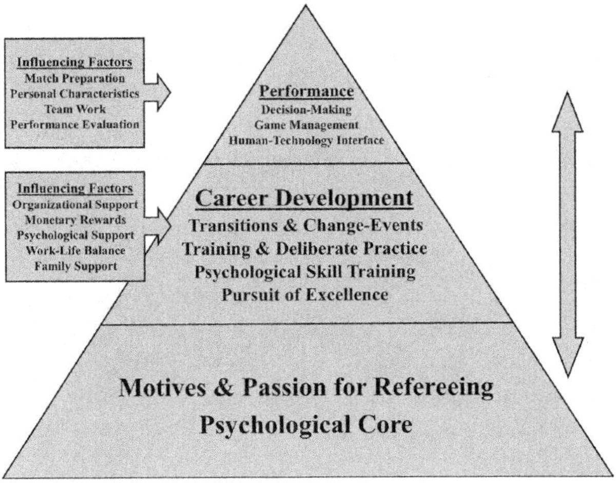

FIGURE 20.1 A hierarchical and holistic perspective of the interactor referee's role.

a study of 514 referees from various Québec sport federations, referees typically reported intrinsic motives (e.g., to prove that one could do it, personal development, enjoyment) and sport-related reasons (e.g., being active in and serving their sports; Hancock et al., 2015). Intrinsic motivation for refereeing, specifically love for the sport and excitement, was also dominant in Johansen's (2015) study of 83 Norwegian soccer referees. In some cases, retired or injured players might wish to continue participating in their beloved sport and maintain a sportive lifestyle (Schnyder & Hossner, 2016). In other cases, soccer fans might be attracted to refereeing as they wish to influence the sport environment (Auger, Fortier, Thibault, Magny, & Gravelle, 2010) or join a sport community (Johansen, 2015). Furthermore, there might be personality-related motives, such as the need to express self-control (Samuel, Englert, Zhang, & Basevitch, 2018) or extraversion (Balch & Scott, 2007). Research has shown that referees tend to maintain high motivation in spite of experiencing stress and aggression (Folkesson, Nyberg, Archer, & Norlander, 2002; Wolfson & Neave, 2007).

Examining the influence of monetary rewards on referees' motivation, a unique trend is evident. At an early stage, referees tend to be intrinsically motivated, although some may be attracted by financial remuneration (Livingston et al., 2017). Yet, as referees develop within their sport, they tend to balance work or academic studies with refereeing demands (Samuel, 2019). Adequate financial compensation then becomes more significant. For example, Bryson, Buraimo, and Simmons (2011) examined the impact of switching from short-term contracts to salaried contracts on English soccer referees' performance, as measured by the number of yellow cards issued per match. Indeed, referees who switched to salaried contracts issued, on average, fewer cards. Bryson et al. (2011) suggested that this process forced them to be more committed to professional training to become successful in their careers.

Importantly, career concerns might also be associated with developing an obsessive passion for refereeing, leading to poorer performance (Philippe et al., 2009, Samuel, 2015). Specifically, Philippe et al. (2009) examined the influence of harmonious and obsessive types of passion on flow experiences among soccer, volleyball, and basketball referees. They found that, in general, the referees had a moderate-to-high passion for refereeing. Elite referees showed higher levels of harmonious passion than non-elite referees. A positive and weak correlation between a harmonious passion for refereeing and flow during matches was also observed. On the other hand, an obsessive passion for refereeing was weakly and positively correlated with the experience of negative emotions during matches and unrelated to positive emotions or flow. These findings supported the importance of developing a harmonious, rather than an obsessive, passion for refereeing, and have important implications for practitioners who support elite referees (see Samuel, 2015, 2019).

Career development

Psychological research on referees has rarely focused on career development. To address this gap, Samuel et al. (2017) examined the career change-events (i.e., transitions, crisis transitions, and longitudinal processes that disrupt the refereeing engagement status quo objectively or subjectively) of 154 Israeli soccer referees and assistant referees from several professional levels. The referees experienced multiple types of change-events (on average more than 10) in their careers, with *a transition to a higher league* (97%), *excelling in a big match* (86%), and *a very poor performance or a decision error in a big match* (74%) being the most common ones. These change-events mainly reflected performance and referee-status issues. International referees experienced an offense by a fellow referee (i.e., ethical misconduct) in higher frequency compared to the lower levels, reflecting the competitiveness of this unique group. The most significant change-events were *receiving an international badge*, *changing from the referee group to the assistant referee group*, *a transition to a higher league*, and *a transition to a lower league*. These results indicated that soccer referees' careers are highly dynamic, requiring special consideration and coping during change-events.

More recently, Samuel (2019) conducted a case study on the experiences of four Israeli soccer referees who transitioned from the second division to the Premier League. He observed that this transition is indeed a multifaceted process, involving professional, physical, psycho-social, and occupational-familial demands. To cope with these demands, the referees consulted with others, received psychological support, and made active decisions to change related attitudes and behaviors. The case study further presented a consultation process designed to facilitate an effective change process in the transition (e.g., promote a harmonious passion for refereeing; see Philippe et al., 2009). The results emphasized the importance of balancing refereeing with other life roles, thereby maintaining a multidimensional refereeing identity and a dual career. Also, it was suggested that sport psychology practitioners should adhere to a whole person perspective when consulting referees in career transitions.

Refereeing excellence

Several scholars have attempted to identify key factors underlying refereeing excellence (e.g., Pina, Passos, Carvalho, & Maynard, 2018; Schnyder & Hossner, 2016; Slack, Maynard, Butt, Olusoga, 2013). For example, Slack et al. (2013) interviewed 15 English Premier League soccer referees and identified eight themes related to being a successful referee. Concerning career development, the referees emphasized the importance of being affiliated to the Premier League select group, self-reflection on performance, and being appointed to numerous challenging Premier League and international matches. These authors concluded that a mixture of physical, environmental, and psychological factors influence refereeing excellence. Similarly, Schnyder and Hossner (2016) interviewed 23 European elite referees. They identified the following characteristics of a good elite referee: educability, game management qualities, mental attributes, fitness, personal characteristics, football intelligence, and experience.

Referee attrition

High refereeing demands combined with lack of support, lack of quality training, and lack of recognition often lead to referee attrition. Annual attrition rates of 20% have been reported for various sports around the world, making attrition a pervasive, persistent, and global problem (Livingston et al., 2017). Attrition rates are typically higher during the first year of refereeing, as a result of realizing the role commitment and requirements, and being exposed to abuse. Experienced officials are more likely to retire as a result of career or family demands (Livingston et al., 2017). For instance, interviews with 15 retired American basketball referees revealed that the main reasons for deciding to retire were problematic social interactions with the sporting community (e.g., players, coaches, parents), lack of training processes or mentoring, lack of a referee community, lack of support from the referee organization, and issues related to career development (Warner, Tingle, & Kellett, 2013). A study with 12 English soccer referees further confirmed the significant impact of organizational issues (lack of support, inadequate training) on referees' intention to retire (Dell, Gervis, & Rhind, 2016).

Referee training

Training

Soccer referees' decision-making accuracy levels for foul incidents, as reported in the literature, range between 55% and 86% (*Mdn* = 64%; see Catteeuw, Helsen,

Gilis, & Wagemans, 2009; Mallo, Gonzalez Frutos, Juárez, & Navarro, 2012; Spitz et al., 2018). This relatively high error rate is not surprising, given the complexity of the soccer refereeing task, which involves various physical, technical, tactical, and mental aspects. In this context, several authors have suggested that effective training of soccer referees' decision-making remains a challenge (e.g., Catteeuw et al., 2009; MacMahon, Helsen, Starkes, & Weston, 2007). Structured training programs for FIFA (Fédération Internationale de Football Association) referees were initiated in 1998. Examining the effects of such programs, MacMahon et al. (2007) asked 26 elite European referees to recall how much time they had spent in various training activities and the associated relevance to improving their refereeing ability in 1998 and in 2003. The results indicated that in 2003 the referees devoted considerable time to on-field (e.g., high-intensity training, speed endurance training) and off-field activities (e.g., video training) each week. Speed endurance and high-intensity training were considered as very relevant for improving refereeing, whereas video training was rated as moderately relevant. The main changes in training reported from 1998 to 2003 were in speed endurance, coordination, agility, recovery training, video training, and psychological skill training. Similarly, Webb, Dicks, Thelwell, and Nevill (2018) charted the evolution of referee training in English association football and conducted interviews with Premier League referees and refereeing-affiliated individuals. The results indicated a marked increase in the level of support and training that referees receive, contributing to an increase in refereeing performance and reduction in home advantage.

In 2010, UEFA (Union of European Football Associations) initiated a specialized training program for young referees of high potential, named CORE (Center of Refereeing Excellence). This program is comprised of a 10-day introductory course followed by an eight-day consolidation course, after four to six months. It focuses on various areas of refereeing, such as fitness training, match preparation, player management, and stress management (Chaplin, 2014). The CORE model was adopted by various UEFA-affiliated referee unions. For example, the Israel Referee Union developed an Excellence Program to select and train referees (Samuel, 2017). Each aspect of the program was designed in line with the deliberate practice perspective for developing expertise in referees (Catteeuw et al., 2009; MacMahon et al., 2007), including identification, selection, training, and monitoring. Unlike CORE, the Israeli program operates over a full season and across seasons. Overall, each trainee receives 85–90 hours of direct instruction per season, including refereeing lectures, video match-analysis, on-field refereeing simulations, refereeing psychology lectures, one-on-one psychology consultations, and fitness training. This program proved highly effective in facilitating referees' career development. Specifically, the majority of the trainees were promoted to higher leagues, including the Israeli Premier League and onto an international track. The referees typically evaluated the program favorably, including training methods and content, staff, and personal progress (Samuel, 2017).

In addition to classic training modalities, researchers have also attempted to develop unique tools for improving refereeing performance. Schweizer, Plessner, Kahlert, and Brand (2011) designed a video-based decision-making training program for foul situations. During each training session, the referee observes several video clips of possible foul situations, with no match contextual information. The referee indicates his/her decision via a mouse click and is then provided with feedback on the correctness of the decision, although no explanation concerning the underlying reason for the decision is provided. Evaluation of this training method indicated large improvements ($d = 1.47$) compared to pre-test. Nevertheless, Schweizer et al. (2011) concluded that there was no evidence that learning effects obtained may be transferred to the real world. To address this issue, Put, Wagemans, Jaspers, and Helsen (2013) examined the extent to which off-field, web-based, offside decision-making training transferred to real-life offside situations. The training included four sessions with 30 video simulations and 30 computer animations of potential offside situations in each session. Unlike Schweizer et al.'s (2011) tool, here the trainees received feedback on their performance and viewed a slow-motion and freeze frame of the offside situation. The findings indicated that the training group increased in response accuracy and decreased in the number of flag errors from pre- to post-test, in both on- and off-field transfer tests. These authors suggested that the online learning environment could be used to simulate some of the perceptual difficulties of real-match situations.

While web-based training tools might facilitate perceptual skills, a real match typically presents additional demands (e.g., crowd, fatigue, stress), currently not simulated in training modalities. Also, current training modalities do not consider the match contextual information (i.e., time of play, previous events, characteristics of teams), which might influence referees' decision-making via game management considerations. Therefore, Samuel (2015) has previously called for the development of simulators that better present referees with the actual refereeing task. These simulators should better reflect refereeing performance, either by combining a decision-making task with a physical task or by using a 3-D environment to create an emotional experience that is closer to reality (see Gulec, Yilmaza, Isler, O'Connord, & Clarke, 2019; Put et al., 2014). For example, Samuel, Galily, Guy, Sharoni, and Tenenbaum (2019) recently developed an easy-to-use decision-making simulator for soccer referees. Twenty-two referees ran on a treadmill for 60 minutes at varying paces while watching on a regular tablet two video sections depicting events from real (unfamiliar) matches, in context and in mixed order, calling their match decisions (i.e., overall 104 decisions) out loud. They completed pre- and post-test assessments of their feelings (i.e., motivation, confidence, focus), within-test perceived exertion (i.e., every 15 min), and a post-test assessment of their performance. The referees reported positive feelings prior to and following the test and rated their performance positively. They felt the simulator was moderately representative of a real match and offered suggestions for improvement. Their perceived exertion increased progressively during the test. Decision accuracy levels peaked in the third quarter and decreased during the final quarter. Decision accuracy levels were higher for simple decisions, such as out of play (73.81%), than for careless fouls (62.86%) or yellow/red cards (25.97%). Decision accuracy levels for yellow/red cards decisions were significantly higher in the in-context section (28.91%) than in the mixed section (20.83%). Perceived self-control correlated moderately with overall accuracy. Careless fouls accuracy level was on par with previous studies, supporting the simulator's validity. The authors concluded that the findings supported the use of the new simulator as a potentially innovative method for training referees in sequential decision-making.

Psychological skill training

Guillén and Feltz (2011) presented a conceptual model of efficacy for sports referees (i.e., termed *refficacy*). The model outlines the sources of refficacy information (i.e., mastery experiences, significant others, preparation, and partner qualifications), the refficacy dimensions (i.e., knowledge of game, decision-making skills, psychological and strategic skills, communication/control, and physical fitness) and the outcomes (e.g., performance, satisfaction). Mental preparation is a key source of refficacy in this model, involving goal setting, arousal regulation, coping with stress, employing self-talk, visualizing good performance, and believing one is ready to give maximum effort. The model suggests that efficacious referees perform better in terms of decision-making accuracy, fitness levels, effective communication with players, and external feedback, as well as feeling less stress and higher satisfaction (Guillén & Feltz, 2011). Johansen, Ommundsen, and Haugen (2018) examined whether refficacy mediated the relationship between sources of efficacy information and positive affective experience, among Norwegian soccer referees. They found that refficacy was a significant mediator only in two instances, namely task orientation and years of referee experience as antecedents. Their findings provided only partial support for Guillén and Feltz's (2011) model.

Mathers and Brodie (2011) presented a case study of a Scottish elite soccer referee who had undergone a psychological skills training intervention, with the following phases: (1) education, (2) assessment, (3) mental skill learning, (4) application of mental skills in context, and (5) evaluation. The intervention focused mainly on performance goals and mental simulation. The referee was assigned to an increasing number of international matches in the season of the intervention and the season immediately post intervention and acknowledged the positive impact of the mental skills intervention.

Based on the author's applied experience with elite referees and several existing mental preparation models, a comprehensive framework was developed to orient the psychological preparation of elite soccer referees (Samuel, 2015). During pre-season, the consultant assesses referees' motivation, mental skills usage, and current abilities. At the end of each season, a comprehensive referee evaluation occurs, including performance, mental skills usage, and the referee union assessments. Accordingly, adjustments are made in the referee's preparation program and new goals are set. The framework includes five stages, constituting the psychological preparation for a given match: (1) allocation of a match and a referee crew, (2) evaluation of match demands, (3) motivational decisions, (4) physiological, technical, tactical, and mental planning, and (5) mental simulation. Upon the completion of the match performance, a post-match analysis is conducted. This framework was applied over the past nine years with several soccer referees, indicating positive outcomes in referees' subjective skills (e.g., self-confidence, attentional focus, coping skills) as well as objective progress (i.e., transition to a higher league or UEFA category, match assignments).

Performance considerations

Referees at different developmental stages might experience different performance-related demands. At the early stages, referees mainly cope with balancing the physical demands with laws of the game knowledge and making correct decisions. They might also experience some abuse from coaches and players' parents regarding their decisions. Much of the existing research focused on the high school, college, and amateur levels of refereeing, has indicated low-to-moderate stress levels (e.g., Ritchie, Basevitch, Rodenberg, & Tenenbaum, 2017; Voight, 2009). It is possible that non-elite referees do not experience high performance-related stress in general but rather experience match-specific stressful moments. In a study of 108 U.S. high-school basketball referees, the participants were asked to evaluate their stress levels at nine game situations. The results showed that as the situation became more critical (a close game score and less time to play), stress levels were higher (Ritchie et al., 2017).

At the elite level, performance demands become more taxing, integrating several dimensions. Interactors need to make numerous sequential decisions, cope with pressure, and manage the game. Next, these performance demands are reviewed in detail.

Decision-making

Referees identify decision-making skills as a significant aspect of their performance (e.g., Slack et al., 2013; Voight, 2009). Interactors must be in the correct location to identify static and dynamic environmental cues (e.g., players, ball, field lines) in order to make accurate decisions (e.g., Hüttermann, Helsen, Put, & Memmert, 2018; Lex, Pizzera, Kurtes, & Schack, 2015). At the elite level, referees interact with their assistants, rapidly process information, and make significant decisions under high pressure (Schnyder & Hossner, 2016; Slack et al., 2013). For example, a study examining the decision-making of the Euro 2000 soccer referees showed that on average, they performed at 85% ± 5% of their maximal heart rate (HR_{max}), making about 200 decisions per match, most of which were based on communication with their assistants (Helsen & Bultynck, 2004). Similarly, elite basketball referees perform at an intensity above 70% HR_{max} for the majority of each match quarter (Leicht, 2008). Thus, at the elite level, referees make numerous sequential decisions under high biopsychosocial stress (Weston, 2015). In this context, Mallo et al. (2012) examined soccer referees' decision-making during the 2009 Confederations Cup and concluded that most errors occurred in the last 15-minute match period, supposedly as the referees were fatigued and the players' tactics changed to long-distance passes. Yet it seems that the effects of fatigue on refereeing performance is complex, and experimental studies are needed to examine these effects (Weston, 2015).

Referee-related research has also been focused on the underlying mechanism of the decision-making process (e.g., Lane, Nevill, Ahmad, & Blamer, 2006; Russell, Renshaw & Davids, 2019). For example, Plessner and Haar (2006) argued that referees' decision-making follows a sequence of (1) perception of a stimulus in the field of play (e.g., a tackle situation); (2) categorization (e.g., a foul); (3) memory processes, and (4) information integration (e.g., awarding a free kick and issuing a card). In addition, research has focused on the various factors influencing referees' decisions, often guided by a motivation to identify various biases in refereeing. These include, among others, the referee's positioning in the field of play (Mallo, et al., 2012), playing time (Unkelbach & Memmert, 2008), home advantage (Picazo-Tadeo, González-Gómez, & Guardiola, 2017), player vocalization (Lex et al., 2015), teams' and players' characteristics (Jones, Paull, & Erskine, 2002; van Quaquebeke & Giessner, 2010), and extreme weather conditions (Gaoua, de Oliveira, & Hunter, 2017). For example, van Quaquebeke and Giessner (2010) reported a bias related to players' height in ambiguous foul decision-making; assumed foul perpetrators were taller than their assumed victims. Overall, previous research has emphasized the significance of contextual factors (i.e., factors related to the specific match characteristics such as score, playing time, and previous decisions) in referees' decision-making.

Other than match characteristics, referees' personal characteristics might also affect their performance. For example, using a laboratory setting, Spitz et al. (2018) examined whether domain-specific (e.g., video-based foul decision-making) and/or domain-generic (e.g., processing speed) perceptual-cognitive skill variables could discriminate between elite and sub-elite referees. The results indicated skill-level differences are due to domain-specific rather than domain-generic factors. Specifically, elite referees were more accurate than sub-elite referees in making decisions as well as more accurate in anticipating what would happen next when the video clip was occluded just before the moment of contact. These results emphasized the importance of specificity in soccer referee training.

Furthermore, Samuel et al. (2018) evaluated the role of self-control strength in soccer referees' real match performance. They found that the referees exhibited high levels of trait and state self-control. Significant reductions in state self-control compared to pre-match levels (i.e., a state of *ego-depletion*) were evident in almost half of the matches and were negatively related to self-rated match performance. The experience of pre-match daily hassles and long travel time to the match were related to lower pre-match self-control. These results highlighted the important role of self-control strength in soccer refereeing (e.g., managing endurance and fatigue, being able to maintain focus and make numerous decisions, managing players calmly) and emphasized the importance of teaching self-management skills as well as supporting referees in establishing effective match-day routines.

Game management

Referees need to manage the players and coaches, in terms of "selling" their decisions (Schnyder & Hossner, 2016; Slack et al., 2013), coping with aggression (Folkesson et al., 2002), and reacting to player vocalizations (Lex et al., 2015). A famous game management example occurred in the second leg of the 2017–2018 UEFA Champions League quarter-final match between Real Madrid and Juventus. English referee, Michael Oliver, awarded a penalty to Real Madrid during extra time, when Juventus were leading 3-0. Following this critical decision, several Juventus players mobbed the referee, who eventually issued a red card to Juventus goalkeeper and captain, Buffon, for dissent. As English Premier League referees identified, game management is an important factor underpinning their performance success, manifested in building players' trust, conveying positive body language, and communicating with players and managers (Slack et al., 2013). The importance of game management was also identified by top-level European referees, especially having leadership skills, being proactive, being assertive, and "selling" their decisions (Schnyder & Hossner, 2016).

Mascarenhas, Collins, & Mortimer (2002) suggested that game management reflects the art rather than the science of refereeing. Expert referees make decisions that are specifically appropriate for the match, allowing it to flow and intervening only when the consequences of not doing so may adversely affect the game. Indeed, research has supported this notion, indicating that referees use deliberate game management when making decisions. For example, Brand, Schmidt, and Schneeloch (2006) showed videotaped contact situations to basketball referees either in their original game sequence or as random successions of individual scenes. They found that referees who watched the clips in their sequential order applied game management and judged the contacts as less severe, awarding less rigorous sanctions. Similar results were reported by Unkelbach and Memmert (2008), who found that soccer referees used both deliberate game management (i.e., purposely postponing cards early in the match) and calibration of the fouls' scale (i.e., setting a severity criterion for issuing a card) in their issuance of yellow cards.

Communication between referees and players is another important aspect of game management (e.g., Cunningham, Simmons, & Mascarenhas, 2018; Mellick, Bull, Laugharne, & Fleming, 2005). Skillful referee decision communication practice involves engaging the offender/s attention and instigating a decision interaction episode, projecting confidence in the decision made, and promoting the perception of the decision as fair and just (Russell et al., 2019). Thereby, referees attempt to "sell their decision" to the players and crowd. This is achieved by using effective communication skills with players and coaches, such as gaze, posture, and movement, and verbal explanation (Mellick et al., 2005). Cunningham et al. (2018) suggested that referees communicate under time pressure in dynamic circumstances that demand spontaneous responses with players. They showed that referees adapt and modify identity and messages (i.e., maintaining various social "faces") appropriately for different players and contexts, by (1) anticipating players' reactions and modifying the presentation of one's social self, (2) asserting and preserving the referee's own social "face," and (3) giving and restoring players' social "face." For example, one of the referees interviewed by Cunningham et al. (2018) commented on his interest in preserving face during interactions with players while projecting outward demonstrations of control of game activities to others:

> Sometimes you need to stop everything. Slow it all down, and make sure others see you are doing that. You might be just giving a regular yellow [card] out, but people see that the player was provoked. Like, "Okay, I've dealt with you and now I am dealing with this guy". The crowd needs to see that and the players need to go, "Okay he didn't just send our guy off because he punched him, he actually saw what happened and is stamping that by making a point here."
>
> *(p. 159)*

Human-technology interface

Various sport organizations have decided to incorporate technology (e.g., instant replay, Hawk-Eye, goal-line technology) into the refereeing process, mainly to support referees' decision-making (Kolbinger & Lames, 2017). In this context, the 2018 Football World Cup was a significant landmark, with the first introduction of Video Assistant Referee (VAR; International Football Association Board — IFAB, 2017). VAR presents a unique human-technology interface, in which the human factor (i.e., the video referee and the on-field referee) heavily influences the quality of the system. In terms of psychological effects, while technological aids might add to decision-making accuracy, they can also undermine the referee's authority and credibility in the eyes of players and fans (Kolbinger & Lames, 2017) as well as impair fans' enjoyment of the game (Winand & Fergusson, 2018). For example, while VAR created much interest and even showed some positive effects in the 2018 World Cup, it also produced controversy. As Iran's coach, Carlos Queiroz, commented (Ganguly, 2018):

> This is not good for the prestige of the game. The game must be clear, it needs to be obvious... People sitting in the stands need to know what the rules are. Who is refereeing the game? We need to know.

These words reflect an important aspect of refereeing – the credibility and authority of the referee is a critical aspect in creating justice and fairness in sport (Russell et al., 2019). Furthermore, referees might need to apply self-control skills (Samuel et al., 2018) in cases of technological intervention, to maintain confidence, focus, and authority. Moreover, inserting technological aids such as VAR into the refereeing process requires tailored training methods (e.g., see IFAB, 2017). Also, it requires adaptations to shared mental models and effective communication within the referee team (Samuel, 2015). Thus, additional research is required to determine the psychological effects of technological aids in refereeing, considering both the referees' perspective as well as the players' and fans' perspectives.

Performance evaluation

Referees are under the scrutiny of professional factors (e.g., the match observer, the Referee Union Professional Committee), the sport community (e.g., coaches, players, fans), and the media. For example, in formal soccer matches, an experienced former referee is usually sent to the stadium to conduct a match performance assessment. This is done by attending to various aspects of the referee's performance, including running patterns and field locations, decision-making, game management (including the referee's personality) and communication, and referee team performance. The match observer then provides the referee team with verbal feedback, a written report, and a performance mark (for each team member). This mark uses a scale ranging from six to ten. Typically, poor performance is reflected in a mark of 7.9–8.2, and very poor performance in a mark lower than 7.9, whereas good performance is reflected in a mark of 8.3–8.4 and very good performance in a mark of 8.5–8.6. If a referee officiated well, yet made one critical decision error (e.g., incorrectly awarding a penalty or red card), then the mark would be 7.9. In addition, the match difficulty is also indicated in the assessment (i.e., "normal," "quite challenging," "very challenging"). This assessment is then sent to the referee's governing body for evaluation by the professional committee. Assessments made over the season have much influence on the referee's professional development (Chaplin, 2007; Samuel, 2015).

The inclusion of VAR in soccer refereeing has created a unique psychological situation for referees. On the one hand, they might feel more confident that this system can help them to avoid critical decision errors that can significantly influence the match and lead to public scrutiny. On the other hand, going to an on-field review as a result of VAR intervention (for VAR protocol see IFAB, 2017), and then changing a critical decision, means that the referee will automatically receive a match mark of 7.9. This can lead to referees feeling internal pressure not to adhere to the VAR's recommendation.

Future developments and research

The world of sport is gradually modifying its view of referees, addressing them as performers on their own merit, with unique developmental, performance, and training considerations. Attempts are being made to reduce the attrition rates of referees, by providing better psychological support and by offering adequate salaries. At the same time technological aids are constantly introduced in various sports, as a result of refereeing limitations. An important debate exists around developing better technological aids to minimize the human factor in refereeing or alternatively developing better training methods to improve referees' skills. Researchers should examine how technological aids are perceived by referees and whether they influence their motivation for refereeing. Also, investigation is warranted into how these aids might affect refereeing performance, not only in major decision-making but also in areas where intervention is not permitted, and in game management. Specifically, how referees effectively communicate during VAR interventions to achieve accurate decisions is not yet well understood. Finally, the question of how technology aids impact the views of fans and players of referees' credibility should be addressed by researchers.

In spite of the considerable volume of research on refereeing, there are few conceptual frameworks specifically developed to explain refereeing performance. Therefore, it is important to theorize the performance of referees in various sports, considering the particularities of the sport and specific performance demands. Developing specific conceptual models can also advance more accurate referee training, integrating the relevant systems into a comprehensive training modality.

Referee training has shown considerable advancements, and there are scientific approaches to using sport science and deliberate practice in developing referees (e.g., MacMahon et al., 2007; Samuel, 2017). Further research is required to establish effective training methods to accurately simulate the refereeing task, in a manner that results in genuine transfers to real-world performance. Developing effective 2-D and 3-D simulators (e.g., Gulec et al., 2019; Put et al., 2014; Samuel et al., 2019) provides new opportunities and should receive more research attention. Yet, to achieve this, a methodological shift should occur, with less focus on refereeing bias and more focus on refereeing advancement. Specifically, while a major line of research has focused on refereeing bias (e.g., Jones et al., 2002; Picazo-Tadeo et al., 2017), a study by Morgulev, Azar, Lidor, Sabag, and Bar-Eli (2018) found that in basketball offensive foul decisions, common biases (e.g., home advantage, star players) are not very robust, and are context sensitive. Furthermore, research should provide more tools for applied practice in refereeing. Currently, only a few studies have examined psychological support aspects in refereeing. Additional research is needed to offer best practices for supporting referees in career development (e.g., maintain a dual-career) as well as in optimizing performance (e.g., developing stress management skills, establishing match-day routines). In this context, it is important that practitioners should perceive referees as performers on their own merits, with unique demands both on and off the field. Adopting a whole-person approach and supporting a dual-career is also imperative. Practitioners who consult referees should become immersed in their world (e.g., by conducting research, attending matches) as well as be familiar with their professional jargon (Samuel, 2019).

Conclusions

In this chapter, a holistic perspective was used to discuss the various aspects pertaining to interactor referees (specifically soccer and basketball referees), in terms of motivation and personal characteristics, career development and training, and performance. Referees typically show high intrinsic motivation and passion to develop within their organizations, with several excellence models supporting their progress. The referee's career, much like the athlete's career, is characterized by various change-events and transitions, emphasizing the need to show resilience as well as receive adequate psychological support. Still, high attrition rates among referees from various sports indicate the difficulties in maintaining a successful long-term career, especially at high levels. Researchers should view referees as performers on their own merit with unique performance considerations and develop effective training methods, as well as sport science support systems to bring these performers to the best of their abilities. This entails a conceptual and methodological shift from emphasizing refereeing bias to focusing on refereeing advancement. Understanding the influence of technology on refereeing is also of paramount significance, as the human-technology interface is complex and has various potential implications for referees' motivation, performance, and development.

References

Auger, D., Fortier, J., Thibault, A., Magny, D., & Gravelle, F. (2010). Characteristics and motivations of sports officials in the Province of Québec. *International Journal of Sport Management Recreation & Tourism*, *5*, 29–50. doi:10.5199/ijsmart-1791-874X-5b

Balch, M. J., & Scott, D. (2007). Contrary to popular belief, refs are people too! Personality and perceptions of officials. *Journal of Sport Behavior*, *30*, 3–20.

Brand, R., Schmidt, G., & Schneeloch, Y. (2006). Sequential effects in elite basketball referees' foul decisions: An experimental study on the concept of game management. *Journal of Sport & Exercise Psychology*, *28*, 93–99. doi:10.1123/jsep.28.1.93

Bryson, A., Buraimo, B., & Simmons, R. (2011). Do salaries improve worker performance? *Labour Economics*, *18*, 424–433. doi:10.1016/j.labeco.2010.12.005

Catteeuw, P., Helsen, W., Gilis, B., & Wagemans, J. (2009). Decision-making skills, role specificity, and deliberate practice in association football refereeing. *Journal of Sports Sciences*, *27*, 1125–1136. doi:10.1080/02640410903079179

Chaplin, M. (2014). *CORE's notable milestones*. Retrieved from http://www.uefa.org/protectingthe-game/refereeing/news/newsid=2076324.html

Cunningham, I., Simmons, P., & Mascarenhas, D. (2018). Sport officials' strategies for managing interactions with players: Face-work on the front-stage. *Psychology of Sport and Exercise*, *39*, 154–162. doi:10.1016/j.psychsport.2018.08.009

Dell, C., Gervis, M., & Rhind, D. J. A. (2016). Factors influencing soccer referee's intentions to quit the game. *Soccer and Society*, *17*, 109–119. doi:10.1080/14660970.2014.919275

Dictionary of Sport and Exercise Science. (2006). *Referee* (p. 175). London, UK: A & C Black Publishers.

Dosseville, F., & Laborde, S. (2015). Introduction to the special issue: Officials in sports. *Movement & Sport Sciences*, *87*, 3–10. doi:10.1051/sm/2015006

Folkesson, P., Nyberg, C., Archer, T., & Norlander, T. (2002). Soccer referees' experience of threat and aggression: Effects of age, experience, and life orientation on outcome of coping strategy. *Aggressive Behavior, 28*, 317–327. doi:10.1002/ab.90028

Ganguly, S. (2018, June 24). Who is refereeing the game, asks Queiroz in slamming VAR. *IOL*. Retrieved from https://www.iol.co.za/sport/soccer/who-is-refereeing-the-game-asks-queiroz-in-slamming-var-15663135

Gaoua, N., de Oliveira, R. F., & Hunter, S. (2017). Perception, action, and cognition of football referees in extreme temperatures: Impact on decision performance. *Frontiers in Psychology, 8*, 1479. doi:10.3389/fpsyg.2017.01479

Guillén, F., & Feltz, D. (2011). A conceptual model of referee efficacy. *Frontiers in Psychology, 2*, 1–5. doi:10.3389/fpsyg.2011.00025

Gulec, U., Yilmaz, M., Isler, V., O'Connor, R. V., & Clarke, P. M. (2019). A 3D virtual environment for training soccer referees. *Computer Standards & Interfaces, 64*, 1–10. doi:10.1016/j.csi.2018.11.004

Hancock, D. J., Dawson, D. J., & Auger, D. (2015). Why ref? Understanding sport officials' motivations to begin, continue, and quit. *Movement & Sport Sciences, 87*, 31–39. doi:10.1051/sm/2014018

Helsen, W., & Bultynck, J. B. (2004). Physical and perceptual-cognitive demands of top class refereeing in association football. *Journal of Sports Sciences, 22*, 179–189. doi:10.1080/02640410310001641502

Hüttermann, S., Helsen, W. F., Put, K., & Memmert, D. (2018). Does visual attention impact on decision making in complex dynamic events? *Journal of Sport & Exercise Psychology, 40*, 163–166. doi:10.1123/jsep.2017-0169

International Football Association Board. (2017). *Video assistant referees (VARs) experiment – protocol (summary)*. Zurich, Switzerland: IFAB

Johansen, B. T. (2015). Reasons for officiating soccer: The role of passion-based motivations among Norwegian elite and non-elite referees. *Movement & Sport Sciences, 87*, 23–30. doi:10.1051/sm/2014012

Johansen, B. T., Ommundsen, Y., & Haugen, T. (2018). Referee efficacy in the context of Norwegian soccer referees – a meaningful construct? *Psychology of Sport and Exercise, 38*, 184–191. doi:10.1016/j.psychsport.2018.06.013

Jones, M. V., Paull, G. C., & Erskine, J. (2002). The impact of a team's aggressive reputation on the decisions of association football referees. *Journal of Sports Sciences, 20*, 991–1000.

Kolbinger, O., & Lames, M. (2017). Scientific approaches to technological officiating aids in game sports. *Current Issues in Sport Science, 2*, 001. doi:10.15203/CISS_2017.001

Lane, A. M., Nevill, A. M., Ahmed, W. S., & Balmer, N. (2006). Soccer referee decision making: Shall I blow the whistle? *Journal of Sports Science & Medicine, 5*, 243–253.

Leicht, A. S. (2008). Physiological demands of basketball refereeing during international competition. *Journal of Science and Medicine in Sport, 11*, 357–360. doi:10.1016/j.jsams.2007.05.006

Lex, H., Pizzera, A., Kurtes, M., & Schack, T. (2015). Influence of players' vocalizations on soccer referees' decisions. *European Journal of Sport Science, 15*, 424–428. doi:10.1080/17461391.2014.962620

Livingston, L. A., Forbes, S. L., Pearson, N., Camacho, T., Wattie, N., & Varian, P. (2017). Sport officiating recruitment, development, and retention: A call to action. *Current Issues in Sport Science, 2*, 011. doi:10.15203/CISS_2017.011

MacMahon, C., Helsen, W. F., Starkes, J. L., & Weston, M. (2007). Decision-making skills and deliberate practice in elite association football referees. *Journal of Sports Sciences, 25*, 65–78. doi:10.1080/02640410600718640

MacMahon, C., Mascarhenhas, D. R. D., Plessner, H., Pizzera, A., Oudejans, R. R. D., & Raab, M. (2014). *Sport officials and officiating: Science and practice*. New York, NY: Routledge.

MacMahon, C., & Plessner, H. (2008). The sport official in research and practice. In D. Farrow, J. Baker, & C. MacMahon (Eds.), *Developing sport expertise: Researchers and coaches put theory into practice* (pp. 172–192). Abingdon, UK: Routledge.

Mallo, J., Gonzalez Frutos, P., Juárez, D., & Navarro, E. (2012). Effect of positioning on the accuracy of decision-making of association football top-class referees and assistant referees during competitive matches. *Journal of Sports Sciences, 30*, 1437–1445. doi:10.1080/02640414.2012.711485

Mascarenhas, D. R. D., Collins, D., & Mortimer, P. (2002). The art of reason versus the exactness of science in elite refereeing: Comments on Plessner and Betsch (2001). *Journal of Sport & Exercise Psychology, 24*, 328–333. doi:10.1123/jsep.24.3.328

Mathers, J. F., & Brodie, K. (2011). Elite refereeing in professional soccer: A case study of mental skills support. *Journal of Sport Psychology in Action, 2*, 171–182. doi:10.1080/21520704.2011.609018

Mellick, M., Bull, P., Laugharne, E., & Fleming, S. (2005). Identifying best practice for referee decision communication in association and rugby union football: A microanalytic approach. *Football Studies, 8*, 42–57.

Morgulev, E., Azar, O. H., Lidor, R., Sabag, E., & Bar-Eli, M. (2018). Searching for judgment biases among elite basketball referees. *Frontiers in Psychology, 9*, 2637. doi:10.3389/fpsyg.2018.02637

Philippe, F. L., Vallerand, R. J., Andrianarisoa, J., & Brunel, P. (2009). Passion in referees: Examining their affective and cognitive experiences in sport situations. *Journal of Sport & Exercise Psychology, 31*, 77–96.

Picazo-Tadeo, A. J., González-Gómez, F., & Guardiola, J. (2017). Does the crowd matter in refereeing decisions? Evidence from Spanish soccer. *International Journal of Sport and Exercise Psychology, 15*, 447–459. doi:10.1080/1612197X.2015.1126852

Pina, J. A., Passos, A.-M., Araújo, D., & Maynard, M. T. (2018). Football refereeing: An integrative review. *Psychology of Sport and Exercise, 35*, 10–26. doi:10.1016/j.psychsport.2017.10.006

Pina, J. A., Passos, A.-M., Carvalho, H., & Maynard, M. T. (2018). To be or not to be an excellent football referee: Different experts' viewpoints. *Journal of Sports Sciences, 37*, 692–700. doi:10.1080/02640414.2018.1522940

Plessner, H., & Betsch, T. (2001). Sequential effects in important referee decisions: The case of penalties in soccer. *Journal of Sport & Exercise Psychology, 23*, 254–259. doi:10.1123/jsep.23.3.254

Plessner, H., & Haar, T. (2006). Sports performance judgments from a social cognitive perspective. *Psychology of Sport and Exercise, 7*, 555–575. doi:10.1016/j.psychsport.2006.03.007

Put, K., Wagemans, J., Jaspers, A., & Helsen, W. F. (2013). Web-based training improves on-field offside decision-making performance. *Psychology of Sport and Exercise, 14*, 577–585. doi:10.1016/j.psychsport.2013.03.005

Put, K., Wagemans, J., Spitz, J., Gallardo, M. A., Williams, A. M., & Helsen, W. F. (2014). The use of 2D and 3D information in a perceptual-cognitive judgement task. *Journal of Sports Sciences, 32*, 1688–1697. doi:10.1080/02640414.2014.912760

Ritchie, J., Basevitch, I., Rodenberg, R., & Tenenbaum, G. (2017). Situation criticality and basketball officials' stress levels. *Journal of Sports Sciences, 35*, 2080–2087. doi:10.1080/02640414.2016.1255770

Russell, S., Renshaw, I., & Davids, K. (2019). How interacting constraints shape emergent decision-making of national-level football referees. *Qualitative Research in Sport, Exercise and Health, 11*, 573–588. doi:10.1080/2159676X.2018.1493525

Samuel, R. D. (2015). A psychological preparation framework for elite soccer referees: A practitioner's perspective. *Journal of Sport Psychology in Action, 6*, 170–187. doi:10.1080/21520704.2015.1065938

Samuel, R. D. (2017). Training prospective soccer referees using a deliberate practice perspective: The Israeli excellence program. *Journal of Sport Psychology in Action, 3*, 184–196. doi:10.1080/21520704.2017.1287798

Samuel, R. D. (2019). Soccer referees' transition to the Premier League: A case study reflecting individual experiences and consultancy. *Case Studies in Sport and Exercise Psychology, 3*, 1–10. doi:10.1123/cssep.2018-0017

Samuel, R. D., Engelrt, C., Zhang, Q., & Basevitch, I. (2018). Hi ref, are you in control? Self-control, ego-depletion, and performance in soccer referees. *Psychology of Sport and Exercise, 38*, 167–175. doi:10.1016/j.psychsport.2018.06.009

Samuel, R. D., Galily, Y., Guy, O., Sharoni, E., & Tenenbaum, G. (2019). A decision-making simulator for soccer referees. *International Journal of Sports Science & Coaching, 14*, 480–489. doi:10.1177/1747954119858696

Samuel, R. D., Galily, Y., & Tenenbaum, G. (2017). Who are you, ref? Defining the soccer referee's career using a change-based perspective. *International Journal of Sport & Exercise Psychology, 15*, 118–130. doi:10.1080/1612197X.2015.1079792

Schnyder, U., & Hossner, E.-J. (2016). Psychological issues in football officiating: An interview study with top-level referees. *Current Issues in Sport Science, 1*, 004. doi:10.15203/CISS_2016.004

Schweizer, G., Plessner, H., Kahlert, D., & Brand, R. (2011). A video-based training method for improving soccer referees' intuitive decision-making skills. *Journal of Applied Sport Psychology, 23*, 1–14. doi:10.1080/10413200.2011.555346

Slack, L. A., Maynard, I. W., Butt, J., & Olusoga, P. (2013). Factors underpinning football officiating excellence: Perceptions of English Premier League referees. *Journal of Applied Sport Psychology, 25*, 298–315. doi:10.1080/10413200.2012.726935

Spitz, J., Put, K., Wagemans, J., Williams, A. M., & Helsen, W. F. (2018). The role of domain-generic and domain-specific perceptual-cognitive skills in association football referees. *Psychology of Sport and Exercise, 34*, 47–56. doi:10.1016/j.psychsport.2017.09.010

Unkelbach, C., & Memmert, D. (2008). Game management, context effects, and calibration: The case of yellow cards in soccer. *Journal of Sport & Exercise Psychology, 30*, 95–109. doi:10.1123/jsep.30.1.95

van Quaquebeke, N., & Giessner, S. R. (2010). How embodied cognitions affect judgments: Height-related attribution bias in football foul calls. *Journal of Sport & Exercise Psychology, 32*, 3–22. doi:10.1123/jsep.32.1.3

Voight, M. (2009). Sources of stress and coping strategies of U.S. soccer officials. *Stress and Health, 25*, 91–101. doi:10.1002/smi.1231

Warner, S., Tingle, J. K., & Kellett, P. (2013). Officiating attrition: The experiences of former referees via a sport development lens. *Journal of Sport Management, 27*, 316–328. doi:10.1123/jsm.27.4.316

Webb, T., Dicks, M., Thelwell, R., & Nevill, A. (2018). The impact of referee training: Reflections on the reduction of home advantage in association football. *Soccer & Society, 19*, 1024–1037. doi:10.1080/14660970.2016.1267626

Weston, M. (2015). Match performances of soccer referees: The role of sport science. *Movement and Sport Sciences, 87*, 113–117. doi:10.1051/sm/2014011

Winand, M., & Fergusson, C. (2018). More decision-aid technology in sport? An analysis of football supporters' perceptions on goal line technology. *Soccer & Society, 19*, 966–985. doi:10.1080/14660970.2016.1267629

Wolfson, S., & Neave, N. (2007). Coping under pressure: Cognitive strategies for maintaining confidence among soccer referees. *Journal of Sport Behavior, 30*, 232–247.

INDEX

Note: **Bold** page numbers refer to tables and *italic* page numbers refer to figures.

Printed in Great Britain
by Amazon

69735262R00174